QUMRAN STUDIES

QUMRAN STUDIES

• •

New Approaches,
New Questions

Edited by

Michael Thomas Davis *&* Brent A. Strawn

Foreword by

James A. Sanders

WILLIAM B. EERDMANS PUBLISHING COMPANY
GRAND RAPIDS, MICHIGAN / CAMBRIDGE, U.K.

Published 2007 by
Wm. B. Eerdmans Publishing Co.
2140 Oak Industrial Drive N.E., Grand Rapids, Michigan 49505 /
P.O. Box 163, Cambridge CB3 9PU U.K.

Printed in the United States of America

12 11 10 09 08 07   7 6 5 4 3 2 1

Library of Congress Cataloging-in-Publication Data

Qumran studies: new approaches, new questions /
edited by Michael Thomas Davis & Brent A. Strawn;
foreword by James A. Sanders.
p.   cm.
Includes bibliographical references and index.
ISBN 978-0-8028-6080-4 (pbk.: alk. paper)
1. Dead Sea scrolls. 4Q. 2. Qumran community.
I. Davis, Michael T.   II. Strawn, Brent A.

BM488.5.Q86   2007
296.1'55 — dc22

2007009302

www.eerdmans.com

למשכילנו

James H. Charlesworth

Contents

Foreword

Now that publication of the Qumran scrolls is, some fifty years after the discovery of the first caves, virtually complete, the field has begun to enter new phases in the study of the Scrolls, led in some measure by younger or third-generation scholars entering the field, bringing with them fresh questions, re-addressing old ones, and questioning some "assured results." This was to be expected and should be welcomed by us all.

The present volume heralds this new phase as a tribute by its authors to their former teacher and colleague, James H. Charlesworth. Each contribution, based in good part on recent publications of Cave 4 fragments, in one way or another questions earlier theses. Major facets of the first phase of study of the Scrolls included: historical identification of the sect and the apparent titles it used to describe its struggles; textual work on the biblical scrolls and the *pesharim;* review of the whole issue of canon(s); and attempts to discern the literary scope of the library — some of that work is continued in this volume. Other essays, however, reflect an important aspect of the new phase in Scrolls study, namely, further literary-critical work on the "sectarian" literature from Qumran, as well as further work on the history of its formation. Focus on the process or history of formation of the literature peculiar to Qumran will undoubtedly shed light on how canonical literature, both Jewish and Christian, was continually adapted to the ongoing and changing situations of Early Judaism and Christianity. And, just as the earlier work necessitated in-depth review of the very concept of "canon," so now there is openness to seeing multiple canons in Early Judaism and how that was manifest at Qumran.[1]

1. See David M. Carr, "Canonization in the Context of Community: An Outline of the

Earlier work on the two-messiah concept at Qumran has now opened up the concept of messiah to the idea of a *messianic era* less focused on an *individual* messiah. Whereas previous work largely dealt with whether or not the finds in the Qumran caves constituted a discrete Jewish library in Early Judaism, those who adhere to that regnant theory now realize that the diversity in the library has to be addressed, particularly its "acquisition policy." The "discrete library" theory, which has held sway largely because of the (unofficial) solar calendar common to most of its diverse literature, is now seen as reflective of the diversity in Early Judaism more generally. The religion practiced at Qumran is also now receiving attention beyond the earlier issues of how a priestly community was so apocalyptic, or how its eschatology was expressed.

It was clear rather early on that Qumran represented a sect in Early Judaism that valiantly resisted the inroads of Hellenism (the modernism of the time) and yet expressed some of its own ideas in the common, cultural terms of the era. The issue of what it meant at Qumran to live and act like the community that had earlier gathered at the foot of Mt. Sinai in the first place needs now to be worked out in greater detail. What did living in the end-time mean for them? What did it mean to them to be the "true Israel" of their day and in what various ways did they express that conviction? Looking beyond the *pesharim,* how exactly did the faithful at Qumran view Torah and tradition and their authority in their lives? What was their hermeneutic of "canon" (whatever that was for them) and in what precise ways did it function for them, besides their belief that Scripture above all addressed the end-time in which they lived and hence addressed their situation directly?

These studies dedicated to Charlesworth, one of the most prolific editors of Early Jewish texts of our time, offer some indications of how further study of the Scrolls will now proceed. Soon the supporting volumes of indices, complete concordances, and catalogs of various sorts in the *Discoveries in the Judaean Desert* series will provide tools for much more in-depth study of the impact of the Scrolls in the ongoing critical study of Early Judaism. The present volume is a harbinger, with others, of the work of those who are forging ahead into the third, perhaps most valuable, phase in the study of Qumran literature and the light it may yet shed on Early Judaism, the cradle of Early Christianity and Rabbinic Judaism. It is important now that what

---

Formation of the Tanakh and the Christian Bible," in *A Gift of God in Due Season: Essays on Scripture and Community in Honor of James A. Sanders* (ed. Richard D. Weis and David M. Carr; JSOTSup 225; Sheffield: Sheffield Academic Press, 1996), 22-64; and Peter W. Flint, *The Dead Sea Psalms Scrolls and the Book of Psalms* (STDJ 17; Leiden: E. J. Brill, 1997).

can be learned from the study of the Qumran library interacts with a broad spectrum of disciplines.[2] Charlesworth, whose professional home is the New Testament, is one of a very few New Testament scholars also at home in the full gamut of the literature of Early Judaism. The work of his students collected here well reflects the broad-based work of their teacher and friend.

Claremont, California   JAMES A. SANDERS
Founder and President emeritus,
The Ancient Biblical Manuscript Center
and
Professor of Biblical Studies emeritus,
Claremont School of Theology
and Claremont Graduate University

---

2. See the interview of Emanuel Tov by Hershel Shanks in *BAR* 28/3 (May/June 2002): 32-35, 62.

Preface

Five of the papers collected here were originally delivered in two special sessions devoted to Qumran and Related Studies at the Mid-Atlantic Region of the Society of Biblical Literature held in New Brunswick, New Jersey in March 2001.[1] The sessions were organized and planned by Michael Thomas Davis at the kind invitation of Professor Jin Hee Han of New York Theological Seminary and Professor Christina Bucher of Elizabethtown College, then-coordinator of the Mid-Atlantic Region of the Society of Biblical Literature. Because the theme of the sessions was "Papers from the Princeton Theological Seminary Dead Sea Scrolls Project" (PTSDSSP), it was decided to collect the papers, together with papers from other members of the PTSDSSP, revise them, and publish them as a tribute to the Project's editor, Professor James H. Charlesworth. Although this is not a *Festschrift* proper — and certainly insufficient by itself to honor the career of someone of Professor Charlesworth's stature — we nevertheless offer it to him as a small token of our gratitude for his leadership of the Scrolls Project and, indeed, of so many other projects that have placed the scholarly world firmly in his debt.

It remains to list the many people who have helped make this volume possible. First of all, we thank our fellow contributors for their good work and patience. We are grateful to Professor James A. Sanders, who kindly agreed to write the Foreword, and Cameron Howard, for her editorial help. Howard and Katie Heffelfinger produced the index. We also express our appreciation to Rev. Dr. Thomas W. Gillespie, President and Professor of New

---

1. The papers by Novakovic, Elledge, Miller, Rietz, and Strawn; both sessions were chaired by Davis.

Testament emeritus of Princeton Theological Seminary, for his encouragement and support of this volume, as well as for his long-standing commitment to the PTSDSSP. We would also like to thank President Gillespie's successor, President Iain R. Torrance, for his continued support of the Project. And last, we would be remiss if we did not acknowledge the long-term support of the Dean of Academic Affairs and Helena Professor of Old Testament Language and Exegesis emeritus, Dr. James F. Armstrong.

Princeton/Atlanta   MTD/BAS

Abbreviations

1. Literature

AB	Anchor Bible
ABD	D. N. Freedman et al., eds., *The Anchor Bible Dictionary* (6 vols.; New York: Doubleday, 1992)
ABRL	Anchor Bible Reference Library
ALUOS	*Annual of Leeds University Oriental Society*
AnOr	Analecta orientalia
AOAT	Alter Orient und Altes Testament
ASOR	American Schools of Oriental Research
BA	*Biblical Archaeologist*
BAR	*Biblical Archaeology Review*
BASOR	*Bulletin of the American Schools of Oriental Research*
BASORSup	Bulletin of the American Schools of Oriental Research Supplement Series
BBB	Bonner biblische Beiträge
BETL	Bibliotheca ephemeridum theologicarum lovaniensium
BHT	Beiträge zur historischen Theologie
Bib	*Biblica*
BibOr	Biblica et orientalia
BibSem	The Biblical Seminar
BIOSCS	*Bulletin of the International Organization for Septuagint and Cognate Studies*
BIS	Biblical Interpretation Series
BJS	Brown Judaic Studies

BJSUCSD	Biblical and Judaic Studies from the University of California, San Diego
BThSt	Biblisch-theologische Studien
CahRB	Cahiers de la Revue biblique
CAT	(see *KTU*)
CBQ	*Catholic Biblical Quarterly*
CBQMS	Catholic Biblical Quarterly Monograph Series
CHJ	*Cambridge History of Judaism* (ed. W. D. Davies et al.; 3 vols. to date; Cambridge: Cambridge University Press, 1984-)
ConBOT	Coniectanea biblica Old Testament Series
CRINT	Compendia rerum iudaicarum ad Novum Testamentum
CTU	(see *KTU*)
DJD	Discoveries in the Judaean Desert
DSD	*Dead Sea Discoveries*
DSSC	M. G. Abegg, Jr. with J. E. Bowley and E. M. Cook and in consultation with E. Tov, *The Dead Sea Scrolls Concordance,* Vol. 1: *The Non-Biblical Texts from Qumran* (2 vols.; Leiden: Brill, 2003)
DSSSE	F. García Martínez and E. J. C. Tigchelaar, eds., *The Dead Sea Scrolls Study Edition* (2 vols.; Leiden: Brill, 1997-1998)
ECDSS	Eerdmans Commentaries on the Dead Sea Scrolls
EDSS	L. Schiffman and J. VanderKam, eds., *Encyclopedia of the Dead Sea Scrolls* (2 vols.; Oxford: Oxford University Press, 2000)
EKKNT	Evangelisch-katholischer Kommentar zum Neuen Testament
EtB.NS	Etudes bibliques, nouv. sér.
GC	J. H. Charlesworth et al., eds., *Graphic Concordance to the Dead Sea Scrolls* (Tübingen: J. C. B. Mohr [Paul Siebeck] and Louisville: Westminster/John Knox, 1991)
GKC	E. Kautzsch, ed., *Gesenius' Hebrew Grammar* (2d ed.; trans. A. E. Cowley; Oxford: Oxford University Press, 1910)
HALOT	L. Koehler, W. Baumgartner, and J. J. Stamm, *The Hebrew and Aramaic Lexicon of the Old Testament* (trans. and ed. M. E. J. Richardson; 5 vols.; Leiden: Brill, 1994-2000)
HdO	Handbuch der Orientalistik
HSM	Harvard Semitic Monographs
HSS	Harvard Semitic Studies
HTR	*Harvard Theological Review*
HUCA	*Hebrew Union College Annual*
ICC	International Critical Commentary
IEJ	*Israel Exploration Journal*
IG	*Inscriptiones graecae* (editio minor; Berlin, 1924-)
JANES(CU)	*Journal of the Ancient Near Eastern Society (of Columbia University)*

JAOS	*Journal of the American Oriental Society*
JBL	*Journal of Biblical Literature*
JJS	*Journal of Jewish Studies*
JQR	*Jewish Quarterly Review*
JSJ	*Journal for the Study of Judaism in the Persian, Hellenistic, and Roman Periods*
JSOT	*Journal for the Study of the Old Testament*
JSOTSup	Journal for the Study of the Old Testament Supplement Series
JSP	*Journal for the Study of the Pseudepigrapha*
JSPSup	Journal for the Study of the Pseudepigrapha Supplement Series
JSS	*Journal of Semitic Studies*
KEK	Kritisch-exegetischer Kommentar über das Neue Testament (Meyer-Kommentar)
KTU	M. Dietrich, O. Loretz, and J. Sanmartín, eds., *The Cuneiform Alphabetic Texts from Ugarit, Ras Ibn Hani, and Other Places (KTU: second, enlarged edition)* (Münster: Ugarit-Verlag, 1995)
LAI	Library of Ancient Israel
MGWJ	*Monatschrift für Geschichte und Wissenschaft des Judentums*
Neot	*Neotestamentica*
NJPSV	*Tanakh: A New Translation of the Holy Scriptures According to the Traditional Hebrew Text* (Philadelphia: Jewish Publication Society, 1985)
NovT	*Novum Testamentum*
NovTSup	Novum Testamentum Supplements
NRSV	New Revised Standard Version
NTD	Das Neue Testament Deutsch
NTL	New Testament Library
NTOA	Novum Testamentum et Orbis Antiquus
NTS	*New Testament Studies*
OCD	S. Hornblower and A. Spawforth, eds., *Oxford Classical Dictionary* (3d ed.; Oxford: Oxford University Press, 1996)
OTL	Old Testament Library
OTP	J. H. Charlesworth, ed., *The Old Testament Pseudepigrapha* (2 vols.; New York: Doubleday, 1983-1985)
OTS	*Old Testament Studies* or *Oudtestamentische Studiën*
PTSDSSP	Princeton Theological Seminary Dead Sea Scrolls Project
PTSDSSP 1	*The Dead Sea Scrolls: Hebrew, Aramaic, and Greek Texts with English Translations*, Vol. 1: *The Rule of the Community and Related Documents* (ed. J. H. Charlesworth et al.; PTSDSSP 1; Tübingen: J. C. B. Mohr [Paul Siebeck] and Louisville: Westminster John Knox, 1994)
PTSDSSP 2	*The Dead Sea Scrolls: Hebrew, Aramaic, and Greek Texts with English Translations*, Vol. 2: *Damascus Document, War Scroll, and*

	Related Documents (ed. J. H. Charlesworth et al.; PTSDSSP 2; Tübingen: J. C. B. Mohr [Paul Siebeck] and Louisville: Westminster John Knox, 1995)
PTSDSSP 4A	*The Dead Sea Scrolls: Hebrew, Aramaic, and Greek Texts with English Translations*, Vol. 4A: *Pseudepigraphic and Non-Masoretic Psalms and Prayers* (ed. J. H. Charlesworth et al.; PTSDSSP 4A; Tübingen: Mohr Siebeck and Louisville: Westminster John Knox, 1997)
PTSDSSP 4B	*The Dead Sea Scrolls: Hebrew, Aramaic, and Greek Texts with English Translations*, Vol. 4B: *Angelic Liturgy: Songs of the Sabbath Sacrifice* (ed. J. H. Charlesworth, C. A. Newsom, et al.; PTSDSSP 4B; Tübingen: Mohr Siebeck and Louisville: Westminster John Knox, 1999)
PTSDSSP 6B	*The Dead Sea Scrolls: Hebrew, Aramaic, and Greek Texts with English Translations*, Vol. 6B: *Pesharim, Other Commentaries, and Related Documents* (ed. J. H. Charlesworth et al.; PTSDSSP 6B; Tübingen: Mohr Siebeck and Louisville: Westminster John Knox, 2002)
QC	*Qumran Chronicle*
RB	*Revue biblique*
RevQ	*Revue de Qumran*
RHPR	*Revue d'histoire et de philosophie religieuses*
RHR	*Revue de l'histoire des religions*
SBLEJL	Society of Biblical Literature Early Judaism and Its Literature
SBLMS	Society of Biblical Literature Monograph Series
SBLRBS	Society of Biblical Literature Resources for Biblical Study
SBT	Studies in Biblical Theology
SDSSRL	Studies in the Dead Sea Scrolls and Related Literature
Sem	*Semitica*
SFSHJ	South Florida Studies in the History of Judaism
SJLA	Studies in Judaism in Late Antiquity
SNTSMS	Society for New Testament Studies Monograph Series
SPB	Studia post-biblica
SSN	Studia semitica neerlandica
STDJ	Studies on the Texts of the Desert of Judah
SubBi	*Subsidia biblica*
SUNT	Studien zur Umwelt des Neuen Testaments
SVTP	Studia in Veteris Testamenti pseudepigraphica
Tanakh	(see NJPSV)
TANZ	Texte und Arbeiten zum neutestamentlichen Zeitalter
TDNT	G. Kittel and G. Friedrich, eds., *Theological Dictionary of the New Testament* (trans. G. W. Bromiley; 10 vols.; Grand Rapids: Eerdmans, 1964-1976)

TDOT	G. J. Botterweck and H. Ringgren, eds., *Theological Dictionary of the Old Testament* (trans. J. T. Willis et al.; 11 vols. to date; Grand Rapids: Eerdmans, 1974-)
ThViat	*Theologia viatorum*
TLZ	*Theologische Literaturzeitung*
TRu	*Theologische Rundschau*
TSAJ	Texte und Studien zum antiken Judentum
TSK	*Theologische Studien und Kritiken*
UT	C. H. Gordon, *Ugaritic Textbook* (AnOr 38; Rome: Pontifical Biblical Institute, 1965)
VT	*Vetus Testamentum*
VTSup	Supplements to Vetus Testamentum
WBC	Word Biblical Commentary
WUNT	Wissenschaftliche Untersuchungen zum Neuen Testament
ZAW	*Zeitschrift für die alttestamentliche Wissenschaft*
ZBK	Zürcher Bibelkommentare
ZDMG	*Zeitschrift der deutschen morgenländischen Gesellschaft*
ZTK	*Zeitschrift für Theologie und Kirche*

2. Other

ad . . . fin	to . . . end
AD/A.D.	Anno Domini
BC/B.C.	Before Christ
BCE/B.C.E.	Before Common Era
BH	Biblical Hebrew
CE/C.E.	Common Era
chap(s).	chapter(s)
cm	centimeter(s)
col(s).	column(s)
ed(s).	edited by/editor(s) or edition (see also ed in Sigla)
LXX	The Septuagint (cf. 𝕆 in Sigla)
m	meter(s)
MH	Mishnaic Hebrew
MS(S)	Manuscript(s)
MT	Masoretic Text (cf. 𝔐 in Sigla)
NT	New Testament
OT	Old Testament
par(s).	parallel(s)
Q	Qumran (in text numbers) or *Quelle* (in Synoptic discussions)
QL	Qumran library/literature

3. Sigla

√	root
//	parallel to/in parallel with
+	plus, in addition to
\x/	supralinear character
[x]	restored character
[. . .]	lacuna, broken text not restored
⟨x⟩	corrected, emended text
[[x]]	physical join
*	original reading
A	Codex Alexandrinus
B	Codex Vaticanus
ed	edition
F	Codex Ambrosianus
frg(s).	fragment(s)
𝔊 (𝔊ed)	The Septuagint according to the Göttingen edition
𝔊B	(see B)
𝔐	The Masoretic Text
mg	marginal reading
SamP	Samaritan Pentateuch
𝔗J	Targum Jonathan

NOTE: Other abbreviations, especially the abbreviation of ancient works, follows Patrick H. Alexander et al., eds., *The SBL Handbook of Style for Ancient Near Eastern, Biblical, and Early Christian Studies* (Peabody: Hendrickson, 1999).

Contributors

Shane A. Berg is a doctoral candidate in Religious Studies (New Testament) at Yale University and an instructor in New Testament at Princeton Theological Seminary. His dissertation focuses on the relationship between religious epistemology and sectarian identity in the Dead Sea Scrolls. He has published a variety of ancient Greek papyri and is currently part of a team working on the *editio princeps* of a fourth-century CE codex of epigrams.

Carsten Claussen is Wissenschaftlicher Assistent in New Testament Theology at the Protestant Theological Faculty, University of Munich, Germany. He holds degrees from the University of Durham, the University of Tübingen, and the University of Munich. His publications include the monograph *Versammlung, Gemeinde, Synagoge: Das hellenistisch-jüdische Umfeld der frühchristlichen Gemeinden* (2002) and articles about the Gospel of John and the Jewish background to early Christianity. From 2001 to 2003 he was a visiting scholar and lecturer at Princeton Theological Seminary.

Michael A. Daise is Assistant Professor of Religious Studies at the College of William and Mary (Williamsburg, Virginia), where he teaches Formative Judaism and Christian Origins. He has published articles on the Old Testament Pseudepigrapha, the Dead Sea Scrolls, and the Gospel of John. His monograph on feasts in the Gospel of John is forthcoming in the WUNT series (Mohr Siebeck).

Michael Thomas Davis studied Hebrew Bible and Semitic languages at St. Mary's Seminary and University (Baltimore, Maryland), and at Princeton Theological Seminary (Princeton, New Jersey). His work on the PTSDSSP includes editions of both the *Rule of the Community* (1994) and the *Damascus Document* fragments from Cave 4 (1995). He has served as adjunct professor at both New York Theological Seminary and Rider University.

C. D. Elledge is an assistant professor of Religion at Gustavus Adolphus College in Saint Peter, Minnesota. He holds degrees from Princeton Theological Seminary and studied at the Ecole Biblique de Jerusalem, taking the Elève Titulaire there while also serving as a Fulbright scholar at the Hebrew University of Jerusalem. He has written for the PTSDSSP and *Revue de Qumran,* and is the author of three books: *The Statutes of the King: The Temple Scroll's Legislation on Kingship* (2004), *The Bible and the Dead Sea Scrolls: Understanding Qumran and Its Literature* (2005), and *Life After Death in Early Judaism: The Evidence of Josephus* (2006).

Loren L. Johns is Associate Professor of New Testament at Associated Mennonite Biblical Seminary (Elkhart, Indiana). He holds degrees from Associated Mennonite Biblical Seminary and Princeton Theological Seminary. He is the author or editor of several books, including *The Lamb Christology of the Apocalypse of John* (2003).

John B. Faulkenberry Miller is an assistant professor of Religion at McMurry University (Abilene, Texas). He holds degrees from the University of California at Berkeley and Princeton Theological Seminary. He has written for the PTSDSSP, and is the author of *Convinced That God Had Called Us: Dreams, Visions, and the Perception of God's Will in Luke-Acts* (2006).

Lidija Novakovic is an associate professor of New Testament at Baylor University (Waco, Texas). She took degrees at the University of Belgrade (former Yugoslavia), the Baptist Theological Seminary in Rüschlikon (Switzerland), and Princeton Theological Seminary. Her monograph, *Messiah, the Healer of the Sick: A Study of Jesus as the Son of David in the Gospel of Matthew,* appeared in 2003.

Henry W. Morisada Rietz is an associate professor of Religious Studies at Grinnell College (Grinnell, Iowa). He holds degrees from Grinnell College and Princeton Theological Seminary. He is currently the associate editor of the PTSDSSP, and his monograph, *Time in the Sectarian Dead Sea Scrolls,* is forthcoming in the WUNT series (Mohr Siebeck).

Brent A. Strawn is Associate Professor of Old Testament/Hebrew Bible at the Candler School of Theology and in the Graduate Division of Religion at Emory University (Atlanta, Georgia). He joined the PTSDSSP in 1993 and has worked on the Project's editions of the *War Scroll* (1995) and the *Songs of the*

Sabbath Sacrifice (1999). His most recent book is *What Is Stronger than a Lion? Leonine Image and Metaphor in the Hebrew Bible and the Ancient Near East* (2005).

Loren T. Stuckenbruck is B. F. Westcott Professor in Biblical Studies at the University of Durham. His books include *Angel Veneration and Christology: A Study in Early Judaism and in the Christology of the Apocalypse of John* (1995), *The Book of Giants from Qumran: Texts, Translation, and Commentary* (1997), and, with Stuart Weeks and Simon Gathercole, *The Book of Tobit: Texts from the Principal Ancient and Medieval Traditions with Synopsis, Concordances, and Annotated Texts in Aramaic, Hebrew, Greek, Latin, and Syriac* (2004). He has published extensively in the areas of ancient Jewish apocalyptic thought and the Dead Sea Scrolls. Since 2003, he has been Chief Editor of the Commentaries on Early Jewish Literature series (Walter de Gruyter).

Introduction

MICHAEL THOMAS DAVIS AND BRENT A. STRAWN

It would be a vast understatement to say that the Dead Sea Scrolls have revolutionized scholarly understanding on a number of fronts, including especially the textual criticism of the Old Testament/Hebrew Bible and the history of Early Judaism in the late Second Temple Period. It was, upon their discovery, immediately apparent that they would do so. And so they have. The revolution has been going on for over fifty years and it shows no signs of letting up. This is especially true now that the publication of the Scrolls in the Discoveries in the Judaean Desert series (DJD) is virtually complete, with the re-edition of the non-biblical manuscripts continuing steadily in the Princeton Theological Seminary Dead Sea Scrolls Project (PTSDSSP). With all of the manuscripts published (or nearly so) — and with many of these re-published — the important work of interpretation and analysis that took place prior to final publication can proceed in new ways. In some ways, that is, we are only now in a position to look at Qumran and the Scrolls *in the round*. This means that earlier analyses will inevitably need to be rethought and reassessed in light of the full evidence.

The present collection of papers is to be found in this latter vein. Although most of the studies published here do not deal with only recently- or lately-published manuscripts, they all evidence in one way or another a *reassessment* of the materials that they consider. In many ways, the texts are old but the questions are new. Older consensuses and opinions are reanalyzed, often with new data, new methods, or — at the very least — new eyes. In this way, it is hoped, the conversation is furthered — whether that is by means of critique and new (re)construction or by means of offering a more secure foundation to, and furthering the cause and conclusions of, previous insights.

The first essay, "4QLXXLev[a] and Proto-Septuagint Studies: Reassessing Qumran Evidence for the *Urtext* Theory," by John B. Faulkenberry Miller, is another installment in the ongoing story of the Scrolls' contribution to the study of the text of the Hebrew Bible and, in this case, the text of the Septuagint as well. Miller revisits the near total consensus of textual critics that the Septuagint texts at Qumran support the *Urtext* theory of Paul de Lagarde over the theory of multiple texts put forth by Paul Kahle. By means of a careful review of the variants from 4QLXXLev[a] (4Q119), Miller demonstrates that a number of these readings, which have typically been presented in support of the *Urtext* theory, in fact do *not* support such a view — at least not unequivocally. Miller stresses that his work is not to be taken as the reverse — that Kahle's theory of Septuagintal origins is correct — but it demonstrates that underlying the "hard data" of textual criticism are the more subjective assumptions of textual critics, many of which cannot be proved or disproved.

In "Identifying Compositions and Traditions of the Qumran Community: The *Songs of the Sabbath Sacrifice* as a Test Case," Henry W. Morisada Rietz concerns himself with a crucial issue: how does one determine whether a "sectarian" document is a composition of the Qumran Community itself as opposed to one that was imported to the library from the outside on the basis of certain theological or ideological affinities? Rietz explores the development of criteria for determining texts that are Qumran compositions vs. texts that were inherited by the Community and functioned as important traditions for the group. He then applies his criteria to a specific and debatable composition: the *Songs of the Sabbath Sacrifice*. In this case, Rietz rightly points out that at the very least this composition functioned as an authoritative tradition at Qumran and can therefore be used to access the group's beliefs. But Rietz also points out that a specific and unusual dependence of *Sabbath Song 5* on the *Rule of the Community* tips the balance from tradition to composition, offering evidence that the *Songs of the Sabbath Sacrifice* originated within the Qumran Community. In a jointly-authored "sequel" to Rietz's essay, "(More) Sectarian Terminology in the *Songs of the Sabbath Sacrifice:* The Case of תמימי דרך," Brent A. Strawn and Rietz examine another piece of data that is pertinent to the argument and that supports Rietz's conclusions.

The next essay, "Excerpted 'Non-Biblical' Scrolls at Qumran? Background, Analogies, Function," by Brent A. Strawn considers whether or not the phenomenon of excerption, which is attested among the Qumran biblical scrolls, might also be found among *non-biblical* texts — particularly those considered authoritative by the Community (most notably, perhaps, the *Rule of the Community*). Strawn argues that *both* variant texts in the classic sense and also deliberately modified texts like excerpted manuscripts provide crucial data in assessing reconstructions of the textual history of documents like the *Rule of the Community;* excerpted manuscripts, in particular, have an important role to play in the development of such reconstructions in the future. Moreover, these manuscripts cast significant light on the possible socio-textual function(s) of certain compositions (and functionaries) at Qumran.

Loren T. Stuckenbruck, "Temporal Shifts from Text to Interpretation: Concerning the Use of the Perfect and Imperfect in the *Habakkuk Pesher* (1QpHab)," revisits the thorny questions surrounding the interpretation of the verbal tenses in the *pesharim,* especially 1QpHab. The point of his essay is not simply syntactical, however. Instead, Stuckenbruck presents a detailed study of the linguistic problems in service to a fresh assessment of this important text and its contribution to the reconstruction of the history of the Qumran Community.

In his essay, "The Temporal Relationship between the Covenant Renewal Rite and the Initiation Process in 1QS," Michael A. Daise returns to a long-standing question regarding the *Rule of the Community* and the Community's liturgical processes. Despite prior conclusions to the contrary, Daise argues that there is no compelling reason to believe that the covenant renewal ceremony described in 1QS 1.18–2.25 coincided with the initiation procedure recounted in 1QS 6.13-23 and 5.7-11. Daise's study has important bearing, not only on prior analyses of this question and 1QS, but also on the interpretation of the actual functioning of the Community insofar as it addresses whether or not the Qumranites calibrated periods of initiation with periods of punishment and covenant renewal.

Shane A. Berg, "An Elite Group within the *Yaḥad:* Revisiting 1QS 8–9," takes up an intriguing aspect of the structure and functioning of the Community. By means of a careful analysis of 1QS 8.1–9.21, Berg furthers the argument that these columns have to do with the formation of an elite group chosen from among members of the wider Community. The creation of this elite group is found in 1QS 8.1–9.11; the group was apparently commissioned by the larger Community to separate itself in order to achieve a higher level of holiness and to perform some atoning function. Since the remainder of 1QS 9 deals with precepts for the Maskil, Berg suggests that this figure played an important role in the creation and formation of the elite group. Here, too, then — as in other studies in this volume — Berg's contribution has important implications for the study of the text of 1QS and for the socio-historical reconstruction of the Qumran Community.

C. D. Elledge tackles a methodological problem in studies of Qumran messianism in the following essay: "The Prince of the Congregation: Qumran 'Messianism' in the Context of *Milḥāmâ*." That problem, in brief, is whether or not it is legitimate to harmonize different texts and different terms so as to produce a conglomerate picture of "Qumran Messianism." Elledge critiques this harmonizing tendency, especially in the popular identification of "the Prince of the Congregation" as "the Davidic Messiah." After reviewing the pertinent texts, Elledge concludes that a more precise and accurate understanding of the former figure would be something like "the Qumran latter-day warrior." Moreover, while the Prince apparently emerges as the much expected "Branch of David" of Isa 11:1-5, his role is almost completely restricted to military actions. He may have little (or no) royal or messianic authority and, regardless, is ultimately peripheral to the dominant priestly authority of the Community's ideology. Attention to the specific manuscripts in question and the Community's creative use of the biblical title "Prince" (see Numbers 7, 34; Ezekiel 34–37, 40–48) clarifies key aspects of their messianic thought.

Lidija Novakovic continues to clarify Qumran messianism in "4Q521: The Works of the Messiah or the Signs of the Messianic Time?" 4Q521 has been much discussed, largely because it mentions end-time miracles immediately after a reference to a messianic figure. Novakovic points out that the fragmentary status of the manuscript complicates certainty regarding the precise relationship between the messiah and the miracles. Even so, after comparing similar thematics in Early Jewish documents, including the New Testament, Novakovic is able to show that what is important about the miracles is not their association with the *messiah's person,* but their temporal aspect — namely, that they are signs of the *messianic time.* This interpretation chastens some of the scholarly speculation surrounding 4Q521 but at the same time anchors this text to a widespread messianic tradition, thus pointing a way forward for future research on this text and similar messianic compositions.

In their joint contribution, "The Concept of Unity at Qumran," Carsten Claussen and Michael Thomas Davis investigate the Qumranites' self-designation as the "Community" (יחד). An overview of the Semitic and biblical background of this term shows that its two primary significations (associative and *dis*-associative) are aptly suited to the Qumran Community, which is a tightly-knit group that is, at the same time, strongly demarcated from outsiders. Even so, the grammatical articulation of יחד in the Hebrew Bible is *not* well suited for Qumran in that the noun form rarely occurs in the Bible. This leads Claussen and Davis to look for precedents or parallels elsewhere in the Greco-Roman world — an unsuccessful task, at least in part — before turning to a thorough reconsideration of the meaning of יחד in Qumran itself and the social-organizational and moral-religious significance of the term there. Not surprisingly, these various considerations urge Claussen and Davis to return finally to the origins of the Qumran Community. The likely reconstruction of the Community as one that was expelled from its original location within the Jerusalem temple and its priesthood makes perfect sense of, and is simultaneously further rounded out by, the Qumranic usage of יחד.

In the final essay, "Identity and Resistance: The Varieties of Competing Models in Early Judaism," Loren L. Johns opens up a new avenue of approach to the Qumran material, though his study ranges widely across the literature and history of Early Judaism. Most studies of Qumran and the "sectarian" documents are read *historically* in order to reconstruct the "theology" or "belief system" of the Community. In this study, Johns asks questions concerning the Community's *moral* thought. How did the Qumranites' self-understanding as "Sons of Light" impact their perception of their responsibilities and participation in the final struggle against the earthly and cosmic forces that would be vanquished at the end of time? Central to this question is the Community's participation in *violent* struggle against the "Sons of Belial." Obviously, the question of violence was not exclusive to Qumran. Johns thus explores a number of conceptions and models of resistance that emerged in response to the Hellenizing crisis in Judea, which began under the reign of Antiochus IV Epiphanes and continued through the Roman period to the First Jewish Revolt. In each case, Johns is concerned with how the conception of resistance reflects differing opinions concerning the efficacy and ethical propriety of human violence. He delineates a range of responses running from passivity (accomodationism) to resistance. But resistance, in turn, must be carefully delineated and differentiated insofar as it includes both *active and violent* resistance (as in the *War Scroll*) and *active but nonviolent* resistance (as in Daniel and the Apocalypse of John). The latter option has often been misunderstood or undervalued in previous research on these texts, but has significant (moral) bearing on the ever-present problem of religion and violence.

The Qumran revolution will continue — that is our belief and our hope. If the essays in the present collection play a small part in that ongoing process or contribute in some small way to that continuing discussion, then all who have been concerned with its production will be satisfied.

4QLXXLevᵃ and Proto-Septuagint Studies: Reassessing Qumran Evidence for the *Urtext* Theory

JOHN B. FAULKENBERRY MILLER

4QLXXLevᵃ (4Q119)[1] is one of the oldest extant Greek translations of Jewish Scripture, dated to the late second or first century B.C.E.[2] Despite its antiquity, this manuscript from Cave 4 has spawned surprisingly few studies.[3] The

1. Designated as manuscript 801 in John William Wevers' Göttingen apparatus. See Wevers, ed., *Leviticus* (Septuaginta: Vetus Testamentum Graecum 2.2; Göttingen: Vandenhoeck & Ruprecht, 1986). Throughout this discussion, I will refer to this document by the more descriptive title, 4QLXXLevᵃ.

2. See the discussion of P. J. Parsons in P. W. Skehan, E. Ulrich, and J. Sanderson, *Qumran Cave 4.4: Palaeo-Hebrew and Greek Biblical Manuscripts* (DJD 9; Oxford: Clarendon, 1992), 9-10.

3. Like the study in DJD 9 mentioned above, all of these studies have discussed 4QLXXLevᵃ along with other Greek texts from Qumran. The preliminary publication of 4QLXXLevᵃ is found in Patrick Skehan's "The Qumran Manuscripts and Textual Criticism," in *Volume du congrès, Strasbourg 1956* (VTSup 4; Leiden: Brill, 1957), 148-60. Skehan also discusses this material in a later article entitled, "The Biblical Scrolls from Qumran and the Text of the Old Testament" (*BA* 28 [1965]: 87-100), but this article focuses more on 4QLXXNum. A. R. C. Leaney discusses various aspects of the Qumran texts in "Greek Manuscripts from the Judean

This essay is dedicated to James H. Charlesworth, with great appreciation for the immeasurable contribution he has made to my education. It was Professor Charlesworth who first encouraged me to apply for a Fulbright grant to study in Israel during the academic year 1997-1998, and it was he who introduced me to the two scholars who would become my primary mentors during that year: Professors Doron Mendels and Emanuel Tov. My work with Professor Tov has provided the basis for this essay. I would like to thank him for supervising this part of my Fulbright research, and for his tireless patience in dealing with a student whose ideas differed so much from his own. I would also like to thank the United States Information Agency and the United States–Israel Education Foundation for providing me with the opportunity to live and study in Jerusalem.

scholars who have engaged it, however, include some of the most prominent figures in Septuagint and Qumran studies from the latter half of the twentieth century. Although none of the published examinations focuses exclusively on the Qumran text as it relates to the question of Septuagint origins, all make at least brief mention of the notion that this text supports the "Lagardian" view.[4] In his initial publication of this text, for example, Patrick Skehan concluded: "The general impression with which the writer is left is that we have here one more book of the O.T. in which a *single* early Greek rendering seems to have undergone a good deal of what we would today call critical revision, in the period even before Origen."[5] The tone of this conclusion became much stronger a few years later when Skehan cited the Greek material from Qumran in the context of an argument against Kahle's multiple translation theory: "the Qumran caves have added the four LXX manuscripts of Exodus, Leviticus, and Numbers. . . . All fit *quite clearly* into the textual tradition that we know from the great 4th century [C.E.] manuscripts and thus counter the *sweeping theory* of Kahle with *tangible facts*."[6] This forceful conclusion is reiterated in the thorough studies of 4QLXXLev[a] done by Eugene Ulrich and Emanuel Tov.[7] In relation to the debate over Septuagint origins, it is interest-

---

Desert" in *Studies in New Testament Language and Text: Essays in Honour of George D. Kilpatrick on the Occasion of his Sixty-Fifth Birthday* ([ed. J. K. Elliott; NovTSup 44; Leiden: Brill, 1976], 283-300). Eugene Ulrich published a preliminary collation of the variants found in 4QLXXLev[a] without analysis in "The Greek Manuscripts of the Pentateuch from Qumrân, Including Newly-Identified Fragments of Deuteronomy (4QLXXDeut)," in *De Septuaginta: Studies in Honour of John William Wevers on his Sixty-Fifth Birthday* (ed. Albert Pietersma and Claude Cox; Mississauga, Ontario: Benben, 1984), 71-82. In 1992, Ulrich published a full analysis of the 4QLXXLev[a] variants in "The Septuagint Manuscripts from Qumran: A Reappraisal of Their Value," in *Septuagint, Scrolls, and Cognate Writings* (ed. George Brooke and Barnabas Lindars; Septuagint and Cognate Studies; Atlanta: Scholars, 1992), 49-80. The most recent analysis of this text is found in Emanuel Tov, "The Greek Biblical Texts from the Judean Desert," in *The Bible as Book: The Transmission of the Greek Text* (ed. Scot McKendrick and Orlaith A. O'Sullivan; London: The British Library and New Castle: Oak Knoll Press, 2003), 97-122. Some of the conclusions found in this essay have already appeared in Tov's earlier essay: "Greek Texts from the Judean Desert," *QC* 8 (1999): 161-68.

4. Named after its founder, Paul de Lagarde. In the most simplified of terms, this is the view that there was one original Greek translation of Jewish Scripture. The primary challenge to de Lagarde's view is found in the multiple translation theory of Paul Kahle. A thorough discussion of both viewpoints is included in the next section.

5. Skehan, "Qumran Manuscripts and Textual Criticism," 158 (emphasis added).

6. Skehan, "Biblical Scrolls from Qumran," 91-92 (emphasis added).

7. Ulrich ("Greek Manuscripts of the Pentateuch," 82; "Reappraisal," 74-76) and Tov ("Greek Texts from the Judean Desert," 167; "Greek Biblical Texts," 118). The analysis provided by Ulrich and Tov will be discussed below.

ing to note that the Greek texts from Qumran were reconciled by some with the *Urtext* theory even *before* thorough analyses of the variants had been published.[8] This is perhaps less surprising when one considers the tenor and scope of the proto-Septuagint debate.

De Lagarde's *Urtext* theory has prevailed so strongly in the discussion of Septuagint origins that it seems to have taken on the status of presupposition in most LXX scholarship of the twentieth century.[9] The antiquity of the Qumran texts, however, combined with the number of variant readings they witness, invites further discussion of the evidence they provide for the proto-LXX question. Indeed, the data provided by 4QLXXLev[a] are at least somewhat more diverse than the aforementioned conclusions might suggest. Some aspects of this text support the *Urtext* theory; others do not. Since previous studies have argued that 4QLXXLev[a] supports the *Urtext* theory, the purpose of this investigation will be to highlight the counterevidence. As with many of the essays in the present volume, the point of this study is not to discard or dismiss earlier discussions of this important textual evidence. Rather, the point is to reexamine presuppositions and conclusions long since taken for granted. After recapitulating the salient features of the proto-Septuagint debate, I will discuss the analyses of both Ulrich and Tov and suggest some evidence that may call into question the extent to which 4QLXXLev[a] can be cited as evidence for de Lagarde's *Urtext* theory.

1. The Debate over the Origins of the Septuagint

The battle lines of the proto-Septuagint debate can be described in deceptively simple terms. On one side are those who accept the view of Paul de Lagarde, who claimed that there was one original Greek translation of the Hebrew Scriptures, and that this translation is the common ancestor of all extant manuscripts of the LXX.[10] On the other side are those who accept the view of Paul Kahle, who argued that various Greek translations arose in Egypt in much the same way that the Aramaic Targums arose in Palestine, and that these multiple translations were eventually replaced by an "official" translation commissioned by Alexandrian Jews in the latter half of the second century B.C.E.[11] The initial simplicity of both lines fades, however, as

---

8. This is true both of Skehan's initial study and of Leaney's agreement with it.

9. See the comments of Jellicoe noted below.

10. See, for example, the introductory discussion in de Lagarde's *Anmerkungen zur griechischen Übersetzung der Proverbien* (Leipzig: F. A. Brockhaus, 1863), 1-4.

11. Kahle's initial publication of this theory came in his "Untersuchungen zur Geschichte

one begins to examine the background of, and theoretical pay-off for, each side of the debate.

De Lagarde's theory has always been particularly appealing to many textual critics for whom study of the LXX is primarily a means to the end of understanding Hebrew text tradition(s) pre-dating MT. Since most of the significant revisions of the LXX appear to represent closer approximations to a proto-MT or to the MT itself, the proposed "original" Greek translation would logically represent an older Hebrew text — a Hebrew text that might be different from the prevailing proto-MT and MT traditions. The goal of de Lagarde (and his adherents), therefore, was to sift through the extant evidence in order to produce an eclectic text representing the nearest approximation to the *original* Greek translation. This original translation could then be used to better understand a Hebrew text *earlier* than MT: "wollen wir über den hebräischen text ins klare kommen, so gilt es zunächst die urform der griechischen übersetzung zu finden."[12]

Even de Lagarde's initial outline involved the delicate unraveling of recensional materials in order to get back to the original translation,[13] but subsequent discoveries further complicated the practicability of his theory. Papyrus Greek 458 in the Rylands Library, containing fragments of Deuteronomy 23–28 and dated by some to the middle of the second century B.C.E.,[14] is remarkably similar to a recensional text-type that scholars had previously associated with the fourth-century C.E. figure of Lucian.[15] In practical terms, Barthélemy's publication of a Minor Prophets text, dated to the latter half of the first century C.E.,[16] has added even more confusion.[17] There has been uni-

---

des Pentateuchtextes," *TSK* 88 (1915): 399-439. A broader explication of his theory is found in idem, *The Cairo Geniza* (2d ed.; Oxford: Basil Blackwell, 1959).

12. De Lagarde, *Anmerkungen*, 2.

13. See the discussion in de Lagarde, *Anmerkungen*, 1-4.

14. This is the dating given by Kahle (*Cairo Geniza*, 220), presumably based on the analysis of C. H. Roberts.

15. The proto-Lucianic problem, of course, did not begin with the discovery of this manuscript. Both the Old Latin and the quotations of Jewish Scripture in Josephus have affinities with the text-type originally associated with the fourth-century martyr (John William Wevers, "Proto-Septuagint Studies," in *The Seed of Wisdom: Essays in Honour of T. J. Meek* [ed. William McCullough; Toronto: Toronto University Press, 1964], 69; repr. in *Studies in the Septuagint: Origins, Recensions, and Interpretations* [ed. S. Jellicoe; New York: Ktav, 1974], 149). Wevers describes the issue of a "proto-Lucianic text" as "the most difficult problem in modern Septuagint work" (149).

16. This is Dominique Barthélemy's assessment of the date ("Redécouverte d'un chaînon manquant de l'histoire de la Septante," *RB* 60 [1953]: 19; and see Barthélemy, *Les devanciers d'Aquila* [VTSup 10; Leiden: Brill, 1963], 167). Based on the analysis of C. H. Roberts, Kahle argued for an earlier dating of 50 B.C.E.–50 C.E. (*Cairo Geniza*, 226-27).

17. This Minor Prophets text characteristically employs καίγε to translate the Hebrew גם,

versal agreement that this text is revisional in nature.[18] What is confusing is that it shares significant traits with what was previously considered to be the so-called "Old Greek" (i.e., the *original* translation) of a significant amount of material in the LXX (particularly in Samuel-Kings).[19] For this material in Samuel-Kings, therefore, the best approximation to the *original* Greek translation is now widely accepted as a revision of that theoretical original![20] De-

---

exhibiting a literalism that would later be magnified by the use of σύν to translate את in the recension labeled Aquila. Indeed, it is this characteristic of Aquila that helps Barthélemy to formulate his hypothesis regarding the recensional nature of the Minor Prophets scroll: "Si l'on remarque d'autre part qu'il existe toute une série de livres de la Bible grecque où les traducteurs ou recenseurs se sont également appliqués à distinguer גם par καίγε, sans pourtant se préoccuper de traduire la particule d'accusatif, une hypothèse se présente tout de suite à l'esprit: les traductions ou recensions de la Bible grecque ainsi caractérisées n'auraient-elles pas été faites sous l'égide du rabbinat palestinien à une époque où florissait déjà un littéralisme minutieux, mais avant qu'Aqiba n'ait à la fois poussé à son comble et monopolisé cette tendance?" (*Les devanciers*, 31). Barthélemy, therefore, labeled the Minor Prophets scroll and other witnesses conforming to this recensional text type as "groupe καίγε" and devoted the first part of *Les devanciers* to delineating the characteristics of this recension.

18. Some of the references to this text in subsequent scholarship may be misleading. S. Jellicoe cites part of the debate over the Minor Prophets scroll in his description of the significant opposition to Kahle's theory: "Barthélemy, whose whole volume *Les Devanciers d'Aquila* constitutes a powerful rejoinder to Kahle's assault on [Barthélemy's] earlier article announcing the Dodekapropheton discovery . . ." (*The Septuagint and Modern Study* [repr. ed.; Winona Lake, Indiana: Eisenbrauns, 1989], 62). F. M. Cross asserts: "The καίγε Recension is of decisive bearing on the debate over Septuagint origins. It brings a qualified victory to the Lagarde school, despite Paul Kahle's protestations to the contrary" ("The History of the Biblical Text in the Light of Discoveries in the Judaean Desert," *HTR* 57 [1964]: 283; repr. in *Qumran and the History of the Biblical Text* [ed. F. M. Cross and S. Talmon; Cambridge: Harvard University Press, 1975], 179). Such comments make it sound as though Kahle contended with Barthélemy over the question of whether the Minor Prophets scroll represented a revision of an older Greek translation. He did not. On the contrary, Kahle refers to the "adaptations" to the Hebrew found in this text ("A Leather Scroll of the Greek Minor Prophets and the Problem of the Septuagint," in Kahle, *Opera Minora* [Leiden: Brill, 1956], 117; trans. of German original in *TLZ* 79 [1954]: coll. 81-94). Kahle's contention with Barthélemy centered on the dating of the scroll (along with C. H. Roberts, Kahle wanted to date it 50 B.C.E.–50 C.E. ["A Leather Scroll," 113]) and Barthélemy's extension of this recensional group to include a significant amount of material previously thought to be a part of the so-called "Old Greek" (see Kahle, *Cairo Geniza*, 246).

19. For a complete discussion of biblical material that may fall into this καίγε group, see Barthélemy's *Les devanciers d'Aquila* (especially Parts 1 and 2).

20. Here, one enters a complex arena befitting Cross' tongue-in-cheek description: "the miasmal precincts of text-critical labors" ("History of the Biblical Text," 177). How can a "revision" be considered "original"? In the introduction to Tov's *The Text-Critical Use of the Septuagint in Biblical Research* (rev. ed.; Jerusalem: Simor Ltd., 1997), we find some of the subtle shifts necessary for keeping all of the extant evidence within the confines of a single theory of Septuagint origins. Tov begins with the assumption of an *Urtext*: "one Greek translation

spite these considerable challenges, scholars have argued that the extant LXX manuscripts support de Lagarde's *Urtext* theory: variations from the prevailing witnesses to the so-called "Old Greek," they say, are attributable either to scribal error, scribal correction, or to larger scale revisional endeavors, such as the hexaplaric witnesses often regarded as Theodotion, Aquila, and Symmachus. Indeed, as Jellicoe observes, de Lagarde's theory went uncontested until the work of Paul Kahle appeared in 1915.[21]

Kahle's challenge to de Lagarde's *Urtext* theory was based on his understanding of the Aramaic Targums and the way these traditions developed through various oral and written stages in Palestine.[22] Just as it seemed reasonable to de Lagarde that there was a single, original Greek translation, so it seemed reasonable to Kahle that the Greek translations of the Hebrew Scripture should fit the same pattern of development as the Palestinian Aramaic translations.[23] In this view, the standardized Greek translation on which later revisions were based was not an "original" translation, but a translation commissioned by Jewish authorities in Alexandria to supersede the multiple

---

must be presupposed as the base of the manuscripts of most, if not all, the books of the LXX. . . . the assumption of an *Urtext* that may be reconstructed . . . remains methodologically correct" (11-12). As we have noted, however, a revision cannot logically be the original. Therefore, an adjustment is made: "As already noted, it stands to reason that all known manuscripts and papyri of the LXX . . . derive from one *archetypal* text, which *may* have been identical with the *original* translation" (13, emphasis added). So, we have now moved from the presumed "original" translation to an "archetypal" text, which *may* be identical with that "original." Presuming an "archetype" that has been distinguished from the original, "original" texts and "revisions" can be mixed together without upsetting our pursuit of an *Urtext*, which can now be identified with an archetype rather than the original: "The anonymous person(s) responsible for selecting the translations included in the collection of Jewish-Greek Scripture apparently did not pay much attention to their uniformity, probably because there were not many copies of each individual translated book from which to choose. Hence the 'LXX' contains translations of *different types, early and late, original and revised*, official and private" (16, emphasis added).

21. Jellicoe, *Septuagint and Modern Study*, 61; here Jellicoe is referring to Kahle's "Untersuchungen zur Geschichte des Pentateuchtextes" *TSK* 88 (1915): 399-439.

22. For a concise summary of Kahle's reasoning, see *Cairo Geniza*, 213-14.

23. Despite the attempts of scholars on both sides of the debate to demonstrate the way that the extant manuscript evidence supports one theory or another, we should not pass lightly over this issue of what "seems reasonable." Critical assumptions that "make sense" to the participants are a pervasive part of many arguments in this ongoing discussion: "it *stands to reason* that all known manuscripts and papyri . . . derive from one archetypal text" (Tov, *Text-Critical Use of the Septuagint*, 13 [emphasis added]); "That this was an oral Targum *seems far more likely* than another Ur-Document, in this case an Ur-Theodotion. One Ur-Document, an Ur-Lucian (or better, the Antiochian text) which cannot be avoided, is enough" (Wevers, "Proto-Septuagint Studies," 72 [emphasis added]).

translations being used at that time.[24] Kahle's theory suffered severe attacks on three fronts: lack of evidence, historical speculation, and the subsequent (and unsound) work of his student, Alexander Sperber.

Although Kahle's multiple translation theory was plausible enough in itself, there has been no manuscript evidence that definitively supported his argument and simultaneously opposed that of de Lagarde. Indeed, one of the strangest facets of the debate over Septuagint origins is this question of "evidence." Strictly speaking, there is not much. This is not to ignore the rich and complex body of manuscripts witnessing the Greek translation of Jewish Scripture. The problem is that almost all of these manuscripts are relatively late when one considers the dates proposed by either school for the actual *origins* of the Septuagint. Only a tiny handful of very fragmentary texts can be dated before the common era. In their criticisms of Kahle's theory, Lagardians regularly lambaste him for not providing tangible supporting evidence.[25] That the extant manuscripts can be massaged into line with the *Urtext* theory is somewhat vitiated, however, by the fact that all of the witnesses of any significant length to a text-type identified with the so-called "Old Greek" are dated several centuries *after* the presumed original translation. That the extant evidence can be categorized into manuscripts largely representing "older" readings and others representing revised readings *does* suggest that a particular Greek translation was considered the "standard" Greek text prior to the common era, but both schools of thought already acknowledge this point. What the evidence does not prove is *when* that "standard" text became standardized.[26] Furthermore, the evidence does not prove anything about translations that may or may not have come before it. There is simply *not enough evidence* to *prove* either theory. The demand for supporting evidence from Kahle, therefore, is interesting when one considers that the Lagardian theory is primarily supported by a lack of early evidence *against it*.

While there may be a dearth of early manuscript evidence, legends de-

24. Kahle, *Cairo Geniza*, 214-15.

25. Harry M. Orlinsky's comments are representative: "Kahle presented no specific evidence to prove his hypothesis with regard to the Septuagint. . . . All talk of independent and equally original Greek translations is without foundation" ("On the Present State of Proto-Septuagint Studies," *JAOS* 61 [1941]: 86-87).

26. This may be one of the issues Tov hints at when he states: "The two theories have developed beyond the original formulations of de Lagarde and Kahle, but in scholarship these subsequent developments are often ascribed to them. Furthermore, the usual polarized description of these theories is not justified because they are, in fact, not mutually exclusive" (*Text-Critical Use of the Septuagint*, 11).

scribing the magnificent, and even miraculous, beginnings of the Greek Bible are not lacking. Both the pseudepigraphical *Letter of Aristeas* and Philo's *On the Life of Moses* describe the circumstances in which the Jewish Law was translated from Hebrew into Greek. The accounts differ from one another, and the historicity of each, of course, has long been doubted.[27] Despite suspicions regarding the historicity of particular claims in these legends, the legends themselves continue to have a remarkable influence in the debate over Septuagint origins.[28] De Lagarde's *Urtext* theory presumed at least a historical kernel behind these legendary accounts, and Kahle had to deal with them as well. His solution was to view the *Letter of Aristeas* as propaganda, written around 100 B.C.E., for the newly produced "standardized" translation.[29] Arguing that the *Letter of Aristeas* was propaganda necessitated an alternative explanation of the real impetus for the translation, and Kahle suggested that this probably came in the form of a commission made by Alexandrian Jews to have a standard Greek translation of Scripture.[30] These speculations were difficult for many scholars to accept, and seem to have hurt Kahle's argument as much as they may have helped.[31]

The most damning attacks on Kahle's theory have resulted inadvertently from the work of his student, Alexander Sperber. Presumably in his zeal to prove the theory of his teacher, Sperber produced a number of unsound arguments that were easily dismantled by his Lagardian opponents. In 1937, for example, Sperber published "Wiederherstellung einer griechischen Textgestalt des Buches Ruth,"[32] in which he argues against a connection between the Old Latin and Codex Vaticanus.[33] In order to demonstrate this hypothesis, Sperber produces a retroversion of the Old Latin into Greek, and then shows where his created retroversion differs from Vaticanus. This is so

27. See Jellicoe's discussion in *Septuagint and Modern Study*, 29-41. Particularly "fantastic" is Philo's claim that multiple translators produced perfectly identical translations (*Moses* 2, 7.37-40).

28. Referring to Philo's account, for example, Wevers contends that the legend suggests something greater than Kahle's proposed commissioned translation: "It should be remembered that Philo records an annual feast held on the Island of Pharos to commemorate the events producing the Septuagint. . . . The tradition was apparently an old one, and one *feels* that more than a recension of the Greek Old Testament was here at stake" ("Proto-Septuagint Studies," 65 [emphasis added]).

29. See, for example, Kahle, *Cairo Geniza*, 209-14.

30. Ibid., 214-15.

31. See, for example, the discussion of Wevers, "Proto-Septuagint Studies," 62-66.

32. Alexander Sperber, "Wiederherstellung einer griechischen Textgestalt des Buches Ruth," *MGWJ* 81 (1937): 55-65.

33. Orlinsky, "Present State," 89.

methodologically unsound as to deserve scorn, but Orlinsky's critique reveals even deeper, fundamental problems:

> One can but agree that this new translation is different from any devised heretofore. It is characterized by its artificial Latin-into-Greek dictionary and concordance translation. Witness, e.g., the omission at times of the definite article in this new Greek version simply because the Old Latin lacked one, ignoring the fact that Latin did not operate with the definite article![34]

In fact, Sperber's repeated attempts to support his teacher's theory were so poor that even an opponent of Kahle was inclined to assert: "One doubts whether Kahle would be happy to accept some of the wild statements of his disciple, and yet this is the kind of chaos that can result from theories inadequately founded in fact."[35]

As the subsequent history of scholarship indicates, the proto-Septuagint debate has been rather one-sided. De Lagarde's *Urtext* theory has prevailed over the challenges of Kahle. Jellicoe's observations are some of the most diplomatic:

> Prima facie [Kahle's] hypothesis is reasonable enough in the light of the Targum analogy, but apart from the proponent's pupil, Alexander

---

34. Ibid.

35. Wevers, "Proto-Septuagint Studies," 76-77. The latter portion of this statement is especially interesting given the number of unsupported, sweeping claims Wevers himself makes in this article. The following, for example, would make many New Testament scholars cringe: "What Kahle presupposes with respect to the New Testament quotations . . . is that the New Testament writers actually had a Greek text of the Old Testament and quoted it verbatim. This conclusion I find quite unacceptable. The New Testament writers *were Semitic speaking. Greek was only their second language. Their Bible was the Hebrew Bible;* the translation to which they were accustomed was *an oral Aramaic Targum.* . . . the New Testament writers were *well acquainted with the Old Testament in Hebrew, and it would be far easier to translate de novo*" (151-52, emphasis added). Compare, for example, the comments of both Joseph Fitzmyer and Jacob Jervell on the author of Luke-Acts: "It is not surprising that [Luke's] quotations of the OT have been drawn from a Greek translation, akin to the LXX, if not the LXX as we know it" (Joseph A. Fitzmyer, *The Acts of the Apostles: A New Translation with Introduction and Commentary* [AB 31; New York: Doubleday, 1998], 91); and "Wichtiger noch sind die semitischen syntaktischen Wendungen, von denen die meisten offenbar aus der Septuaginta kommen" (Jacob Jervell, *Die Apostelgeschichte: Übersetzt und Erklärt* [KEK 17; Göttingen: Vandenhoeck & Ruprecht, 1998], 75). Jervell also suggests some possible influence from Aramaic and Hebrew sources (75), but the primary source is the Septuagint. For both scholars, the likelihood that the author of Luke-Acts was Semitic does *not* further indicate that the author's primary source material for the OT was Hebrew or Aramaic.

Sperber, and a few others who have been favourably disposed, the consensus of opinion has been overwhelmingly contrary. The very data adduced by Kahle have been increasingly turned against him in vindication of the Lagardian hypothesis, a theory which has motivated the entire work of the Göttingen school, the researches of a number of independent workers of whom Max Leopold Margolis may be taken as typical, and which was accepted, if no more than tacitly, by the Cambridge school.[36]

Other assessments have been far less kind, ranging from the inexplicably vituperative[37] to the condescendingly dismissive.[38]

As Jellicoe has stated, the question of Septuagint origins reaches farther than competing hypotheses and speculation. As a point of fact, de Lagarde's basic theory has provided the foundation for most of the significant work in LXX studies during the twentieth century. The idea that scholars can construct an eclectic text that somehow approximates the "original" Greek translation continues to fuel the ongoing production of the Göttingen series. Moreover, this "original" translation is of fundamental importance among those for whom the Septuagint is primarily valuable as evidence in the larger framework of textual criticism of the Hebrew Bible.[39] One wonders whether the zeal with which Kahle's opponents have derided his theory might have some basis in the implications of Kahle's theory for these studies.[40] In any case, it is clear that de Lagarde's theory has become a presupposition in most LXX research. The limited studies of the Greek material at Qumran are no exception as the following section will demonstrate.

36. Jellicoe, *Septuagint and Modern Study,* 61-62.

37. Note, for example, the acerbic tone of Orlinsky: "Kahle presented no specific evidence to prove his hypothesis with regard to the Septuagint, any more than he did with regard to the Masorah. *Excellent organizer that he is* . . . Kahle later entrusted the task of refuting the Lagardian theory, with facts, to his pupil, Alexander Sperber" ("Present State," 86 [emphasis added]).

38. See, for example, Wevers' comment: "Up to this point the argument between Kahle and the Lagarde school has been purely speculative, Kahle's objections hinging on a rather dubious interpretation of an obscure passage" ("Proto-Septuagint Studies, 146).

39. See Tov's *Text-Critical Use of the Septuagint,* and Chapter 2 of his *Textual Criticism of the Hebrew Bible* (rev. ed.; Minneapolis: Fortress and Assen: Royal Van Gorcum, 2001).

40. Kahle described these implications in the following way: "The task which the Septuagint presents to scholars is not the 'reconstruction' of an imaginary 'Urtext' nor the discovery of it, but a careful collection and investigation of all the remains and traces of earlier versions of the Greek Bible which differed from the Christian standard text" (*Cairo Geniza,* 264).

Chart 1
4QLXXLev^a (4Q119)[41]

Frg. 1 (Lev 26:2-16)

top margin

1	[²	μο]ὺ φοβηθησεσθε εγ[ω ειμι	³	]
2	[	π]ὸρευησθε και τας εντ[ολας μου		]
3	[⁴	τον υετον τ]ῆι γηι υμων εν καιρωι αὺ[του		]
4	[	κ]ὰι τον ξυλινὸν καρῆ[ον	⁵	]
5	[	]ὸ αμητος[τον]σπορὺ[ητον		]
6	[	σ]πορον κὰ[ι φα]ῆεσθ[ε		]
7	[	κ]ὰτὸικὴὸ[ετε		]
8	[⁶	ε]ἰρηνην εν τ[ηι γηι υμων]κὰἱ[		]
9	[	ο]ἐκφοβων υμας κ̇[αι α]π̇ολω[		]
10	[	κ]ὰι πολεμὸς ου δ̇[ιελε]ὺσετ̇[αι	⁷	]
11	[διωξεσθ]ε τους εχθρους υμων [κ]αι π̇[εσουνται		]
12	[⁸	διωξ]ονται πεντε υμων εκ̇[ατον	διω]
13	[ξοντ]ὰἱ μυριαδας και πεσουντὰ[ι		]
14	[μαχαιρα]ι ⁹και ἐπ̇ιβλεψω εφ υμας[		]
15	[και εσται μο]ὺ η διαθηκη ἐν ὑμῖν̇[¹⁰		]
16	[εξοισετ]ε μετὰ των νεων[¹¹		]
17	κ̇αι ου β̇δελυξομαι υμας ¹²και εσομ[αι υμιν θεος		]

(Line 5 has superscript "τρυ·" above "σπορὺ[ητον")

---

41. Cf. the edition by Skehan, Ulrich, and Sanderson, "119. 4QLXXLeviticus^a," in DJD 9: 161-65, esp. 162 and Pl. 38.

18 και υμεις εσεσθε μοι εθν[ος ¹³   ε]

19 ξαγαγων υμας εγ γης Αιγὺ[πτου   ]

20 συνετριψα τὸν ζυγον τὸ[υ δεσμου   ]

21_μετα παρρησιας ¹⁴εαν[   ]

22 προσταγματα μου   ¹⁵αὶ[λα   προστα]

23 γμασι μου προσοχθιὸ[ηι   ]

24 τας εντολας μου α[λλα ωστε (?)   ]

25 ¹⁶και εγω ποιησὼ[   ]

26 ψωραν και το[ν   ]

27 και την ψυ[χην   ]

28 υμων [¹⁷   ]

bottom margin

12

LXX of Leviticus 26:2-16[42]

²τὰ σάββατά μου φυλάξεσθε καὶ ἀπὸ τῶν ἁγίων μου φοβηθήσεσθε · ἐγώ εἰμι κύριος.

³᾿Εὰν τοῖς προστάγμασίν μου πορεύησθε, καὶ τὰς ἐντολάς μου φυλάσσησθε καὶ ποιήσητε αὐτάς, ⁴καὶ δώσω τὸν ὑετὸν ὑμῖν ἐν καιρῷ αὐτοῦ, καὶ ἡ γῆ δώσει τὰ γενήματα αὐτῆς, καὶ τὰ ξύλα τῶν πεδίων ἀποδώσει τὸν καρπὸν αὐτῶν · ⁵καὶ καταλήμψεται ὑμῖν ὁ ἀλοητὸς τὸν τρύγητον, καὶ ὁ τρύγητος καταλήμψεται τὸν σπόρον, καὶ φάγεσθε τὸν ἄρτον ὑμῶν εἰς πλησμονήν, καὶ κατοικήσετε μετὰ ἀσφαλείας ἐπὶ τῆς γῆς ὑμῶν · ⁶καὶ πόλεμος οὐ διελεύσεται διὰ τῆς γῆς ὑμῶν, καὶ δώσω εἰρήνην ἐν τῇ γῇ ὑμῶν, καὶ κοιμηθήσεσθε, καὶ οὐκ ἔσται ὑμᾶς ὁ ἐκφοβῶν, καὶ ἀπολῶ θηρία πονηρὰ ἐκ τῆς γῆς ὑμῶν. ⁷καὶ διώξεσθε τοὺς ἐχθροὺς ὑμῶν, καὶ πεσοῦνται ἐναντίον ὑμῶν φόνῳ · ⁸καὶ διώξονται ἐξ ὑμῶν πέντε ἑκατόν, καὶ ἑκατὸν ὑμῶν διώξονται μυριάδας, καὶ πεσοῦνται οἱ ἐχθροὶ ὑμῶν ἐναντίον ὑμῶν μαχαίρᾳ. ⁹καὶ ἐπιβλέψω ἐφ᾿ ὑμᾶς καὶ αὐξανῶ ὑμᾶς καὶ πληθυνῶ ὑμᾶς καὶ στήσω τὴν διαθήκην μου μεθ᾿ ὑμῶν. ¹⁰καὶ φάγεσθε παλαιὰ καὶ παλαιὰ παλαιῶν, καὶ παλαιὰ ἐκ προσώπου νέων ἐξοίσετε. ¹¹καὶ θήσω τὴν σκηνήν μου ἐν ὑμῖν, καὶ οὐ βδελύξεται ἡ ψυχή μου ὑμᾶς. ¹²καὶ ἐμπεριπατήσω ἐν ὑμῖν καὶ ἔσομαι ὑμῶν θεός, καὶ ὑμεῖς ἔσεσθέ μου λαός. ¹³ἐγώ εἰμι κύριος ὁ θεὸς ὑμῶν ὁ ἐξαγαγὼν ὑμᾶς ἐκ γῆς Αἰγύπτου, ὄντων ὑμῶν δούλων, καὶ συνέτριψα τὸν δεσμὸν τοῦ ζυγοῦ ὑμῶν καὶ ἤγαγον ὑμᾶς μετὰ παρρησίας.

¹⁴᾿Εὰν δὲ μὴ ὑπακούσητέ μου μηδὲ ποιήσητε τὰ προστάγματά μου ταῦτα, ¹⁵ἀλλὰ ἀπειθήσητε αὐτοῖς, καὶ τοῖς κρίμασίν μου προσοχθίσῃ ἡ ψυχὴ ὑμῶν, ὥστε ὑμᾶς μὴ ποιεῖν πάσας τὰς ἐντολάς μου, ὥστε διασκεδάσαι τὴν διαθήκην μου, ¹⁶καὶ ἐγὼ ποιήσω οὕτως ὑμῖν, καὶ ἐπισυστήσω ἐφ᾿ ὑμᾶς τὴν ἀπορίαν τήν τε ψῶραν καὶ τὸν ἴκτερον καὶ σφακελίζοντας τοὺς ὀφθαλμοὺς ὑμῶν καὶ τὴν ψυχὴν ὑμῶν ἐκτήκουσαν, καὶ σπερεῖτε διὰ κενῆς τὰ σπέρματα ὑμῶν, καὶ ἔδονται οἱ ὑπεναντίοι ὑμῶν ·

---

42. The text follows the Göttingen edition (see note 1).

MT of Leviticus 26:2-16[43]

‫2את־שבתתי תשמרו ומקדשי תיראו אני יהוה:‬
‫3אם־בחקתי תלכו ואת־מצותי תשמרו ועשיתם אתם:‬
‫4ונתתי גשמיכם בעתם ונתנה הארץ יבולה ועץ השדה יתן פריו:‬
‫5והשיג לכם דיש את־בציר ובציר ישיג‬
‫את־זרע ואכלתם לחמכם לשבע וישבתם לבטח בארצכם:‬
‫6ונתתי שלום בארץ ושכבתם ואין מחריד והשבתי חיה‬
‫רעה מן־הארץ וחרב לא־תעבר בארצכם: 7ורדפתם‬
‫את־איביכם ונפלו לפניכם לחרב: 8ורדפו מכם חמשה‬
‫מאה ומאה מכם רבבה ירדפו ונפלו איביכם לפניכם‬
‫לחרב: 9ופניתי אליכם והפריתי אתכם והרביתי אתכם‬
‫והקימתי את־בריתי אתכם: 10ואכלתם ישן נושן וישן מפני‬
‫חדש תוציאו: 11ונתתי משכני בתוככם ולא־תגעל נפשי‬
‫אתכם: 12והתהלכתי בתוככם והייתי לכם לאלהים ואתם‬
‫תהיו־לי לעם: 13אני יהוה אלהיכם אשר הוצאתי אתכם‬
‫מארץ מצרים מהית להם עבדים ואשבר מטת עלכם‬
‫ואולך אתכם קוממיות: 14ואם־לא תשמעו לי ולא‬
‫תעשו את כל־המצות האלה: 15ואם־בחקתי תמאסו ואם‬
‫את־משפטי תגעל נפשכם לבלתי עשות את־כל־מצותי‬
‫להפרכם את־בריתי: 16אף־אני אעשה־זאת לכם והפקדתי‬
‫עליכם בהלה את־השחפת ואת־הקדחת מכלות עינים‬
‫ומדיבת נפש וזרעתם לריק זרעכם ואכלהו איביכם:‬

---

43. The text follows that of Leningradensis (MS B19[A]) as edited by G. Quell in *Biblia Hebraica Stuttgartensia* (ed. K. Elliger and W. Rudolph; 4th ed.; Stuttgart: Deutsche Bibelgesellschaft, 1990), 203-4.

2. Assessing the Evidence from Qumran

The following is a simplified version of the 4QLXXLevᵃ variants collated in DJD 9 (for the text see Chart 1):[44]

Variant 1: 4QLXXLevᵃ frg. 1 line 3 (Lev 26:4)
τον υετον τ]ῆι γηι υμων 𝕮ᴶ (מיטריא דארעכון)] τον υετον υμιν 𝕲 = גשמיכם MT SamP

Variant 2: 4QLXXLevᵃ frg. 1 line 4 (Lev 26:4)
τον ξυλινὸν καρπ̂[ ] τα ξυλα των πεδιων αποδωσει τον καρπον αυτων 𝕲 = (ו)עץ השדה יתן פריו MT SamP

Variant 3: 4QLXXLevᵃ frg. 1 line 5 (Lev 26:5)
αμητος A B* MSS] αλοητος 𝕲 = דיש MT SamP

Variant 4: 4QLXXLevᵃ frg. 1 line 9 (Lev 26:6)
ο]ἐκφοβων υμας F MSS] υμας ο εκφοβων 𝕲

Variant 5: 4QLXXLevᵃ frg. 1 line 10 (Lev 26:6)
κ]ὰι πολεμὸ̣ς — [υμων = MT SamP] ad 5 fin 𝕲; ad 5 fin et 6 fin A Bᵐᵍ F MSS

Variant 6: 4QLXXLevᵃ frg. 1 line 12 (Lev 26:8)
πεντε υμων] εξ υμων πεντε 𝕲; מכם חמשה MT SamP

Variant 7: 4QLXXLevᵃ frg. 1 line 15 (Lev 26:9)
και εσται μο]ὺ η διαθηκη ἐν ὑμῖν̂] και στησω την διαθηκην μου μεθ υμων 𝕲 = והק(י)מתי את בריתי אתכם MT SamP

Variant 8: 4QLXXLevᵃ frg. 1 line 16 (Lev 26:10)
εξοισετ]ε μετὰ των νεων] εκ προσωπου νεων εξοισετε 𝕲 = מפני חדש תוציאו MT SamP

Variant 9: 4QLXXLevᵃ frg. 1 line 17 (Lev 26:11)
βδ̂ελυξομαι] βδελυξεται η ψυχη μου 𝕲 = תגעל נפשי MT SamP

---

44. Cf. DJD 9:164-65.

Variant 10: 4QLXXLevᵃ frg. 1 line 17 (Lev 26:12)

και εσομ̣[αι υμιν θεος] και εμπεριπατησω εν υμιν και εσομαι υμων θεος 𝕲 = והתהלכתי בתוככם והייתי לכם לאלהים MT SamP

Variant 11: 4QLXXLevᵃ frg. 1 line 18 (Lev 26:12)

εσεσθε μοι εθν[ος] εσεσθε μου λαος 𝕲; תהיו לי לעם MT SamP

Variant 12: 4QLXXLevᵃ frg. 1 line 20 (Lev 26:13)

τὸν ζυγον τὸ[υ δεσμου] τον δεσμον του ζυγου 𝕲; מטת על(כם) MT

Variant 13: 4QLXXLevᵃ frg. 1 line 22 (Lev 26:14)

μου] + ταυτα 𝕲 = האלה MT SamP

Variant 14: 4QLXXLevᵃ frg. 1 line 22 (Lev 26:15)

αλ̀[λα 𝕲] ואם MT SamP

Variant 15: 4QLXXLevᵃ frg. 1 lines 22-23 (Lev 26:15)

[προστα]/γμασι μου] κριμασιν μου 𝕲; משפטי MT SamP

Variant 16: 4QLXXLevᵃ frg. 1 line 24 (Lev 26:15)

α[λλα ωστε (?)] ωστε 𝕲 = ל(הפרכם) MT SamP

In 1992, the same year that 4QLXXLevᵃ and the other Greek texts from Cave 4 were published in DJD IX, Eugene Ulrich published "The Septuagint Manuscripts from Qumran: A Reappraisal of Their Value."[45] A significant portion of this article is devoted to an evaluation of the variant readings found in 4QLXXLevᵃ.[46] For each variant, Ulrich provides a thorough discussion of possible explanations for the different reading, as well as an evaluation of potential correction or revision.[47] With reference to Variant 1, for example, Ulrich notes the possibility of a different Hebrew *Vorlage* behind 4QLXXLevᵃ based on the agreement with 𝕮ᴶ.[48] In terms of correction/revision, he observes that if 𝕲 is original, it represents a "translation of a text like MT [and SamP], and 4QLXXLevᵃ is either a legitimate, free translation of the same Hebrew or a literal reflection of a slightly different Hebrew *Vorlage*."[49] If, on the

---

45. See note 3 above.

46. Ulrich, "Reappraisal," esp. 52-63 and 74-76.

47. That is, he considers the circumstances in which 𝕲 might represent a revision/correction of a text like 4QLXXLevᵃ and vice versa.

48. Ulrich, "Reappraisal," 53.

49. Ibid.

other hand, 4QLXXLev^a is closer to the "Old Greek," 𝕲 "is probably the result of a revision toward MT."[50] Although couched in cautious language, Ulrich's eventual conclusion is that 4QLXXLev^a "penetrates further behind" the prevailing witnesses to the so-called Old Greek, and that the readings found in 𝕲 can be characterized more consistently as "a revision toward the proto-MT."[51] It is interesting to note, however, that Ulrich's language regarding text tradition is far from tentative:

> 4QLXXLev^a displays 15 variants from the text of 𝕲^ed . . . 15 variants in 28 less-than-half-extant lines of manuscript! But none of these variants are errors. . . . Is Kahle correct that prior to the LXX translation there were divergent Greek targumim? No. These variants are embedded in a text that shows 75% agreement with 𝕲^ed. Thus, 4QLXXLev^a and 𝕲^ed are two representatives of the same translation.[52]

I will return to this conclusion, and to this issue of statistical agreement, below.

The only other systematic study of the 4QLXXLev^a variants has been produced by Emanuel Tov.[53] Following a similar method to that employed earlier by Skehan, Tov augments his analysis of the variant readings with a discussion of unusual translation equivalents shared by 4QLXXLev^a and 𝕲.[54] Tov discusses these equivalents, along with the variants, in four categories: (1) "4QLXXLev^a and the Septuagint have a common background";[55] (2) "4QLXXLev^a reflects the original text of the LXX, while the main LXX tradition probably reflects a revision";[56] (3) "4QLXXLev^a represents the Hebrew

---

50. Ibid.

51. Ibid., 75-76.

52. Ibid., 74-75. Ulrich employs the modified siglum "𝕲^ed" to denote the Göttingen LXX, for which I am using the unmodified siglum 𝕲.

53. See Tov, "Greek Biblical Texts," 97-122.

54. See Skehan's comments on the similar use of [προ]κειμενην in 4QLXXNum and the 𝕲 text of Num 4:7 ("Biblical Scrolls from Qumran," 92).

55. In this category, Tov cites what he regards as shared "unusual renderings" that indicate a common text tradition. An example of evidence in this section is the mutual reading of σπόρος for זרע, an equivalent that "recurs elsewhere only six times in the LXX, while the usual LXX equivalent is σπέρμα" ("Greek Biblical Texts," 106).

56. This category is further subdivided into two sections: "4QLXXLev^a represents an unusual rendering or equivalent," and "4QLXXLev^a probably reflects a Hebrew variant." An example of evidence Tov includes in this section is Variant 6 (πεντε υμων] εξ υμων πεντε): "the unusual sequence of 4QLXXLev^a . . . probably represents the original translation. . . . LXX reflects an approximation to MT" (ibid., 107). For the second section, Variant 2 is given as one example (τον ξυλινον καρπ[ ] τα ξυλα των πεδιων αποδωσει τον καρπον αυτων). Tov suggests that the reading in 4QLXXLev^a "could reflect פרי(ה) עץ" (ibid., 109).

more closely than the 'LXX'";[57] and (4) "Indecisive evidence."[58] Like Ulrich, Tov rather cautiously suggests that 𝕲 represents a revision to the text witnessed in 4QLXXLevᵃ. Also like Ulrich, Tov's conclusions about text tradition are far from tentative:

> If de Lagarde's theory on the history of LXX *needed any further support,* it is provided by the texts from the Judean Desert. The newly found texts share important details with the manuscript tradition of LXX known so far, so that all the known Greek texts reflect *one single translation,* rather than different translations, as suggested by Kahle.[59]

Ulrich and Tov have reached essentially the same conclusions using slightly different methods. Both assert unequivocally that 4QLXXLevᵃ and 𝕲 are part of the same translation tradition. Similarly, both are more tentative in their conclusion that 𝕲 represents a revision of the Qumran text. As we have already observed, explaining the *Urtext* theory in a way that takes all available evidence into account is a complicated endeavor.[60] Superficially, it would seem that the *Urtext* theory would demand a particular relationship between two LXX manuscripts at variance with one another: any newly discovered text should have a determinable relationship with the prevailing witnesses to the so-called Old Greek. If the text represents a revision, the relationship is clear. If the discovered text appears to be more original than the prevailing witnesses, it would make sense that the prevailing witnesses correct the earlier text in some way. The respective methods and conclusions of both Tov and Ulrich bear out this fundamental idea, but even this element of textual relationships must be further nuanced. As Ulrich has observed:

> But it must constantly be borne in mind that all texts are quite stratified — they contain many original readings, a certain number of unique errors, a certain number of errors inherited from parent texts, usually some intentional expansions or clarifications, and often some revisions (whether fresh or inherited) for a variety of purposes. It is perfectly logi-

57. Tov cites only three readings for this category, one of which is Variant 11 (μοι εθν[ος] μου λαος). Tov observes that "לי is more precisely rendered by μοι in 4QLXXLevᵃ than by μου in LXX" (ibid., 110).

58. The only reading adduced for this category is Variant 4 ( ]εκφοβων υμας] υμας ο εκφοβων) (ibid., 110).

59. Ibid., 118. This conclusion is found almost verbatim in Tov's "Greek Texts from the Judean Desert," 167. In both cases, Tov notes the similar conclusions of Skehan and Leaney.

60. See note 20 above.

cal, therefore, to maintain that the same text is original in one reading and secondary in the very next reading.[61]

The stratification of which Ulrich speaks will be important for our understanding of the Qumran material as it relates to the prevailing LXX witnesses. In terms of correction and revision, however, it is also important to note that stratification does not erase general indications of whether one text revises another toward proto-MT or MT itself. As Ulrich continues:

> It is unlikely . . . that we should accept the hypothesis that correction of the original Greek toward the Hebrew text which became dominant in the Masoretic *textus receptus* is randomly scattered. For example, it is a plausible hypothesis that 4QLXXLevᵃ might represent a revision toward proto-MT of a text like that transmitted in the fourth-century Codex Vaticanus (𝕲ᴮ); conversely it is also a plausible hypothesis that the text in 𝕲ᴮ might represent a revision toward the proto-MT of a text like that in 4QLXXLevᵃ. But it is implausible that both 4QLXXLevᵃ and 𝕲ᴮ could each be revised toward the proto-MT in 40-50% of their readings. That is, although all texts are to a certain degree mixed texts and systematic revision toward the eventually dominant MT is to be expected in certain early texts, such revision is not to be expected to have permeated one text in half measure and a different text in different half measure.[62]

These comments help one understand the caution with which both Ulrich and Tov suggest that 𝕲 is a revision of 4QLXXLevᵃ.[63] Still, there is a good reason why both scholars argue for a revisional relationship: some of the variant readings fit the correctional model quite well. Variant 9 (βδελυξομαι] βδελυξεται η ψυχη μου) is an excellent example. Although βδελύξομαι[64] could

---

61. Ulrich, "Reappraisal," 51.

62. Ibid., 51-52.

63. Since much of this discussion is devoted to arguments concerning revision, a point of clarification is in order. For the sake of brevity, I will talk about evidence supporting the argument that 𝕲 is a revision of 4QLXXLevᵃ, and counterevidence supporting the argument that 4QLXXLevᵃ is a revision of 𝕲. It should be understood that 4QLXXLevᵃ is not regarded as a tradition unto itself. Rather, the point is to determine whether 𝕲 represents a revision of the translation tradition witnessed by 4QLXXLevᵃ, and vice versa.

64. When giving variants in collated form, I have followed the DJD convention of excluding breathing marks and accents. When citing a Greek word or phrase in the body of the discussion, however, I have included them. The same pattern applies to the representation of *iota* subscripts (in Variant 1, for example). When citing the collation of the variant, I have followed the DJD convention of transliterating what is in the manuscript. In the body of the discussion, they are printed according to standard conventions.

be the result of a Hebrew *Vorlage* different from MT, it could just as easily be a free rendering of MT. The reading in 𝔊, on the other hand, can be most readily understood as a more literal revision of the 4QLXXLevᵃ reading toward a Hebrew text like MT.[65] A number of other variants between 4QLXXLevᵃ and 𝔊 fit more or less into this general pattern.[66] It is much more difficult, however, to argue for 4QLXXLevᵃ as a revision of 𝔊. Only one of the variants, Variant 5, would support such a theory.

Indeed, if 4QLXXLevᵃ and 𝔊 belong to the same translation tradition, it seems highly likely that the latter represents some sort of revision of the former. Although I agree with much in the analyses of both Ulrich and Tov, their overly-cautious suggestion about the revisional relationship between the two texts seems odd. Given the collective nature of the variants, such a relationship seems to be a foregone conclusion. This is true despite Ulrich's observations on the textual complexities cited above. Again, *if* 4QLXXLevᵃ and 𝔊 belong to the same translation tradition, it is difficult to avoid the conclusion that the latter is a revision of the former.[67]

I would like to suggest, however, that the *presupposition* of a shared textual tradition is worthy of further consideration. How to go about questioning this presupposition is somewhat difficult. Ulrich's observations about revisional probability seem to provide one of the best opportunities for renewing the dialogue on this question. Assuming both the same textual tradition and textual stratification, it is possible for *both* 4QLXXLevᵃ and 𝔊 to contain *both* original and secondary readings. It is "implausible," however, that *both* might represent a correction of the other. Since it is implausible that both texts might correct one another, and since 𝔊 can be easily understood as a correction of 4QLXXLevᵃ (while it is implausible to argue that 4QLXXLevᵃ is a correction of 𝔊), it seems reasonable to question the presupposition of a single text tradition by highlighting those instances in which 𝔊 differs from the Qumran text in a way that represents an inferior reading: a reading that would be difficult to regard as a "correction." If 𝔊

---

65. See similar conclusions for this variant in Ulrich, "Reappraisal," 59.

66. Variants 2, 3, 7, 12, and 15, for example, fit the suggested revisional pattern nicely.

67. Even here, what seems like firm footing may be transitory. Although this conclusion makes sense, it still rests on one significant presumption: an identical Hebrew *Vorlage*. As Ulrich has observed, the widespread acceptance of various Hebrew traditions pre-dating MT has far reaching implications for understanding the relationship between two Greek translations at variance with one another (see his discussion in "Reappraisal," 63-69). One must always reckon with the possibility of a different Hebrew *Vorlage* when assessing any variant. Fortunately, this consideration does not significantly affect the discussion of variants in the next section. Where it is a factor, I have included mention of it in the notes.

often presents readings that more accurately reflect MT, one would not expect to find variants in which 𝕲 *corrects* the "earlier" witness of 4QLXXLevᵃ with inferior readings vis-à-vis MT. We turn now, therefore, to some variants that may call into question whether these witnesses share the same text tradition.

3. Some of the Qumran Evidence Reconsidered

Variant 1: 4QLXXLevᵃ frg. 1 line 3 (Lev 26:4)

τον υετον τ]ῇι γηι υμων 𝕮ᴶ (מיטריא דארעכון)] τον υετον υμιν 𝕲 = גשמיכם MT SamP

In the first variant listed for 4QLXXLevᵃ, we find the addition of τῇ γῇ followed by the possessive genitive plural ὑμῶν.[68] The addition of τῇ γῇ could be a free rendering of a Hebrew text much like MT based on formulaic language found in passages like Deut 11:14 and 28:12, 24.[69] It is also possible, however, that 4QLXXLevᵃ reflects a different Hebrew *Vorlage;* the similar variation found in 𝕮ᴶ may support the latter possibility.[70]

Both Tov and Ulrich note that 𝕲 is closer to MT, but it is still only approximate; the second person plural suffix of גשמיכם has not been rendered literally.[71] This aspect of the variant raises a question for our consideration: if 𝕲 represents a correction/revision of the Qumran version toward MT, why would the reviser "correct" the more accurate ὑμῶν to the less accurate ὑμῖν? Freely rendering the second person plural suffix of גשמיכם by the dative ὑμῖν is all the more striking when we consider the 𝕲 translation of the same suffix elsewhere in the immediate context of Leviticus 26. In 26:5, לחמכם is translated τὸν ἄρτον ὑμῶν, and the translation of בארצכם similarly employs the genitive: ἐπὶ τῆς γῆς ὑμῶν. 𝕲 adds the possessive in ἐν τῇ γῇ ὑμῶν even though it is not in the Hebrew of 26:6 (בארץ), and לא־תעבר בארצכם וחרב later in the same verse is rendered accurately with the genitive form of the pronoun: καὶ πόλεμος οὐ διελεύσεται διὰ τῆς γῆς ὑμῶν. Leviticus 26:7 again

68. My discussion of this variant is based on an acceptance of the reconstruction offered by the editors of the DJD edition.

69. So also Ulrich, "Reappraisal," 53; and Tov, "Greek Biblical Texts," 107.

70. Ulrich, "Reappraisal," 53. The possibility of a different *Vorlage,* however, does not affect the question of this discussion. The most likely suggestion for a different *Vorlage* is to postulate something similar to the Hebrew of Deut 11:14; 28:12 and 24. In each of these verses, the second person possessive suffix is used, just as it is in גשמיכם.

71. Ulrich, "Reappraisal," 53; Tov, "Greek Biblical Texts," 107.

contains the possessive genitive τοὺς ἐχθροὺς ὑμῶν for את־איביכם.[72] The genitive plural is used again in verse 13 as ἐγώ εἰμι κύριος ὁ θεὸς ὑμῶν is used to render אני יהוה אלהיכם. In Lev 26:15, ἡ ψυχὴ ὑμῶν renders נפשכם. Finally, in 26:16, זרעכם and איביכם are rendered as τὰ σπέρματα ὑμῶν and οἱ ὑπεναντίοι ὑμῶν, respectively. It is noteworthy to find such consistency in the use of the genitive plural ὑμῶν when rendering the possessive second person plural suffix in MT. In fact, in the immediate context of Lev 26:2-16 this consistency is almost universal; the only exceptions are our passage, and the idiomatic rendering ἐν ὑμῖν for בתוככם in verses 11 and 12.[73] If there were no surrounding context for comparison, a *correction* of ὑμῶν to ὑμῖν in our passage would be odd. Fortunately, we have ample context for comparison, and that context shows the translator of 𝔊 using the genitive again and again and again. The extant evidence is clear: the translator represented by the prevailing witnesses of 𝔊 did use ὑμῖν. What is not clear — indeed, what is difficult to conceive — is that this translator *corrected* the text to read ὑμῖν instead of ὑμῶν.

Variant 5: 4QLXXLevᵃ frg. 1 line 10 (Lev 26:6)
κ]ἀὶ πολεμὸς — [υμων = MT SamP] ad 5 fin 𝔊; ad 5 fin et 6 fin A Bᵐᵍ F MSS

In this variant, we find 4QLXXLevᵃ in agreement with a number of other witnesses, including MT and SamP. Ulrich argues that the variant placement in 𝔊 is best explained by a possible problem with the Hebrew text.[74] Both Ulrich and Tov have observed that the Greek phrase fits the context at the end of both verses.[75] The issue at hand, however, is whether one can argue that the 𝔊 reading is a *correction* of that found in 4QLXXLevᵃ. As Ulrich has suggested, the only way to make such an argument is to posit "an early variant" in the Hebrew text used by the corrector.[76] At best, such a scenario seems unlikely.

Variant 6: 4QLXXLevᵃ frg. 1 line 12 (Lev 26:8)
πεντε υμων] εξ υμων πεντε 𝔊; מכם חמשה MT SamP

---

72. See also the similar rendering in Lev 26:8.
73. Indeed, ἐν ὑμῖν appears to be the stereotype translation equivalent for בתוככם in the Pentateuch. There, בתוככם occurs ten times (Gen 23:9; Exod 12:49; Lev 16:29, 17:12, 18:26, 20:14, 26:11, 26:12, 26:25; Num 15:14). In nine of these ten passages, it is translated as ἐν ὑμῖν.
74. Ulrich, "Reappraisal," 56.
75. Ibid.; Tov, "Greek Biblical Texts," 109.
76. Ulrich, "Reappraisal," 57.

At first glance, the text found in 𝕲 looks like it could be explained easily as a correction of 4QLXXLev^a. That is, 𝕲 represents a much more literal rendering of MT.[77] If this is a correction, however, the surrounding context of Lev 26:8 in 𝕲 is difficult to explain. If someone took the trouble to correct πέντε ὑμῶν to ἐξ ὑμῶν πέντε in order to more accurately and literally represent the Hebrew מכם חמשה, why would that same person not similarly correct the expression ἑκατὸν ὑμῶν two words later in the same verse to more accurately and literally reflect the Hebrew parallel מכם ומאה? If this *were* a correction, we would expect to see something like ἑκατὸν ἐξ ὑμῶν. It seems implausible that someone would take the trouble to revise one clause, but not the next parallel clause in the very same sentence.

Variant 11: 4QLXXLev^a frg. 1 line 18 (Lev 26:12)

εσεσθε μοι εθν[ος] εσεσθε μου λαος 𝕲; תהיו לי לעם MT SamP

This variant poses a rather complex problem. Although one could argue that λαός is an exegetical correction of the more neutral ἔθνος,[78] both serve as equivalents for עם.[79] Indeed, both are used to translate עם in the context of Leviticus (19:16).[80] I would suggest that, once again, the difference in pronouns is the most striking part of the variant. Although the argument for a correction from ἔθνος to λαός is plausible enough, a correction of μοι to μου is implausible assuming a Hebrew reading of לי. The dative is the more accurate rendering of the Hebrew. לי occurs eleven times in Leviticus. Of these, it is translated only once by μου without a specific reason, and this is in a confusing rendering of ὥσπερ ἀφὴ ἑώραταί μου ἐν τῇ οἰκίᾳ for כנגע נראה לי בבית (Lev 14:35). It is translated by μου in Lev 26:14, 18, and 21, but in each case μου is rendered in Greek as the direct object of a form of ὑπακούω (which takes the genitive). Elsewhere it is translated literally as μοι (Lev 20:26 [twice], 22:2, and 25:55), or rendered by an adjective or prepositional phrase (Lev 25:23, 26:23, and 26:27).

---

77. Tov mentions nothing about the possibility of a variant in the Hebrew, and Ulrich explicitly states: "there is no reason to suppose" such a variant ("Reappraisal," 58).

78. Ulrich, "Reappraisal," 60-61; Tov, "Greek Biblical Texts," 108. Tov, in fact, suggests that ἔθνος in 4QLXXLev^a "probably reflects the Old Greek translation" prior to the standardization of λαός for עם (ibid.).

79. Neither Ulrich nor Tov suggest the need to consider a variant in the Hebrew *Vorlage*.

80. See Ulrich, "Reappraisal," 60-61. Although Ulrich notes that λαός is the usual equivalent for עם, he is quick to include exceptions. Skehan's earlier evaluation shows how tone can skew such data: "[4QLXXLev^a], in rendering 'am by εθνος, *violates the pattern* by which the LXX *regularly* applies εθνος to the gentiles, and λαος to the people of Israel" ("Qumran Manuscripts and Textual Criticism," 158 [emphasis added]).

The preceding phrase in 𝔊, καὶ ἔσομαι ὑμῶν θεός for והייתי לכם
לאלהים, is also somewhat difficult to understand. This portion of the text is
not extant in the Qumran manuscript, but the editors have reconstructed that
text to read καὶ ἔσομ[αι ὑμῖν θεός, based on the use of μοι in the next line. If
we accept the reconstruction of the editors, we are challenged to see how the
genitive ὑμῶν can be regarded as a correction of the more accurate ὑμῖν. For
such a "correction," however, we do find some compelling evidence. In Exod
6:7, we find exactly the same formula in the Hebrew (והייתי לכם לאלהים),
and in Lev 25:38 the phrase is repeated with only slight variation (להיות לכם
לאלהים). In both texts, we find לכם translated by ὑμῶν.[81] One could argue,
therefore, that the use of the genitive is based on a stereotyped translation
equivalent for this important formulaic language.[82] Given the translator's use
of the dative for almost all other occurrences of לכם, such a stereotyped
equivalent is the only way to understand ὑμῶν in Lev 26:12. This same argument, however, works *against* any attempt to suggest that μου is a correction
for μοι later in the same verse.

Similar formulaic precedents for תהיו־לי לעם can be found in passages
like Exod 19:5 (והייתם לי סגלה) and 19:6 (תהיו־לי ממלכת כהנים). In both
cases, we find the dative in the text of 𝔊: ἔσεσθέ μοι λαός and ἔσεσθέ μοι
βασίλειον ἱεράτευμα, respectively. The importance and formulaic nature of
both Greek phrases can be seen in the fact that they are repeated in the 𝔊 text
of Exod 23:22, an expansionary passage not found in MT. The use of μου in
the 𝔊 text of Lev 26:12, therefore, goes against formulaic, stereotypical equivalents. If such equivalents are behind the odd rendering of ἔσομαι ὑμῶν θεός in
𝔊, it seems highly unlikely that the same translator would both *ignore* similar
formulae and *correct* ἔσεσθέ μοι to the less accurate and less formulaic ἔσεσθέ
μου.

4. The Implications of These Readings

The variant readings discussed in the previous section raise issues concerning
earlier conclusions that 4QLXXLev^a provides supporting evidence for de
Lagarde's theory. Although not overwhelming, these data are important.

---

81. The Hebrew לכם occurs fifteen times in the immediate context of Lev 25–26. It is
translated by the genitive ὑμῶν only in 25:38. At 26:26, we find a strange rendering using ὑμᾶς,
and the translation of 26:37 does not employ a personal pronoun at all. In all twelve of the other
occurrences, לכם is rendered by a dative form of the second person personal pronoun in Greek.

82. But compare the use of the dative for rendering the same formula in Jer 7:23 and Ezek
27:37.

Having found a few possible exceptions to the status of 𝕲 as a revision of 4QLXXLev^a, we must look once again at the arguments that have placed these two texts within the same text tradition.

For Tov, unusual translation equivalents provide the proof needed to link 4QLXXLev^a to 𝕲. His treatment of these equivalents is both thorough and thought-provoking. Taken as a cumulative whole, the equivalents he adduces seem convincing. Taken individually, however, one finds that each example is open to alternative interpretations. In most cases, Tov has highlighted translation equivalents that occur elsewhere in the LXX, but that are less common than other equivalents.[83] Such evidence leads to questions of degree: How "unusual" does an equivalent need to be in order to establish a common translation tradition? Tov includes in this category of his discussion the LXX *hapax* μετὰ παρρησίας used to translate the Hebrew *hapax* קוממיות.[84] Such *hapax legomena* leave us with another problem; by definition, they are absolutely unique renderings and provide no context for comparison. The best evidence provided by Tov in this category is the verb βδελύσσομαι, found both in 4QLXXLev^a frg. 1 line 17 (βδελυξομαι) and in the 𝕲 translation of Lev 26:11 (βδελύξεται).[85] The question is whether this is enough evidence to carry the argument. Methodologically, Tov's category is sound. The problem is that 4QLXXLev^a does not provide enough evidence in this category for such an argument to be decisive.

Ulrich's similar conclusions about textual tradition are based on the idea of statistical agreement: "these variants are embedded in a text that shows 75% agreement with 𝕲^ed."[86] Unfortunately, the method for arriving at

---

83. An example is the use of ἀπολῶ in both 4QLXXLev^a and 𝕲 to render the *hiphil* והשבתי (in 4QLXXLev^a, the verb is partially restored: α]πολω). Tov observes: "This equivalent is unique in the Pentateuch, while it occurs elsewhere in Isaiah, Jeremiah, and Ezekiel. The regular equivalent in the Pentateuch is καταπαύω" ("Greek Biblical Texts," 106). An examination of Hatch-Redpath does indicate that καταπαύω is the regular equivalent in the Pentateuch. Looking more broadly at the whole LXX, however, we find that ἀπόλλυμι is used to translate שבת seven times (five when it is in the *hiphil*), and καταπαύω is used fifteen times (eight when it is in the *hiphil*). In the text of Leviticus, the verb καταπαύω is not found for שבת. In fact, the most common rendering for this Hebrew is the Greek verb σαββατίζω (Lev 23:32, 26:34, and twice in 26:35). Certainly, σαββατίζω would not make sense in 26:6. Indeed, the sense of the passage favors ἀπόλλυμι more than any of the other common equivalents.

84. Tov, "Greek Biblical Texts," 107.

85. Ibid. It should be noted that this is a lexical, but not a grammatical, equivalent (see Variant 9). The use of this equivalent is even more striking when one notices that the more common equivalent of געל, προσοχθίζω, is also found in both 4QLXXLev^a (line 23) and 𝕲 (Lev 26:15). I would suggest that this combination is by far the most compelling evidence available for Tov's argument.

86. Ulrich, "Reappraisal," 75.

this percentage is not delineated, and arguments based on such statistics are beset with a number of difficulties. First, 4QLXXLev^a is a fragmentary piece of evidence. How does one count agreement for words that are only partially extant? This question seems especially pertinent since "4QLXXLev^a . . . displays 15 variants in 28 less-than-half-extant lines of manuscript!"[87] Whatever method one uses for counting agreement between the Qumran text and 𝔊, one has to make a very significant assumption: that the number of variants in the portions of the text now lost will average out to be the same as those in the extant text. But how can we make such an assumption? A text with this many extant variants could easily have twice as many variants in the material now lost. The material now lost could also agree completely with 𝔊. We simply do not know, and this renders statistical agreement as tenuous evidence at best.

The idea of statistical agreement raises another important question: how much variation is required to conclude that two texts represent independent translations? The idea that different translators are at work in different books of the LXX is widely accepted. In Swete's discussion of the evidence proving this phenomenon, he points to two passages that are extremely similar in the Hebrew of MT, but are represented by two very different Greek translations (LXX Ps 17:3-6 and 2 Kgdms 22:2-6).[88] The two Greek texts are presented on page 27 alongside the Hebrew text. Material found in the Hebrew of 2 Sam 22:2-6, but not in the Hebrew of Ps 18:3-6, is marked with a single underline in both the Hebrew and Greek texts. Material found in the Hebrew of Ps 18:3-6, but not in the Hebrew of 2 Sam 22:2-6, is marked by parentheses in both the Hebrew and Greek texts. Othographic variants between the two Hebrew texts are marked by a double underline. See the chart on the following page.

Although one could use different criteria to measure the percentage of agreement between the two translations, it seems best in this case to accept only exact lexical and grammatical parallels. Employing this rather conservative measure, we find roughly 67% agreement between these two "different hands."[89] Since these two translations are considered to be from "different hands,"[90] one must ask where the line is to be drawn. Is it somewhere between

87. Ibid., 74.

88. H. B. Swete, *An Introduction to the Old Testament in Greek* (rev. ed. of R. R. Ottley; New York: Ktav, 1968), 316.

89. Ibid.

90. After citing these texts, Swete states: "One of these versions has *doubtless* influenced the other" (*An Introduction*, 317 [emphasis added]). Unfortunately, he provides no argument or support for the assumption that one translation influenced the other, nor does he suggest which text is primary and which is secondary. It is possible that what underlies this assumption is the similarity between two translations that inarguably come from different translators.

Chart 2

Ps 17:3-6 (LXX)	Ps 18:3-6//2 Sam 22:2-6	2 Kgdms 22:2-6 (LXX)
³κύριος στερέωμά μου καὶ κατάφυγη μου καὶ ῥύστης μου ὁ θεός μου βοηθός μου καὶ ἐλπιῶ ἐπ' αὐτόν ὑπερασπιστής μου καὶ κέρας σωτηρίας μου ἀντιλήμπτωρ μου ⁴αἰνῶν ἐπικαλέσομαι κύριον καὶ ἐκ τῶν ἐχθρῶν μου σωθήσομαι ⁵περιέσχον με (ὠδῖνες) θανάτου (καὶ) χείμαρροι ἀνομίας ἐξετάραξάν με ⁶ὠδῖνες ᾅδου περιεκύκλωσάν με προέφθασάν με παγίδες θανάτου	יהוה סלעי וּמְצֻדָתִי וּמְפַלְטִי־לִי׃ אֱלֹהַי צוּרִי אֶחֱסֶה־בּוֹ מָגִנִּי וְקֶרֶן יִשְׁעִי מִשְׂגַּבִּי וּמְנוּסִי מֹשִׁעִי מֵחָמָס תֹּשִׁעֵנִי׃ מְהֻלָּל אֶקְרָא יהוה וּמֵאֹיְבַי אִוָּשֵׁעַ׃ כִּי אֲפָפֻנִי מִשְׁבְּרֵי (חֶבְלֵי)־מָוֶת (וְ)נַחֲלֵי בְלִיַּעַל יְבַעֲתֻנִי׃ חֶבְלֵי שְׁאוֹל סַבֻּנִי קִדְּמֻנִי מֹקְשֵׁי־מָוֶת׃	²κύριε πέτρα μου καὶ ὀχύρωμά μου καὶ ἐξαιρούμενός με ἐμοί ³ὁ θεός μου φύλαξ ἔσται μου πεποιθὼς ἔσομαι ἐπ' αὐτῷ ὑπερασπιστής μου καὶ κέρας σωτηρίας μου ἀντιλήμπτωρ μου καὶ κατάφυγή μου σωτηρίας μου ἐξ ἀδίκου σώσεις με ⁴αἰνετὸν ἐπικαλέσομαι κύριον καὶ ἐκ τῶν ἐχθρῶν μου σωθήσομαι ⁵ὅτι περιέσχον με συντριμμοὶ θανάτου χείμαρροι ἀνομίας ἐθάμβησάν με ⁶ὠδῖνες θανάτου ἐκύκλωσάν με προέφθασάν με σκληρότητες θανάτου

67% and 75%? Perhaps this example indicates that percentage of agreement between texts is a faulty measuring device. Or perhaps it indicates that two different translators with roughly the same level of expertise in both the source language and destination language of a translation will produce translations that share *both* similarities *and* differences. Or perhaps this example, compared with our studies of 4QLXXLevᵃ, demonstrates that our conclusions about textual traditions are shaped largely by assumptions that can be neither proved nor disproved.

5. Conclusion

The casual reader of this essay may get the impression that I am arguing for Kahle's theory of Septuagint origins. That is not precisely the case. Kahle's theory involves a great deal of historical speculation, of which I want no part. My purpose, instead, has been to highlight a question for which the answer has long been presupposed: Does 4QLXXLevᵃ, one of our oldest extant Greek translations of Jewish Scripture, consistently support de Lagarde's *Urtext* theory? Although some of the 4QLXXLevᵃ readings fit well within this model of a single translation tradition, I have suggested that some do not. Since this text represents some of the earliest available LXX evidence, readings in this latter category are all the more important. Precisely because it resists simple categorization in terms of textual tradition, 4QLXXLev[a] should be an intriguing centerpiece for future discussions of Septuagint origins.

At this point, it seems fitting to make a few observations regarding possible directions such future conversations might take. Magisterial studies like Margolis' work on Joshua have been, and should continue to be, landmarks in the broader discussion of text tradition encompassing all of the available LXX evidence. On the other hand, these studies — many of which were produced before the discovery of the Dead Sea Scrolls — should not predetermine the way we look at "newly" discovered evidence. Since the earliest LXX evidence is very fragmentary, it seems necessary to develop some special criteria for evaluating the place of this evidence in relation to what we know of (later) LXX text traditions. The criterion of unusual translation equivalents employed by both Skehan and Tov is useful, depending on the degree to which a rendering is unusual. Another excellent criterion would be the determination of shared mistranslations.[91] Ulrich's observations about correction criteria are equally important: if an early text *seems* to fit into a particular text tradition, and if there seems to be a particular correctional/revisional relationship between the early text and the prevailing witnesses of its tradition, it is necessary to look for variant readings that go against that pattern of correction/revision; it is implausible that two texts would correct each other to any significant degree. Finally, I would suggest further consideration of independent Greek translations of identical Hebrew texts and what these would look like. Despite Philo's propagandistic statements in *Moses* 2, it seems reasonable that two independent translations would contain both similarities and differences.

91. See Wevers' discussion of this type of evidence ("Proto-Septuagint Studies," 149).

Identifying Compositions
and Traditions of the Qumran Community:
The *Songs of the Sabbath Sacrifice* as a Test Case

Henry W. Morisada Rietz

1. Introduction

Scholars have long recognized that the collection of documents found in the eleven caves near Khirbet Qumran constitute a sort of "library" of the Community whose ruins are adjacent to the caves.[1] The significance of this collec-

1. In this article, "the Community" (היחד) refers to the Qumran Community, whose members composed the sectarian Dead Sea Scrolls. The evidence of the association between the manuscripts, the caves, and the ruins is, for this author, compelling. The dates of occupation as well as pottery remains found in the ruins corresponds to that of the caves (see R. de Vaux, *Archaeology and the Dead Sea Scrolls: The Schweich Lectures of the British Academy 1959* [rev. ed.; London: Oxford University Press, 1973], 53-57). Caves 5-10, which are situated on marl below the ruins, are only accessible from the ruins (see ibid., pl. XL). Recent excavations by M. Broshi and H. Eshel along the trail leading from the ruins to the area of caves 1, 2, 3, and 11 have uncovered coins, nails, and pottery from the first century CE indicating foot-traffic between the ruins and the caves (see M. Broshi and H. Eshel, "Residential Caves at Qumran," *DSD* 6 [1999]: 328-48; A. Rabinovich, "Qumran: First Western Monastery," *Jerusalem Post International Edition* [(week ending) May 11, 1996]: 19). The palaeographic dating of the manuscripts, confirmed in large part by AMSC-14, coincides with the dates for the occupation of the ruins as established by pottery and coins. For palaeographical dating, see F. M. Cross, "The Development of the Jewish

It is my pleasure to dedicate this essay is James H. Charlesworth, my teacher, mentor, and friend. It is impossible to express fully my gratitude to him. For reading and commenting on earlier versions of the arguments in this article, I am also indebted to Dennis T. Olson, Donald H. Juel, and Brian K. Blount, as well as my colleagues and friends on the staff of the Princeton Theological Seminary Dead Sea Scrolls Project, especially Brent A. Strawn, Michael T. Davis, Casey D. Elledge, Lidija Novakovic, M. Ellen Anderson, and Shane A. Berg. I also thank my research assistants at Grinnell College, Mary W. Nelson and Rachel Fleming.

tion's nature as a "library" lies in the recognition that the documents represented are from a variety of sources. Thus, in order to understand the thought
of members of the Qumran Community, it is necessary to identify those documents that were actually composed by members of the Community — that
is, those texts that are often termed the "sectarian" Dead Sea Scrolls. Considerable work has already been done by scholars to provide criteria to identify
such "Qumran compositions," and I will briefly summarize the most useful
criteria below (§2). There is, however, another category of documents that are
significant for understanding the Qumran Community, namely those documents that functioned as traditions for the Community but that did not orig-
inate within the Community. Thus, the third section of the paper (§3) will
provide some criteria to identify the documents that were not necessarily
composed by the Community but, because they were used by the group, influenced the theology and practice of the Qumranites. Finally, I will apply the
two sets of criteria to the *Songs of the Sabbath Sacrifice* in order to revisit the
question of whether or not it is a Qumran composition (§4).

2. Compositions of the Qumran Community

The most useful criterion for determining Qumran authorship is the distinctive use of certain technical terms.[2] Devorah Dimant provides a helpful sur-

---

Scripts," in *The Bible and the Ancient Near East: Essays in Honor of William Foxwell Albright* (ed.
G. E. Wright; Garden City: Doubleday, 1961), 133-202; idem, "Excursus on the Dating of the
Copper Scroll," in *Les 'Petites Grottes' de Qumrân: Exploration de la falaise, les grottes 2Q, 3Q, 5Q,
6Q, 7Q, à 10Q, le rouleau de cuivre* (ed. M. Baillet, J. T. Milik, and R. de Vaux; 2 vols.; DJD 3; Ox-
ford: Clarendon, 1962), 1:217-21; and N. Avigad, "The Palaeography of the Dead Sea Scrolls and
Related Documents," in *Aspects of the Dead Sea Scrolls* (ed. C. Rabin and Y. Yadin; 2d ed.; Scripta
Hierosolymitana 4; Jerusalem: Magnes, 1965), 56-87. For AMSC-14, see G. Bonani, S. Ivy,
W. Wölfli, M. Broshi, I. Carmi, and J. Strugnell, "Radio Carbon Dating of Fourteen Dead Sea
Scrolls," *'Atiqot* 20 [1991]: 27-32 and *Radiocarbon* 34 [1992]: 843-49; A. J. T. Jull, D. J. Donahue,
M. Broshi, and E. Tov, "Radiocarbon Dating of Scrolls and Linen Fragments from the Judean
Desert," *Radiocarbon* 37 [1995]: 11-19. For the dates of the occupation of the ruins, see de Vaux,
Archaeology and the Dead Sea Scrolls.

The few proposals that seek to separate the connection between the ruins and the manu-
scripts do not have the same archaeological support. See, e.g., N. Golb, who disassociates the
scrolls from the ruins at Qumran and suggests that they are the remains of the Jerusalem
Temple's library which were hidden in the caves during the first revolt ("Who Hid the Dead Sea
Scrolls?" *BA* 48 [1985]: 68-82; idem, *Who Wrote the Dead Sea Scrolls? The Search for the Secret of
Qumran* [New York: Scribners, 1995], 3-171).

2. See the classic but now dated work of Friedrich Nötscher, *Zur theologischen Terminolo-
gie der Qumran Texte* (BBB 10; Bonn: Hanstein, 1956).

vey using this criterion to distinguish the documents composed by members of the Qumran Community from the rest of the Dead Sea Scrolls. She classifies the technical terms into four major categories:

(1) the practices and organization of a particular community, (2) the history of this community and its contemporary circumstances, (3) the theological and metaphysical outlook of that community, and (4) the peculiar biblical exegesis espoused by that community.[3]

As examples of the distinctive practices and organization of the Community, Dimant highlights terms such as יחד, סרך, and מבקר,[4] to which may be added בני צדק, בני חושך, בני אמת, בני אור, פקיד, משכיל, and בני שחר. She illustrates references to historical situations and figures of the Community with מורה הצדק, דורשי החלקות, and איש/מטיף הכזב,[5] to which may be added הכוהן הרשע. The examples Dimant provides in the category of Qumran theology are "terms related to dualism, such as the Spirits of Light

---

3. D. Dimant, "The Qumran Manuscripts: Contents and Significance," in *Time to Prepare the Way in the Wilderness: Papers on the Qumran Scrolls by Fellows of the Institute for Advanced Studies of the Hebrew University, Jerusalem, 1989-1990* (ed. D. Dimant and L. H. Schiffman; STDJ 16; Leiden: E. J. Brill, 1995), 23-58; citation from 27-28. Compare the criteria suggested by H. Stegemann:

> Als "spezifische Qumrantexte" können zunächst nur solche Werke aus den Qumranfunden gelten, die der Gestalt des "Lehrers der Gerechtigkeit" eine autoritative Funktion beimessen, die die spezifische Ordnung der Qumrangemeinde kennen, auf andere Weise deren Sonderstellung im Rahmen des Judentums reflektieren oder wegen ihres formalen oder terminologischen Konnexes mit solchen Schriften diesen *notwendigerweise* zuzuordnen sind.

(See H. Stegemann, "Die Bedeutung der Qumranfunde für die Erforschung der Apokalyptic," in *Apocalypticism in the Mediterranean World and the Near East: Proceedings of the International Colloquium on Apocalypticism Uppsala, August 12-17, 1979* [ed. D. Hellholm; 2d ed.; Tübingen: J. C. B. Mohr (Paul Siebeck), 1989], 495-530; citation from 511.) Newsom discusses the identification of documents as "sectarian," which can refer to "authorship" or "use" (i.e., "readership"), and settles on a third, "more restrictive category," that of "rhetorical function":

> A sectarian text would be one that calls upon its readers to understand themselves as set apart within the larger religious community of Israel and as preserving the true values of Israel against the failures of the larger community.

(See C. A. Newsom, "'Sectually Explicit' Literature from Qumran," in *The Hebrew Bible and Its Interpreters* [ed. B. Halpern, W. H. Propp, and D. N. Freedman; BJSUCSD 1; Winona Lake: Eisenbrauns, 1990], 167-87; citation from 178-79.)

4. Dimant, "The Qumran Manuscripts," 27 n. 10.

5. Ibid., 27 n. 11.

and Darkness . . . and to predestination, such as "תעודה" and רזי אל.[6] Finally, the most distinctive term in the category of biblical exegesis is פשר,[7] to which one can add the various formulae used to introduce quotations of biblical texts.[8] So, on the basis of such technical terms, Dimant distinguishes between "[w]orks containing terminology linked with the Qumran Community (CT)" and "[w]orks not containing such terminology (NCT)."[9] She subsequently provides a long list of documents that are to be included in the first category: "Literary works with terminology related to the Community."[10]

Several observations on Dimant's list of Qumran sectarian documents are to be noted. First, all of the works that can be identified as probably sectarian are written in Hebrew; none are in Aramaic.[11] Moreover, none of the

---

6. Ibid., 27-28 n. 12. Dimant cautions that this is a problematic category since these technical terms may also appear in non-sectarian documents. However, she judiciously is unwilling to abandon it.

7. Ibid., 28 n. 13.

8. These formulae are compiled by M. P. Horgan, *Pesharim: Qumran Interpretation of Biblical Books* (CBQMS 8; Washington, D.C.: Catholic Biblical Association, 1979), 239-44; and see also C. D. Elledge, "Appendix: A Graphic Index of Citation and Commentary Formulae in the Dead Sea Scrolls," in *The Dead Sea Scrolls: Hebrew, Aramaic, and Greek Texts with English Translations*, Vol. 6B: *Pesharim, Other Commentaries, and Related Documents* (ed. J. H. Charlesworth et al.; PTSDSSP 6B; Tübingen: Mohr Siebeck and Louisville: Westminster John Knox, 2002), 367-77.

9. Dimant classifies biblical manuscripts under a third category. She cautions that there is a margin of error since it is possible that a document composed in the Community does not employ the Community's technical terms or other elements that associate it with documents that are clearly sectarian. She rightly asserts that there must be positive evidence to consider a document to be a sectarian composition. See also J. H. Charlesworth, who suggests the following categories of Dead Sea Scrolls: "Biblical Texts," "Texts of the Old Testament Apocrypha and Pseudepigrapha," "Qumran-Edited Documents" (which includes the *Damascus Document* and the *Temple Scroll*), "Non-Qumran Documents," and "Scrolls Composed at Qumran" (*The Dead Sea Scrolls: Rule of the Community Photographic Multi-Language Edition* [ed. J. H. Charlesworth, H. W. Rietz, M. T. Davis, and B. A. Strawn; New York: Continuum, 1996], 15-17).

10. See Dimant, "The Qumran Manuscripts," 37-44.

11. The use of Hebrew is probably a reflection of the belief that Hebrew was considered to be the divine language. See *Jub.* 12:25-26:

> And the LORD God said to me, "Open his mouth and his ears so that he might hear and speak with his mouth in the language which is revealed. . . ." And I opened his mouth and his ears and his lips and I began to speak with him in Hebrew, the tongue of creation. (translation from O. S. Wintermute in *OTP* 2:82)

See further B. Z. Wacholder who discusses the "renaissance" of Hebrew during the Maccabean period and suggests that some Aramaic texts should be considered pre-Qumran ("The Ancient Judeo-Aramaic Literature (500-164 BCE): A Classification of Pre-Qumran Texts," in *Archaeology and History in the Dead Sea Scrolls* [ed. L. H. Schiffman; JSPSup 8; Sheffield: JSOT Press, 1990], 257-81, esp. 273-74). See also F. García Martínez, who identifies at least two Aramaic texts (4Q246

documents that belong to the genre of apocalypse can be positively identified as originating in the Qumran Community.[12] Thirdly, there are documents that do not contain the Community's technical terms, but that positively correspond to the sectarian documents. These documents include halakhic texts whose rules are consistent with those preserved in clearly sectarian documents,[13] along with calendrical, chronological, and astrological texts.

3. Traditions Used by the Qumran Community

In addition to the documents composed by the Qumranites, there is another category of documents that is useful for understanding the Qumran Community. This category comprises those documents that can be identified as the "traditions" inherited and used by members of the Qumran Community, although probably not composed by them. Of the two categories of documents — composition and tradition — that of authoritative traditions is the more controversial and difficult to assess. While one cannot fully understand the Qumran Community by looking only at the traditions it inherited and utilized, it is nevertheless important to consider this material in order to provide a wholistic picture of the Community. A similar situation occurs in the study of Early Christianity which inherited, among other traditions, the Torah, the Prophets, and the Writings as authoritative traditions. While a study of those writings alone would not yield a comprehensively accurate picture of Early Christianity, knowledge of that literature is essential in order to understand the thought world of the early followers of Jesus. The situation is similar for studying the Qumran Community. At the same time, it is important to stress that not every document that a community possesses or even considers as an ideal authoritative tradition may actually function authoritatively.[14]

---

and *New Jerusalem*) as apocalypses that originated within the Qumran Community (*Qumran and Apocalyptic: Studies on the Aramaic Texts from Qumran* [STDJ 9; Leiden: E. J. Brill, 1992], esp. xi, 162-213).

12. See also Dimant, "Apocalyptic Texts at Qumran," in *The Community of the Renewed Covenant: The Notre Dame Symposium on the Dead Sea Scrolls* (ed. E. Ulrich and J. Vanderkam; Notre Dame: University of Notre Dame Press, 1994), 175-91; citation from 179. In contrast, F. García Martínez considers the *New Jerusalem, Visions of Amram,* and *4QpsDan ar* to be examples of apocalypses that were produced by the Qumran Community (*Qumran and Apocalyptic,* esp. 212-13).

13. Dimant cites as examples 4Q251 and the *Temple Scroll.*

14. For example, many Christians consider the Hebrew Bible/Old Testament to be authoritative; however, in reality, it is often only the New Testament that actually *functions* authoritatively, and, further, perhaps only portions of certain Gospels and/or letters of Paul.

Thus, it is important to try to distinguish those documents that the Community actually used from those that were merely in their library.

The criteria that may be adduced to identify traditions actually used by the Community include the following: (1) the number of extant manuscript copies; (2) evidence that the manuscripts were copied at Qumran; and (3) references, allusions, and quotations in Qumran compositions. I would also suggest that when discussing traditions inherited by the Qumran Community, it is important to distinguish between *ideal* traditions and *functional* traditions. That is to say, one must distinguish between traditions that *are asserted to be authoritative* by members of the Community and those for which we can discern evidence of *actual authoritative function*.

As with most other Early Jewish groups, the Torah, the Prophets, the Psalms, and many of the documents later collected as the Writings were important traditions inherited by the Community.[15] The *Rule of the Community* commands that the members engage in studying the Torah,[16] indicating that it was, at the very least, an ideal source of traditions. Although not definitive by itself, the number of copies of a document provides an initial indication of which documents actually functioned as the Community's traditions.[17] Of the approximately two hundred biblical manuscripts,[18] the most well attested

15. The Samaritans would be the single exception, if one considers them within the category of Early Judaism.

16. 1QS 6.6-8: "And where there are ten (members) there must not be lacking there a man who studies the Torah [דורש בתורה] day and night continually, each man relieving another. The Many shall spend the third part of every night of the year in unity, reading the Book [לקרוא בספר], studying judgment [ולדרוש משפט], and saying benedictions in unity [ולברך ביחד]" (text and translation follow that of E. Qimron and J. H. Charlesworth, "Rule of the Community," in *The Dead Sea Scrolls: Hebrew, Aramaic, and Greek Texts with English Translations*, Vol. 1: *Rule of the Community and Related Documents* (ed. J. H. Charlesworth et al.; PTSDSSP 1; Tübingen: J. C. B. Mohr [Paul Siebeck] and Louisville: Westminster John Knox, 1994], 26-27).

17. See G. J. Brooke, "'The Canon within the Canon' at Qumran and in the New Testament," in *The Scrolls and the Scriptures: Qumran after Fifty Years* (ed. S. E. Porter and C. A. Evans; JSPSup 26 and Roehampton Institute London Papers 3; Sheffield: Sheffield Academic Press, 1997), 242-66. Cf. D. Dimant, who finds that the proportion of biblical, sectarian, and non-sectarian documents is fairly consistent in the various caves. J. C. VanderKam suggests that the use of the archaic paleo-Hebrew script in some manuscripts of the Pentateuch and Job "may be a way of expressing the esteem in which they were held" (*The Dead Sea Scrolls Today* [Grand Rapids: Eerdmans, 1994], 32).

18. This count is based on lists of manuscripts provided in E. Tov, "A Categorized List of all the 'Biblical Texts' Found in the Judaean Desert," *DSD* 8 (2001): 67-84; cf. earlier, E. Tov, *Companion Volume to the Dead Sea Scrolls Microfiche Edition* (2d ed.; Leiden: E. J. Brill, 1995); S. A. Reed, *The Dead Sea Scrolls Catalogue* (SBLRBS 32; Atlanta: Scholars Press, 1994); and P. W. Flint, *The Dead Sea Psalms Scrolls and the Book of Psalms* (STDJ 17; Leiden: E. J. Brill, 1997).

are the book of Psalms with thirty-five copies,[19] Deuteronomy with twenty-eight,[20] Isaiah with twenty-one,[21] Genesis with eighteen,[22] Exodus with sixteen,[23] and Leviticus with twelve.[24] Also worth mentioning are Daniel[25] and the Twelve Prophets[26] each with eight copies, and Numbers[27] with six copies. The only biblical document that has not been identified at Qumran is Esther,[28] and, interestingly, neither is there a reference to Purim extant in the Qumran corpus.[29] While the omission of Esther may be the result of chance

19. 1Q10-12 (1QPs^{a-c}), 2Q14 (2QPs), 3Q2 (3QPs), 4Q83-98 (4QPs^{a-q}), 4Q98a-g (4QPs^{r-x}), 5Q5 (5QPs), 8Q2 (8QPs), and 11Q5-8 (11QPs^{a-d}); cf. 6Q5 (6QpapPs?), 11Q9 (11QPs^{e}?), 11Q11 (11QPsAp^{a}).

20. 1Q4-5 (1QDeut^{a-b}), 2Q10-12 (2QDeut^{a-c}), 4Q28-37 (4QDeut^{a-j}), 4Q38-38b (4QDeut^{k1-k3}), 4Q39-46 (4QDeut^{l-s}), 5Q1 (5QDeut), 11Q3 (11QDeut); cf. 4Q122 (4QLXXDeut), 6Q3 (6QDeut?), and 6Q20 (6QDeut?).

21. 1QIsa^{a}, 1Q8 (1QIsa^{b}), 4Q55-61 (4QIsa^{a-g}), 4Q62-62a (4QIsa^{h-i}), 4Q63-69 (4QIsa^{j-p}), 4Q69a-b (4QIsa^{q-r}), and 5Q3 (5QIsa).

22. 1Q1 (1QGen), 2Q1 (2QGen), 4Q1-7 (4QGen^{a-g}), 4Q8a-b (4QGen^{h1-2}), 4Q9-10 (4QGen^{j-k}), 4Q11 (4QpaleoGen-Exod^{l}), 4Q12 (4QpaleoGen^{m}), 4Q576 (4QGen^{n}), 6Q1 (6QpaleoGen), and 8Q1 (8QGen); cf. 4Q483 (4QpaleoGen^{o}?).

23. 1Q2 (1QExod), 2Q2-4 (2QExod^{a-c}), 4Q1 (4QGen-Exod^{a}), 4Q11 (4QpaleoGen-Exod^{l}), 4Q13-16 (4QExod^{b-e}), 4Q17 (4QExod-Lev^{f}), 4Q18-21 (4QExod^{g-k}), 4Q22 (4QpaleoExod^{m}); cf. 4Q37 (4QDeut^{j}) [contains portions of Exod 12-13] and 7Q1 (7QpapLXXExod).

24. 1Q3 (1QpaleoLev), 2Q5 (2QpaleoLev), 4Q17 (4QExod-Lev^{f}), 4Q23 (4QLev-Num^{a}), 4Q24-26 (4QLev^{b-d}), 4Q26a-26b (4QLev^{e,g}), 6Q2 (6QpaleoLev), 11Q1 (11QpaleoLev^{a}), and 11Q2 (11QLev^{b}); cf. 4Q119-120 (4QLXXLev^{a-b}) and 4Q249j (4Qpap cryptA Lev^{h}?).

25. 1Q71-72 (1QDan^{a-b}), 4Q112-116 (4QDan^{a-e}), and 6Q7 (6QDan).

26. 4Q76-82 (4QXII^{a-g}) and 5Q4 (5QAmos = 5QXII); cf. 4Q168 (4QMic? or 4QpMic?).

27. 1Q3 (1QpaleoNum), 2Q6-8 (2QNum^{a-c}), 4Q23 (4QLev-Num^{a}), and 4Q27 (4QNum^{b}); cf. 2Q9 (2QNum^{d}?) and 4Q121 (4QLXXNum).

28. Assuming that Ezra-Nehemiah already formed one document; otherwise Nehemiah is not extant.

29. J. Jarick rightly argues that Purim was rejected at Qumran because according to Esth 9:20-22 it was to be celebrated on the fourteenth and fifteenth day of Adar, the twelfth month. According to the calendar followed at Qumran, the fourteenth day of the twelfth month is the Sabbath, and the Qumranites' 364-day calendar avoided having festivals occur on the Sabbath. This plausibly explains why Purim is not mentioned as well as why Esther has not been found. See J. Jarick, "The Bible's 'Festival Scrolls' among the Dead Sea Scrolls," in *The Scrolls and the Scriptures: Qumran Fifty Years After,* 170-82, esp. 179-82. So also J. C. Vanderkam, "Authoritative Literature in the Dead Sea Scrolls," *DSD* 5 (1998): 382-402, esp. 384-85. S. Talmon, however, cites eight phrases from the sectarian Dead Sea Scrolls which parallel *hapax legomena* from Esther ("Was the Book of Esther Known at Qumran?" *DSD* 2 [1995]: 249-67). See also S. White Crawford, who critiques Milik's analysis of 4Q550a-d (J. T. Milik, "Les Modèles Araméens du Livre d'Esther dans la Grotte 4 de Qumrân," *RevQ* 15 [1992]: 321-99) and concludes that this composition, which she entitles *"Tales of the Persian Court,"* may have been a source for Esther ("Has *Esther* Been Found at Qumran? 4QProto-Esther and the *Esther* Corpus," *RevQ* 17 [1996]: 307-25).

considering the fragmentary state of the library, it may also reflect, I suspect, the tendentious character of the library.[30]

On the basis of the sheer number of copies of manuscripts, other documents also must be considered as functional sources of traditions for the Community.[31] The non-Qumran sectarian documents with the most extant copies are *Jubilees* with sixteen manuscripts,[32] *1 Enoch* with eleven,[33] and the *Book of Giants* with ten.[34] Other non-sectarian documents with multiple ex-

30. That is to say, the Qumran "library" did not consist of a random sampling of Jewish literature of the time, but rather on the whole its contents generally reflected the perspective of the Community itself. Cf. F. García Martínez and A. S. van der Woude, "A 'Groningen' Hypothesis of Qumran Origins and Early History," *RevQ* 14 (1990): 521-41, esp. 521-26.

31. See also Newsom, who counts the non-biblical manuscripts that occur in multiple copies and concludes "[w]hat appears from this simple count is that most of the nonbiblical texts that exist in two or more copies and the great majority of those found in more than one of the caves are either products of the Qumran community or are closely related to central aspects of its theology and praxis" ("'Sectually Explicit' Literature," 169-71; citation from 171). In discussing what it means to call a text "sectarian," Newsom suggests as one possibility "that it was the way a particular text was read that made it a sectarian text, no matter who had written it. . . . One might argue that the criterion of use (rather than authorship) corresponds more closely to the ancient sense of what are 'our writings' as opposed to 'not ours' or 'theirs.'" If this definition is employed, then documents that were not composed by the Qumranites could be labelled "sectarian," and this could even include documents later collected in the Hebrew Bible/Old Testament. While Newsom ultimately rejects this use of the label "sectarian," the heuristic value of her discussion is that it demonstrates that documents that were not composed at Qumran may still be significant for understanding the Qumranites: "[w]hether or not these texts were written by members of the Qumran community, it is plausible that they may have influenced the self-understanding of the community as deeply as the pesharim or the Hodayot" (ibid., 173).

32. 1Q17-18, 2Q19-20, 3Q5, 4Q176 frgs. 19-20, 4Q216, 4Q218-224, 11Q12; and XQ5a. Cf. also 4Q217, 4Q482-483.

33. 4Q201-202, 4Q204-212. *First Enoch,* as preserved in the Ethiopic versions, has long been recognized as composite, comprising five large divisions, each of which is also composite: "the Book of Watchers" (chaps. 1–36), "the Book of the Similitudes" (chaps. 37–71), "the Book of Astronomical Writings" (chaps. 72–82), "the Book of Dream Visions" (chaps. 83–90), and "the Book of the Epistle of Enoch" (chaps. 91–107). Of these, only the "Similitudes" section is not attested at Qumran. The Qumran manuscripts provide evidence that these "books" were collected together fairly early. 4QEn[c] (4Q204) brought together "the Book of Watchers," "the Book of Dreams," and "the Epistle." Portions of "the Book of Watchers" and "the Book of Dreams" are preserved in 4QEn[d] (4Q205) and 4QEn[e] (4Q206). 4QEn[a] (4Q201) and 4QEn[b] (4Q202) probably only contained "the Book of Watchers," 4QEn[g] (4Q212) "the Epistle," and 4QEnastr[a-d] (4Q208-211) "the Astronomical Book." See J. T. Milik, *The Books of Enoch: Aramaic Fragments of Qumran Cave 4* (Oxford: Clarendon, 1976), 5.

34. 1Q23, 1Q24, 2Q26, 4Q203, 4Q206 frgs. 2-3, 4Q530-533, 6Q8. Milik suggests that the *Book of Giants* was considered to be the fifth book in the Enoch cycle at Qumran, in place of the so-called "Similitudes" or "Parables of Enoch" (Ethiopic chaps. 37–71), which is not extant at Qumran (*The Books of Enoch,* 58). Contrast D. Dimant, who rejects this suggestion in "The Bi-

tant copies are *Testament of Levi* with seven,[35] *New Jerusalem* with five,[36] *Visions of Amram* with six,[37] *Tohorot* with four,[38] and the *Temple Scroll* with three.[39] Similarly, the *Words of Lights*, which is extant in three manuscript copies (4Q504-6), can be identified as a tradition used by the Community.[40] There are also numerous calendrical documents; however, they are not all identical. While some of the calendrical documents may have been composed by members of the Community, it is difficult to establish because these documents do not typically use the technical terms of the Community.[41]

In addition to the existence of multiple copies, the provenience of the manuscript — that is, whether it was copied by a member of the Community — might indicate the function of a document as tradition. Scribal tendencies have been suggested as distinguishing the manuscripts that were copied by members of the Qumran Community from those manuscripts that were

---

ography of Enoch and the Books of Enoch," *VT* 33 (1983): 16 n. 8. For a reconstruction of the *Book of Giants*, see L. T. Stuckenbruck, "The Sequencing of Fragments Belonging to the Qumran *Book of Giants:* An Inquiry into the Structure and Purpose of an Early Jewish Composition," *JSP* 16 (1997): 3-24; and idem, *Book of Giants from Qumran: Texts, Translation, and Commentary* (TSAJ 63; Tübingen: Mohr Siebeck, 1997).

35. 1Q21, 4Q213, 4Q213a-b, 4Q214, 4Q214a, 4Q214b.

36. 2Q24, 4Q554-4Q555, 5Q15, 11Q18; cf. also 1Q32, 4Q232.

37. 4Q543-4Q548; cf. also 4Q549.

38. 4Q274, 4Q276-4Q278.

39. 11Q19-11Q20, 4Q524; cf. also 4Q365a and 11Q21.

40. While the terminology of this document does not positively establish it as a sectarian document and the paleographic dating of one of the manuscripts (4Q504) may be prior to the founding of the Community at Qumran, the presence of three manuscripts that date from the middle of the second century B.C.E. to the middle of the first century C.E. justifies E. Chazon's statement that "we can safely conclude that *Divrei Ha-me'orot* was copied and used by the sect over a period of nearly two centuries" ("Is *Divrei Ha-me'orot* a Sectarian Prayer?" in *The Dead Sea Scrolls: Forty Years of Research* [ed. D. Dimant and U. Rappaport; STDJ 10; Leiden: E. J. Brill, 1992], 3-17; citation from 17).

41. Significantly, however, a calender begins one extant copy of *Some Works (Prescribed by) the Torah* (4QMMT), specifically 4Q394 frgs. 1-2, 3-7 col. 1 (see E. Qimron and J. Strugnell, *Qumran Cave 4.5: Miqṣat Maʿaśe ha-Torah* [DJD 10; Oxford: Clarendon, 1994]); and another calendar may have been part of one manuscript of the Rule of the Community (4Q319 and 4Q259; see the two articles by U. Glessmer, "Investigation of the Otot-text [4Q319] and Questions about Methodology," in *Methods of Investigation of the Dead Sea Scrolls and the Khirbet Qumran Site* [ed. N. Golb, M. O. Wise, and J. J. Collins; Annals of the New York Academy of Sciences 722; New York: Annals of the New York Academy of Sciences, 1994], 429-40; and "The Otot-Texts [4Q319] and the Problem of Intercalations in the Context of the 364-Day Calendar," in *Qumranstudien: Vorträge und Beiträge der Teilnehmer des Qumranseminars auf dem Internationalen Treffen der Society of Biblical Literature, Münster, 25-26 Juli 1993* [ed. A. Lange, H.-J. Fabry, and H. Lichtenberger; Göttingen: Vandenhoeck & Ruprecht, 1996], 125-64).

brought into the Community. Since the manuscripts that can be identified as Qumran compositions on the basis of terminology often also display a distinctive set of scribal features, Emanuel Tov has suggested that these features may be used to identify other manuscripts that were copied at Qumran.[42] He identifies the following scribal practices as distinctive: (1) a tendency towards a rather full orthography and morphology,[43] (2) use of paleo-Hebrew or four dots for the Tetragrammaton[44] along with other scribal marks, and (3) the

42. See E. Tov, "The Orthography and Language of the Hebrew Scrolls Found at Qumran and the Origin of These Scrolls," *Textus* 13 (1986): 31-57; idem, "Hebrew Biblical Manuscripts from the Judaean Desert: Their Contribution to Textual Criticism," *JJS* 39 (1988): 5-37; and idem, *Textual Criticism of the Hebrew Bible* (2d ed.; Minneapolis: Fortress and Assent: Royal Van Gorcum, 2001), esp. 100-117. F. M. Cross calls the rather full orthography found in several of the Qumran manuscripts the "baroque style." In his opinion, "the baroque style is a learned attempt at archaism, much like the Massoretic pointing correcting the Rabbinic consonantal text, and was known in Palestine in the Hasmonaean and Herodian eras quite widely. At the same time I think it is true that the scribes in the Qumrân scriptorium were enchanted with this archaizing style, and that Tov is correct in recognizing that many if not all baroque texts were copied at Qumrân" ("Notes on a Generation of Qumrân Studies," in *The Ancient Library of Qumran* [3rd rev. ed.; Minneapolis: Fortress, 1995], 176-77). Cf. E. Ulrich's critique in his "A Theory of the History of the Biblical Text," in *Current Research and Technical Developments on the Dead Sea Scrolls* [ed. D. W. Parry and S. D. Ricks; STDJ 20; Leiden: E. J. Brill, 1996], 78-105, esp. 93-96).

43. Under this category Tov provides the following list:
1. Lengthened independent pronouns: אתנה‎, אתמה‎, היאה‎, הואה‎;
2. Lengthened pronominal suffixes for 2nd and 3rd persons plural, e.g. מלכמה‎, מלככמה‎;
3. Forms that serve in the MT as "pausal," e.g. יקטולו(ו)‎, תקטולו(ו)‎;
4. Lengthened future forms: e.g., אקטלה(ו)‎;
5. Verbal forms with pronominal suffixes construed as יקוטלנו‎;
6. The form קטלתמה(ו)‎ for the 2nd person plural;
7. The forms מודה‎, מואדה‎, מאודה‎.

In general, the writing is full: "o" and "u" sounds tend to be represented by ו‎; י‎ is used to represent "i" sounds along with ṣērê; in final position "i" is sometimes represented by אי‎, and "a" and "e" by ה‎ or א‎. In addition to the works by Tov cited earlier, see also E. Y. Kutscher, *The Language and Linguistic Background of the Isaiah Scroll (1QIsaᵃ)* (STDJ 6; Leiden: E. J. Brill, 1974) and E. Qimron, *The Hebrew of the Dead Sea Scrolls* (HSS 29; Atlanta: Scholars Press, 1986).

44. Tov lists the various marks that indicate deletions (dots above and/or below characters, horizontal line through a character), paragraphing, along with other undecipherable marks (for these marks see Tov, "Letters of the Cryptic A Script and Paleo-Hebrew Letters Used as Scribal Marks in Some Qumran Scrolls," *DSD* 2 [1995]: 330-39; and idem, "Scribal Markings in the Texts from the Judean Desert," in *Current Research and Technological Developments on the Dead Sea Scrolls*, 41-77). Other distinctive scribal practices include the avoidance of the Tetragrammaton by writing it in paleo-Hebrew script or by four dots, and the use of medial characters in final position. Cf. H. Stegemann, "Religionsgeschichtliche Erwägungen zu den Gottesbezeichnungen in den Qumrantexten," in *Qumrân, sa piété, sa théologie et son milieu* [ed. M. Delcor; BETL 46; Paris: Leuven University Press, 1978], 200-217).

use of "cryptic script."[45] Since these scribal features provide evidence that a manuscript was copied by members of the Community, they also indicate that the composition was valued by members of the Community and functioned as a tradition.[46] Likewise, absence of these scribal features *may* indicate that a manuscript was not copied by a member of the Community.[47] Thus, by identifying which manuscripts may have been copied at Qumran, we have some basis for identifying those documents that, though composed elsewhere, were valued by the Community and thus served as traditions for the Community.[48]

45. See 4Q298, which is written in cryptic script. The title, written in square script, refers to the משכיל and the בני שחר, technical terms of the Community. The edition of the text is S. J. Pfann and M. Kister, "298. 4QcryptA Words of the Maskil to All Sons of Dawn," in *Qumran Cave 4.15: Sapiential Texts, Part 1* (ed. T. Elgvin et al.; DJD 20; Oxford: Clarendon, 1997), 1-30 and Pls. I-II. This leads Dimant to consider works written in cryptic script to be sectarian ("The Qumran Manuscripts," 44 n. 55). Pfann suggests that Cryptic Script A, used in 4Q238, is sectarian and an attempt to restrict the reading of the manuscripts to certain members of the Community: "The size of the scroll permitted it to be safely carried (or hidden) while travelling. The use of the esoteric script (aside from the title) protected the scroll's contents from being read by anyone except the *Maskil* and other elite members of the group. In case the scroll was stolen or lost, the legible title made it possible for the scroll to be returned to its rightful owner(s)" ("298. 4QcryptA Words of the Maskil," 17).

46. While these scribal features may provide evidence that a manuscript was copied by the Community, that does not positively establish that a document was composed by a member of the Community. Note, e.g., 11QPs^a (11Q5), which employs a rather full orthography and consistently has the Tetragrammaton written in paleo-Hebrew script, and which refers to the 364-day calendar (see 27.6-7) used by the Community (see J. A. Sanders, *The Psalms Scroll from Qumran Cave 11 (11QPs^a)* [DJD 4; Oxford: Clarendon, 1965]; and idem, *The Dead Sea Psalms Scroll* [Ithaca: Cornell University Press, 1967]). Although a portion of this manuscript may have been composed by a member of the Community, specifically "David's Compositions," which refers to the 364-day calendar, the rest of the compositions are probably not sectarian (this is clearly the case with the so-called canonical Psalms since they predate the Community).

47. So, e.g., the *Qumran Pseudepigraphic Psalms* (4Q380 and 4Q381), both of which tend to use defective orthography and have the Tetragrammaton written in normal script (see E. Schuller, *Non-Canonical Psalms from Qumran: A Pseudepigraphic Collection* [HSS 28; Atlanta: Scholars Press, 1986], esp. 38-41, 64, 242). The concepts and terminology of the psalms do not positively connect them with the Qumran Community and 4Q381 frg. 33 line 2 might refer to the lunar calendar (the reference, however, is far from clear; see the discussion in ibid., 22-23, 146, 148, 150-52). However, at least one copy of the *Rule of the Community* (4Q264), a clearly sectarian document, is written in defective orthography (note the unpublished paper by E. Qimron cited in Dimant, "The Qumran Manuscripts," 29 n. 15). For a transcription of 4Q264 (4QS^j) see Qimron and Charlesworth, PTSDSSP 1:102.

48. Tov, e.g., has used these criteria to identify the biblical manuscripts that were probably copied at Qumran: five copies of Deuteronomy (1QDeut^a, 2QDeut^c, 4QDeut^{j,k,m}); at least four copies of Psalms (1QPs^{b,c}, 11QPs^{a,b}; other manuscripts from Cave 4 are reported to follow

There are other more explicit clues that a document functioned as an authoritative source of traditions for the Qumran Community. These involve positive references, allusions, and quotations in the sectarian documents.[49] The most obvious of these are the biblical books that serve as the traditions interpreted in the *Pesharim:*[50] Isaiah,[51] Psalms,[52] Hosea,[53] Micah,[54] Zephaniah,[55] Nahum,[56] Habakkuk,[57] and Genesis.[58] Quotations of at least the following biblical books occur in the sectarian Dead Sea Scrolls: Genesis, Exodus, Leviticus, Numbers, Deuteronomy, Joshua, 1-2 Samuel, Isaiah, Ezekiel, Hosea, Amos, Micah, Zechariah, Malachi, Psalms, Proverbs, and Daniel.[59] Using the criterion of citation and allusion we also find that at least *Jubilees* and what later became known as *1 Enoch* were considered to be authoritative sources of tradition for the Community.[60]

---

his "Qumran scribal practice"); two copies each of Isaiah (1QIsa[a], 4QIsa[c]), Exodus (2QExod[a,b]), Lamentations (3QLam, 4QLam), and the Twelve Prophets (4QXII[c,e]); and one copy of Numbers (2QNum[b]), Leviticus (11QLev[b]), Samuel (4QSam[c]), Jeremiah (2QJer), Qohelet (4QQoh[a]), and Daniel (4QDan[b]). Tov also identifies three copies of *Reworked Pentateuch* (4Q158, 4Q364, 4Q365), at least two copies of *Jubilees* (3Q5 and 4QJub[d]), several copies of the *Songs of the Sabbath Sacrifice* (4Q401-403, 4Q405), and 11QTemple as probably copied at Qumran. For Tov's analysis, see his "Groups of Biblical Texts Found at Qumran," in *Time to Prepare the Way in the Wilderness*, 85-102, esp. 98-101; see also idem, *Textual Criticism of the Hebrew Bible*, 109; and "The Orthography and Language of the Hebrew Scrolls," 31-57, esp. 50-55. It is important to note that, for many manuscripts — given their state of preservation — it is difficult to determine whether or not they follow Tov's delineation of the Qumran scribal practice.

49. For quotation formulae, see J. C. Vanderkam, "Authoritative Literature in the Dead Sea Scrolls," 382-402 and C. D. Elledge, PTSDSSP 6B:367-77.

50. For publication of the *Pesharim*, see M. P. Horgan in PTSDSSP 6B:1-193 and *Pesharim: Qumran Interpretations of Biblical Books;* J. Strugnell, "Notes en marge du volume V des 'Discoveries in the Judaean Desert of Jordan,'" *RevQ* 7 (1969-71): 163-276; J. M. Allegro, *Qumran Cave 4.1 (4Q158-4Q186)* (by J. M. Allegro with A. A. Anderson; DJD 5; Oxford: Clarendon, 1968).

51. 4Q161-165, 3Q4.

52. 1Q16, 4Q171, 4Q173.

53. 4Q166-167.

54. 1Q14, 4Q168.

55. 1Q15, 4Q170.

56. 4Q169.

57. 1QpHab.

58. 4Q252, 4Q253, 4Q253a, 4Q254, 4Q254a.

59. See the discussion in VanderKam, *The Dead Sea Scrolls Today*, 149-53.

60. Also to be noted is the now lost "Book of Hagu" or "Hagi" (ספר ההגו/י) mentioned in CD MS A 10.6 (//4Q270 frg. 6 4.17), 13.2, 14.8 (//4Q267 frg. 9 5.12); 1QSa 1.7. L. H. Schiffman, among others, has argued that the "Book of Hagu/i" refers to the study of the Torah (*The Eschatological Community of the Dead Sea Scrolls* [SBLMS 38; Atlanta, Scholars Press, 1989], 15; and idem, *The Halakhah at Qumran* [SJLA 16; Leiden: E. J. Brill, 1975], 44 and n. 144). J. M.

To summarize to this point: The purpose of the previous discussion has been to provide a theoretical basis for evaluating which documents found in the diverse Qumran library are useful for understanding the Community that collected and preserved them. That is to say, the attempt has been made to provide criteria that can be used to identify those documents that are compositions of, or authoritative traditions inherited by, members of the Qumran Community. These criteria include:

1. the number of extant manuscript copies;
2. evidence that the manuscripts were copied at Qumran; and
3. references, allusions, and quotations in Qumran compositions.

Before proceeding to apply these criteria to a test case — the *Songs of the Sabbath Sacrifice* — it is important to note that certain categories of documents have *not* been found at Qumran. These include pre-70 Jewish Greek compositions such as the *Wisdom of Solomon,* the *Letter of Aristeas,* and the *Psalms of Solomon.* Scholars also have not found pro-Hasmonean documents such as *1 Maccabees* and *Judith.*[61] While it is always perilous to argue from silence, the sheer number of manuscripts found at Qumran reduces the statistical possibility that these omissions are the result of chance.[62] Rather, it is probable that the omissions reflect the tendencies of the Qumran Community.[63] In particular, these omissions exclude the partisan documents of the so-called

---

Baumgarten, however, suggests that this "Book" may have been "a collection of Torah interpretations by Qumran teachers" ("Damascus Document," in *The Dead Sea Scrolls: Hebrew, Aramaic, and Greek Texts with English Translations,* Vol. 2: *Damascus Document, War Scroll, and Related Documents* (ed. J. H. Charlesworth et al.; PTSDSSP 2; Tübingen: J. C. B. Mohr [Paul Siebeck] and Louisville: Westminster John Knox, 1995), 45 n. 153; see also L. T. Stuckenbruck and J. H. Charlesworth, "Rule of the Congregation (1QSa)," in PTSDSSP 1:111 n. 14).

61. The probable exception is the so-called *Prayer for King Jonathan* (4Q448). The identification of the king referred to in this prayer is debated. E. Eshel and H. Eshel understand this composition as a "prayer for the welfare of King Jonathan" whom they identify as Alexander Jannaeus (see E. Eshel, H. Eshel, and A. Yardeni, "A Qumran Composition Containing Part of Ps. 154 and a Prayer for the Welfare of King Jonathan and his Kingdom," *IEJ* 42 [1992]: 199-229, esp. 208, 216-19). G. Vermes, in contrast, identifies "King Jonathan" as Jonathan Maccabeus (G. Vermes, "The So-Called King Jonathan Fragment (4Q448)," *JJS* 44 [1993]: 294-300, esp. 299-300). Either way, the document, which does not reflect the technical terminology or the scribal tendencies of the Community, reflects a political position that is counter to what we know of the Community.

62. The total count is estimated by Dimant at 760 ("The Qumran Manuscripts," 57).

63. So Dimant, "The Qumran Manuscripts," 32-33: "One cannot, then, escape the conclusion that the collection was intentional and not a haphazard assemblage of disparate works."

"Hellenizers" of the early second century B.C.E., as well as their Hasmonean opponents.

4. The *Songs of the Sabbath Sacrifice:* A Test Case

The *Songs of the Sabbath Sacrifice* is a document whose provenience in the Qumran Community has been disputed. Originally identified as stemming from the Qumran Community itself, it has been argued more recently that the *Songs of the Sabbath Sacrifice* is a composition that predates the Qumran Community. Thus, this document provides a useful test case for the criteria for determining whether a document was used as a tradition by the Qumran Community and/or whether it may have been composed by members of the Community. It will become clear below that, according to these criteria, the *Songs of the Sabbath Sacrifice* clearly functioned as a tradition for the Qumran Community. Moreover, I will argue for the probability that the *Songs* were not only a tradition at Qumran but *were also composed* by members of the Community.

The *Songs of the Sabbath Sacrifice* comprise a collection of "songs" (שירות) for the first thirteen sabbaths of the year according to the 364-day calendar used by the Qumran Community.[64] The thirteen *Songs* describe the celebration of "the Sabbath sacrifice" (עולת השבת) in the heavens.[65]

---

64. Apart from a superscription and an initial call to praise, the structure of the individual *Songs* vary. The superscription for each *Song* includes an address "To the Master" (למשכיל) followed by a title identifying the composition as a "Song" of a specifically numbered "Sabbath sacrifice" (e.g., שיר עולת השבת הריאישונה) and a date formula such as, "on the fourth (day) of the first month" (בארבעה לחודש הראישון). The body of each *Song* begins with a call to praise (הללו) followed by an epithet for God (the direct object, occasionally indicated by a prefixed -ל) addressed to a group of heavenly beings (plural vocative). For a composite Hebrew text and translation of the *Sabbath Songs* reconstructed from the individual manuscripts, see C. A. Newsom, H. W. Rietz, and B. A. Strawn, "Composite Text," in *The Dead Sea Scrolls: Hebrew, Aramaic, and Greek Texts with English Translations*, Vol. 4B: *Angelic Liturgy: Songs of the Sabbath Sacrifice* [ed. J. H. Charlesworth et al.; PTSDSSP 4B; Tübingen: Mohr Siebeck and Louisville: Westminster John Knox, 1999], 138-89.

65. The question of how the *Sabbath Songs* functioned in the life of the Qumran Community has occasioned a spectrum of views. Schiffman suggests that the collection of *Sabbath Songs* is an exegetical description of angelic worship ("Merkavah Speculation at Qumran: The 4Q Serekh Shirot 'Olat ha-Shabbat," in *Mystics, Philosophers, and Politicians: Alexander Altmann Festschrift* [ed. J. Reiharz and D. Swetschinski; Duke Monographs in Medieval and Renaissance Studies 5; Durham: Duke University Press, 1982], 15-47). J. Maier understands the *Sabbath Songs* as functioning in the context of the Qumran Community, which was estranged from the cult of the Jerusalem Temple. In this context, the Qumran Community "offered as

Carol A. Newsom has discerned a pyramidal structure of three sections, with *Songs 1-5*, *Songs 6-8*, and *Songs 9-13* each comprising a section, with *Song 7* centrally located as a climax.[66] In Newsom's summary of the contents of the individual sections, the movement of the *Songs* progresses from the establish-

---

substitutes [for the real Sabbath offerings] the Songs, in solemn form describing and in a certain sense also staging and participating in the performance of the corresponding ritual in the heavenly cult act" ("Shîrê ʿÔlat hash-Shabbat: Some Observations on Their Calendric Implications and on Their Style," in *The Madrid Qumran Congress: Proceedings of the International Congress on the Dead Sea Scrolls Madrid 18-21 March, 1991* [ed. J. Trebolle Barrera and L. Vegas Montaner; 2 vols.; STDJ 11; Leiden: E. J. Brill, 1992], 2:543-60; citation from 553). Maier suggests that the *Sabbath Songs* were accompanied with the traditional prayers and songs appropriate to the sacrifice (ibid., 553). B. Nitzan also understands the *Sabbath Songs* as a liturgical replacement for sacrifice (*Qumran Prayer and Religious Poetry* [trans. J. Chipman; STDJ 12; Leiden: E. J. Brill, 1994], 282-96). Nitzan points to the phrases "in the chiefs of offering (are) tongues of knowledge" (ברא שי תרומות לשוני דעת; 4Q405 frg. 23 2.12), "and the offering of their tongues" (ותרומת לשוניהם; 4Q403 frg. 1 2.26), and "the offering of our tongue of dust" (תרומת לשון עפרנו; 4Q400 frg. 2 line 7) in support of her interpretation (ibid., 290-91). While Newsom acknowledges that the *Sabbath Songs* may have been recited at the time of the Sabbath offering, she emphasizes the mystical rather than the cultic function of the *Songs*:

> During the thirteen week cycle the community which recited the *Sabbath Songs* is led through a progressive experience. The mysteries of the angelic priesthood are described, an ecstatic celebration of the sabbatical number seven produces an anticipatory climax at the center of the work, and finally the community is led through the spiritually animate heavenly temple until the worshippers experience the holiness of the *merkābāh* and of the Sabbath sacrifice conducted by the angelic high priests. (C. A. Newsom, "Angelic Liturgy: Songs of the Sabbath Sacrifice," in PTSDSSP 4B:4; see also her earlier essay, "'He Has Established for Himself Priests': Human and Angelic Priesthood in the Qumran Sabbath *Shirot*," in *Archaeology and History in the Dead Sea Scrolls* [ed. L. H. Schiffman; JSPSup 8; ASOR Monographs 2; Sheffield: JSOT Press, 1990], 101-20, esp. 114)

Rather than limit the function of the *Sabbath Songs* to one of these options or to a single point on this spectrum of viewpoints, it seems better to broaden the understanding of the function to include all of these views since, in their broad strokes, they are not mutually exclusive. Maier's suggestion that the *Sabbath Songs* function as a sort of script for staging the Sabbath sacrifice and that they would be accompanied by other elements of the traditional service, short of actual blood sacrifice, does not exclude, and in fact would heighten, their use as "instruments of mystical praxis." Newsom, who emphasizes the visual and aural aspects of the *Sabbath Songs* as vehicles of mystical experience, ignores the ways that the physical actions of liturgy may also serve a similar function. I would suggest, rather, that the liturgical and mystical experiences facilitated by the *Sabbath Songs* probably substituted for the actual blood sacrifice of the sabbath, which the members of the Qumran Community could not perform outside of the Jerusalem Temple.

66. Newsom, *Songs of the Sabbath Sacrifice: A Critical Edition* (HSS 27; Atlanta: Scholars Press, 1985), 13-17; idem, "He Has Established for Himself Priests"; and, more recently, idem, PTSDSSP 4B:3-4.

ment of the angelic priesthood and its praise *(Songs 1-5)* to an elaboration of angelic praise and blessing *(Songs 6-8)*, then to the description of the heavenly temple and its praise, and finally to the blessing of the *merkābāh* and the heavenly highpriests (*Songs 9-13; anticipated already in Song 7).*[67] Newsom argues further that the structure of the collection of *Songs* indicates that the *Songs* were recited together.[68] Moreover, she has observed that in the extant portions of the *Songs,* there seems to be only one place in which the vocabulary of sacrifice and the high priestly vestments occurs, and that is at the beginning of *Song 13:*[69]

> [. . .]° for the sacrifices of[70] the Holy Ones °[. . .] the odor of their offerings (ריח מנחותם) °°[. . .]*lm* and the o[do]r of their drink offerings (ור[י]ח נסכיהם) *lms*[. . .]*m* of purity with a spirit of holine[ss . . .] eternity, with [majesty and] splendor *l*°[. . .]° wonder and the form of the breastplates of (חשני) [. . . be]auty [. . .] multicolored like wo[rks of . . .] brightly blended, dyed [. . .]°°[. . .]*mw* for images [. . .]*š'* ephod (אפוד) [. . .] angels of [. . .] his [holi]ness [. . .][71]

According to Newsom's interpretation, the recitation of the *Sabbath Songs* cycle would culminate in this single reference to heavenly sacrifice in the last *Song.*[72] The highly structured arrangement of the individual *Songs* indicates that the collection as a whole is a unified composition.

The *Songs of the Sabbath Sacrifice* are preserved by eight manuscript witnesses found in the Qumran caves, along with one copy found at Masada. Newsom dates the earliest manuscript witnesses, 4Q400 and 4Q407, to the

---

67. Newsom, PTSDSSP 4B:3-4.

68. See Newsom, *Songs of the Sabbath Sacrifice,* 18-19. Newsom points out that "whole burnt-offering" (עולה) is preserved only in the headings and not in the extant portions of the bodies of the *Songs.* She suggests, however, that since *Song 13* mentions "their offerings" (מנחותם) and "their drink offerings" (נסכיהם), the reference to "whole burnt-offering" (עולה) may be lost. She refers to Lev 23:37 and Ezek 45:17, where all three types of offerings are mentioned together (ibid., 372).

69. Ibid., 371-72.

70. Note: לזבחי. The only other extant occurrence of "sacrifice" is in a small fragment, 4Q405 frg. 94 line 2: "[. . .] the sacrifices ʿ[. . .]" ([. . .]ע הזבחים[. . .]).

71. *Song 13,* lines 5-10 of the composite text.

72. Newsom's proposal, however, does not account for the specificity of the date formula assigning each *Song* to a particular Sabbath. In contrast to Newsom, Maier and Nitzan suggest that the individual *Songs* were for specific Sabbaths in each quarter of the year and that the cycle of *Songs* was repeated throughout the year. See Maier, "Shîrê ʿÔlat hash-Shabbat," 544-52; Nitzan, *Qumran Prayer and Religious Poetry,* 284. There is no clear evidence, however, that the cycle of *Songs* was repeated throughout the year.

late Hasmonean period, ca. 75-50 B.C.E.[73] Slightly later are 4Q401, 4Q402, and 4Q404, all of which Newsom dates to the late Hasmonean or early Herodian period, ca. 25 B.C.E. She dates the rest of the manuscripts to the Herodian period with 4Q403 earlier, between 25 and 1 B.C.E., and 11Q17 to the late Herodian period, ca. 20-50 C.E.[74] She assigns the copy from Masada to the end of the Herodian period, ca. 50 C.E. Because of the poor state of preservation Newsom wisely does not offer a date for 4Q406.[75] The orthography of the manuscripts tends to be rather full, including that of the copy found at Masada,[76] suggesting — according to Tov's theory — that the manuscripts may have been copied by the members of the Community. The rather large number of copies spanning several generations and the probability that the manuscripts were copied by members of the Qumran Community indicate that they viewed the *Songs* as an important tradition.[77]

The earliest manuscript witnesses, 4Q400 and 4Q407, set the latest possible date of composition to ca. 75-50 B.C.E. The earliest possible date is more difficult to discern. Since there are no clear references or allusions to known historical persons or events preserved in the manuscripts, the question of the *terminus a quo* rests in part on the issue of provenience. In 1959, John Strugnell argued that the *Songs of the Sabbath Sacrifice* was a Qumran composition,[78] a position followed by Newsom in her *editio princeps*[79] and then by many others. More recently, however, Newsom has reversed her earlier position; she now favors a non-Qumran origin.[80] She rightly assesses much of the evidence concerning provenience as ambiguous, whether for or against Qumran provenience. Newsom points out that this ambiguous evi-

---

73. This paleographic dating follows that of Newsom, most recently in PTSDSSP 4B:1-3. See her earlier discussion in *Songs of the Sabbath Sacrifice*, 86, 126, 147-48, 168, 186-87, 249-50, 258-59, 355, 359, 363.

74. F. García Martínez and E. J. C. Tigchelaar also date 11Q17 to the early to middle Herodian period; see their discussion in "17. 11QShirot 'Olat ha-Shabbat," in *Qumran Cave 11.2: 11Q2-18, 11Q20-31* (ed. F. García Martínez et al.; DJD 23; Oxford: Clarendon, 1998), 263-65.

75. See Newsom, *Songs of the Sabbath Sacrifice*, Pl. 15.

76. For discussion of the orthography, see Newsom, *Songs of the Sabbath Sacrifice*, 85-86, 125, 147, 167-68, 185-86, 249, 258, 363.

77. That the *Sabbath Songs* functioned as a tradition does not necessarily imply that the collection is pre-Qumranic. A composition of a member of the Community could become a tradition that was then used by other members.

78. J. Strugnell, "The Angelic Liturgy at Qumrân—4Q Serek Šîrôt 'Ôlat Haššabbāt," in *Congress Volume: Oxford 1959* (VTSup 7; Leiden: Brill, 1960), 318-45.

79. Newsom, *Songs of the Sabbath Sacrifice*, 1-4.

80. Newsom, "'Sectually Explicit' Literature," 179-85. Newsom continues to favor a pre-Qumran provenience in PTSDSSP 4B:4-5.

dence includes the lack of polemical language (one would not necessarily expect a liturgical work to be polemical), the dependence on the 364-day calendar (which is attested in other works judged as having a pre-Qumran provenience — e.g., portions of *1 Enoch* and *Jubilees*), and the presence of a copy at Masada (while the orthography is suggestive, there is no conclusive evidence to favor the suggestion that it was carried there from Qumran or to prove that it originated from outside the movement with which Qumran is to be associated).[81]

There is other evidence that could point in the direction of a Qumran provenience, but much of it is still not definitive. For example, each *Sabbath Song* is introduced by the heading למשכיל. There are several possible interpretations of this heading. The prefixed -ל may be translated as "by" or "of," indicating putative authorship as, perhaps, in the Psalms (cf. לדוד). The prefix may also be translated as "to" or "for," indicating addressee, also attested in the Psalms (cf. למנצח). In psalmic contexts, both uses are often attested *in the same superscription*,[82] so the precise meaning of the prefixed -ל remains elusive. But what of משכיל? Newsom suggests that the interpretation of משכיל may be similarly uncertain, since משכיל might refer merely to a "wise one"[83] (√שכל) or, alternatively, to a particular office in the Qumran Community — the "Master."[84] Newsom is correct, of course, but it seems plausible that the use of למשכיל in the *Songs of the Sabbath Sacrifice* parallels the construction used to address the "Master" in 1QS and, even more to the point, in the *Songs of the Master* (4Q510-511 = 4QShir^{a-b}). In light of this usage, I would suggest that the superscription למשכיל should be interpreted as addressing the *Songs*

81. On the ambiguity of these points I am in agreement with Newsom.

82. See, e.g., the superscription to Psalm 51 which is attested both in the MT as well as at Qumran in 4Q85 (4QPs^c). See Flint's "Synopsis of Superscriptions, Postscripts and Doxologies in the MT, the Scrolls, and the LXX," in *The Dead Sea Psalms Scrolls*, 117-34.

83. So Newsom refers to Dan 11:33, 12:3; *1 En.* 100:6, 104:12. As examples in the Qumran literature where משכיל has the non-technical meaning of "wise one," Newsom cites CD MS A 12.21 and 1QH 22.11 [12.11 in Sukenik's old numbering] (see PTSDSSP 4B:4-5). Even in these examples, however, משכיל may refer to the sectarian office of "Master." See also the discussion in Newsom, *Songs of the Sabbath Sacrifice*, 3.

84. 1QS 3.13; 1QSb 1.1, 3.22, 5.20. 1QS 9.12 and 9.21 are more ambiguous. Note that the parallels between 1QS 9.12 and CD MS A 12.20-21 (which Newsom cites as a non-technical occurrence of משכיל), highlighted by underlining, indicates a genetic relationship of some sort between the two texts:

אלה החוקים למשכיל להתהלך בם עם כול חי לתכון עת ועת ולמשקל איש ואיש

(1QS 9.12)

ואלה החקים למשכיל להתהלך בם עם כל חי למשפט עת ועת

(CD MS A 12.20-21)

of the Sabbath Sacrifice to the sectarian official, the "Master." This would mean that at least the superscription reflects the work of the Qumran sectarians. It might be argued, however, that the Community inherited the tradition of the *Sabbath Songs* and simply added the superscription; the provenience of the compositions themselves is thus still in need of further discussion.

Further evidence indicating the provenience of the *Sabbath Songs* is provided by its genetic relationship with other clearly sectarian compositions. Newsom has discussed the possible relationship between the *Sabbath Songs* and the *Songs of the Master* and *Blessings and Curses* (4Q286-90). The *Songs of the Master*[85] are found in two manuscripts that date to the Herodian period, with 4Q510 slightly earlier.[86] The presence in this composition of the "Master" (משכיל)[87] in an official capacity coupled with references to the "Community" (יחד)[88] and the "Sons of Lig[ht]" (בני או[ר])[89] along with other similarities to the sectarian material[90] point to a provenience for the *Songs of the Master* within the Qumran Community.

Newsom has argued for particular points of contact between the *Songs of the Master* and the *Songs of the Sabbath Sacrifice*.[91] Note, for example, the following considerations: (1) Each individual composition is called a "song" (שיר) and (2) is directed "to the Master" (למשכיל).[92] (3) Both collections share a number of similar expressions: "highest heights" (רום מרומי; 4Q511 frg. 41 line 1; cf. 4Q400 frg. 1 1.20, 2.4; frg. 2 line 4); "holy cherubim" (כרובי קודש; 4Q511 frg. 41 line 2; cf. 4Q405 frgs. 20-22 2.3; 11Q17 frgs. 3-4 line 4); and "laud" (תשבוחה; 4Q511 frg. 2 1.8, 4Q510 frg. 1 line 1; cf., e.g., 4Q403 frg. 1 1.31-33).[93] Newsom also finds similarities in the (4) consecration of priests in 4Q511 frg. 35 and that described in 4Q400 frg. 1 column 1. Her assessment of these data leads her to propose that the *Sabbath Songs* were one of the major

---

85. Published by M. Baillet, *Qumran Grotte 4.3: 4Q482-4Q520* (DJD 7; Oxford, Clarendon, 1982), 215-62 and Pls. 55-71. The title of the document is derived from the superscription to one of the *Songs* preserved on 4Q511 frg. 2 1.1: למשכיל שיר. See B. Nitzan, who describes the *Songs* as "a protection against evil spirits" ("Hymns from Qumran — 4Q510-511," in *The Dead Sea Scrolls: Forty Years of Research*, 53-63; citation from 53).

86. Baillet, DJD 7:215, 219.

87. 4Q510 frg. 1 line 4.

88. 4Q511 frg. 2 1.9.

89. 4Q510 frg. 1 line 7.

90. E.g., 4Q511 frgs. 28-29 lines 3-4: אני מצירוק יצר חמר] קורצתי and 1QS 11.21-22: והואה מצירוק חמר קורצ (restoration follows Baillet; see there for parallels to 1QH); and 4Q511 frg. 63 lines 1-2 and 1QH 16.16 [= 8.16 in Sukenik].

91. Newsom, "'Sectually Explicit' Literature," 183.

92. For למשכיל שיר in the *Songs of the Master*, see 4Q511 frg. 2 1.1.

93. See Newsom, "'Sectually Explicit Literature,'" 183.

traditions influencing the *Songs of the Master*.[94] This proposal, I would add, might account for the free use of the usually-avoided אלוהים in the *Songs of the Master*.[95] But, while the similarities between the *Songs of the Master* and the *Sabbath Songs* are suggestive, they do not conclusively establish a genetic link between the two.

The relationship between the *Sabbath Songs* and *Blessings and Curses* (4Q286-290) is closer and more readily discerned.[96] *Blessings and Curses* is found in five manuscripts that date to the Herodian period.[97] Milik suggests that *Blessings and Curses* was recited at the covenant renewal ceremony described in 1QS 1.16–3.12.[98] Its Qumran provenience is indicated by the reference to the technical terminology "Council of the Community" (עצת היחד; 4Q286 frg. 10 2.1) as well as by its connections to other, clearly sectarian compositions.[99] The similarities between the *Sabbath Songs* and *Blessings and Curses* center on the terminology used to describe the heavenly sanctuary (see esp. 4Q286 frg. 1 col. 1).[100] Newsom originally argued that the relationship between these two compositions indicated a Qumran provenience for the *Sabbath Songs*.[101] Now, however, she finds this evidence inconclusive, since it is

94. See Newsom in PTSDSSP 4B:5, where she suggests that the *Songs of the Master* are "almost certainly dependent upon the Sabbath Songs." Cf. Newsom, "'Sectually Explicit' Literature," 184.

95. Newsom does not explicitly make this point.

96. 4Q286-90 are published by B. Nitzan in "286-290. 4QBerakhot[a-e]," in *Qumran Cave 4.6: Poetical and Liturgical Texts, Part 1* (ed. E. Eshel et al.; DJD 11; Oxford: Clarendon, 1998), 1-74 and Pls. 1-7. J. T. Milik previously published portions of 4Q286 and 4Q287 in "*Milkî-ṣedeq et Milkî-rešaʿ dans les Anciens Écrits Juif et Chrétiens*," *JJS* 23 (1972): 99-144, esp. 130-35 and Pl. 2. The materials were re-examined by P. Kobelski in *Melchizedek and Melchirešaʿ* (CBQMS 10; Washington, D.C.: Catholic Bible Association, 1981), 42-48. B. Nitzan published portions of 4Q286, 4Q288, and 4Q289 in "4QBerakhot (4Q286-290): A Preliminary Report," in *New Qumran Texts and Studies: Proceedings of the First Meeting of the International Organization for Qumran Studies, Paris 1992* (ed. G. J. Brooke; STJD 15; Leiden: E. J. Brill, 1994), 53-71 and Pl. 3; and in "4QBerakhot[a-e] (4Q286-290): A Covenantal Ceremony in the Light of Related Texts," *RevQ* 16 (1995): 487-506. Milik and Nitzan refer to the document as *4QBerakot/4QBerakhot*; however, the name *Blessings and Curses* more accurately reflects the contents of the document, which contains both "blessings" (ברכות) and "curses" (אררות).

97. Milik, "*Milkî-ṣedeq et Milkî-rešaʿ*," 96.

98. Ibid., 135. Cf. B. Nitzan, "4QBerakot[a-e] (4Q286-290): A Covenantal Ceremony," 487-506.

99. E.g., 4Q286 frg. 7 2.1-5 and 1QM 13.4-6.

100. Newsom, *Songs of the Sabbath Sacrifice*, 2; see B. Nitzan's publication of 4Q286 frg. 1 col. 2 and her notes, which highlight many of the parallels between the *Blessings and Curses* and the *Sabbath Songs* ("4QBerakot [4Q286-290]: A Preliminary Report," 56-63).

101. Newsom, *Songs of the Sabbath Sacrifice*, 2.

possible that the *Sabbath Songs* are pre-Qumranic and yet still influenced the composition of sectarian texts.[102]

Newsom's present position is that the *Sabbath Songs* are a pre-Qumran composition. The decisive evidence for her current position is the abundant use of אלוהים for God, which is uncharacteristic of the sectarian Dead Sea Scrolls.[103] But even this evidence is far from conclusive. While it is true that the sectarian Qumran compositions tend to avoid using אלוהים apart from quotations of scriptural traditions, there are exceptions to this "rule." Note, first, that the use of אלוהים also occurs in other liturgical compositions of the Community, such as the *Blessings* (1QSb).[104] Second, אלוהים is widely used in the *Songs of the Master,* and, again, there is abundant evidence that this composition is a Qumran composition. Newsom, however, explains this unusual use of אלוהים in the *Songs of the Master* by appealing to the document's incantational function:[105]

> That the normally avoided divine epithet *'ĕlōhîm* should be used in this sectarian composition [*Songs of the Master*] is not as surprising as it might first appear. According to the Songs of the Maśkil [i.e., *Songs of the Master*], the description of the "splendor of His beauty" (4Q510 [frg.] 1 [line] 4) serves a quasi-magical purpose, "to frighten and ter[rify] all the spirits of the angels of destruction . . ." (4Q510 [frg.] 1 [lines] 4-5). The Songs of the Maśkil are conceived of as words of power. In such a context the use of a normally restricted divine name is readily explicable.[106]

What Newsom does not consider, however, is that such an explanation *is equally applicable* to the *Songs of the Sabbath Sacrifice* — a composition that describes the inner sanctums of the heavenly sanctuary and the angelic liturgy that transpires there. Thus, Newsom's argument for the pre-Qumran

---

102. Newsom, "'Sectually Explicit' Literature," 183-84; and idem, PTSDSSP 4B:5.

103. Newsom, "'Sectually Explicit' Literature," 182-83; and idem, PTSDSSP 4B:5. See also H. Stegemann, "Religionsgeschichtliche Erwägungen," 195-217; and P. Skehan, "The Divine Name at Qumran, in the Masada Scroll, and in the Septuagint," *BIOSCS* 13 (1980): 14-44, esp. 14-18, 20-28.

104. *Blessings* (1QSb) 4.25: ". . . for the glory of the God of host[s . . .]" (לכבוד אלהי צבא[ות); cf. *Daily Prayers* (4Q503) frg. 13 line 1: "[. . .] God of lights [. . .]" (אלוהי אורים[), and frgs. 37-38 line 14: "the God of all the Holy One[s . . .]" (אלוהי כול קודש[ים).

105. Although Newsom suggests that the *Sabbath Songs* are a source or influence on the *Songs of the Master,* she does not suggest that the genetic link accounts for the use of אלוהים in the *Songs of the Master.*

106. Newsom, "'Sectually Explicit' Literature," 184-85.

character of the *Sabbath Songs* on the basis of the use of אלוהים, while possible, is scarcely conclusive.

There is, however, at least one more piece of evidence, not considered by Newsom, that I would argue is decisive in the question of the provenience of the *Sabbath Songs*.[107] It is a passage in *Sabbath Song 5* that is paralleled in the *Rule of the Community* and other Qumran compositions. *Sabbath Song 5* is witnessed by 4Q402 frg. 4 and Masık col. 1. The relevant section, lines 15-17 of the composite text, reads as follows:

כיא מאלוהי דעת נהיו כול הוי עד ומדעתו
ראישונות [. . .]תיו היו כול תעודות עולמים עושה [. . .]תיהם ואחרונות
למועדיהם

For from the God of knowledge came into being all that is forever. And from his knowledge [. . .]*tyw* is all the eternally fixed times. He (is) making the former things [. . .]*tyhm* and the latter things in their appointed times.

This passage bears marked similarity to 1QS 3.15b-16a:

מאל הדעות כול הויה ונהייה ולפני היותם[108] הכין כול מחשבתם
ובהיותם לתעודותם כמחשבת כבודו ימלאו פעולתם

From the God of knowledge (comes) all that is and (all) that shall be. And before their coming into being[109] (God) has established all their design(s). And when they come into being for their fixed times[110] according to his (God's) glorious design they fulfill their deeds.[111]

Besides the obvious affinities in thought, the almost exact parallel phrase "from the God of knowledge (comes) all that is" and the presence of the un-

---

107. See also the contribution by Strawn with Rietz in the present volume.

108. See also the same construction, לפני היותם, in the composite text of *Sabbath Song 5* (line 18).

109. For the construction לפני followed by an infinitive construction indicating the time "before," cf., e.g., Gen 13:10; 1 Sam 9:15.

110. While in biblical Hebrew תעודה is derived from עוד meaning "testimony" (see Isa 8:16, 20) or "custom" (Ruth 4:7), in Qumran Hebrew תעודה seems to be semantically related to יעד and has the following meanings: "fixed time," "assembly," and "destination" (see Qimron, *Hebrew of the Dead Sea Scrolls*, 115; cf. B. W. Dombrowski, "The Meaning of the Qumran Terms T'wdh and Mdh," *RevQ* 7 [1971]: 567-74; Newsom, *Songs of the Sabbath Sacrifice*, 161). For examples of תעודה meaning "fixed time," cf. 1QS 1.9, 3.10; 1QM 2.8, 14.13; Masık 1.3//4Q402 frg. 4 lines 12-13.

111. 1QS 3.15b-16a; cf. 1QS 11.11. My translation leaves ambiguous whether the clause כמחשבת כבודו modifies the preceding or succeeding phrase. It probably modifies both.

usual niphal of היה[112] in both passages indicate some sort of genetic relationship between these texts. The question that then needs to be raised is the direction of influence. While it is possible that both passages are dependent on
an earlier common source or tradition, there is no positive evidence to indicate this. Therefore one must ask: Is the *Sabbath Song* dependent on the *Rule
of the Community* or vice versa?[113] At first glace, Newsom's argument regarding the use of אלוהים might seem to tip the scale conclusively in favor of the
Sabbath Songs' priority. That is, one might suppose that it is more probable
that the author of the *Rule of the Community* would avoid אלוהים and change
it to אל than for the author of the *Sabbath Songs* — which use both אל and
אלוהים for God — to change אל to אלוהים. But, again, further evidence must
be considered. In this case, the direction of influence can be assessed by noting that the phrase "God of knowledge" ultimately derives from Hannah's
song in 1 Sam 2:3b where the form is אל דעות.[114] The form אל דעות in
Hannah's song suggests, therefore, that the *Rule of the Community* is prior to
the *Sabbath Songs*. Therefore, it is probable that the *Songs of the Sabbath Sacrifice* is a Qumran composition.

5. Conclusion

In conclusion, there is clear evidence that the *Songs of the Sabbath Sacrifice*
functioned as an influential tradition at Qumran.[115] That evidence includes,
again, the presence of multiple copies that cover a period of several generations and that reflect the scribal practices of the Community. Moreover, even
if the למשכיל superscriptions — addressing the *Sabbath Songs* to the "Master" for his use — are merely the redaction of the Community and constitute
the Community's sole contribution to the composition, that superscription
still indicates that the *Sabbath Songs* were used in the Community, apparently
by important functionaries. Finally, if the *Sabbath Songs* influenced the composition of clearly sectarian documents, this establishes that the *Sabbath*

---

112. For discussion of the niphal participle of היה, see W. H. Brownlee, *The Dead Sea
Manual of Discipline: Translation and Notes* (BASORSup 10-12; New Haven: American Schools
of Oriental Research, 1951), 9 n. 1 and 54-55 ("Appendix H: The Niph'al Participle of the Verb
היה").

113. This question does not necessarily assume that the influence is unmediated. The
question is instead one of priority.

114. I am indebted to M. Ellen Anderson for pointing out this reference to me. It is the
only occurrence of "God of knowledge" (whether אל דעות or אלוהי דעות) in the Hebrew Bible.

115. So also Newsom, "'Sectually Explicit' Literature," 181-82.

Songs were an authoritative tradition used by the Community. I have argued, moreover, that the *Songs of the Sabbath Sacrifice* not only functioned as a tradition for the Qumran Community, but that they were *composed by members* of the Qumran Community. The decisive piece of evidence in my judgment is that it is probable that *Sabbath Song 5* is dependent upon the language of the *Rule of the Community.* This dependence on an undisputed Qumran composition, in turn, indicates that the *Songs of the Sabbath Sacrifice* originated within the Qumran Community.

(More) Sectarian Terminology
in the *Songs of the Sabbath Sacrifice:*
The Case of תמימי דרך

BRENT A. STRAWN WITH HENRY W. MORISADA RIETZ

A further piece of evidence that may be pertinent to the preceding essay and that may also support arguments for a sectarian, Qumranic origin for the *Songs of the Sabbath Sacrifice* is the use of the phrase תמימי דרך in this composition. The occurrence of תמימי דרך in the *Sabbath Songs* is significant because this phrase is found elsewhere (in either identical or near-identical constructions) almost exclusively in other, clearly sectarian compositions — most notably, the *Rule of the Community.* Moreover, not only is such terminology found in these documents, it is frequently used there as a sobriquet or self-designation for the Community itself, and is, therefore, fraught with theological meaning and significance.[1] In short, תמימי דרך seems to be tech-

---

1. The origins of the phrase, while important, are not under discussion here. For biblical antecedents that collocate דרך and √תמם, see Ezek 28:15; Pss 101:2, 6; 119:1; Prov 10:29; 11:20; 13:6; 28:6; Job 4:6; cf. LXX Ps 36:18; see also *HALOT* 4:1742-43; 1748-50 and, further, note 25 below. Of this list, the dualistic presentation of Psalm 101 (note esp. v. 2, which also utilizes a verbal form

---

Both of the authors, working independently, but also as a result of their joint editorial work on *The Dead Sea Scrolls: Hebrew, Aramaic, and Greek Texts with English Translations,* Vol. 4B: *Angelic Liturgy: Songs of the Sabbath Sacrifice* (ed. James H. Charlesworth, Carol A. Newsom, H. W. Rietz, B. A. Strawn, and R. E. Whitaker; PTSDSSP 4B; Tübingen: Mohr Siebeck and Louisville: Westminster John Knox, 1999), arrived at similar conclusions about certain terminology that might indicate a Qumranic provenience for the *Sabbath Songs.* For Rietz, the telling phrase was אל דעת (see the preceding article); for Strawn, the revealing phrase was תמימי דרך. In order to retain the integrity of its original oral presentation, it was decided to publish Rietz's paper as it was, and to coauthor this second treatment, which can be seen as a kind of appendix to the preceding essay by Rietz. The authors' thanks go to Michael Thomas Davis for his comments on an earlier draft.

nical terminology that further underscores a possible connection (or influence) between the *Rule of the Community* and the *Sabbath Songs,* on the one hand, and between the *Sabbath Songs* and other Qumranic compositions, on the other hand. If so, the use of תמימי דרך in the *Songs of the Sabbath Sacrifice* might be taken as additional evidence that it is not completely devoid of sectarian terminology and that it may, in fact, be a Qumranic composition.

תמימי דרך appears three times in the extant manuscripts of the *Sabbath Songs:*[2]

- 4Q403 frg. 1 1.22: וברך לכול תמימי דרך בֹּ[ש]בעה דֹּבֹרי פלא; "and he will bless all (the) perfect of way with [se]ven wondrous words."
- 4Q404 frg. 2 line 3: וברך לכול תמימֹ[י] דרך בשבעֹ[ה]; "and he will bless all (the) perfec[[t]] of way with seve[n. . . .]"
- 4Q405 frg. 13 line 6: וב[ו]רך לכוֹל תמימי דֹרֹ[ך]; "[and] he [will bl]ess all (the) perfect of way [. . .]."

Since 4Q403 frg. 1 parallels 4Q404 frg. 2 at this point, both preserving portions of *Sabbath Song 6,* there are really only two distinct passages that preserve the phrase תמימי דרך. Moreover, while 4Q405 frg. 13 belongs to *Sabbath Song 8,* the descriptions of the blessings of the seven princes (chief and deputy, respectively) in both *Songs 6* and *8* are so similar and formulaic that one can be used to reconstruct the other; the two units are obviously related. Regardless of these facts, the phrase תמימי דרך is extant in three different manuscripts of the *Sabbath Songs* and at two different points in the overall composition.[3]

---

of שכל) may have been particularly instructive for and generative of Qumran usage. The specific phrase תמימי דרך occurs only twice in the Hebrew Bible: Ps 119:1, which specifically includes a mention of תורת יהוה; and Prov 11:20, where the תמימי דרך are said to be God's pleasure (רצונו). (Cf. also, perhaps, Prov 13:6 where the singular תם־דרך is said to be protected by צדקה.) In each case, there are significant points of contact with Qumran vocabulary, indicating that these verses may contain the sentiments that were seized upon and appropriated by the Community for use as a self-designation.

2. Texts are cited from Carol A. Newsom, "Angelic Liturgy: Songs of the Sabbath Sacrifice (4Q400-4Q407, 11Q17, Masık)," in PTSDSSP 4B:50, 62, 86. Newsom's DJD edition ("Shirot Olat Hashabbat," in *Qumran Cave 4.6: Poetical and Liturgical Texts, Part 1* [ed. E. Eshel et al.; DJD 11; Oxford: Clarendon, 1998], 257, 295, 329) is identical, as is her earlier work: *Songs of the Sabbath Sacrifice: A Critical Edition* (HSS 27; Atlanta: Scholars Press, 1985), 189, 250, 277. For instances of the terms, see the concordances in DJD 11:445-72, esp. 450, 472; and DSSC 2:765. Translations are our own unless otherwise indicated and intentionally tend toward the literal; diacritics are only provided for texts from the *Sabbath Songs.*

3. Given the fragmentary state of preservation, it is always possible that the phrase could have occurred elsewhere as well.

In Newsom's critical editions of the *Sabbath Songs,* she has translated the clause לכול תמימי דרך as "all those whose way is perfect."[4] James R. Davila, in his commentary on the text, offers a translation that follows Newsom's closely: "all whose way is sound."[5] Both translations treat the construct chain as a kind of unmarked relative clause. This is both acceptable and accurate given (1) comparable adjectival uses of the construct elsewhere in the composition;[6] and (2) the absence of the relative אשר from the extant sections of the *Sabbath Songs* — a fact that might at first strike one as somewhat unusual, especially given the lateness of Qumran Hebrew,[7] but which is probably to be understood as the result of the poetic or hymnic nature of the Songs.[8] Even so, these translations may unfortunately obscure somewhat the marked similarity the construction and vocabulary of this phrase shares with closely related and clearly sectarian terminology elsewhere in Qumran Literature. A listing of passages that collocate דרך with the adjective תמים follows:[9]

- 1QS 2.2: "the men of God's lot, those walking perfectly in all his ways (תמים בכול דרכיו)."

---

4. Newsom, PTSDSSP 4B:51, 63, 87 (the latter *sans* "those"); DJD 11:261, 295, 330; cf. *Songs of the Sabbath Sacrifice,* 194.

5. James R. Davila, *Liturgical Works* (ECDSS 6; Grand Rapids: Eerdmans, 2000), 119: "And he blesses all whose way is sound" (for 4Q403//4Q404; ditto for 4Q405 [see ibid., 136]).

6. As in Hebrew generally. For this usage in biblical Hebrew, e.g., see Bruce K. Waltke and M. O'Connor, *An Introduction to Biblical Hebrew Syntax* (Winona Lake: Eisenbrauns, 1990), 255-56 (§14.1b), 261-62 (§14.3.3b).

7. I.e., in contrast to earlier periods, there is a general tendency to employ אשר (or –ש) in relative clauses in later stages of the language. See, e.g., Angel Sáenz-Badillos, *A History of the Hebrew Language* (Cambridge: Cambridge University Press, 1993), 58-59, 123-24, 127, 141, 145-46. See also, more generally, the important study by William M. Schniedewind, "Qumran Hebrew as an Antilanguage," *JBL* 118 (1999): 235-52.

8. See, e.g., Stanislav Segert, "Observations on Poetic Structures in the Songs of the Sabbath Sacrifice," *RevQ* 13 (1988): 215-23; Elisha Qimron, "A Review Article of *Songs of the Sabbath Sacrifices* [sic]: *A Critical Edition,* by Carol Newsom," *HTR* 79 (1986): 358; and Davila, *Liturgical Works,* 86-88. Note, esp., Segert, "Observations," 216 and n. 11 on the self-categorization of the composition as שירות. Segert also instructively compares 4Q405 frgs. 20-22 2.8-9 with the biblical text that inspired it (Ezek 1:26) and notes, among other things, the omission of "the typically prosaic relative pronoun 'ŠR" in 4Q405. See the previous note.

9. See *DSSC* 2:764-66; *GC* 112-13, 125. For the boldfaced passages, see further below. The texts follow the editions in PTSDSSP wherever possible; otherwise DJD has been used. See also, conveniently *DSSSE.* More passages could be listed if תמים and √תמם are collocated solely with הלך, which is the most obvious verb of motion associated with דרך. See esp. CD 7.5//4Q266 (4QDᵃ) frg. 3 3.6; 1QSb 1.2; 4Q415 (4QInstructionᵃ) frg. 2 col. 1 + frg. 1 col. 2 line 3; 4Q417 (4QInstructionᶜ) frg 1 1.12, 2.5; 4Q525 (4QBeatitudes) frg. 5 line 11.

- 1QS 3.9-10 (//4Q255 [4QpapSᵃ] frg. 2 line 5): "May he establish his steps by walking perfectly in all the ways of God (תמים בכול דרכי אל)."[10]
- 1QS 4.22: "in order that the upright might have insight into the knowledge of the Most High and the wisdom of the Sons of Heaven, (and) in order that the perfect of way (תמימי דרך) might receive understanding."
- 1QS 8.10: "when these are established in the counsel of the community for two years in/with/among (the) perfect of way (בתמים דרך)."[11]
- 1QS 8.18: "until his deeds are purified from all iniquity by walking in/with/among (the) perfect of way (בתמים דרך)."
- 1QS 8.21: "every one who enters into the holy council, those walking in/with/among (the) perfect of way (בתמים דרך), just as he commanded."
- 1QS 9.2: "he will be tested two years for the perfection of his way (לתמים דרכו)."[12]
- 1QS 9.5: "and (the) perfect of way (ותמים דרך) are like a pleasing freewill offering."
- 1QS 9.9: "and walking in/with/among (the) perfect of way (בתמים דרך)."
- 1QSa 1.28: "the sa[ges of] the Congregation, and the insightful ones, and the knowledgeable (ones), the perfect (ones) of the way (תמימי הדרך), and the men of valor."
- 1QSb 5.22: "and to walk before him (i.e., God) perfectly in all [the] wa[ys of God] ([תמים בכול דר[כי אל)."
- 1QM 14.7 (//4Q491 [4QM1] frgs. 8-10 1.5): "and through/in/by (the) perfect (ones) of way (ובתמימי דרך) will all the wicked nations be destroyed."
- 1QHᵃ 9.36: "Righteous ones, put an end to iniquity; and be stron[g] all (you) perfect (ones) of way (תמימי דרך)."
- 4Q266 (4QDᵃ) frg. 2 1.4: "[for] those [examin]ing his commandments and those walking in/with/among (the) perfect of way (בתמים דרך)."
- 4Q266 frg. 5 1.19: "[. . .] in his way by walking perfect[ly . . .] (בדרכו[להתהלך /ת\מ]ים)."

---

10. Cf. also the // in 4Q257 (4QpapSᶜ) frg. 1 2.13, which is very broken.

11. בתמים דרך was also written above line 10 but subsequently erased. See the discussion in Elisha Qimron and James H. Charlesworth, "Rule of the Community (1QS; cf. 4QS MSS A-J, 5Q11)," in *The Dead Sea Scrolls: Hebrew, Aramaic, and Greek Texts with English Translations*, Vol. 1: *Rule of the Community and Related Documents* (ed. James H. Charlesworth et al.; PTSDSSP 1; Tübingen: J. C. B. Mohr [Paul Siebeck] and Louisville: Westminster John Knox, 1994), 34 n. 242.

12. Slightly different in the // in 4Q258 (4QSᵈ) frg. 3 line 3 but לתמים דרכו is also preserved there.

- CD MS A 2.15-16: "and choose that which he [i.e., God] desires and reject that which he hates by walking perfectly in all his ways (תמים בכל דרכיו)."[13]
- 4Q418 (4QInstruction[d]) frg. 172 line 4: "[. . .] in/with/among (the) perfect of way (בתמים דרך[)."
- 4Q510 (4QShir[a]) frg. 1 line 9//4Q511 (4QShir[b]) frg. 10 line 8: "All (the) perfect (ones) of way (כול תמימי דרך)[will] exalt him."[14]
- 4Q511 (4QShir[b]) frg. 63 3.2-3: "and the intentions (?) of the deeds of (the) perfect (ones) of way (תמימי דרך)."
- 4Q525 (4QBeatitudes) frgs. 11-12 line 3: "perfect in all my way(s) (תמים[בכול דרכי)."

This is no insignificant collection of texts. It could be rounded out still further by adding those instances where the verb תמם is conjoined with דרך,[15] or similar and related phraseology that employs תמים, especially.[16] The listing presented above is sufficient, however, to raise the question of the possible sectarian provenience of תמימי + דרך in the *Sabbath Songs* and elsewhere.

It is should be underscored that the above listing has not been "doctored" — that is, *all passages* that conjoin דרך and תמים and that can be meaningfully translated have been presented above.[17] Moreover, all of the attestations occur in documents that are closely related to the Qumran Community (see further below). Especially important is the fact that *the particular construction* תמימי דרך occurs *exclusively* in documents that are clearly Qumran compositions.[18] It is also of no small significance that the majority of passages that conjoin דרך and תמים are found in the *Rule of the Community* (1QS).[19]

---

13. Cf. also the // in 4Q266 (4QD[a]) frg. 2 2.15-16, which is very broken.

14. The citation is composite, derived mostly from 4Q511, which is the more complete text.

15. See, e.g., 1QS 8.25; 10.21; 11.17; 1QM 14.7//4Q491 frgs. 8-10 1.5; 1QH[a] 12.32; 4Q259 (4QS[e]) frg. 1 3.17; 4Q260 (4QS[f]) frg. 3 lines 1-2 (see *DSSC* 2:765-66).

16. E.g., אנשי תמים (sometimes with a further complement such as הקדש) in CD MS B 20.2, 5, 7; 1QS 8.20; 4Q525 frg. 27 line 4; cf. 1QM 8.5.

17. Perhaps one should add to the listing above 4Q223-224 (4QpapJub[h]) unit 2 3.18-19, which is very broken, but where similar phraseology is plausibly reconstructed on the basis of the Ethiopic text of *Jub.* 36:23.

18. One should note, too, other important sectarian texts that employ תמים, though not with דרך: 4Q287 (4QBer[b]) frg. 2 line 10; 4Q491 frg. 11 1.11 (= 4Q491c frg. 1 line 4 in *DSSSE*). Cf., however, 4Q528 frg. 1 line 4 (bis), which is probably pre-Qumranic. See Émile Puech, "528. 4QOuvrage hymnique ou sapientiel B," in *Qumrân Grotte 4.18: Textes Hébreux (4Q521-4Q528, 4Q576-4Q579)* (DJD 25; Oxford: Clarendon, 1998), 188.

19. Note the 4QS //s, which are limited in number. Additional passages from 1QS that are pertinent but that do not include דרך (but sometimes הלך; see note 9 above) include: 1.8;

To be sure, תמים is not, by itself, a sectarian term — or, put differently, it is not sufficient by itself to indicate sectarian provenience. An illustrative example can be found in the use of תמים in 11Q5 (11QPsª) 18.1 and 22.8.

- 11Q5 18.1: "to/for the good (ones) (are) your souls and to/for the perfect (ones) (ולתמימים) to glorify the Most High."
- 11Q5 22.8: "your perfect ones (תמיך) have mourned over you."

The former text is, of course, from Psalm 154, attested also in the Peshitta;[20] the latter is from the Apostrophe to Zion.[21] It may be doubted whether these passages, especially the first given its attestation in the Syriac tradition, can be properly labeled "sectarian" or "Qumranic" if that is understood narrowly as composed by the Community.[22] Even so, it is crucial to note that these two passages employ תמים *only;* it is *not* collocated with דרך. Hence, they may actually underscore the point made above regarding the sectarian provenience of the construction דרך + תמים. That said, it must immediately be stated that there is another instance in 11Q5 that *does* employ the whole phrase. It is

---

3.3 (//4Q257 [4QpapSᶜ] frg. 1 2.5); 8.1, 9 (//4Q259 [4QSᵉ] frg. 1 2.16); 9.6 (//4Q258 [4QSᵈ] frg. 3 1.7), 8 (//4Q258 [4QSᵈ] frg. 3 1.8), 19 (//4Q256 [4QSᵇ] frg. 8 1.2//4Q258 [4QSᵈ] frg. 3 2.3). Note that the vast majority of instances of תמים itself are located in 1QS: 18 out of 80 or 22.5%. If the 4QS materials are included, they add 10 hits, totaling 28 out of 80 or 35%. The next closest manuscript is CD with 7 instances (8.8%); the 4QD texts add 5 more, for a total of 12 instances or 15%. The *Temple Scroll* (11Q19-20) has 7 hits (8.75%). Not all hits, of course, are equally applicable to the matter under discussion (e.g., 6 of the 7 references in the Temple Scroll are irrelevant).

20. Ps 154:3: ܪܡܝܫܠܐܐ. See the edition by J. A. Sanders, J. H. Charlesworth, and H. W. Rietz, "Non-Masoretic Psalms (4Q88 = 4QPsᶠ, 11Q5 = 11QPsª, 11Q6 = 11QPsᵇ), in *The Dead Sea Scrolls: Hebrew, Aramaic, and Greek Texts with English Translations,* Vol. 4A: *Pseudepigraphic and Non-Masoretic Psalms and Prayers* (ed. James H. Charlesworth et al.; PTSDSSP 4A; Tübingen: Mohr Siebeck and Louisville: Westminster John Knox, 1997), 174. Cf. also 4Q448 1.7 and the discussion in E. Eshel, H. Eshel, and A. Yardeni, "448. 4QApocryphal Psalm and Prayer," in DJD 11:409-10, 416, 418.

21. Cf. also 4Q88 (4QPsᶠ) 7.14-8.15 and 11Q6 (11QPsᵇ) frg. 6 lines 1-2, but the specific passage is not extant in either of these.

22. See, however, the excellent article by Carol A. Newsom, "'Sectually Explicit' Literature from Qumran," in *The Hebrew Bible and Its Interpreters* [ed. B. Halpern, W. H. Propp, and D. N. Freedman; BJSUCSD 1; Winona Lake: Eisenbrauns, 1990], 167-87 for other uses of the term "sectarian," including, esp., the notions of sectarian reception and use. In these ways, both compositions could be seen as sectarian. For more on 11Q5, especially compositions therein that were previously unknown, see further below. In the case of Psalm 154, another possibility would be that a Qumranic tradition was somehow adopted into a larger stream of tradition, eventually finding its way into the Syriac tradition. This is an intriguing scenario but one that is impossible to demonstrate with certainty. (We thank Michael Thomas Davis for discussions on Psalm 154.)

found in the prose insert known as *David's Compositions* (11Q5 27.2-11), which states that David was wise and a scribe (see 27.2):

- 11Q5 27.3: "and discerning and perfect in all his ways (ותמים בכול דרכיו) before God and men."

What might be said about this passage? First, the sectarian nature of this specific composition cannot be definitively ruled out insofar as it has not yet appeared elsewhere in Early Jewish literature; moreover, in many respects the debate still continues over the "sectarian" or "secondary" nature of 11QPs[a] as a whole.[23] Second, the passage might be influenced, in part, by biblical language like that which is found in 2 Sam 22:24, 26, and 33 (//Ps 18:24, 26, 33).[24] Only one of these verses (v. 33) employs תמים with דרך,[25] and even here the sense is not entirely clear.[26] Third, it is not at all certain that the route of influence runs from 11Q5 (DavComp) to the other instances of the phrase. Indeed, given the weight of instances elsewhere, it seems equally possible that the influence runs *from* them *to* DavComp. Thus, the appearance of דרך + תמים in

23. Cf. Sanders's remarks in PTSDSSP 4A:213; and, further, idem, "Variorum in the Psalms Scroll (11QPs[a])," *HTR* 59 (1966): 83-94; idem, "Cave 11 Surprises and the Question of Canon," *McCormick Quarterly* 21 (1968): 1-15; and idem, "The Qumran Scroll (11QPs[a]) Reviewed," in *On Language, Culture, and Religion: In Honor of Eugene A. Nida* (ed. M. Black and W. A. Smalley; The Hague: Mouton, 1974), 79-99. Joining Sanders in arguing that 11QPs[a] is a "true, Scriptural" psalter is Peter W. Flint. See his numerous studies on the subject, especially *The Dead Sea Psalms Scrolls and the Book of Psalms* (STDJ 17; Leiden: Brill, 1997); idem, "The Contribution of the Cave 4 Psalms Scrolls to the Psalms Debate," *DSD* 5 (1998): 320-33; and "The '11QPs[a]-Psalter' in the Dead Sea Scrolls, Including the Preliminary Edition of 4QPs[e]," in *The Quest for Context and Meaning: Studies in Biblical Intertextuality in Honor of James A. Sanders* (ed. C. A. Evans and S. Talmon; Leiden: Brill, 1997), 173-99. Others have argued that 11QPs[a] is a "secondary, liturgical" collection. See, e.g., S. Talmon, "Pisqah Be'emsa' Pasuq and 11QPs[a]," *Textus* 5 (1966): 11-21; P. W. Skehan, "A Liturgical Complex in 11QPs[a]," *CBQ* 35 (1973): 195-205; M. Haran, "11QPs[a] and the Canonical Book of Psalms," in *Minhah le-Nahum: Biblical and Other Studies Presented to Nahum M. Sarna in Honour of His 70th Birthday* (ed. M. Brettler and M. Fishbane; JSOTSup 154; Sheffield: JSOT Press, 1993), 193-201; and M. H. Goshen-Gottstein, "The Psalms Scroll (11QPs[a]): A Problem of Canon and Text," *Textus* 5 (1966): 22-33.

24. On this point, compare 11Q19 60.21: תמים תהיה עם יהוה אלוהיכה ("you shall be perfect with the LORD your God") with Lev 19:2: קדשים תהיו כי קדוש אני יהוה אלהיכם ("you shall be holy, for I, the LORD your God, am holy"). Cf. also Matt 5:48: ἔσεσθε οὖν ὑμεῖς τέλειοι ὡς ὁ πατὴρ ὑμῶν ὁ οὐράνιος τέλειός ἐστιν ("Therefore, be perfect, as your heavenly father is perfect").

25. 2 Sam 22:33: ויתר תמים דרכו (K; Q: דרכי), "he [i.e., God] has opened wide (?) his [K; Q: "my"] path" (so NRSV); Ps 18:33: ויתן תמים דרכי, "he [i.e., God] made my way safe" (so NRSV). For other biblical passages that make use of דרך and √תמם, see note 1 above.

26. See the previous note and, further, the commentaries.

DavComp cannot and does not, on its own, obviate the widespread attestation of this phrase in the sectarian scrolls. On the contrary, the numerous instances of דרך + תמים in those texts, conjoined with its appearance in DavComp, could be taken as data pertinent to, if not actually indicative of, the latter's origin and provenience.[27]

With the evidence from 11QPs[a] accounted for, it remains to say a few words about the phrase תמימי דרך in the *Sabbath Songs* in light of its use elsewhere in the Qumran Literature:

1. To begin with, it must be granted that not every collocation of דרך and תמים occurs in clearly sectarian texts. The uses in 11QPs[a], for example, have already been mentioned and addressed. Nevertheless, the vast majority of occurrences appear in documents that are either Qumran compositions or traditions that significantly influenced the Community. The *Rule of the Community* (1QS), the *Rule of the Congregation* (1QSa), and the *Blessings* (1QSb) are clearly Qumran compositions, as are the *War Scroll* (1QM, 4QM1) and the *Thanksgiving Hymns* (1QH[a]).[28] As Newsom rightly argues, the *Songs of the Master* (4Q510-511) are also probably Qumran compositions.[29] The *Damascus Document* (CD and 4Q266) is closely related to the Qumran Community, and may reflect the perspective of a different branch of the movement, while *Instruction* (4Q418)[30] and *Beatitudes* (4Q525)[31] are probably traditions inherited by the Community.[32]

2. Identical attestations of the specific construction תמימי דרך are few and far between. The handful of instances (in boldface in the above list) are

27. If not also, more broadly, 11QPs[a] as a whole (see note 23 above).

28. Only the *specific manuscripts* found in the bulleted list above are included in this and the following statements.

29. See Newsom, "'Sectually Explicit' Literature," 167-87.

30. See D. J. Harrington, "Wisdom at Qumran," in *The Community of the Renewed Covenant: The Notre Dame Symposium on the Dead Sea Scrolls* (ed. E. Ulrich and J. VanderKam; Notre Dame: University of Notre Dame Press, 1994), 137-52; Carol A. Newsom "Songs of the Sabbath Sacrifice," in *EDSS* 2:887.

31. Cf. Puech, who has argued that 4Q525 is a tradition that influenced the Qumran Community ("525. 4QBéatitudes," in DJD 25:119) with J. C. R. de Roo, who believes that it is a Qumran composition ("Is 4Q525 a Qumran Sectarian Document?" in *The Scrolls and the Scriptures: Qumran Fifty Years After* [ed. S. E. Porter and C. A. Evans; JSPSup 26; Roehampton Institute London Papers 3; Sheffield: Sheffield Academic Press, 1997], 338-67).

32. For discussion of the category of "traditions" that influenced Qumran, see the essay by Rietz in the present volume. See note 17 above for the possibility that *Jubilees* should be added to this latter category, in which case, see Henry W. Morisada Rietz, "Synchronizing Worship: Jubilees as a Tradition for the Qumran Community," in *Enoch and Qumran Origins: New Light on a Forgotten Connection* (ed. G. Boccaccini with J. H. Ellens and J. Waddell; Grand Rapids: Eerdmans, 2005), 111-18.

found in 1QS (4.22: תמימי דרך), 1QSa (1.28: תמימי הדרך), 1QM/4QM1 (1QM 14.7//4QM1 frgs. 8-10 1.5: ובתמימי דרך), 1QH^a (9.36: תמימי דרך), and 4Q510 and 4Q511 (תמימי דרך). As already noted, there is wide agreement among scholars that these documents are compositions of the Qumran Community itself. These passages, moreover, are the *only* ones where this precise phrase occurs outside its use in the *Sabbath Songs*. A problem immediately presents itself, however, with regard to the possible relationships between these five compositions and the *Sabbath Songs*. Newsom, for instance, has argued that 4Q510-11 (Qumranic in her view) is dependent on the *Sabbath Songs* (non-Qumranic in her view).[33] If she is correct, this scenario could easily explain the use of תמימי דרך in both compositions without any specifically sectarian connotations pertaining to the *Sabbath Songs*. But the evidence Newsom has amassed seems equivocal: the data concerning the use of אלוהים in the *Songs of the Sabbath Sacrifice* and in the *Songs of the Master,* for example, could also (and perhaps just as easily) be understood as establishing a sectarian provenience for the former since such a provenience is clear in the case of the latter. The same might be said for similarities between the *Sabbath Songs* and other texts, such as *Blessings and Curses* (4Q286-290) — namely, that the *Sabbath Songs* look like other sectarian texts not (only) because they have influenced those other texts but because they, too, are sectarian. Indeed, the use of דרך תמימי could be further evidence of this very point, especially given its technical status as a self-designation for the Community.

3. This leads directly to a final and very critical point: the semantics of the phrase תמימי דרך in the *Sabbath Songs* — namely, who is speaking the phrase and who is being addressed by it? In *Sabbath Song 6,* the speaker is the sixth chief prince who is said to "bless in the name of the divine power[s] (גבורו[ת] [אלים) all the insightful powerful ones (גבורי שכל) with seven words of his wondrous power" (lines 54-55). This chief prince then blesses all the תמימי דרך and all who wait for "him" (presumably, God) "with seven wondrous words" (lines 55-56). At that point the speech of the seventh chief prince begins. *Sabbath Song 8* is quite similar, only here it is "the sixth among the wondrous deputy [prin]ces" (lines 36-37: השׁשׁי במשׁני [נשׁי[אי פלא) that blesses all תמימי דרך — presumably in nearly identical fashion as *Sabbath Song 6,* though the text of *Sabbath Song 8* is unfortunately broken. In both cases, then, the speaker of these blessings is an angelic figure of some sort. But of whom are the angels speaking?

There seem to be only two options: the recipients of the angelic bless-

33. See Newsom, "Songs," 887; and, further, the discussion by Rietz in the preceding essay along with his own assessment of the evidence.

ings are either the human community or the divine community. Language that is used both before and after the section containing תמימי דרך is applicable to either one of these referents. The language of "waiting for him (i.e., God)" (חוכי לו: *Sabbath Song 6* line 56; *Sabbath Song 8* line 38), for instance, seems evocative of pious humans,[34] but other statements explicitly state that the recipients of the blessings are the angelic hosts themselves (לכול א[י]לי: *Sabbath Song 6* line 48; *Sabbath Song 8* line 34). Other language, it would seem, could apply to *either* group — (a) human or (b) divine — if not, in fact, (c) *both*.[35]

The collocation of תמים + דרך, and especially the specific phrase תמימי דרך, however, is often and mostly used *of* the Qumran Community itself, *by* the Community itself. As Newsom states:

> The phrase תמימי דרך and close variations (e.g., תמים בכול דרכיו) are frequent in QL . . . often with reference to the members of the Qumran community.[36]

Davila has observed the same but goes somewhat further than Newsom in identifying the specific referents of תמימי דרך:

> With small variations, the phrase "those whose way is sound" appears often in the QL . . . *always* referring to *human beings, especially the sectarians.* Presumably it applies to human beings here [in the *Sabbath Songs*] as well.[37]

But, given the use of the phrase תמימי דרך elsewhere, it may be more accurate to say that in the *Sabbath Songs* it does not refer only or simply to human beings in general but to the Qumran sectarians in particular.

We believe the same could be the case even if the referents of the angelic

---

34. See, e.g., Ps 33:18-22 or 1QHᵃ 11.20-21, 31; 14.6; 15.18; 17.10, 14; 19.31.

35. Note Newsom's careful discussion in DJD 11:262: "One might ask whether the blessings of the seven chief princes are addressed to angelic or human recipients. . . . Most of the phrases are ambiguous, but in view of the overwhelming focus on angels in the *Sabbath Shirot*, I am inclined to see them as referring to the angels who worship in the heavenly temple. . . . The phrases that allude to the moral qualities of those blessed (e.g., לכול הולכי יושר,לכול תמימי דרך) certainly need not be taken as referring to human worshippers. The *Sabbath Shirot* refers to statutes promulgated for the angels through which they attain to purity and holiness (4Q400 1 i 5, 15) and describes the angels as obedient (4Q405 23 i 10-11). It is possible, however, that just as the human community joins with the angels in the praise of God (4Q400 2 6-8), they are also considered to be recipients of the blessings of the chief princes, along with the angelic worshippers."

36. Newsom, *Songs of the Sabbath Sacrifice,* 202; cf. idem, DJD 11:265.

37. Davila, *Liturgical Works,* 121-22 (our emphases).

blessing are opened up to include divine recipients (option c above). This option is, in fact, quite intriguing and telling in our judgment. There was a concern at Qumran, evident in calendrical machinations and in specific Qumranic texts (e.g., 1QM), to align the worship of the Community with that of heaven and the angels.[38] A possible double entendre in תמימי דרך is thus not impossible, nor is it completely unexpected, especially in the poetic context. Such a double referent may, in fact, further underscore the point: that it is the Qumran Community itself that is referenced in the phrase — a Community that understood itself, even by means of this very phrase, as comprised of both earthly and heavenly worshippers.

To summarize: given תמימי דרך's almost exclusive use in other, clearly sectarian compositions, especially as a self-designation of the Community, it is probable that תמימי דרך in the *Sabbath Songs* should be taken as additional evidence that, not only is this composition not devoid of sectarian terminology, it should be considered Qumranic in origin and provenience.[39] If so, any non-Qumranic-like elements in the *Songs of the Sabbath Sacrifice* will need to be accounted for and/or explained in ways other than that of compositional origin.[40] If this scenario is correct it would also indicate that Masık was taken to Masada by a Qumranite after all.[41]

---

38. See Henry W. Morisada Rietz, "The Qumran Concept of Time," in *The Bible and the Dead Sea Scrolls*, Vol. 2: *The Dead Sea Scrolls and the Qumran Community* (ed. James H. Charlesworth; Waco: Baylor University Press, 2006), 203-34; and idem, *Time in the Sectarian Dead Sea Scrolls* (WUNT II; Tübingen: Mohr Siebeck, 2006), 203-34. In several publications, Newsom has argued that the *Sabbath Songs* function as a kind of "communal mysticism" providing "the means for a communion with angels in the act of praise" (so, e.g., "Songs," 888).

39. See, e.g., Rietz's essay in the present volume on the possible sectarian nature of אל דעת, which is used in both the *Rule of the Community* and the *Sabbath Songs*. Note also Qimron, "A Review Article," 363-64 (cf. 356-58, 366-67) for arguments on the basis of dualism and distinctive vocabulary and terminology that "may well establish the common provenance of *ShirShabb* and the DSS." Cf. Davila, *Liturgical Works*, 89.

40. See, e.g., Rietz's argument in the preceding essay regarding the use of אלוהים in the *Sabbath Songs*.

41. Cf. Shemaryahu Talmon in *Masada VI: Yigael Yadin Excavations 1963-1965 Final Reports: Hebrew Fragments from Masada and the Ben Sira Scroll from Masada* (Jerusalem: Israel Exploration Society and the Hebrew University, 1999), 104, 116, 119, who believes that Masım (MasapocrGen), Masıl (MasapocrJosh), and Masıj (MasJub or MaspsJub) were taken to Masada by a member(s) of the Qumran Community who fled the settlement when the Romans overran it. Talmon (ibid., 116) believes the same about Masık (MasShirShabb) as did Yigael Yadin (see ibid., 120, but n. 2 for Newsom's present distance from that position). Perhaps one should also compare Masın (Talmon in ibid., 133-35). Whatever the case, if Talmon is correct about Masım, Mas ıl, and Masıj, there is something of a precedent or context for the importation of Qumran documents to Masada, and Masık, if similar, would therefore not be unusual or out of place.

The debate on the provenience of the *Sabbath Songs* will no doubt continue. Certainty may elude us. This paper, however, has suggested that there may be more sectarian terminology in the *Sabbath Songs* than is often thought to be the case. תמימי דרך is probably another example of what Newsom has called "sectually explicit" language at Qumran. While it cannot conclusively establish the Qumranic provenience of the *Sabbath Songs* by itself, it should nevertheless be taken as additional evidence that points to a probable Qumranic origin for this fascinating composition.

Excerpted "Non-Biblical" Scrolls at Qumran?
Background, Analogies, Function

1. Introduction

The presence of documents that exist in multiple copies — sometimes from different caves — is a notable phenomenon among the Dead Sea Scrolls. Moreover, the fact that the Qumranites preserved multiple copies of "non-biblical" or "sectarian" scrolls alongside multiple copies of "biblical"[1] texts seems tacit proof that the Community viewed at least some of the former to be as important and authoritative as some of the latter.[2]

1. "Non-biblical," "sectarian," and "biblical" are placed in quotation marks to underscore their uncertain nature and (somewhat) anachronistic application to the Qumran evidence. With this caveat duly noted, other instances will generally not be so marked. Note further that "sectarian" is a distinct category from those of biblical/non-biblical — one that relates to the origin and use (not only content) of the manuscript in question. Cf. Carol A. Newsom, "'Sectually Explicit' Literature from Qumran," in *The Hebrew Bible and Its Interpreters* (ed. W. H. Propp, B. Halpern, and D. N. Freedman; BJSUCSD 1; Winona Lake: Eisenbrauns, 1990), 167-87.

2. Attestation in multiple copies is now often cited as a primary indicator of authoritative

It is a privilege and pleasure to dedicate this essay to my teacher and friend, the Reverend Dr. James H. Charlesworth. The extent of my debt and gratitude to him is beyond expression in this brief space (but our common love of basketball must be acknowledged!). In several ways, this article continues ideas that we originally published jointly (see J. H. Charlesworth and B. A. Strawn, "Reflections on the Text of *Serek Ha-Yahad* from Cave IV," *RevQ* 17 [1996]: 403-35, esp. 410-16). I thank the following individuals for reading and commenting on an earlier draft of the current article and/or for discussing its argument with me in various incarnations: Shane A. Berg, James H. Charlesworth, Michael Thomas Davis, Steve Delamarter, C. D. Elledge, Paul Garnet, Henry W. Morisada Rietz, Eileen Schuller, Christine Roy Yoder, and Jürgen Zangenberg. None of these are responsible for the opinions expressed here and several would no doubt take issue with them.

Multiple exemplars of a composition raise a number of questions, not merely the question of authoritative status — as any textual critic knows. Moreover, authoritative status may be signaled in numerous ways, not solely by the number of copies extant. Preeminently, the authoritative status of a manuscript/composition/text[3] is demonstrated by its *use*, an indicator that is now, unfortunately, mostly lost to us. So we must look to other, textual and para-textual, clues for how a composition was used.[4] To return to where this essay began, one such clue is the existence of multiple copies, a factor that indicates something of a composition's importance and, perhaps, its authority, however that is defined.[5]

Elsewhere I have argued that an additional indicator of a composition's authoritative nature and function is if it is excerpted or abbreviated — by itself or with other selections — to form a new text.[6] Excerption is similar to citation, a practice long understood to indicate authoritative status, but is distinct from it insofar as citations are simply that: a source cited in a new composition with additional and often extensive text in the latter that is not contained in the former. In the case of excerption, the *entirety* of the new composition is comprised of the source(s) *without* additional text, whether

---

status. See, e.g., James C. VanderKam, *The Dead Sea Scrolls Today* (Grand Rapids: Eerdmans, 1994), 149-57; idem, "Authoritative Literature in the Dead Sea Scrolls," *DSD* 5 (1998): 382-402; James VanderKam and Peter Flint, *The Meaning of the Dead Sea Scrolls: Their Significance for Understanding the Bible, Judaism, Jesus, and Christianity* (San Francisco: HarperSanFrancisco, 2002), 172-80; Philip R. Davies, *Scribes and Schools: The Canonization of the Hebrew Scriptures* (LAI; Louisville: Westminster John Knox, 1998), 153-55; and the contribution of H. W. Morisada Rietz in the present volume. Note also Peter Flint, "Scriptures in the Dead Sea Scrolls: The Evidence from Qumran," in *Emanuel: Studies in Hebrew Bible, Septuagint, and Dead Sea Scrolls in Honor of Emanuel Tov* (ed. Shalom M. Paul et al.; VTSup 94; Leiden: Brill, 2003), 269-304.

3. These terms are not identical but are used interchangeably in this essay. Even so, let the reader beware of reified notions of "text(s)" that are divorced from the material-cultural reality of the actual manuscripts, which do more than just "witness" to a "composition" or "text." I thank Steve Delamarter for discussions on this point and refer readers to his work. See also D. C. Parker, *The Living Text of the Gospels* (Cambridge: Cambridge University Press, 1997).

4. One cannot assume, therefore, that, in the absence of manifest clues to the contrary, a composition did *not* have authoritative function via its use. It very well might have, it is only that the textual or para-textual clues that would speak to such use are not (or are no longer) present.

5. The question of definition is important but not always addressed in the literature: what does "authoritative" literature or function *mean? What kind* of authoritative functioning?

6. See Brent A. Strawn, "Excerpted Manuscripts at Qumran: Their Significance for the Textual History of the Hebrew Bible and the Socio-Religious History of the Qumran Community and its Literature," in *The Bible and the Dead Sea Scrolls*, Vol. 2: *The Dead Sea Scrolls and the Qumran Community* (ed. J. H. Charlesworth; Waco: Baylor University Press, 2006), esp. 148-57.

that is commentary on the source (as, for example, in the *pesharim*) or additional content of whatever type (as, for example, in *Reworked Pentateuch*).

Authoritative status and function are two of the issues that are evoked by the phenomenon of excerpted manuscripts. A third issue is what the excerpted manuscripts contribute to the complex question of the textual history of the Hebrew Bible at Qumran. But prior to all of these issues is the problem of identification. How does one determine an excerpted manuscript is, in fact, that and not something else? A number of criteria exist but, fundamentally, identification of an excerpted manuscript depends largely on comparison with other, fuller exemplars of the source text. The only setting that affords such a situation is that of multiple-copy documents. Right from the start, then, it should be noted that the existence of excerpted manuscripts, which by definition can be positively identified only among multiple-copy documents, raises the possibility that any number of manuscripts from multiple-copy compositions could also be excerpted.

While previous discussions of excerption at Qumran have focused primarily on excerption of biblical compositions, the present essay revisits the genre of excerpted manuscripts to investigate the possibility that the Qumran Community excerpted from its non-biblical compositions as well, and, if so, what this means for the Community itself, the textual history and development of these particular non-biblical compositions, and the nature and function of the excerpted manuscripts as a genre. The study proceeds in the following manner: First, an overview and taxonomy of the excerpted biblical manuscripts is presented (§2), which is followed by a discussion of excerption-like activities in several non-biblical compositions (§3), before a closer analysis is offered of one particular test case: the Cave 4 manuscripts of the *Rule of the Community* (§4). Finally, by way of conclusion, I will explore some implications of this study for our understanding of the use and functioning — "authoritative" or otherwise — of excerpted manuscripts (§5).

2. Excerpted Biblical Manuscripts at Qumran: Overview, Taxonomy, Problems[7]

Excerption is a widespread practice in the ancient world.[8] It is thus not surprising to find it in the library of Qumran. Excerpted biblical scrolls were first

---

7. This section is indebted to Strawn, "Excerpted Manuscripts at Qumran," esp. 110-30. See there for further discussion.

8. See H. Chadwick, "Florilegium," *Reallexikon für Antike und Christentum* (ed. Theodor

treated in an article-length study in 1967.[9] But already in 1954, P. W. Skehan suspected that 4QDeut^q (4Q44) was an excerpted or abbreviated manuscript because it apparently contained only the Song of Moses (Deut 32:1-43).[10] The existence of a genre of excerpted manuscripts at Qumran was subsequently demonstrated by Sidnie A. White-Crawford and Julie A. Duncan, who identified three additional Deuteronomy manuscripts as excerpts (4QDeut^j [4Q37], 4QDeut^{k1} [4Q38], and 4QDeut^n [4Q41]).[11] On the basis of these four texts, Duncan posited that two copies of Exodus (4QExod^d [4Q15] and 4QExod^e [4Q16]) might also be excerpted. In 1995, Emanuel Tov lent his weighty opinion to the existence of excerpted texts at Qumran in a study of the aforementioned scrolls and others like them (see Table 1).[12]

The excerpted nature of several of these manuscripts might be doubted for a number of reasons (see further below). Despite that, the following five elements are characteristic of the excerpted texts. They are listed in order of decreasing significance.

1. *Excerpted Form.* Excerpted manuscripts resemble other, running biblical texts, with the exception that units from the base-text(s) are *missing, shortened,* and/or *rearranged.* Unlike non-biblical manuscripts that anthologize the biblical text along with interpretation (e.g., the *pesharim*), excerpted biblical manuscripts present small or large segments of text *without* accompanying commentary. The lack of additional, non-source text of any kind also distin-

---

Klauser et al.; 18 vols.; Stuttgart: Hiersemann, 1950-1998), 7:1131-60. Julie A. Duncan, "Excerpted Texts of Deuteronomy at Qumran," *RevQ* 18 (1997): 62, identifies the Nash Papyrus as among the earliest Hebrew examples.

9. H. Stegemann, "Weitere Stücke von 4QpPsalm 37, von 4Q Patriarchal Blessings und Hinweis auf eine unedierte Handschrift aus Höhle 4Q mit Exzerpten aus dem Deuteronomium," *RevQ* 6 (1967): 193-227, esp. 217-27 (on 4QDeut^n).

10. P. W. Skehan, "A Fragment of the 'Song of Moses' (Deut. 32) from Qumran," *BASOR* 136 (1954): 12-15. Cf. 4QPs^{g,h} and 5QPs, which probably contained only Psalm 119.

11. See S. A. White (Crawford), "4QDt^n: Biblical Manuscript or Excerpted Text?" in *Of Scribes and Scrolls: Studies on the Hebrew Bible, Intertestamental Judaism, and Christian Origins Presented to John Strugnell on the Occasion of His Sixtieth Birthday* (ed. H. W. Attridge, J. J. Collins, and T. H. Tobin, S.J.; Lanham: University Press of America, 1990), 13-20; idem, "The All Souls Deuteronomy and the Decalogue," *JBL* 109 (1991): 193-206; idem, "41. 4QDeut^n," in *Qumran Cave 4.9: Deuteronomy, Joshua, Judges, Kings* (ed. E. Ulrich et al.; DJD 14; Oxford: Clarendon, 1995), 117-28; J. A. Duncan, "Considerations of 4QDt^j in Light of the 'All Souls Deuteronomy' and Cave 4 Phylactery Texts," in *The Madrid Qumran Congress: Proceedings of the International Congress on the Dead Sea Scrolls, Madrid 18-21 March, 1991* (ed. J. Trebolle Barrera and L. Vegas Montaner; 2 vols.; STDJ 11; Leiden: E. J. Brill, 1992), 1:199-215; idem, "Excerpted Texts," 43-62; idem, "37. 4QDeut^j" and "38. 4QDeut^{k1}," in DJD 14:75-98.

12. Emanuel Tov, "Excerpted and Abbreviated Biblical Texts from Qumran," *RevQ* 16 (1995): 581-600.

guishes the excerpted biblical manuscripts from "thematic *peshers*" such as *Florilegium* (4Q174) and *Catena*[a] (4Q177).[13] However, excerpted biblical manuscripts are comparable to the *pesharim* (running or thematic) insofar as they, too, can select text from *two different compositions* (e.g., 4QDeut[j], which includes material from Exodus) or from *different sections* within *the same composition* (e.g., 4QDeut[k1,n,q]). In some of the excerpted manuscripts, there is a scribal break or marking between selections (e.g., 4QDeut[n]; *Testimonia* [4Q175]; and the phylacteries and *mezuzot*), but this is not uniform.

2. *Smaller Size.* Excerpted scrolls are usually of small dimensions and their columns, with few exceptions, contain less than 20 lines with many having less than 15 (see Table 1). In the case of both scroll and column size, the smaller dimensions are a fairly certain indicator that the manuscript had limited contents and could not have contained the whole source composition in question.[14] In contrast, column height of many of the (full) biblical scrolls is quite large, with Cave 4 Deuteronomy manuscripts, as a comparison, typically running anywhere from 22 to 40 lines.[15] The smaller size of the excerpted manuscripts would have facilitated their mobility and may also reveal something of their function and use.[16]

3. *Correspondence in Text Selection and Distribution.* It is often the case that excerpted biblical manuscripts select the same portions of biblical text. Both 4QDeut[j] and 4QDeut[n], for example, begin a column with Deut 5:1 and reserve a single column for Deut 8:5-10. Both 4QDeut[j] and 4QDeut[k1] include Deut 11:6-13. Apart from Deuteronomy 8, these biblical passages are also commonly excerpted in the phylacteries and *mezuzot*. This overlap in text selection between the biblical excerpted manuscripts and these latter, highly specialized manuscripts may suggest something about their function: perhaps they too, like the phylacteries and *mezuzot*, were used in liturgical or ritual fashion.[17]

---

13. See ibid., 581, for more on the thematic *peshers*. *Tanḥumim* (4Q176) is one of these, but is somewhat exceptional (see §3 below).

14. See Duncan, "Excerpted Texts," 49; cf. also *b. Bat.* 14a, which indicates that the circumference of a scroll cannot exceed its column height. See E. Tov, "The Dimensions of the Qumran Scrolls," *DSD* 5 (1998): 73-74; and E. Eshel, "4QDeut[n] — A Text That Has Undergone Harmonistic Editing," *HUCA* 62 (1991): 150-51.

15. See Tov, "Dimensions," 81-83; cf. Duncan, "Excerpted Texts," 49 n. 28. The Megilloth are exceptional in that they are all quite small (see Table 2 in Strawn, "Excerpted Manuscripts at Qumran," 164-65, and the discussion there).

16. Cf. E. Tov, "106-108. Introduction to 4QCant[a-c]," in *Qumran Cave 4.11: Psalms to Chronicles* (ed. E. Ulrich et al.; DJD 16; Oxford: Clarendon, 2000), 198; Stephen Pfann, "4Q298: The Maskil's Address to All Sons of Dawn," *JQR* 85 (1994): 213 and n. 14.

17. Not all of the passages preserved in the Deuteronomy excerpts are paralleled in the

4. *Textual Character and Affiliation.* The text-critical data are complex and mixed.[18] Even so, as a general categorization, most of the excerpted Deuteronomy manuscripts tend toward a slightly expanded version of the text and in this way might be classified as belonging to the SamP or Proto-SamP group.[19] However, insofar as this expanded (and harmonistic) text-type, in the case of the Deuteronomy manuscripts at least, can be explained by affinity to other text groups[20] or by other phenomena altogether,[21] the affiliation question should be kept open. It is also possible but, given the fragmentary remains, uncertain that some of the excerpted biblical manuscripts may share textual characteristics amongst themselves.[22] Whatever the case, the "free approach to Scripture"[23] that is reflected in several of these manuscripts complicates the search for precise textual affiliation — at least as that can be analyzed according to the later established families of MT, LXX, and SamP.

5. *"Qumran Scribal Practice."* Tov observes that several of the excerpted manuscripts (e.g., 4QDeut[k1]) are written according to his theory of "Qumran scribal practice," which includes full orthography and morphology, the use of scribal markings, and, at times, writing in cryptic script.[24] Even so, many of

---

phylacteries or *mezuzot.* For more on the phylacteries, esp. those that evidence textual deviation from later rabbinic *halakah,* see Emauel Tov, *"Tefillin* of Different Origin from Qumran?" in *A Light for Jacob: Studies in the Bible and the Dead Sea Scrolls in Memory of Jacob Shalom Licht* (ed. Y. Hoffman and F. H. Polak; Jerusalem: Bialik Institute, 1997), 44*-54*.

18. See Duncan, "Excerpted Texts," 52-60, for a full listing of variants from the Deuteronomy manuscripts.

19. See ibid., 51; idem, "Deuteronomy, Book of," in *EDSS* 1:199. Note esp. 4QDeut[n]'s harmonization of Exod 20:11 with Deut 5:12-13. For this, see White, "4QDt[n]," 15; idem, "The All Souls Deuteronomy," 193-206; and Tov, "Excerpted and Abbreviated," 589, who notes the same harmonization in 4QPhyl G, 8QPhyl, 4QMez A, and the Nash papyrus. See further Eshel, "4QDeut[n]," 117-54.

20. Especially the phylacteries. See Tov, "Excerpted and Abbreviated," 589; White, "4QDt[n]," 15-16; Duncan, "Excerpted Texts," 47-48. Cf. also 4QpaleoExod[m] and 4QNum[b], both of which are related somehow to SamP. See Nathan Jastram, "A Comparison of Two 'Proto-Samaritan' Texts from Qumran: 4QpaleoExod[m] and 4QNum[b]," *DSD* 5 (1998): 264-89. Eshel, "4QDeut[n]," prefers the term "harmonistic" for this text grouping.

21. Such as copying from memory and/or the influence of parallel passages. See Duncan, "Excerpted Texts," 60; idem, "Deuteronomy," 199. For copying from memory, see *b. Meg.* 18b, which permits the writing of phylacteries and *mezuzot* in this fashion.

22. See Duncan, "Considerations of 4QDt[j]," 206.

23. So Tov, "Excerpted and Abbreviated," 600, who thinks this might be evidence that the scrolls were for personal use.

24. Ibid., 587, 600. Tov's theory can be found in several of his essays, most famously perhaps in "The Orthography and Language of the Hebrew Scrolls Found at Qumran and the Origin of These Scrolls," *Textus* 13 (1986): 31-57; and "Hebrew Biblical Manuscripts from the Judaean Desert: Their Contribution to Textual Criticism," *JJS* 39 (1988): 5-37. See also Tov,

these texts are not so written (e.g., 4QExod^d, 4QDeut^{n,q}) and so this is at best a secondary criterion.

These five criteria must be adjudicated. Even large scrolls could be excerpted if they satisfy other criteria.[25] Form, that is, is a more determinative indicator than size, with the excerpted, abbreviated, and/or rearranged form of a base-text(s) being the preeminent characteristic of an excerpted manuscript.

Beyond a manuscript's attestation of these criteria or the adjudication of criteria with reference to a particular scroll, there are two further problems that must be considered when dealing with the excerpted manuscripts. The first problem relates to *the material preservation of the scrolls*. Simply put, how can one be certain a scroll is excerpted when, by definition, so many of the Dead Sea Scrolls exist only in fragments, preserving only pieces of a text that are often unconnected? One realizes quickly that a great deal depends on the material reconstruction of the scrolls. While this has reached a relatively advanced state,[26] questions remain given both the nature of reconstructive methodologies currently available and the scroll fragments themselves.[27] Indeed, one of the perduring questions is prompted by the very existence of excerpted manuscripts. Simply put, this scroll-type urges caution when dealing

---

"*Tefillin* of Different Origin," 44*-54*; idem, "Letters of the Cryptic A Script and Paleo-Hebrew Letters used as Scribal Marks in Some Qumran Scrolls," *DSD* 2 (1995): 330-39; idem, "Scribal Markings in the Texts from the Judean Desert," in *Proceedings of the Judaean Desert Scrolls Conference, Jerusalem, 30 April 1995* (ed. D. W. Parry and S. D. Ricks; Leiden: Brill, 1996), 41-77; and idem, "Groups of Biblical Texts found at Qumran," in *Time to Prepare the Way in the Wilderness: Papers on the Qumran Scrolls by Fellows of the Institute for Advanced Studies of the Hebrew University, Jerusalem, 1989-1990* (ed. D. Dimant and L. H. Schiffman; STDJ 16; Leiden: E. J. Brill, 1995), 85-102. Tov has nuanced the theory in his most recent work, especially by differentiating the categories of scribal practices and that of text type. See Tov, "The Biblical Texts from the Judaean Desert — An Overview and Analysis of the Published Texts," in *The Bible as Book: The Hebrew Bible and the Judaean Desert Discoveries* (ed. Edward D. Herbert and Emanuel Tov; London: The British Library and Oak Knoll Press, 2002), 139-66.

25. Cf. *Testimonia* and, perhaps, 4QEzek^a.

26. See, e.g., Hartmut Stegemann, "Methods for the Reconstruction of Scrolls from Scattered Fragments," in *Archaeology and History in the Dead Sea Scrolls: The New York University Conference in Memory of Yigael Yadin* (ed. Lawrence H. Schiffmann; JSPSup 8; JSOT/ASOR Monographs 2; Sheffield: Sheffield Academic Press, 1990), 189-220; Annette Steudel, "Scroll Reconstruction," in *EDSS* 2:842-44; and idem, "Assembling and Reconstructing Manuscripts," in *The Dead Sea Scrolls after Fifty Years: A Comprehensive Assessment* (ed. P. W. Flint and J. C. VanderKam; 2 vols.; Leiden: Brill, 1998), 1:516-34.

27. See, e.g., Edward D. Herbert, *Reconstructing Biblical Dead Sea Scrolls: A New Method Applied to the Reconstruction of 4QSam^a* (STDJ 22; Leiden: Brill, 1997), 6, for important observations against Stegemann's method. Stegemann himself ("Methods," 191) notes that differently-ordered manuscripts (e.g., various Psalms scrolls or even 4QH^a; see below) complicate reconstruction.

with fragmentary documents. Given the criteria above, small-sized manuscripts from multiple-copy documents are a natural place to look for or even expect excerption,[28] but, in the face of poor preservation, excerpted-status cannot be assumed. One requires recourse to fuller exemplars to be certain a text is excerpted. But one must also guard against the opposite assumption: presuming too confidently that a manuscript must have originally contained the whole composition reflected therein. Perhaps that is so; and perhaps that can be known with a degree of certainty depending on various factors (including material reconstruction). But perhaps it is not so: the manuscript may be an excerpt. This is the conundrum created, on the one hand, by the fragmentary remains at our disposal and, on the other hand, by the existence of a group and genre of excerpted manuscripts.

The second problem is even more complicated than the first: it concerns the *larger theoretical issues regarding the nature of the biblical text* at Qumran and in the late Second Temple Period and how these impact a proper approach to the manuscripts. The larger theoretical questions cannot be addressed or resolved here.[29] It should be stressed, however, that the text-critical significance of the excerpted manuscripts is located, not only in their contents, but also in the overall form, order, and shape of these scrolls. And yet, it is precisely the overall form which is odd insofar as it differs from the base-text(s). That is, it is the variant form that raises the possibility that the manuscript in question is not (simply) a copy of the base-text but an excerpted text. If the scroll is an excerpt, its overall form is not useful for textual criticism even while its constituent parts may still be. And yet, if the overall

---

28. Following the computations of Emanuel Tov, "D. The Biblical Texts from the Judaean Desert," in *The Texts from the Judaean Desert: Indices and an Introduction to the* Discoveries in the Judaean Desert *Series* (ed. E. Tov; DJD 39; Oxford: Clarendon, 2002), 167-78 and the data in Table 1, the statistics are as follows: 18 of 202 "biblical" texts or 8.91% (counting only Hebrew "biblical" texts and excluding *Testimonia*, the phylacteries, and the *mezuzot*) are excerpted. If all of the psalms scrolls thought by Tov to be possible excerptions or abbreviations are included, the computation becomes 27 of 202 or 13.37%. Perhaps a median number of 10-11% is reasonable.

29. See the discussion in Strawn, "Excerpted Manuscripts at Qumran," esp. 130-47. For the biblical text at Qumran and in Early Judaism, see the important essays by Eugene Ulrich, several of which have been collected in his *The Dead Sea Scrolls and the Origins of the Bible* (SDSSRL; Grand Rapids: Eerdmans, 1999), esp. 3-120. See, more recently, idem, "Our Sharper Focus on the Bible and Theology Thanks to the Dead Sea Scrolls," *CBQ* 66 (2004): 1-24; idem, "The Qumran Biblical Scrolls — the Scriptures of Late Second Temple Judaism," in *The Dead Sea Scrolls in Their Historical Context* (ed. T. H. Lim; Edinburgh: T&T Clark, 2000), 67-87; and idem, "The Text of the Hebrew Scriptures at the Time of Hillel and Jesus," in *Congress Volume: Basel 2001* (ed. A. Lemaire; VTSup 92; Leiden: Brill, 2002), 85-108.

form of the manuscript is suspect on the text-critical level, then one should be careful about making too much of the scroll's constituent parts. The function of the manuscript and its manner of composition may have impacted its contents and, correlatively, the text-critical significance and usefulness of its contents. As proof of the point, remember that several of the excerpted biblical manuscripts cannot be easily aligned with the established text-families of MT, LXX, or SamP (see above). It is simply not certain, that is, if several of the excerpted manuscripts were copied from an exemplar that was (and so that they are) aligned with a particular text-type, or if they were composed from memory, and/or if they were created for a specific and highly functional purpose. With these caveats entered, it is safe to conclude that the lack of units or the rearrangement of such — what can be termed "macrovariants" from the base-text(s) — ought to be attributed to excerption or shortening, not to the specific textual character or affiliation of either the scroll and/or its source-text(s). The selectivity of the manuscript, that is, indicates a purpose *beyond* mere textual transmission. In such a scenario, macrovariants — and perhaps even microvariants — are not attributable solely or primarily, and perhaps not at all, to affiliation.

As a concrete example of the complex issues surrounding the excerpted manuscripts, 4QDeut[j] can be briefly assessed: this unusual scroll preserves excerpts from Deut 5:1-11, 13-15, 21, 22-28 (cols. 1-3); 5:29-33; 6:1-3 (col. 4); 8:5-10 (col. 5); 11:6-13 (col. 8); 11:21 (?)[30] + Exod 12:43-44 (col. 9); and 12:46–13:5 (col. 10); before returning to Deut 32:7-8 (col. 12).[31] Each selection of text may, and in this case does, preserve variants from the other main witnesses. These can be assessed and aligned in varying ways. Regardless of that, no one would want to argue that 4QDeut[j] *in its present form* represents an early or variant text-form of Exodus and Deuteronomy.

But it is at exactly this point that the most difficult issues arise. One can only be sure that 4QDeut[j] is not an early text-form with important bearing on the textual-history of Exodus and Deuteronomy by (1) *recourse to other, typically more complete, copies* of Exodus and Deuteronomy — copies that are, in turn, more or less aligned with established text families — and (2) *prior knowledge of the genre* of excerpted manuscripts. In the case of 4QDeut[j], both knowledge-sets are not overly problematic. There are numerous copies of Deuteronomy and Exodus from Qumran, many of which pre-

---

30. So plausibly Duncan (DJD 14:79, 88), who refers to the same order in 4QPhyl A, and I. Tov, "Excerpted and Abbreviated," 588 n. 28, thinks the reading may be Exod 12:42.

31. Data is taken from Duncan, DJD 14:75-91. Only extant verses are listed above. Note that cols. 6-7 and 11 (according to Duncan's reconstruction) are not preserved.

date 4QDeut^j (ca. 50 CE) by a couple of centuries.[32] The extra-textual and *a priori* knowledge in this case is not, therefore, based only on later, chronologically-*posterior* manuscripts. This is an important observation given Eugene Ulrich's work on the history of the biblical text at Qumran, which has criticized Tov's work at this very point. Ulrich disagrees with Tov on several matters and on several specific texts, but a particularly instructive example for our purposes is found in these scholars' treatment of 4QCant^{a-b}. In brief, Tov argues that these texts are abbreviated manuscripts of the biblical book.[33] Ulrich, on the other hand, observes that these manuscripts are the earliest known witnesses to the text of Canticles presently available and believes that it is thus "more likely" that they are early text-forms of what became (only) later the book of Canticles as we now know it.[34]

In my judgment, Tov's argument is slightly more convincing than Ulrich's with respect to the Canticles manuscripts, but Ulrich's general insight is indispensable for the Qumran biblical manuscripts writ large. Ulrich's work has highlighted a key problematic: one simply cannot and must not assume that Qumran texts "align" with later families; the antiquity and chronological priority of the Dead Sea Scrolls means that they must be given preeminence. In many, if not most cases, the Scrolls comprise our "oldest . . . best . . . most authentic" sources.[35] Again, Ulrich's insights do not adversely affect the analysis of 4QDeut^j offered above and may not apply to the Canticles texts. But he has raised the *theoretical problem(s)* facing the excerpted manuscripts that is connected, in some ways inextricably, to the *material problem*. Ulrich has also provided suggestions of how best to proceed — namely, in a more descriptive, less typological fashion (if the typology is in any way anachronistic), and with primacy given to the earliest extant evidence.

Ulrich's theory concerns the biblical manuscripts in general, not the excerpted biblical manuscripts specifically. Be that as it may, his insights urge that alignment of an excerpted biblical manuscript, if it is attempted at all,

---

32. Exodus is preserved in 18 copies at Qumran; Deuteronomy in 31 (see Table 5 in Strawn, "Excerpted Manuscripts at Qumran," and the bibliography there). The earliest Exodus manuscripts are 4Q15 and 4Q17, which date from 250-150 BCE; the earliest Deuteronomy manuscripts are 4Q28, 4Q46, and 5Q1, dating to the same period. For the date of 4QDeut^j, see Duncan, DJD 14:77. Note that 5Q1, a very early manuscript, may be an excerpted scroll (see Table 1).

33. Emanuel Tov, "Three Manuscripts (Abbreviated Texts?) of Canticles from Qumran Cave 4," *JJS* 46 (1995): 88-111.

34. Ulrich, "Our Sharper Focus," 8.

35. See Eugene Ulrich, "The Absence of 'Sectarian Variants' in the Jewish Scriptural Scrolls Found at Qumran," in Herbert and Tov, eds., *The Bible as Book*, 180.

should be done carefully, on a case-by-case basis. Moreover, analysis of alignment will be largely dependent on, and only possible if, one has access to fuller, more extensive manuscripts from established text-families. Any and all such alignment (or its lack) could, however, be inadvertent;[36] or, said differently, alignment may not be the most important question raised by the excerpted biblical manuscripts. Indeed, the second critical piece of knowledge discussed above — namely, awareness of the existence of the genre of excerpted manuscripts — raises one of the most interesting of these questions: did Qumranites excerpt from their non-biblical texts as they did from their biblical ones? To this point in the discussion, the criteria and the considerations that flow from these have concerned excerpted *biblical* manuscripts. But is there such a thing as an excerpted *non-biblical* manuscript?

3. Excerpted *"Non-Biblical"* Manuscripts at Qumran? Homologies and Analogies

The existence of excerpted non-biblical compositions at Qumran is suggested, first, by two scrolls that, ironically enough, do not exist in multiple-copy formats: *Testimonia* and *Tanḥumim*. Further support for this suggestion is found in the work of Joseph Baumgarten on 4QD[a] (4Q266) and Eileen Schuller on 4QH (4Q427-432).

Testimonia *and* Tanḥumim

Testimonia offers irrefutable evidence that Qumran did, in fact, excerpt from its "non-biblical" compositions. This rather unique "scroll" — actually a large, single sheet of leather — preserves four selections, each separated by a scribal mark and containing a *testimonium,* or quotation. The first section is Exod 20:21 in a form similar to (proto-)SamP;[37] the second is Num 24:15-17; and the third is Deut 33:8-11. The fourth *testimonium* is most important for the present study: it preserves a quotation from the *Apocryphon of Joshua*[b] (4Q379) frg. 22 2.7-14. The unifying thread connecting these selections, as-

---

36. Cf. Sidnie White Crawford, "A Response to Elizabeth Owen's '4QDeut[n]: A Pre-Samaritan Text?'" *DSD* 5 (1998): 94: 4QDeut[n] is non-aligned *because* it is an excerpted text.

37. Cf. the notes in Frank Moore Cross, "Testimonia (4Q175 = 4QTestimonia = 4QTestim)," in *The Dead Sea Scrolls: Hebrew, Aramaic, and Greek Texts with English Translations,* Vol. 6B: *Pesharim, Other Commentaries, and Related Documents* (ed. James H. Charlesworth et al.; PTSDSSP 6B; Tübingen: Mohr Siebeck and Louisville: Westminster John Knox, 2002), 312.

suming there was one, need not detain us. It is enough to note that *Testimonia* bears a number of features identifying it as a Qumran composition;[38] the same can probably *not* be said for 4Q379;[39] and the former cites the latter *along with* and in *the same way* as the biblical texts — indeed no less than Torah texts.[40] Hence, *Testimonia,* clearly a kind of excerpted text, cannot be called an excerpted *biblical* manuscript — at least not like the other excerpted biblical manuscripts that select only from (what we now know as) canonical compositions. *Testimonia* is similar to at least one of those biblical excerpts (4QDeut^j; cf. also the phylacteries and *mezuzot*) in that it selects from more than one base-text; it differs, however, from all of the biblical excerpts in that it includes a non-biblical (and apparently non-Qumranic) composition in its selections. Of course, it bears repeating that categories like "biblical" and "canonical" are very much in flux at Qumran, if not downright anachronistic. It may very well be the case, that is, that 4Q379 was "biblical" at Qumran or was considered as such by the scribe of 4Q175.[41] Be that as it may, no other biblical excerpt cites from more than two different base-texts. So, even while it bears some similarity to the excerpted biblical manuscripts, *Testimonia* remains distinctive. But, insofar as *Testimonia* comprises only excerpts, with no commentary or additional non-citation material, it belongs with the other manuscripts listed in Table 1.

The same cannot be said for *Tanḥumim,* or at least the presence of addi-

---

38. E.g., the scribal marks, the use of four dots in place of the Tetragrammaton, and the *plene* style adduced by Tov to be indicative of Qumran (see above). Note also that the scribe of 4Q175 was also responsible for 4QSam^c, 1QS (and adjuncts), and a set of corrections in 1QIsa^a. See Cross, PTSDSSP 6B:308; Eugene Charles Ulrich, "4QSam^c: A Fragmentary Manuscript of 2 Samuel 14-15 from the Scribe of the *Serek Hay-yaḥad* (1QS)," *BASOR* 235 (1979): 1-25; and Eibert Tigchelaar, "In Search of the Scribe of 1QS," in Paul et al., eds., *Emanuel,* 439-52. Both Tigchelaar (ibid., 452) and Ulrich ("Sectarian Variants," 187) believe that the scribe may have been a high-ranking official in the Community. Tigchelaar believes that the somewhat careless scribal style in 4Q175 demonstrates that it "was written for private use" ("In Search of the Scribe," 451).

39. See Carol Newsom, "The 'Psalms of Joshua' from Qumran Cave 4," *JJS* 39 (1988): 56-73, esp. 59; idem, "378-379. 4QApocryphon of Joshua^a-b," in *Qumran Cave 4.17: Parabiblical Texts, Part 3* (ed. G. Brooke et al.; DJD 22; Oxford: Clarendon, 1996), 238, 263, for arguments against a Qumran provenience.

40. Cf. Cross, PTSDSSP 6B:310; and Newsom, "Psalms of Joshua," 59.

41. Perhaps a la Ulrich, one could go so far as to say that 4Q379 is a "version" of Joshua at Qumran, esp. via *Testimonia's* citation. If 4Q378-379 belongs to the category of "rewritten Bible" (see Newsom, "Psalms of Joshua," 58) then perhaps it could be considered alongside *Reworked Pentateuch* — a composition that Ulrich has posited may well be a true version and variant literary edition of the Torah at Qumran (see "Our Sharper Focus," 13; idem, "The Qumran Biblical Scrolls," 76; idem, "The Text of the Hebrew Scriptures," 102-3). But, in the case of 4Q379, this probably stretches Ulrich's insights too far.

tional textual and interpretive material is more likely here even if it remains debatable.[42] But, even if additional material is present, *Tanḥumim* is important insofar as the extra material is quite limited: the composition is almost entirely a pastiche of biblical quotations, virtually all of which come from the same book (Isaiah) and the same section of the book (chaps. 40ff., the so-called "Deutero-Isaiah").[43] In this regard it resembles the thematic *pesharim* but stands even closer to the excerpted biblical manuscripts than they do since non-citation material is severely limited (and uncertain). Moreover, the thematic connection among the various citations is not interpretive in the same way or to the same extent as the other commentary texts. Unlike so many of the *pesharim,* especially the continuous *pesher*s, the reasons for 4Q176's composition are not manifestly some contemporary (historical) concern of the Community.[44] Indeed, instead of "composition," "compilation" may be a better term describing *Tanḥumim's* production. The theme or *raison d'etre* of the compilation is explicitly provided in frgs. 1-2 1.4: "And from the book of Isaiah, consolations [. . .]" (וֹמן ספר ישׁעיה תנחֹומיֹם).[45] This introduction signals that the scroll exists "for the sake of consolation."[46] Immedi-

---

42. Much depends on the contents of 4Q176 frgs. 1-2 1.1-3, 4b; frgs. 4 and 5 line 5; frgs. 8-11 lines 13-17; frg. 14 lines 1-7; frg. 15 lines 5-6; frgs. 16-18, 22-23, 51 and 53 lines 1-9 (cf. also the small frgs. 24-32, 34-41, 43-50, 52, 54-57). The question is whether or not these passages contain non-citation material and if so, of what sort. Both Allegro and Lichtenberger think that frgs. 1-2 1.1-3, e.g., comprise non-citation material. See John M. Allegro, "176. Tanḥûmîm," in *Qumrân Cave 4.1: (4Q158-4Q186)* (DJD 5; Oxford: Clarendon, 1968), 60-61; Hermann Lichtenberger, "Consolations [4Q176 = 4QTanḥ]," in PTSDSSP 6B:332-33; cf. John Strugnell, "Notes en marge du Volume V des 'Discoveries in the Judaean Desert of Jordan,'" *RevQ* 7 (1969-1971): 229. But, as Lichtenberger notes, several of the phrases used here are similar to other biblical language (PTSDSSP 6B:333 nn. 1-4; see also Christopher D. Stanley, "The Importance of 4QTanhumim [4Q176]," *RevQ* 15 [1992]: 570-71, who critiques Allegro's use of the term "pesher" with regard to these passages). The fragmentary state of the scroll's preservation makes certainty in these matters difficult. Even so, it seems probable that 4Q176 includes at least some additional, non-citation material (commentary or otherwise) and so it is not an excerpted manuscript precisely. Note, finally, that Lichtenberger compares 4Q176 frgs. 16, 17, 18, 22, 23, 33, 51, and 53 lines 2-9 with 1QS 3.12–4.26 (PTSDSSP 6B:345 n. 56).

43. Namely, Isa 40:1-5a; 41:8-9; 43:1-2; 43:4-6; 49:7d; 49:13-17; 51:22-23a; 51:8 (?); 52:1-3; 54:4-10a; 52:1; 52:1c-2a. The first extant selection is from Ps 79:3; the last is apparently from Zech 13:9 (see Lichtenberger, PTSDSSP 6B:333, 345).

44. See the remarks of James H. Charlesworth, *The Pesharim and Qumran History: Chaos or Consensus?* (Grand Rapids: Eerdmans, 2002). Note also the comments of Stanley ("The Importance," 576), who distinguishes 4Q176 from both *Testimonia* and 4Q158, on the one hand, and the *pesharim* on the other.

45. Cf. 4Q176 frgs. 8-12 line 13 which mentions "words of consolation" (דברי תנחומים). Stanley thinks this may be an *inclusio* ("The Importance," 570).

46. Lichtenberger, PTSDSSP 6B:330.

ately after this rubric the quotations from Second Isaiah begin with a selection from Isa 40:1-5a followed by one from 41:8-9 with no segue of any kind between the two.

The contribution of *Tanḥumim* to the present investigation is two-fold. First, it provides additional evidence for the practice of excerpting text, and doing so mostly (or exclusively) from one source-text — though, in this case, the selections are accompanied with additional (but minimal) non-base-text content, thus marking the text with characteristics akin to the thematic *pesharim*. Second, the identification of the excerpts that follow 4Q176 frgs. 1-2 1.4 as "consolations" casts significant light on the author and nature of this manuscript. The author is less a composer than a compiler, but that is no less important from an editorial point of view. Indeed, the introductory and editorial rubric demonstrates that the excerpts are *consciously selected* according to genre and function. The *genre* description — consolations drawn from the book of Isaiah — is also a *functional* one. The conscious selection of these particular excerpts, identified as of a particular generic piece, reveals that these *consolations from* Isaiah are *for consolation*. It is obvious, therefore, that the scroll's primary purpose is not to preserve a copy of the book of Isaiah,[47] but, instead, to collect excerpts from it (and, perhaps, other compositions) for an edificatory purpose. *Tanḥumim*, in short, not only raises the question of the function(s) of excerpted texts, but also provides key data toward determining function(s) and how that impacts composition.[48]

4QD[a] and 4QHodayot

Scholars often claim that a particular scroll is a personal copy. Criteria for making this claim are not always clearly delineated and vary widely. Be that as it may, 4QD[a] is of interest since it belongs to a multiple-copy composition and has been identified as a personal copy (or possibly so) by its editor, Joseph M. Baumgarten.

4QD[a] is the earliest of the Cave 4 copies of the Damascus Document,

47. Cf. Strugnell, "Notes en marge," 230-36; Allegro, DJD 5:60-64; and Stanley, "The Importance," 573-75, for textual variants from MT.

48. Cf. Stanley, "The Importance," 576: "What we see . . . is a written record of one person's progressive reading through a limited portion of Scripture . . . in which certain passages that appeared to speak to the concerns of the reader and/or his broader community were copied down for later reference." See also idem, *Paul and the Language of Scripture: Citation Technique in the Pauline Epistles and Contemporary Literature* (SNTSMS 69; Cambridge: Cambridge University Press, 1992), 76-77.

dating to the first half or middle of the first century BCE.[49] It is a rather large scroll, with column heights of 18.4–19.2 cm and 24-25 lines per column. Baumgarten believes that it is an early draft of the composition or, "more likely, a copy written for personal rather than public use."[50] As proof of this point, he notes

> the markedly high number of scribal erasures, deletions, and cancellation dots in 4Q266 [which] is unusual among the Qumran manuscripts. It seems that along with the scrolls that were copied at Qumran by professional scribes, there were some private drafts (e.g. 4Q448, 4Q398, 4Q255) and other fragments in semi-cursive hands.[51]

Baumgarten's inclusion of 4Q398 (pap4QMMT[e]) and 4Q255 (4QS[a]) in the category of private drafts is of interest since both of these manuscripts also belong to multiple-copy compositions. Equally interesting is his correlation of "careless" scribal habits with personal or private copies and how scribal carelessness may reflect a scroll's status as a draft copy. Both possibilities — private copy or early draft — especially the latter, have bearing on 4QD[a]'s contribution to the textual history of the *Damascus Document*. In this particular case, however, while there are a number of scribal corrections and variants from CD and other 4QD manuscripts, 4QD[a] seems to join the latter in generally enhancing the reliability of CD, especially MS A. Moreover, there seems to be a "high degree of compatibility" among the 4QD fragments, when and where that can be determined.[52] So whatever the precise nature and origin of 4QD[a], it does not cast significant *alternative* light on the compositional history of the *Damascus Document* — at least not vis-à-vis the other exemplars.[53] On the other hand, the possibility that 4QD[a] is a personal copy, made for private use, of a document that was clearly of great importance at Qumran is significant: if Baumgarten is correct, this provides insight into the varied functions of manuscripts at Qumran and the possible functions of this *particular manuscript* and this *particular composition* at Qumran. In brief, if 4QD[a] is a "personal copy," it would underscore the importance of the *Damascus Document* on what might be termed the individual, not solely

---

49. See Joseph M. Baumgarten, *Qumran Cave 4.13: The Damascus Document (4Q266-273)* (DJD 18; Oxford: Clarendon, 1996), 2, 30; idem, "Damascus Document," in *EDSS* 1:166.

50. DJD 18:2.

51. Ibid.

52. See ibid., 6-7.

53. See ibid., however, on the incomplete nature and improper order in MS A — "but whether this was haphazard or perhaps due to some selectivity on the part of the presumably Karaite copyists in omitting portions of their *Vorlage* will have to be further investigated."

communal, level. Or, said differently and perhaps more accurately, it would signal the importance of this composition in real, social ways — whether individual *or* communal — not just in abstract ways concerned solely with textual transmission (i.e., the preservation of a "text"). This bears comparison with similar issues in the excerpted biblical manuscripts, particularly with regard to text functionality, despite the fact that the categories of "personal copy" and "excerpted manuscript" are not coterminous.[54]

The *Hodayot* manuscripts from Cave 4 are even more to the point. Like 4QD[a], the nature of the 4QH material does not warrant theories of major recensional activity. In the main, while the 4QH manuscripts have offered additional content, that material is largely in line with what we know from 1QH[a]; variants are minimal and typically minor.[55] This statement is not entirely accurate, however. In fact, while the *text* (microvariants) of the 4QH manuscripts corresponds more or less with what we know from 1QH[a], the *content and order* (macrovariants) of the psalms themselves seem to differ in at least four manuscripts.[56] This situation is comparable to the excerpted biblical manuscripts, especially the first criterion, which includes rearranged form. The Qumran Psalms scrolls, especially those that might be excerpted, are also important analogues (see Table 1).

54. Even though there may be overlap between the two. See above (§2) and cf. Annette Steudel, *Der Midrasch zur Eschatologie aus der Qumrangemeinde (4QMidrEschat[a.b])* (STDJ 13; Leiden: Brill, 1994), 180, for the possibility that *Testimonia* was a "privately used handbill or leaflet [*Handzettel*] for the discussion of eschatological questions."

55. See the work of Eileen Schuller: "427-432. 4QHodayot[a-e] and 4QpapHodayot[f]: Introduction," in *Qumran Cave 4.20: Poetical and Liturgical Texts, Part 2* (ed. E. Chazon et al.; DJD 29; Oxford: Clarendon, 1999), 74; idem, "The Cave 4 *Hôdāyôt* Manuscripts: A Preliminary Description," in *Qumranstudien: Vorträgen und Beiträge der Teilnehmer des Qumranseminars auf dem internationalen Treffen der Society of Biblical Literature, Münster, 25.-26. Juli 1993* (ed. H.-J. Fabry, A. Lange, and H. Lichtenberger; Göttingen: Vandenhoeck & Ruprecht, 1996), 90, 92 (this essay is virtually identical to an earlier one by the same name: "The Cave 4 Hodayot Manuscripts: A Preliminary Description," *JQR* 85 [1994]: 137-50); Émile Puech, "Hodayot," in *EDSS* 1:368. Even the genuine variants that do occur between the 4QH manuscripts are typically small and often difficult to adjudicate (DJD 29:106, 207).

56. See DJD 29:74; also E. M. Schuller, "The Classification *Hodayot* and *Hodayot*-Like (with Particular Attention to 4Q433, 4Q433A and 4Q440)," in *Sapiential, Liturgical and Poetical Texts from Qumran: Proceedings of the Third Meeting of the International Organization for Qumran Studies Oslo 1998: Published in Memory of Maurice Baillet* (ed. D. K. Falk, F. García Martínez, and E. M. Schuller; STDJ 35; Leiden: Brill, 2000), 183-84; and idem, "Some Contributions of the Cave Four Manuscripts (4Q427-432) to the Study of the *Hodayot*," *DSD* 8 (2001): 280 and n. 12. For a synoptic presentation of the manuscripts, see DJD 29:72-73. The column order of 1QH[a] utilized in the present study is that of Stegemann and Puech; line numbers are taken from Sukenik.

The order of the psalms as known from 1QH^a is supported by 4QH^b (4Q428), which is probably the oldest *Hodayot* manuscript. This scroll is carefully executed and is reconstructed at 9.5m in length with 65-68 columns. This indicates that, in addition to the "Hymns of the Teacher" collection, the scroll "must have contained the section corresponding to 1QH^a I-VIII."[57] With methodological cautions on scroll reconstruction already registered above, it nevertheless seems probable that several of the 4QH fragments do not support the content and order of 1QH^a/4QH^b:

- 4QH^c: Given the size of the manuscript (12 lines per column), it is extremely unlikely that the scroll contained all of the material found in 1QH^a/4QH^b.[58] Instead, 4QH^c probably started with the first of the Hymns of the Teacher or, perhaps, with the "Creation Psalm." Like 4QH^b, it is carefully written with almost no corrections. The scroll's small size and likely reconstruction indicates that it "contained a much smaller collection of psalms than did 1QH^a/4QH^b. . . . [it] may have contained only Hymns of the Teacher" — perhaps with an introductory psalm of some sort.[59]
- 4QH^e: While only one psalm has been preserved, this manuscript may have contained all (and only) the Hymns of the Community. Much depends on the scroll's reconstruction, which is uncertain;[60] even so, it seems that 4QH^e had a different order from that of 1QH^a/4QH^b, on the one hand, and from that of 4QH^a, on the other.[61]
- 4QpapH^f: The psalms that are extant in this scroll follow the order known in 1QH^a/4QH^b. The order and content of 4QpapH^f as a whole, however, differs from those manuscripts insofar as it would be over 100 cols. long if it contained all the material that they do.[62] Schuller thinks it is "impossible to know whether the scroll contained only the 'Hymns of the Teacher' or whether it included other material,"[63] but some sort of

---

57. DJD 29:128; for the reconstruction see ibid., 125, 127-28.

58. Otherwise it would have been "impossible to roll" (see DJD 29:179; Schuller, "A Preliminary Description [1996]," 92-93). Cf. the discussion of *b. Bat.* 14a in note 14 above.

59. DJD 29:181, cf. 75, 179; idem, "A Preliminary Description [1996]," 92-93; idem, "Classification," 184; Puech, "Hodayot," 367.

60. See DJD 29:202.

61. Ibid., 75, 86; cf. 78 n. 1.

62. See Schuller, "A Preliminary Description [1996]," 94. 4QpapH^f probably lacked 1QH^a 1-8; if it contained that material, it would have had a different order than 1QH^a because 4QpapH^f begins with a psalm found in 1QH^a 9 (Schuller, "Classification," 184; DJD 29:75).

63. DJD 29:212.

abbreviation seems unavoidable in light of the material reconstruction. She is tempted to suggest that 4QpapH[f] "served some special function, perhaps as an introduction to the Hymns of the Teacher collection."[64] The length (slightly over 5m) and material (papyrus) of the scroll should be noted.[65]

• 4QH[a]: the alternative order of this manuscript is well known. Notably, 4QH[a] contains no Hymns of the Teacher and, therefore, it is quite possible that it contained only Hymns of the Community,[66] though the material reconstruction indicates that it was not long enough to have contained all of those hymns as they are known from 1QH[a].[67] Moreover, 4QH[a] contains some material (see frg. 8 1.13-21 and 2.8-9) that does not overlap with 1QH[a]. Such passages "may correspond with parts of 1QH[a] that have not been preserved, or . . . [may] come from psalms that were not part of the 1QH[a] collection."[68]

Assessment

It is clear that, while the text of 4QH vis-à-vis 1QH may not reflect major recensional activity, the different orders presented in 1QH[a]/4QH[b] vs. 4QH[a] (cf. 4QH[e]) vs. 4QH[c] (cf. 4QpapH[f]) raise "fundamental questions about the nature and compilation of the specific collection which we have long known from 1QH[a]."[69] The possibility that 4QH[c] (and 4QpapH[f]?) contained only Hymns of the Teacher with 4QH[a] (and 4QH[e]?) containing only Hymns of the Community is particularly intriguing. What situation could account for these two facts: (1) lack of major recensional difference; and yet (2) variant order and content? One answer is provided by Ulrich's work on the biblical texts: perhaps what we have in the *Hodayot* manuscripts is evidence of variant literary editions. This is certainly possible, but the amount of (micro)variance among the *Hodayot* texts seems both less than and different from that of the Qumran biblical scrolls and their major text fami-

---

64. Schuller, "A Preliminary Description [1996]," 94.

65. The former places 4QpapH[f] in Tov's medium-sized category ("Dimensions," 79-81; see Table 3, p. 121 below). For the latter, cf. Stegemann, "Methods," 195-96, who states that papyrus was used, in general, for shorter texts.

66. See Schuller, "Classification," 184; idem, "A Preliminary Description [1996]," 97; DJD 29:86. Contrast John J. Collins and Devorah Dimant, "A Thrice-Told Hymn: A Response to Eileen Schuller," *JQR* 85 (1994): 154.

67. DJD 29:75, 86 and n. 18.

68. Schuller, "Contributions," 281; cf. DJD 29:73-74, 81.

69. Schuller, "A Preliminary Description [1996]," 90.

lies. So, a second possible answer is suggested by the excerpted biblical manuscripts. They, too, witness to a text that is similar to a source-text(s) *but that manifests major differences in order.* Could one or more of the 4QH manuscripts be excerpted?

Schuller has already raised this possibility, noting that what is preserved in 4QH[a,c,f] may be "shorter sections excerpted from a larger collection."[70] However, in her estimation, while this possibility "cannot be eliminated," it is "more likely that we are dealing with independent sources which were subsequently combined into the collection which we have in 1QH[a] (and probably 4QH[b])."[71] Schuller apparently deems it preferable to regard the versions of the *Hodayot* preserved in 4QH[a,c,f] as early sources because "there were various *Hodayot* collections as well as other poetic materials more-or-less closely linked."[72] One might compare the work of Émile Puech here: he allows for the possibility that 4QH[a] is a copy of an older manuscript in which case it could preserve an earlier text-form than 1QH[a].[73] Both options — that of early text-form (Puech) and/or early source (Schuller) — are viable, and both have venerable histories (and lineages) in biblical scholarship, especially in the subfields of textual and source criticism.

And yet Schuller's other possibility — that of excerption — should not be too quickly dismissed. In the first place, it is noteworthy that she never indicates why it is "more likely" that the variant versions of 4QH[a,c,f] (or 4QH[e], for that matter) are better understood as "sources" rather than excerpts. Is her estimation a personal hunch or is it based on the weight accorded traditional source-critical and text-critical methods? More to the point: is there any evidence or reason to think otherwise — to make a case that a source-critical understanding is not, in fact, "more likely," and that another option is equally likely?

In my judgment, the excerpted biblical manuscripts provide just such evidence. (1) Their existence is evidently what prompted Schuller to raise the possibility of excerption in 4QH in the first place, and the *alternative or rearranged order* of several of the 4QH manuscripts corresponds to the primary criterion in the taxonomy presented above. Textual variation proper (on the level of microvariants) is minimal, while macrovariants in ordering are relatively secure for several of the 4QH manuscripts. (2) 4QH[c], in particular, but

---

70. Schuller, "A Preliminary Description [1994]," 150. Schuller apparently depends on suggestions offered by Stegemann. One should recall his earlier work on excerpted manuscripts (see note 9 above).

71. Ibid.; cf. 144; also "A Preliminary Description [1996]," 98; and DJD 29:75 n. 13.

72. Schuller, "Classification," 193; cf. DJD 29:75.

73. Puech, "Hodayot," 367.

perhaps also 4QH^e and 4QpapH^f, also attest to *smaller size,* a second important criterion.[74] (3) Moreover, the *specific content* of the 4QH manuscripts
provides insight into the possible motivation(s) for excerption:

(a) In the case of the *Hodayot* as a *collection,* the compositions themselves
    can be arranged or selected generically. So it is that 4QH^c (and perhaps
    4QpapH^f) probably contained only Hymns of the Teacher with 4QH^a
    (and perhaps 4QH^e) containing only Hymns of the Community. Selec-
    tion according to genre is also found in *Tanḥumim* and, to some extent,
    in the excerpted biblical manuscripts, phylacteries, and *mezuzot.* It is
    also found in Greco-Roman examples of excerption.[75] These consider-
    ations, coupled with others,[76] begin to raise suggestions regarding the
    possible function(s) of the 4QH manuscripts, especially if one or more
    are excerpted.

(b) In the case of 4QH^a specifically, it is of considerable importance that
    Schuller notes "a strong doxological, liturgical element, with special
    emphasis on the union of humans and angels in praise" in this manu-
    script.[77] Indeed, 4QH^a has a number of unique or rare features, includ-
    ing: "extended sections in the plural, either first-person plural state-
    ments or plural summons to praise . . . and [a] series of blessings/
    doxological praises . . . [also] the inclusion of the 'List of Appointed
    Time[s]' for praise. . . . The accumulation of these features makes the
    collection of psalms in 4QH^a seem more liturgically oriented than other
    Hodayot collections."[78]

---

74. See Tables 2-3. The reconstruction of 4QH^e at 4.25 m makes it medium-sized according to Tov's categories ("Dimensions," 79-81). See note 65 for 4QpapH^f, also medium-sized.

75. See Stanley, "The Importance"; and Chadwick, "Florilegium."

76. E.g., the careful copying of 4QH^c (but cf. also 4QH^b). Note Puech's theory of struc-
turing 1QH^a into five sections, each introduced by a rubric for the *Maskil* ("Hodayot," 365-69;
idem, "Quelques aspects de la restauration du Rouleau des Hymnes [1QH]," *JJS* 39 [1988]: 38-55,
esp. 52-53; cf. DJD 29:74). See Carol A. Newsom, *The Self as Symbolic Space: Constructing Identity
and Community at Qumran* (STDJ 52; Leiden: Brill, 2004), 287-300, 349, on the use of the
Hodayot of the Leader as compositions employed by Community functionaries. Newsom suggests that the *Hodayot* might have been "a collection of models for oral performance" (see 202-
4), relying in part on Bo Reike, "Remarques sur l'histoire de la form (Formgeschichte) des texts
de Qumran," in *Les manuscripts de la mer Morte: Colloque de Strasbourg 25-27 Mai 1955* (ed.
J. Daniélou; Paris: Paris University Press, 1957), 38-44. Finally, note Puech, "Hodayot," 368, on
the authoritative nature of the 1QH manuscripts.

77. Schuller, "A Preliminary Description [1996]," 97; cf. DJD 29:75.

78. DJD 29:86-87. The Psalms excerpts are important at this juncture. Cf. Table 1.

(4) Finally, the *relative dates of the manuscripts* in question ought to be considered.[79] 4QH[b] (ca. 100-50 BCE) demonstrates that the order of psalms known there and in 1QH[a] is as early as ca. 100 BCE.[80] If 4QH[b] is a copy, then that order is even earlier. 4QH[a], with its different order, is not far behind 4QH[b] (ca. 75-1 BCE), and it too could be a copy of an earlier manuscript.[81] The other scrolls that preserve alternative orders are somewhat later (4QH[c]: 50-25 BCE; 4QH[e,f]: 30-1). Schuller concludes that, despite the relatively early establishment of the 1QH[a]/4QH[b] order, "smaller collections of psalms probably continued to be copied separately" or "independently."[82]

Schuller does not explain why this should be the case, however. Again, Ulrich's language of "multiple editions," conjoined with his broader theoretical insights, could be pertinent and, if so, would indicate that what we have in the *Hodayot* is comparable to other variant editions found at Qumran — for example, in the Book of Jeremiah.[83] But here, too, the calculus of the data on excerpts presented above could provide another, equally possible but quite different response to the question of why alternative text-forms would be preserved later. In brief, the alternative text-form may have nothing to do with text-type or text-family in a compositional or text-critical sense. Instead, a la the excerpted biblical manuscripts, the form of a particular scroll could just as easily stem from its status as an excerpted text. The specific function(s) of that scroll (and composition) could also have dictated its particular (and peculiar) form. In the case of 4QH, we cannot yet be certain which analysis is correct. But the data presented above are neither meager nor miniscule; at the very least they are analogous to what we find elsewhere in the genre of excerpted biblical manuscripts. In the light of those manuscripts it is apparent that a decision on which option — excerpted manuscript, early text-form, or source — is correct for 4QH is no simple matter, nor is it an "academic" exercise. Determining one option as "more likely" than another will only be possible after a sustained and substantial argument.

79. Dates follow, conveniently, Brian Webster, "J. Chronological Index of the Texts from the Judaean Desert," in DJD 39:351-446, esp. 371-75.

80. See DJD 29:74, 130-31; Puech, "Hodayot," 366. 1QH[a] itself is dated to 30-1 BCE.

81. Puech, "Hodayot," 366-67.

82. DJD 29:75 and n. 13.

83. See Ulrich's essays in note 29 above. Add now Ulrich's recent assessment of the biblical texts from Masada: "Two Perspectives on Two Pentateuchal Manuscripts from Masada," in Paul et al., eds., *Emanuel*, 453-64.

Summary

Apart from *Testimonia,* the documents discussed above only *suggest* a positive answer to the question of non-biblical excerpted manuscripts at Qumran, though several of the 4QH manuscripts may well go further than that. Moreover, several of the scrolls, *Testimonia* included, fail to satisfy certain key criteria for excerpted manuscripts. Both *Testimonia* and *Tanḥumim,* for example, do not exist in multiple copies, though since their source-texts do, this does not pose much of a problem. More significant is that both scrolls participate in practices that are not exclusively the purview of excerption: citation in the case of the former; for the latter, the gestalt of the thematic *pesharim.* This complicates identification. 4QD^a and 4QH^a do belong to multiple-copy compositions, but their larger sizes poses a problem vis-à-vis other excerpted manuscripts.[84] While such judgments on these four scrolls are not, in themselves, insurmountable, they do raise questions about how confident we can be that they are excerpted manuscripts properly so-called.[85] So, the basic question remains and must be addressed as directly as possible: Are there clearer, less ambiguous examples of excerpted manuscripts among the non-biblical scrolls? *Prima facie,* it is at least theoretically possible that any number of multiple-copy non-biblical manuscripts (Table 4) could be excerpted.[86] The examples presented above (especially 4QH^{a,c,e,f}), whether considered as homologous or analogous to the excerpted biblical manuscripts, are already on record. And, while others could be added to this list,[87] a partic-

84. But note that for overall length, both 4QD^a (4.23 m; DJD 18:24) and 4QH^a (3.7 m; DJD 29:79) are reconstructed so as to fit Tov's category of medium size (Tov, "Dimensions," 72). Cf. Table 3.

85. Indeed, in the case of 4QD^a, Baumgarten's claim is only that it is a personal copy. Even so, a personal copy could involve additions as well as abbreviations or selections that are not genetically related to issues of textual history or development. Note, in this regard, the comment of Maurice Baillet on 4QM^a (4Q491): "Il est peu probable qu'on ait affaire à une recension plus ancienne que celle reproduite par 1QM. On remarquera en tout cas que le texte suit parfois de près celui de la grotte I, que parfois il semble le résumer, et qu'il a des passages non attestés jusqu'ici. Peut-être s'agit-il après tout *d'extraits,* ou *d'un condense* accompagné d'amplifications, aux fins de *meditation personnelle*" (*Qumrân grotte 4.3: [4Q482-4Q520]* [DJD 7; Oxford: Clarendon, 1982], 12; my emphases). The complex textual relationship between 4QM^a and 1QM makes Baillet's comments particularly important for the present discussion.

86. Especially those of small dimensions. When the data from Table 2 is compared with Table 4, the manuscripts that are of particular importance for further research in this regard are 4Q255 (4QS^a), 4Q256 (4QS^b), 4Q258 (4QS^d), 4Q260 (4QS^f), 4Q264 (4QS^j), 4Q429 (4QH^c), 4Q287 (4QBer^b), 4Q396 (4QMMT^c), 4Q399 (4QMMT^f), and 4Q436 (4QBarki Nafshi^c). As size is not the only, nor decisive, criterion (by itself), compare also Tables 3 and 4.

87. E.g., 4QM^a (see note 85) or the texts in the previous note. Note also 4Q225-227

ularly intriguing and instructive example is found in the Cave 4 manuscripts of the *Rule of the Community.*

4. A Closer Look: The 4QS Manuscripts

The *Rule of the Community* provides an excellent test-case for several reasons. First, the composition is known in at least 12, possibly as many as 15, copies from at least three, perhaps as many as four, different caves (see Table 4). Second, if multiple-copies were not sufficient to establish the case, the *Rule of the Community* manifests itself as a particularly important composition by the fact that at least two other scrolls cite this composition (5Q13 frgs. 4, 12, 14 lines 2-3 [// 1QS 3.4-5], line 4 [// 1QS 2.19];[88] and 4Q502 frg. 16 [// 1QS 4.4-6]) and several others are related to the *Rule of the Community* in some fashion.[89] Third, the composition's content is explicitly related to the functioning of the Community and its leadership. Copies of the composition are likely to have served specific socio-religious functions. Finally, the different copies of the

---

(4Qpseudo Jubilees[a-c]), which could be related to selections from Jubilees. See J. VanderKam and J. T. Milik, "225. 4QpseudoJubilees[a-c]," in *Qumran Cave 4.8: Parabiblical Texts, Part 1* (ed. H. Attridge et al.; DJD 13; Oxford: Clarendon, 1994), 141-75, esp. 142. I thank Henry W. Morisada Rietz for bringing the pseudo-Jubilees material to my attention.

88. Note the order of the parallels. Given the preceding and following lines, Lawrence H. Schiffman rightly points out that "we are not dealing here with a manuscript of the Rule of the Community" ("Sectarian Rule [5Q13]," in *The Dead Sea Scrolls: Hebrew, Aramaic, and Greek Texts with English Translations,* Vol. 1: *Rule of the Community and Related Documents* [ed. James H. Charlesworth et al.; PTSDSSP 1; Tübingen: J. C. B. Mohr (Paul Siebeck) and Louisville: Westminster John Knox, 1994], 137 n. 12). Cf. also 5Q13 frg. 28 line 4, which may also parallel a portion of 1QS (2.19 or 5.24).

89. Note, e.g., 4Q265 (4QSD), 4Q275 (4QCommunal Ceremony), 4Q279 (4QFour Lots), and, especially, 4Q280, which B. Nitzan thinks may have been an early form/source for the *Rule of the Community* or, perhaps, a liturgical piece "like 4Q275, 5Q11, or 5Q13, which are connected with the annual covenantal ceremony in various ways still unknown" ("280. 4QCurses," DJD 29:4). Lists of parallels between 1QS and non-Serekh texts can be found in Philip S. Alexander and Geza Vermes, *Qumran Cave 4.19: Serekh Ha-Yaḥad and Two Related Texts* (DJD 26; Oxford: Clarendon, 1998), 3; and DJD 39:319. A number of these overlaps concern the penal code sections in 4QD, on which see Joseph M. Baumgarten, "The Cave 4 Versions of the Qumran Penal Code," *JJS* 43 (1992): 268-76 (on punishments); and Charlotte Hempel, "The Penal Code Reconsidered," in *Legal Texts and Legal Issues: Proceedings of the Second Meeting of the International Organization for Qumran Studies Cambridge 1995: Published in Honour of Joseph M. Baumgarten* (ed. Moshe Bernstein, Florentino García Martínez, and John Kampen; STDJ 23; Leiden: Brill, 1997), 337-48 (on offenses). Both Baumgarten and Hempel argue for the relative priority of the 4QD traditions.

Serekh date from different periods; this range may be useful in determining relationships among the documents.

Prior to the publication of the 4QS manuscripts, arguments regarding the composition of the *Rule of the Community* were largely restricted to 1QS itself and fell into two main positions encapsulated in the work of two scholars:[90] P. Guilbert, who argued for a structural (and authorial) unity to 1QS,[91] and J. Murphy-O'Connor, who offered a source-critical theory of the development of 1QS.[92] Twenty-five years after Murphy-O'Connor's essay, which carried the day, the Cave 4 fragments of the *Rule of the Community* were published.[93] These texts provide a critical vantage point from which to study the document's compositional history and textual development with studies devoted to this question beginning to appear soon after the 1994 *editio princeps*. These studies have set forth at least two major theories of recensional development in the *Rule of the Community*, each of which has bearing on the positions of Murphy-O'Connor and Guilbert.

Option 1: 4QS Preserves Early Text-Forms that Predate 1QS

Despite some earlier remarks by J. T. Milik on this score,[94] Geza Vermes was the first to articulate Option 1 in two short articles in the *Journal of Jewish Studies*.[95]

90. For a review of the literature, see Robert A. J. Gagnon, "How Did the Rule of the Community Obtain its Final Shape? A Review of Scholarly Research," in *Qumran Questions* (ed. James H. Charlesworth; Biblical Seminar 36; Sheffield: Sheffield Academic Press 1995), 67-85; and Sarianna Metso, *The Textual Development of the Qumran Community Rule* (STDJ 21; Leiden: Brill, 1997), 6-11.

91. P. Guilbert, "Le plan de la Règle de la Communauté," *RevQ* 1 (1958-1959): 323-44.

92. J. Murphy-O'Connor, "La genèse littéraire de la Règle de la Communauté," *RB* 76 (1969): 528-49. Murphy-O'Connor's work was furthered by his student, J. Pouilly, who modified his thesis at only two points, both of which were accepted by Murphy-O'Connor in his Foreword to Pouilly's book (*La Règle de la Communauté e Qumrân: Son évolution littéraire* [CahRB 17; Paris: J. Gablada, 1976], 7-8).

93. Elisha Qimron and James H. Charlesworth, "Cave IV Fragments Related to the Rule of the Community (4Q255-264 = 4QS MSS A-J)," in PTSDSSP 1:53-103.

94. See Milik's review of P. Wernberg-Møller's *The Manual of Discipline* in *RB* 67 (1960): 410-16; and idem, "Numérotation des feuilles des rouleaux dans le Scriptorium de Qumrân," *Sem* 27 (1977): 75-81. Note also Milik's remarks in P. Benoit et al., "Le travail d'édition des manuscrits de Qumrân," *RB* 63 (1956): 61 = idem, "Editing the Manuscript Fragments from Qumran," *BA* 19 (1956): 89.

95. Geza Vermes, "Preliminary Remarks on Unpublished Fragments of the Community Rule from Qumran Cave 4," *JJS* 42 (1991): 250-55; idem, "Qumran Forum Miscellanea I," *JJS* 43 (1992): 299-305, esp. 300-301.

In these studies, Vermes noted that 4QS^d is shorter than 1QS 5 and that the former also lacks many of the biblical quotations found in the latter. In light of these differences, Vermes opined that 4QS^d (and 4QS^b, to which it is related) represented the earlier recension. 1QS 1-4, which is missing from 4QS^d (see below), is therefore to be considered a later addition to the *Rule of the Community*.[96] Other aspects of 1QS, especially the "enlargements . . . and the introduction of the Zadokite priesthood as the Community's leading authority, reflect . . . subsequent editorial activity."[97] So, as a "preliminary guess," Vermes offered that it was "more likely" that 1QS was an expanded edition of the Cave 4 traditions than that the latter were an abridgment of 1QS.[98]

Only slightly after Vermes' essays, Sarianna Metso published the first in a series of important studies on the textual history of the *Rule of the Community*.[99] Her work constitutes the most extensive and careful articulation of Option 1. A brief summary of Metso's research cannot hope to do it justice. Even so, a few salient points reappear throughout her work: (1) Metso bases much of her analysis on a reconstruction of the 4QS manuscripts following Stegemann's methodology.[100] (2) In her work, Metso intends to offer a study that utilizes and, indeed, confirms the "conventional" or "traditional" methods of source-critical and redaction-critical analysis.[101] (3) Pursuant to the last-mentioned approach in particular, Metso emphasizes the noticeable lack of biblical citations (proof-texts) and terms relating to (and, in her assessment, "strengthening") the self-understanding

96. Vermes, "Qumran Forum," 301.

97. Ibid.; cf. Vermes, "Preliminary Remarks," 255.

98. Vermes, "Preliminary Remarks," 255.

99. In chronological order: Sarianna Metso, "The Primary Results of the Reconstruction of 4QS^e," *JJS* 44 (1993): 303-8; idem, *The Textual Development* (1997); idem, "The Textual Traditions of the Qumran Community Rule," in Bernstein, García Martínez, and Kampen, eds., *Legal Texts and Legal Issues,* 141-47 (1997); idem, "The Textual History of the Serek and the Textual Criticism of Legal Material in the Hebrew Bible" (unpublished paper [1997]; I thank Professor Metso for sharing this paper with me); idem, "The Use of Old Testament Quotations in the Qumran Community Rule," in *Qumran between the Old and New Testaments* (ed. Frederick H. Cryer and Thomas L. Thompson; JSOTSup 290; Sheffield: Sheffield Academic Press, 1998), 217-31; idem, "In Search of the *Sitz im Leben* of the *Community Rule*," in *The Provo International Conference on the Dead Sea Scrolls: Technological Innovations, New Texts, and Reformulated Issues* (ed. Donald W. Parry and Eugene Ulrich; STDJ 30; Leiden: Brill, 1999), 306-15; idem, "Biblical Quotations in the Community Rule," in Herbert and Tov, eds., *The Bible as Book,* 81-92 (2002); idem, "Qumran Community Structure and Terminology as Theological Statement," *RevQ* 20 (2002): 429-44.

100. Metso, "The Primary Results," 305-6; idem, *The Textual Development,* 3-4, 151, 155 and *passim.*

101. Metso, *The Textual Development,* 4-5, 154; idem, "The Textual History of the Serek," 6; cf. Michael A. Knibb, "Rule of the Community," *EDSS* 2:796.

of the Community in 4QS^{b,d}.[102] Metso understands the presence of these motifs *(Tendenzen?)* in 1QS as establishing the relative priority of 4QS^{b,d} over 1QS.[103] Similarly, Metso argues that the differences between 1QS and 4QS^e "were motivated by a need to bring the text of 1QS up to date."[104] She believes that a slackening in the Community's devotion explains both why 1QS needed updating and why the additions, especially of the proof-texts, were necessary.[105] Finally, (4) Metso largely ignores the paleographical sequencing of the *Serekh* manuscripts; or, perhaps more precisely, she does not give this methodological priority. Instead, she grants primacy to (a) manuscript reconstruction and (b) source and redaction criticism.[106]

Metso concludes that at least three versions of the *Rule of the Community* are attested: 1QS, 4QS^{b,d}, and 4QS^e. These versions witness to at least five recensions of the composition. The first, original version ("O") has not survived. It was followed by recensions A (= 4QS^e, depending on its date; see below) and B (= 4QS^{b,d}). Later, the redactor of 1QS (or its predecessor) compiled the two lines of tradition represented in A and B into recension C. A final redaction is found in the second, correcting hand present in 1QS 7-8 (recension D).[107] Metso summarizes her analysis by means of a helpful diagram (see Chart 1 on p. 91).

Metso's assessment of the textual history of the *Rule of the Community* has won the support of many. Her analysis is cogent and her argument compelling, especially if one subscribes to her methodological presuppositions as laid out above. If one does not subscribe to those starting points, however — at least not all of them, at least not with every manuscript of the *Rule* — then the discussion is still very much open. In particular, the paleographical sequencing is a large problem for Metso and others who would follow her. This applies to Metso's understanding of the (paleographically) *later* 4QS^{b,d}'s priority over the (paleographically) *earlier* 1QS, but it also applies, perhaps, to an

102. Metso, "The Textual Traditions," 142.

103. Metso, "Biblical Quotations," 87; cf. idem, "The Use of Old Testament Quotations," 226; idem, "In Search of the *Sitz im Leben*," 307.

104. Metso, *The Textual Development,* 105; idem, "In Search of the *Sitz im Leben*," 307; cf. idem, "The Textual History of the Serek," 1; idem, "Biblical Quotations," 87; idem, "The Use of Old Testament Quotations," 226.

105. Metso, "Biblical Quotations," 88; cf. idem, "In Search of the *Sitz im Leben*," 310. For another possible explanation for the differences, see Option 2 below.

106. E.g., Metso, "The Textual Traditions," 142: "Although manuscripts 4QS^b and 4QS^d are palaeographically several decades later than 1QS, there are good grounds for presuming that these manuscripts have preserved a more original text than 1QS."

107. Metso, "The Textual Traditions," 144-47; idem, *The Textual Development,* 69-149, esp. 143-49.

Chart 1
Metso's Stemma of the Textual History of the *Rule of the Community*

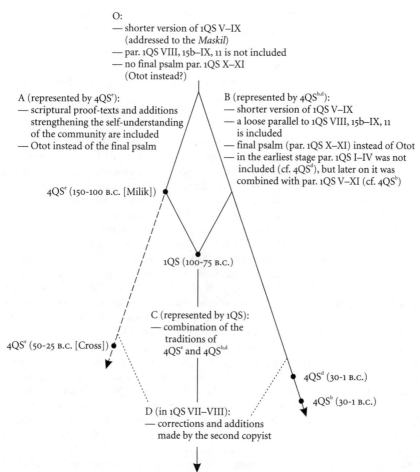

O:
— shorter version of 1QS V–IX
  (addressed to the *Maskil*)
— par. 1QS VIII, 15b–IX, 11 is not included
— no final psalm par. 1QS X–XI
  (Otot instead?)

A (represented by 4QSᵉ):
— scriptural proof-texts and additions
  strengthening the self-understanding
  of the community are included
— Otot instead of the final psalm

B (represented by 4QSᵇ·ᵈ):
— shorter version of 1QS V–IX
— a loose parallel to 1QS VIII, 15b–IX, 11
  is included
— final psalm (par. 1QS X–XI) instead of Otot
— in the earliest stage par. 1QS I–IV was not
  included (cf. 4QSᵈ), but later on it was
  combined with par. 1QS V–XI (cf. 4QSᵇ)

4QSᵉ (150-100 B.C. [Milik])

1QS (100-75 B.C.)

C (represented by 1QS):
— combination of the
  traditions of
  4QSᵉ and 4QSᵇ·ᵈ

4QSᵉ (50-25 B.C. [Cross])

4QSᵈ (30-1 B.C.)

4QSᵇ (30-1 B.C.)

D (in 1QS VII–VIII):
— corrections and additions
  made by the second copyist

Sources: Sarianna Metso, *The Textual Development of the Qumran Community Rule* (STDJ 21; Leiden: Brill, 1997), 147; idem, "The Textual Traditions of the Qumran Community Rule," in *Legal Texts and Legal Issues: Proceedings of the Second Meeting of the International Organization for Qumran Studies Cambridge 1995: Published in Honour of Joseph M. Baumgarten* (ed. Moshe Bernstein, Florentino García Martínez, and John Kampen; STDJ 23; Leiden: Brill, 1997), 145; idem, "In Search of the *Sitz im Leben* of the *Community Rule*," in *The Provo International Conference on the Dead Sea Scrolls: Technological Innovations, New Texts, and Reformulated Issues* (ed. Donald W. Parry and Eugene Ulrich; STDJ 30; Leiden: Brill, 1999), 315.

undervaluation of 4QS^a's contribution to the dating of 1QS 1-4 and Metso's continued entertainment of the earlier but erroneous dating of 4QS^e as the earliest of the 4QS manuscripts.[108] Questions about Metso's use of Stegemann's scroll reconstruction methodology might also be raised,[109] along with questions of whether or not her redaction-critical insights can carry the weight of the historical reconstruction she posits.[110] On this latter point, a major problem is temporal compression. Simply put, is there enough time between the recensions to permit Metso's understanding of the textual

108. The problem is rather complex. Early statements by Frank Moore Cross gave conflicting dates for 4QS^e, which he sometimes called a papyrus manuscript *(sic)*. See Cross, *The Ancient Library of Qumran and Modern Biblical Studies* (Garden City: Doubleday, 1958), 89 = (3d ed.; Sheffield: Sheffield Academic Press, 1995), 95; cf. the revised edition (Grand Rapids: Baker Book House, 1980 [repr.; orig: 1961]), 119. This may have been due in part to changes in scroll sigla. In any event, Cross has now clarified the matter definitively in his appendix on the paleographical sequencing of 4QS in PTSDSSP 1:57. It is now clear that the scroll of which Cross was speaking is 4QS^a not 4QS^e. Unfortunately, Milik followed Cross's earlier, erroneous dating (see esp. Milik in Benoit et al., "Le travail d'édition," 61 = "Editing the Manuscript Fragments," 89) and this has led to widespread confusion in subsequent literature. See Milik, *The Books of Enoch* (Oxford: Clarendon, 1976), 61; idem, *Ten Years of Discovery in the Wilderness of Judaea* (SBT 26; London: SCM, 1959), 123 (though the reference to 4QS^e is not in the French original [*Dix ans découvertes dans les desert de Juda* [Paris: Éditions de Cerf, 1957], 83). Happily, this confusion should now be resolved in light of Cross's appendix. For further discussion and clarification, see, *inter alia,* Michael Thomas Davis, "Methodological Considerations Concerning the Reconstruction of the Textual History of the 'Rule of the Community' from Qumran" (paper presented at the International Meeting of the Society for Textual Scholarship, April 7, 1995; City College of New York, New York); Charlesworth and Strawn, "Reflections," 416-17 n. 60; and H. W. Rietz's review of Metso, *The Textual Development,* in *Koinonia* 11 (1999): 140-43. For Metso's dating of 4QS^e, see, e.g., "The Primary Results," 303 (but n. 1 is tentative); *The Textual Development,* 48 (which leaves the date open); "The Textual History of the Serek," 2; "The Use of Old Testament Quotations," 223 n. 9; "In Search of the *Sitz im Leben,*" 307-8; and also Metso's stemma (see Chart 1 here), which lists both Cross's and Milik's dating. Unfortunately, Milik's dating is not independent but based on a miscommunication with Cross (see Rietz's review, 140-43). A later date for 4QS^e may actually fit Metso's understanding of the textual history better insofar as 4QS^e has the self-understanding and proof-texts that are missing in 4QS^{b,d} but present in 1QS. Finally, note that Émile Puech has recently attempted to date 4QS^e (again) to the same horizon as 1QS. He does this, however, on the basis of his own paleographical study of the text, not simply on the earlier comments of Milik. See Puech, "L'alphabet cryptique A en *4QS^e* (4Q259)," *RevQ* 18 (1998): 429-35; and his review of Metso, *The Textual Development* in *RevQ* 18 (1998): 448.

109. E.g., Metso's suggestion that 4QS^e, like 4QS^d, may also have started with 1QS 5 ("The Primary Results," 307; "The Textual Traditions," 144; *The Textual Development,* 67). Alexander and Vermes find this "rather speculative" (DJD 26:131).

110. See, e.g., Metso, "The Textual History of the Serek," 5. This is a problem inherent in all forms of redaction-criticism, not just Metso's. Note her more flexible comments in "Qumran Community Structure and Terminology."

"development"? How early must recension O (which Metso thinks lacked 1QS 1-4) be in light of 4QS^a — the earliest manuscript — which preserves parallels to those very columns? Questions like these are among the reasons why a second major theory of recensional development exists.[111]

Option 2: 4QS Preserves Later Text-Forms that Postdate 1QS

This formulation of the second option is not precise: only *some* of the 4QS manuscripts preserve later text-forms *because* they postdate 1QS. As with Option 1, there are several proponents of and more than one variation on Option 2. Regardless, Option 2 is largely predicated on the data that proved problematic for Vermes, Metso, et al. — namely, that, in the main, the 4QS manuscripts (especially 4QS^{b,d,e}) are paleographically *later* than 1QS (see Chart 2 on p. 94).

Philip S. Alexander argues that this paleographical sequencing is decisive: "the order in which the manuscripts were copied should hold the key to the order in which the recensions were composed."[112] In fact, he throws down the gauntlet by stating: "we will need very strong grounds for concluding that the later copy actually contains the earlier recension. The burden of proof must rest squarely — and heavily — on the shoulders of those who would make such a paradoxical claim."[113] As Alexander's essay was written prior to the publication

---

111. Another important proponent of Option 1 is Markus Bockmuehl, "Redaction and Ideology in the *Rule of the Community (1QS/4QS),*" *RevQ* 18 (1998): 541-60, whose assessment is quite similar to Metso's and Vermes'. In contrast to them, however, and to his credit, Bockmuehl admits that abridgements, private copies, excerpted notes, and so forth, are possible interpretations of the manuscript data that cannot be ruled out. Even so, Bockmuehl believes Pentateuchal (and rabbinic) texts indicate that such abbreviation is unlikely "in the case of authoritative constitutional texts like a community rule" (ibid., 545). The appeal to Pentateuchal evidence is mislaid, however, insofar as the majority of excerpted biblical manuscripts from Qumran *are precisely Torah manuscripts*. Moreover, the degree of harshness in penalties appealed to by Bockmuehl and others is not a secure indication of chronological priority. Note, e.g., Nahum M. Sarna who, in the case of ancient Near Eastern law, argues that the "direction of the evolutionary process is not from 'an eye for an eye' to pecuniary compensation, but the opposite" and that this is actually a revolutionary and progressive advance given certain factors (especially socio-economic inequities) in the historical context (*Exploring Exodus: The Heritage of Biblical Israel* [New York: Schocken, 1986], 182-85; citation from 184).

112. Philip S. Alexander, "The Redaction-History of *Serekh Ha-Yahad:* A Proposal," *RevQ* 17 (1996): 437, cf. 438; similarly Davis, "Methodological Considerations"; Rietz, review of Metso, 140-43.

113. Alexander, "The Redaction-History," 438, similarly, 453; cf. Charlesworth and Strawn, "Reflections," 408 n. 15.

Chart 2
Paleographical Dates and Groupings of
the Manuscripts of the *Rule of the Community*

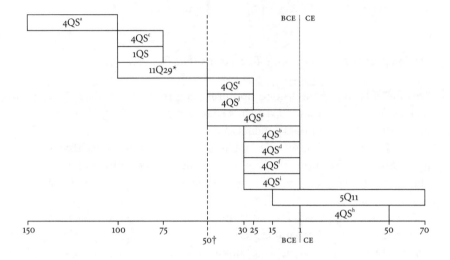

Sources: Frank Moore Cross in PTSDSSP 1:57; J. T. Milik, "13. Règle de la Communauté," in *Les 'Petites Grottes' de Qumrân* (M. Baillet, J. T. Milik, and R. de Vaux; DJD 3; Oxford: Clarendon, 1962), 180, cf. 173; Florentino García Martínez, Eibert J. C. Tigchelaar, and Adam S. van der Woude, "29. 11QFragment Related to Serekh ha-Yaḥad," in idem, *Qumran Cave 11.2: 11Q2-18, 11Q20-31* (DJD 23; Oxford: Clarendon, 1998), 433; Brian Webster, "J. Chronological Index of the Texts from the Judaean Desert," in *The Texts from the Judaean Desert: Indices and an Introduction to the Discoveries in the Judaean Desert Series* (ed. Emanuel Tov; DJD 39; Oxford: Clarendon, 2002), 372, 374, 427; James H. Charlesworth and Brent A. Strawn, "Reflections on the Text of *Serek Ha-Yaḥad* Found in Cave IV," *RevQ* 17 (1996): 418-19.

*This dating follows DJD 39:372; for a slightly earlier range (125-50 BCE) as well as the possibility that the script could be from a much later Hasmonean date, see DJD 23:433.

†For the importance of 50 BCE, see Michael Thomas Davis, "Methodological Considerations Concerning the Reconstruction of the Textual History of the 'Rule of the Community' from Qumran" (paper presented at the International Meeting of the Society for Textual Scholarship, April 7, 1995; City College of New York, New York), 14-16, who sees the manuscripts falling into two periods on either side of 50 BCE, perhaps due to the earthquake of 31 BCE and subsequent desertion and resettlement of the Community.

Chart 3
Paleographical Groupings of the Manuscripts
of the *Rule of the Community*

Early cursive:	4QS^a
Hasmonean Semiformal:	4QS^c, 1QS
Mid- to Late Hasmonean:	11Q29*
Jewish Semicursive:	4QS^e (with Semiformal features), 4QS^g
Late Hasmonean/Early Herodian:	4QS^{b,d,f,i,j}
Vulgar Semicursive:	4QS^h
Mid- to Late Herodian:	5Q11

Sources: see the sources for Chart 2 on p. 94. Cf. Philip S. Alexander, "The Redaction-History of *Serekh Ha-Yaḥad:* A Proposal," *RevQ* 17 (1996): 447, who sees two major groupings: Hasmonean (ca. 100 BCE) and Herodian (ca. 25 BCE).

    *See the note on the dating of 11Q29 in Chart 2.

---

of Metso's monograph, it is uncertain whether he believes her work offers strong enough grounds or attains the burden of proof he requires. Given the distance evident between the DJD edition and Metso's work, it seems that he is not yet fully persuaded.[114] Whatever the case, Alexander's attention to the paleographical dating and the problems that the dating raises for theories like Metso's remains one of the foundational principles of Option 2.

Like Metso, Alexander finds three versions of the *Rule of the Community* attested in 1QS, 4QS^e, and 4QS^{b,d}. Unlike Metso, however, he arranges these in chronological order on the basis of Cross's paleographical analysis; he sees no need to posit recensions before or beyond these three since they are "reasonably well spread out":

1	1QS (and perhaps 4QS^c)	ca. ± 100 BCE
2	4QS^e	ca. ± 50 BCE
3	4QS^b and 4QS^d	ca. ± 25 BCE

Among the manuscripts, Alexander discerns "two distinct clusters": a Hasmonean (ca. 100) and a Herodian (ca. 25) grouping (cf. Chart 3 above).[115] Alexander points out that

114. See DJD 26:xiii.
115. Alexander, "The Redaction-History," 447; cf. DJD 26:9.

Any attempt to advance beyond [statements about the manuscripts themselves] takes us into the field of redaction criticism. This is a highly subjective and inexact mode of analysis, which will not yield incontestable results. . . . The trouble with redaction criticism is that the signs can nearly always be reversed. Arguments are often based on questionable assumptions. It is not inevitable that texts evolve toward greater length and complexity. Abbreviation and epitomizing are well attested editorial activities. . . . Redaction criticism has its place in the historian's armoury, but it should be used with a great deal of irony, and it will be all the stronger if it is subject to external checks and controls.[116]

I will return to these points below; for now, two things should be stressed: (1) For Alexander, "external checks and controls" come down to one thing: Cross's paleographical dating of the manuscripts.[117] (2) Alexander rightly observes that texts do not always evolve toward length and complexity, and that abbreviation and epitomizing also belong to the scribal repertoire. These observations are directly pertinent to the present essay and are demonstrably evident in the excerpted manuscripts.

Paul Garnet has employed insights similar to Alexander's in his study of one of the key passages where the *Serekh* manuscripts most diverge (1QS 5.1-7).[118] In an exact and polar reversal of Metso, he concludes that the absence of Scriptural legitimation and terms relating to the Community's self-understanding in 4QS^{b,d} demonstrates that these, not 1QS, represent the later version. Indeed, independently both he and Alexander argue, *contra* Vermes and Metso, that the Zadokite absence from 4QS^{b,d} and its presence in 1QS 5.2 need not be taken that the former version is early and the latter late.[119] Garnet

116. Alexander, "The Redaction-History," 447.

117. This dating could be challenged, of course, not least from the perspective of time and inner-recensional distance, esp. given the margin of error in paleographical dating (cf. Charlesworth and Strawn, "Reflections," 416, 419-20; PTSDSSP 1:53). Alexander acknowledges problems with paleographical dating, but continues to maintain that order of copying should reflect the order of recension ("The Redaction-History," 449). He also believes that his three recensions are sufficiently spread out so that paleography and textual criticism go hand-in-hand and are mutually supportive of his theory (ibid., 450). Finally, even if the paleographical dating is uncertain, Alexander asserts that "it is arbitrary to dismiss it out of hand" (ibid., 453). One might add to these considerations the evidence from the radiocarbon dating of the Scrolls, which has generally confirmed the paleographical dating (see ibid., 450 n. 31; DJD 26:90 n. 2 and the bibliography there).

118. See Paul Garnet, "Cave 4 MS Parallels to 1QS 5.1-7: Towards a *Serek* Text History," *JSP* 15 (1997): 67-78.

119. See further Geza Vermes, "The Leadership of the Qumran Community: Sons of Zadok-Priests-Congregation," in *Geschichte-Tradition-Reflexion: Festschrift für Martin Hengel*

believes it sensible that the Zadokite connection would decline through time as the Maskil gained in influence.[120] Alexander asks trenchantly: "Why at a [later] time when the Zadokites were in control [so Vermes and Metso] should someone copy a form of the Rule which suggests that they are not?"[121] In Option 2's perspective, then, 4QS^{b,d}, commensurate with their *later* dating, reflect a *later* time period when Zadokite power had waned, perhaps because the line had died out.[122]

Option 2 interprets the same data as Option 1 but comes to opposite conclusions. So, while Metso's observations regarding the absence of Scriptural legitimation and self-understandings in some of the 4QS materials vis-à-vis 1QS stands, the *interpretation* of what those minuses mean for the textual history of the *Rule of the Community* is far from settled. Instead of a *later* waning of interest or fervor that required the insertion of proof-texts and self-designations into a recension (paradoxically known mostly in an *early* manuscript) because *earlier* recensions (paradoxically known only from *later* manuscripts) lacked them so as to "update" the composition (so Metso), it is just as possible that justifications and the like were omitted because they were already well known (so Garnet).[123] Instead of the full text (1QS) being a sign

---

zum 70. Geburtstag (ed. Hubert Cancik, Hermann Lichtenberger, and Peter Schäfer; 3 vols.; Tübingen: J. C. B. Mohr [Paul Siebeck], 1996), 1:375-84. In this article, however, Vermes pushes the Zadokite take-over quite early in the history of the sect, effectively complicating (if not merging) "earlier" and "later" stages. Again, temporal compression is a problem. For a careful argument that continues to hold for a late(r) take-over by the Zadokites in light of the differences between 4QS^{b,d} and 1QS, see A. I. Baumgarten, "The Zadokite Priests at Qumran: A Reconsideration," *DSD* 4 (1997): 137-56. Note, similarly, the more wide-ranging study by Charlotte Hempel, "Interpretive Authority in the Community Rule Tradition," *DSD* 10 (2003): 59-80.

120. Garnet, "Cave 4 MS Parallels," 72. See Newsom, *The Self as Symbolic Space*, 102-3, for 1QS as a guide for the Maskil and/or as a written extension of his teaching. "In either case the document's function has more to do with formation than information" (ibid.; cf. 107; Alexander, "The Redaction-History," 442).

121. Alexander, "The Redaction-History," 451.

122. See Garnet, "Cave 4 MS Parallels," 72 n. 13; Alexander, "The Redaction-History," 451. For still other possible explanations, see Nathan Jastram, "Hierarchy at Qumran," in Bernstein, García Martínez, and Kampen, eds., *Legal Texts and Legal Issues,* 365 who notes that "more than one designation . . . [might have been] used for the same group of priests at the top of the hierarchical structure of the community." Cf. Larry Schiffman, "Utopia and Reality: Political Leadership and Organization in the Dead Sea Scrolls Community," in Paul et al., eds., *Emanuel,* 413-27, who speaks of a general democratization of the sect over time. Note also Philip R. Davies, who does not believe that the Sons of Zadok designate any real community at all ("Redaction and Sectarianism in the Qumran Scrolls," in idem, *Sects and Scrolls: Essays on Qumran and Related Topics* [SFSHJ 134; Atlanta: Scholars Press, 1996], 155).

123. E.g., Garnet, "Cave 4 MS Parallels," 73 and *passim,* esp. 77.

of spiritual laxity (so Metso), the brief text is a sign of spiritual robustness (so Garnet)!

Questions about Serekh "Recensionalism"

Things seem at an impasse. To put it bluntly: redaction-critical arguments are often speculative and unverifiable;[124] as Alexander notes, one can easily argue the opposite case. This is manifestly true from the work of Vermes, Metso, and others, on the one hand, and Alexander and Garnet, on the other. Is there a way beyond this impasse?

Alexander has suggested a way forward: "Faced with a composite document such as [the] S[erekh], our starting-point should be *the objective facts* of the manuscript and what these tell us about *the scribe's understanding* of the limits, redactional identity and structure of the work."[125] The objective facts of the manuscript are, however, only able to take us so far; even they can be debated. Metso's material reconstruction of some of the 4QS manuscripts, for instance, can be challenged or at least queried.[126] But, even if Metso is correct in all of her reconstructions, the weighty matters of *interpreting* the differences between manuscripts and *assessing* the development and compositional history of the *Rule of the Community* remain.

Alexander's other suggestion that could move us beyond the impasse – the paleographical dating of the manuscripts — has already been discussed. Here too the data are not definitive given the margin of error involved in paleography and the relatively limited period of time between manuscripts. So, while paleography ought to be given significant credence as one of our few pieces of "hard data" (with appropriate qualifications), the matter is still not resolved. What then?

Enter the excerpted manuscripts. The existence of the excerpted biblical manuscripts along with the homologues and analogues discussed in §3, makes it possible if not probable that certain scrolls of multiple-copy compositions could also be excerpted. This is to say that the excerpted biblical manuscripts comprise another piece of "hard data"; they provide another "external control" and are among the "observable facts" (Alexander) about the manuscripts from Qumran. We know that excerption is an attested scribal

---

124. Cf. Davies, "Redaction and Sectarianism," 151.

125. Alexander, "The Redaction-History," 438 (my emphases).

126. Note that in their edition, Alexander and Vermes often do not follow Metso (see DJD 26:15-16). The problem, in part, is the fragmentary status of several of the 4QS manuscripts, which renders their reconstruction impossible.

practice at Qumran and that, at least for *Testimonia,* scribes felt free to excerpt from "non-biblical" compositions. We also know of the importance of the *Rule of the Community* among the Dead Sea Scrolls. These factors connect with Alexander's emphasis on *real scribes.* The calculus of the data is that it seems not only possible, but perhaps quite likely, that excerpted scrolls of the *Rule of the Community* could exist. To clarify, however, Alexander does not intend his insights for the observable facts of *all* Qumran manuscripts but of *specific manuscripts.* So, while the broader context makes it possible that one of the *Serekh* scrolls is excerpted, can one say more than that? Can one identify *specific manuscripts* as excerpts?

Problems immediately beset such an endeavor. One of the main issues is related to the *material problem* discussed in §2 above. Without full scrolls, it is difficult if not impossible to be certain that a text is excerpted or not. The latter qualification is crucial, because it reminds us that the situation is two-edged: if we cannot be certain that a scroll is excerpted, we also cannot be completely certain that it is not. It may well be; the possibility must be entertained, perhaps even sustained and retained throughout our work with these scrolls, given the hard data of excerpted biblical manuscripts and their non-biblical homologues and analogues at Qumran. And this is not even to mention that we have a rather full and early exemplar in 1QS.

The *theoretical problem* that plagues the excerpted biblical manuscripts (see §2) also obtains for the *Rule of the Community* though scholars rarely treat it explicitly. That problem raises the question of how we should view the various versions of the *Rule of the Community.* How should they be approached in the first place? It is obviously possible to see and approach them via the standard methods of source criticism, textual criticism, and redaction criticism. Metso, in fact, believes one of the outcomes of her work to be confirmation that such standard approaches are applicable to the non-biblical scrolls.[127] Metso's approach is viable, but the reverse is also true: the Dead Sea Scrolls have demonstrated that some of the standard approaches and theories, *especially regarding textual history and development,* are inadequate. The biblical text at Qumran seems far too fluid and pluriform to hold to the "standard" theories of direct, genetic relationship.[128] Indeed, it was largely the Qumran evidence that helped to expose such theories as inadequate for these texts in the first place. I will return to this point below. But first it is important to test the 4QS manuscripts

---

127. See at note 101 above.

128. In addition to the work of Ulrich (already cited above), see the insightful comments of George J. Brooke, "*E Pluribus Unum:* Textual Variety and Definitive Interpretation in the Qumran Scrolls," in *The Dead Sea Scrolls in Their Historical Context* (ed. T. H. Lim et al.; Edinburgh: T&T Clark, 2000), 107-19.

against the taxonomy of excerpted biblical manuscripts to see if the *possibility* of an excerpted *Serekh* manuscript might be, in fact, a *reality.*

The Serekh *Manuscripts and Criteria for Excerpted Status*

1. Excerpted Form

Several of the *Serekh* manuscripts satisfy this criterion insofar as units (sometimes lengthy) are missing or shortened. 4QS[b,d] represent a distinctly shorter text than 1QS. 4QS[d] is even shorter as it seems to begin with 1QS 5. It is possible, but uncertain, that 4QS[e] also lacked an equivalent to 1QS 1-4.[129] There is no evidence of disordering or rearrangement in 4QS; this makes identification of excerption more difficult because a fragmentary manuscript that was an abbreviation of its source text looks very much like a fragmentary manuscript that was once a full copy. One possible case of rearrangement is found in 5Q13 frgs. 4, 12, and 14 lines 2-4, which apparently move from 1QS 3.4-5 *back* to 1QS 2.19. However, given the poor state of preservation and the likelihood that 5Q13 is not (solely) a copy of the *Rule of the Community,* this scroll is of only tangential significance.

The 4QS manuscripts contain no overt commentary on the base text. In this regard, they resemble the excerpted biblical manuscripts in contrast to the *pesharim,* whether continuous or thematic. However, given the nature of the composition ("non-biblical"), one does not necessarily expect commentary and so this correlation with excerpted biblical texts may be little more than coincidence. But perhaps one should not be too hasty on this score: it is possible that commentary texts on "non-biblical" compositions existed at Qumran;[130] and the *Rule of the Community* is present in several scrolls that are not copies of the *Serekh* (see above). That said, two or three of the 4QS manuscripts may have contained *additional* material not known from 1QS, though in each case the argument depends on reconstruction and is thus somewhat uncertain.

---

129. See at note 109 above.

130. E.g., 4Q247, which is probably a commentary on 1 Enoch. See Peter W. Flint, "Noncanonical Writings in the Dead Sea Scrolls: Apocrypha, Other Previously Known Writings, Pseudepigrapha," in *The Bible at Qumran: Text, Shape, and Interpretation* (ed. P. W. Flint; SDSSRL; Grand Rapids: Eerdmans, 2001), 119; and M. Broshi, "247. 4QPesher on the Apocalypse of Weeks," in *Qumran Cave 4.26: Cryptic Texts and Miscellanea, Part 1* (by S. J. Pfann et al.; DJD 36; Oxford: Clarendon, 2000), 187-91. Of course, the "elevated" (ibid., 188) — if not "biblical" — status of Enoch at Qumran must be kept in mind, along with the anachronistic application of the terms "biblical" and "non-biblical" at Qumran. See further Flint, "Noncanonical Writings," *passim.*

- *4QS^b* frg. 8 apparently contained additional material after 1QS 11.22.[131] Milik speculated that this could have been from 1QSa and/or 1QSb,[132] but Alexander and Vermes are appropriately cautious about identifying the contents; they are not even certain that frg. 8 belongs to 4QS^b. If it does, Alexander and Vermes believe that this "recension of [the] S[erekh] contained material regarded by the redactor of 4QS^b as integral to [the] S[erekh], but not attested in any other recension."[133] However, the fact that excerpted manuscripts can select text from more than one source composition (see 4QDeut^j, *Testimonia*) renders their conclusion only one of several possibilities. The shorter version of 4QS^b (and 4QS^d, see next) vis-à-vis 1QS should also be kept in mind. It is possible that 4QS^b did not contain the two spirits treatise (1QS 3.13–4.26) or the penal code (1QS 6.24–7.25) since the scroll seems to have covered the entirety of 1QS but these two units are surprisingly absent. However, this may be due to the accidents of preservation; in Alexander and Vermes' judgment, "[t]he absence of some form of the Penal Code would certainly be very surprising."[134] The level of surprise depends, however, on the nature of the scroll.

- Given the large right-hand margin and lack of stitching, it seems safe to conclude that *4QS^d* did not contain any of 1QS 1-4, but started, instead, only with col. 5.[135] This is a very large minus, and it is hard to believe it is not intentional. Whether or not it is recensional, however, is quite another question. In fact, the lack of cols. 1-4 probably explains the variants between 4QS^d 1.1 (frgs. 1a col. 1 + 1b)//4QS^b 9.1 (frg. 4) from 1QS 5.1:

וזה הסרך לאנשי היחד :1QS –

מדרש למשכיל על אנשי התורה :4QS^d/b –

The latter version, especially in 4QS^d, may be a title of a sort. But there is no need to speculate with Hempel that this was the original title of the *Rule of the Community* itself at some point in its history.[136] It suffices to posit that this could have been the title of *this particular scroll* and/or the materials contained therein. The explicit and highly func-

---

131. DJD 26:1, 11, 63-64.
132. See Milik's review of Wernberg-Møller's *The Manual of Discipline*, 415.
133. DJD 26:63.
134. Ibid., 42; cf. 55, 57.
135. See ibid., 85.
136. See Charlotte Hempel, "Comments on the Translation of 4QS^d I, 1," *JJS* 44 (1993): 127-28.

tional rubrics present in the 4QS version are striking (cf. *Tanhumim* above and see further §5 below). Again, the distinctly shorter form of 4QS^d, like 4QS^b, should be kept in mind.

- It is now widely agreed that *4QS^e* did not contain an equivalent to the Maskil's Hymn (1QS 10.5–11.22) but had, in its place, *Otot* (4Q319).[137] However, one should not make too much of the lack of the Hymn given its attestation in 4QS^{b,d,f,j}. At the same time, one should not make too much of the presence of *Otot*. If 4QS^e was identified as an excerpted manuscript — and its famous minus (abbreviation?) of 1QS 8.15–9.11 is especially notable in this regard (see below) — it is possible that the function of the manuscript required the inclusion of selected text from another composition. Such a scenario is not unparalleled in excerpted biblical manuscripts (4QDeut^j; cf. *Testimonia*) and is widely attested in excerpted texts outside of Qumran.[138] So, even if *Otot* did follow the *Rule of the Community* in 4QS^e,[139] this need not be directly related to recensional development.[140] Indeed, the lack of a comparable scenario in any other *Serekh* manuscript

137. E.g., Knibb, "Rule of the Community," 794; Alexander, "The Redaction-History," 444-45; Metso, "The Primary Results"; Uwe Glessmer, "The Otot-Texts (4Q319) and the Problem of Intercalations in the Context of the 364-Day Calendar," in Fabry, Lange, and Lichtenberger, eds., *Qumranstudien*, 125-64; DJD 26:11, 129-31; Jonathan Ben-Dov, "319. 4QOtot," in *Qumran Cave 4.16: Calendrical Texts* (by Shemaryahu Talmon, Jonathan Ben-Dov, Uwe Glessmer; DJD 21; Oxford: Clarendon, 2001), 195-201.

138. See above, esp. Stanley, "The Importance"; and Chadwick, "Florilegium." Also J. Ross Wagner, *Heralds of the Good News: Isaiah and Paul in Concert in the Letter to the Romans* (NovTSup 101; Leiden: Brill, 2002), 20-21 and the bibliography in n. 75.

139. While it is true that the material remains of *Otot* and 4QS^e are remarkably similar (and the scribal hand identical), such that they probably belonged to the same scroll, it bears repeating that no material join is extant (Glessmer, "The Otot-Texts," 125). Also, that *Otot* began in col. 4 of 4QS^e, with only a line (if that) or *vacat* between the two texts, while possible, depends entirely on reconstruction of the manuscript's original extent (see DJD 26:130-31; DJD 21:200-201). Moreover, even if 4QS^e and *Otot* belong to the same scroll, that does not mean they belong to the same composition (cf., perhaps, 1QS and 1QSa and 1QSb; *contra* DJD 26:12). Still further, even if they belong to the same column, if the manuscript is excerpted, the two compositions are shown only to be connected in the newly produced excerpt text. If this was the case, the connection between the two compositions would have nothing to do with original recension but would represent only the connection between them that was evident in the mind of the compiler (cf. Stanley, "The Importance," 582). Indeed, the presence of a *vacat* between 4QS^e and *Otot* (if there was one) could well be taken as evidence that the scribe considered them to be distinct selections (*contra* DJD 26:152). Cf. the scribal breaks of various sorts that are often used in the excerpted biblical manuscripts, phylacteries, and *mezuzot*, as well as *Testimonia*.

140. Note Milik's original opinion that *Otot* should be considered separately from 4QS^e given the difference in subject matter and style between the two compositions (see Ben-Dov in DJD 21:196; cf. 201).

(contrast 4QS^{b,d,f,j}) could be taken as evidence that 4QS^e + *Otot* is *not* a recensional phenomenon. Quite the contrary: it could be evidence that 4QS^e is an excerpted, special-use manuscript.

- All that remains of 4QS^j belongs to the Maskil's Hymn. Given the poetic-liturgical nature of this unit and the small dimensions of the scroll (see below), it is tempting to speculate that 4QS^j may have contained *only* that composition.[141] If so, it would be a liturgical-hymnic excerpt not unlike 4QDeut^q, 4QPs^{g,h}, and 5QPs, each of which probably contained only one poetic selection (cf. also the 4QH manuscripts discussed above). There are stitch marks on the left edge of 4QS^j, which may "indicate that the fragment comes from the left side of the sheet, and that another sheet followed."[142] What followed is, of course, unknown, but the presence of additional text need not be understood as directly pertinent to *Serekh*-recensionalism *per se*. Perhaps 4QS^j was not *followed* by additional text so much as it was *prefixed* to another text(s) as a kind of introduction. Or perhaps it was *infixed* between different selected texts. Whatever the case, the prefixing of Deut 8:5-10 at the beginning of 4QDeut^n is an interesting potential analogue.

- *Other 4QS manuscripts?* The physical state of several of the 4QS manuscripts complicates analysis, but the following observations on several scrolls may be pertinent:

  — 4QpapS^a has two fragments that do not correlate with any known portion of 1QS. Fragment A bears some lexical similarity to the two spirits treatise. Alexander and Vermes speculate that "we may have here the remnants of an alternative version of this text," especially given the early dating of 4QpapS^a.[143] Fragment B cannot be identified with any part of 1QS; from this Alexander and Vermes believe that 4QpapS^a contained a different recension of the *Rule of the Community*. Enough has been said above, however, to query this kind of conclusion on the basis of such fragments, whatever their precise contents.[144] Moreover,

---

141. Cf. DJD 26:201, where Alexander and Vermes posit "a short liturgical miscellany, which included the Maskil's Hymn."

142. Ibid.

143. Ibid., 37; cf. 31.

144. Namely, that in light of excerpted analogues, the presence of additional material does not necessarily prove that 4QpapS^a is a different recension of the *Rule* properly so called (*contra* ibid., 31). There may well be a different version of the *Serekh* in 4QpapS^a, but that may have to do with this particular scroll and have little or nothing to do with text-type or recension. A similar situation may hold for 4QpapS^c, which also has an unidentified fragment, though Alexander and Vermes think it may represent a parallel to 1QS 4.10-12 (ibid., 69, 82).

given the use of סֶפֶר in *Tanḥumim,* Alexander and Vermes' conclusion that סֶפֶר in 4QpapS[a] means that it was a complete version of the *Rule of the Community* "and not a miscellany of quotations from diverse sources" is neither foregone nor demonstrable.[145] Finally, several physical characteristics of 4QpapS[a] are noteworthy: the papyrus medium, the scribal hand, and the fact that it is written on the *verso* of a *liturgical* composition (4Q433a).[146]

— 4QS[g] has three unidentified fragments, but they probably belong to 1QS 5-7.[147] More significant is that 4QS[g] may have lacked the material on the session of the Many (1QS 6.8-23).[148] Whether the lack, if it existed (the fact depends on material reconstruction), is related to textual development or manuscript selection and function is, however, unknown.

— 4QS[h] has two unidentified fragments. If frg. A belonged to frg. 1, "4QS[h] may have included material not attested in the other S[erekh]-recensions. However, it is also possible that 4QS[h] was not a full copy of [the] S[erekh], but an anthology of different texts which contained some S[erekh] material."[149]

2. Smaller Size

While not determinative on its own, small size is important in that it indicates (a) that a manuscript is unlikely to have contained all of its source-text; and (b) that it was designed for portable and, perhaps, personal use. Five of the ten (!) 4QS manuscripts are small according to Tov's categorization (see Table 2). 4QS[f,j] each contain only 10 lines per column, 4QpapS[a] contains 12 lines, and 4QS[b,d] each have 13 lines. 4QS[j] is among the tiniest of Qumran scrolls; though it contains 10 lines per column, the writing is very small, with the column height only 4.4 cm. It is extremely unlikely, then, and probably impossible, that 4QS[j] could have contained all of 1QS. Alexander and Vermes think the small dimensions of 4QS[j] and 4QS[f] facilitated easy transport: "It is hard to imagine that skin would have been in such short supply at Qumran as to make such small scrolls a necessity. Rather, both 4QS[f] and 4QS[j] are probably examples of miniature scrolls, designed to be carried around on the person."[150]

---

145. DJD 26:10.
146. For the first two aspects, see at notes 51 and 65 above.
147. Alexander, "The Redaction-History," 455; DJD 26:170, 186.
148. DJD 26:170-71, 173.
149. Ibid., 190; cf. 11.
150. Ibid., 5; cf. 154, 201.

Two more of the 4QS manuscripts are medium-sized, according to Tov's dimensions (see Table 3): 4QS^e has 19 lines, 4QpapS^c has 20-21. These are not far from the line counts of 1QS (25-27 lines) itself. Nearer the small-sized manuscripts is 5Q11 with 14 lines per column.

3. Correspondence in Text Selection and Distribution

Unfortunately, despite the careful text-critical work on the different versions of the *Serekh* manuscripts, it is sometimes the case that too little of the manuscripts has been preserved to permit us to say much about the text.[151] To be sure, there is a good degree of overlap among several manuscripts and the overlaps manifest varying degrees of agreement or disagreement with each other and with or against 1QS. But here too, fragmentary preservation often prevents one from being sure about the stemmatic relationship between certain 4QS manuscripts and 1QS.[152] A very important textual correspondence is found, of course, in the relationship between 4QS^b and 4QS^d. These two manuscripts (and traditions, if they are that) are not to be simplistically identified, however, insofar as 4QS^b apparently covered all of 1QS, whereas 4QS^d seems to have begun only with 1QS 5. The two are thus "different, though cognate" recensions.[153] The correlation of these two pieces of data — (a) the agreement of 4QS^{b,d} against 1QS; and (b) the large minus of 4QS^d from 1QS and 4QS^b — raises the intriguing possibility that 4QS^d could be an excerpt made from 4QS^b.[154] Such a scenario is only possible, of course, if 4QS^d is truly an excerpted manuscript. If *both* 4QS^b and 4QS^d were excerpted, the (at least partial) correspondence in text selection and distribution would parallel a similar phenomenon in some of the excerpted biblical manuscripts (see above) and would attest to a popular, probably utilitarian, "version" of the *Rule of the Community*.[155]

---

151. E.g., in 4QS^{a,c,h,j}. See DJD 26:30, 69, 190.

152. Cf. ibid., 158 on 4QS^f.

153. Ibid., 46; cf. 11.

154. Cf. Alexander, "The Redaction-History," 447: "Stemmatically it would be natural to see 4QS^d as derived from 4QS^b, or from a form of text very close to it, or vice versa." See further ibid., 452 and DJD 26:90 for the possibility that 4QS^d may have had a minus about the two messiahs akin to 4QS^e, though it is probable that 4QS^d contained at least some of 1QS 8.15–9.11. See note 109 above for the possibility that 4QS^e, like 4QS^d, began with 1QS 5.

155. 4QS^i, too, may have had a shorter text similar to 4QS^d (DJD 26:198). Perhaps one might compare the edition — variant literary or popular liturgical? — of 11QPs^a, which is also represented in 4QPs^e and 11QPs^b. See Strawn, "Excerpted Manuscripts at Qumran," 153-57.

4. Textual Character and Affiliation

The material realities of the manuscripts that complicate analysis of the third criterion also pertain to the fourth. Despite many overlaps and various textual correlations, the extant remains simply are not sufficient to answer all of our questions. The agreement of 4QS[b,d] and their shorter nature vis-à-vis 1QS has already been discussed, as has the two major options for understanding of the textual development of the *Serekh*.[156]

5. Scribal Practice

According to Tov's theory of Qumran scribal practice, the 4QS evidence is varied. 4QS[d] and 4QS[j] are defective and the same may be true for 4QS[g] and 4QS[i].[157] As for scribal practices writ large, one might note that several of the manuscripts are neatly and cleanly done (e.g., 4QS[d,j]), while others are less so (e.g., 4QpapS[a]). The possible use of cryptic script in 4QS[e] is especially noteworthy.[158] Bockmuehl wonders if the "more casual execution" of 4QS[e] and 4QS[h] might be explained by their being "copies or excerpted notes for private study"[159] — a suggestion that is particularly germane to the present essay.

Summary

While the data are suggestive, the case is not yet proven. Indeed, in light of the material and theoretical problems that beset analysis of the excerpted biblical manuscripts, and which also obtain for 4QS, it may well be impossible to prove (or disprove) the case definitively. The question must remain open, that

---

156. See above. Note, additionally, that Alexander and Vermes posit four distinct recensions (DJD 26:12):

Recension	Manuscript(s)
A	1QS
B	
B[1]	4QS[b]
B[2]	4QS[d]
C	4QS[e]
D	4QS[g]

157. See ibid., 20-21.
158. So Puech, "L'alphabet cryptique A," 429-35; DJD 39:337; contrast DJD 26:9.
159. Bockmuehl, "Redaction and Ideology," 543.

is, but it is important that it at least be considered. Indeed, the data presented above insist that the option of a 4QS excerpt must be entertained.

As a way of concluding this section, it is instructive to consider the difference it would make if the two large minuses in 4QS^d and 4QS^e were explained as the result of excerption rather than textual evolution. In the case of the famous lack of 1QS 8.15–9.11 in 4QS^e, it remains possible — as James H. Charlesworth carefully argues — that 4QS^e preserves an older, non-Messianic tradition stemming from the earliest days of Qumran when its theology was not messianic; 1QS then represents a later Messianic redaction.[160] But, as Charlesworth rightly insists, other interpretations are possible, including ones that would see in 4QS^e a copy for private use or an abbreviation for some institutional use. Charlesworth makes a strong case for his own interpretation, but the question we encountered before continues to loom large: why would an *early* form (and theology) be preserved and copied in a *later* manuscript?[161] If 4QS^e was excerpted, there is no need to answer such a question; it is obviated. The minus is not related — at least not directly — to issues of *text-type, recension, or family*. It is, instead, due to textual *selection, abridgment, abbreviation* — that is, *excerption*. But even if this latter scenario is true, there is an equally large question facing it: why would this particular section be left out of 4QS^e?

The second example, from 4QS^d, may suggest an answer. As already noted, much has been made of the lack of 1QS 1-4 in this manuscript. The minus has been interpreted as meaning that 1QS 1-4 is a secondary unit, added only later to the *Rule of the Community* in its textual development. 4QS^d would thus preserve the earlier text-form. This interpretation is faced by several problems, some of which were discussed above. Note that, in addition to 4QpapS^a — the earliest 4QS manuscript, which contains parallels to 1QS 1 and 3 — 4QS^b, 4QpapS^c, and 4QS^h also contain textual overlaps with 1QS 1-4. Further, the relationship between 4QS^b and 4QS^d is significant insofar as the two manuscripts are clearly related, but it is *only* 4QS^d that lacks 1QS 1-4.

In fact, as intimated previously, the important variant in 4QS^d (and 4QS^b) from 1QS 5.1 may be the interpretive key for the minus. Perhaps 4QS^d

---

160. See James H. Charlesworth, "Challenging the *Consensus Communis* Regarding Qumran Messianism (1QS, 4QS MSS)," in *Qumran-Messianism: Studies on the Messianic Expectations in the Dead Sea Scrolls* (ed. James H. Charlesworth, Hermann Lichtenberger, and Gerbern S. Oegema; Tübingen: Mohr Siebeck, 1998), 120-34. Cf. PTSDSSP 1:54.

161. Here the date of 4QS^e reemerges as an important factor. See note 108 above. Metso (e.g., "The Textual History of the Serek," 2) has appealed to the Jeremiah data (4QJer^{a,b}) as a way to answer this question. But the situations are not exactly the same: differences in genre and, especially, temporal range are operative between Jeremiah and the *Rule of the Community*. On the problem of temporal compression for Metso's reconstruction, see above.

was never intended to be a copy of the *Rule of the Community* in the transmissional sense: that is, it was not intended to be "only" or "merely" a "copy" of "the text" of the "composition." Instead, perhaps 4QS^d ought to be taken at its word — that is, it was an *instruction* (מדרש) for the *Master* (למשכיל) *concerning* (על) the men of the Torah. Hempel points out that על might be better translated "over" the men of the Torah.[162] Her translation may emphasize the Master more, especially his *position* or *status;* but this only makes explicit what is already implicit in the term משכיל. Moreover, "concerning" emphasizes the Maskil's *task* insofar as the term designates the important Community functionary whose responsibilities included instruction of novices.[163] But, *contra* Hempel et al., the 4QS^d variant does not necessarily suggest that this scroll (or its tradition) is older than the version in 1QS. Instead, למשכיל — a *functional* rubric for a Community/cultic *functionary* — makes "it the responsibility of this official to see to it that members follow the rule."[164] This functional explanation of the scroll could easily account for the large omission of 1QS 1-4: it simply was not needed in this particular scroll given the scroll's function and usefulness. It may still be the case that 1QS 1-4 belongs to a later stage in the literary growth of the *Rule of the Community,* but the scroll-form of 4QS^d would not directly bear on that. Instead, if excerpted, 4QS^d would be a manuscript for *a specific use,* perhaps a highly specialized function of the Maskil, in his teaching and/or liturgical duties with other members of the Community. To put it differently, in terms similar to those used for the excerpted biblical manuscripts: if excerpted, the *constituent parts* of 4QS^d may or may not be significant for understanding the textual development of the *Rule of the Community.* And, if excerpted, 4QS^d's *overall shape* is likely to be mostly insignificant and perhaps even totally irrelevant.

162. Hempel, "Comments," 128.

163. See 4Q298; cf. 4Q510-511. For secondary literature, see James H. Charlesworth, "Community Organization in the Rule of the Community," in *EDSS* 1:135; Carol A. Newsom, "The Sage in the Literature of Qumran: The Functions of the Maśkîl," in *The Sage in Israel and the Ancient Near East* (ed. John G. Gammie and Leo G. Perdue; Winona Lake: Eisenbrauns, 1990), 373-82; Jastram, "Hierarchy at Qumran," 349-76, esp. 358-60; and Hans Kosmala, "Maśkîl," *JANES(CU)* 5 (1973): 235-41. Note also Pfann, "4Q298," 224-25 on the function of 4Q298: "Since it is the responsibility of the *Maskîl* to teach all members of the community [cf. 1QS 1.1; 3.13], and the novices have not yet been fully inducted into the community [cf. 1QS 6.13b-23], he must leave the community premises in order to teach them. The size of the scroll permitted it to be safely carried (or hidden) while traveling. The use of the esoteric script (aside from the title) protected the scroll's contents from being read by anyone except the *Maskîl*." The small size of several of the 4QS manuscripts and the possible use of cryptic script in 4QS^e immediately come to mind.

164. Garnet, "Cave 4 MS Parallels," 71.

These two possible interpretations of minuses in 4QS[d,e] are evocative. More evidence is needed to decide the case, and it may be that such evidence will never be forthcoming, that it is irretrievably lost in the missing sections of the manuscript. Be that as it may, Metso is certainly correct that the *entirety* of the manuscripts (as we have them) must be considered in a discussion like the present one. The overall pattern of variants, not just one or two, even if they are large minuses, must be assessed. At this point Metso's work, especially, along with that of Alexander and Vermes in DJD, must be accorded all due respect, even though these three scholars do not agree in every detail. Even so, the fact remains: the existence of excerpted biblical manuscripts is another piece of "hard data" that, along with the paleographical sequencing of the 4QS manuscripts (so Alexander), may serve to complicate "traditional" or overly simplistic and linear recensional theories. Again, Qumran has taught us nothing if not that the textual evidence is typically far more fluid and pluriform than was thought heretofore. All of this should not be taken as an argument that the *Rule of the Community* did not go through a complex process of growth or that none of the 4QS manuscripts contribute to understanding that process. Clearly it did and clearly they do. But this can be true even if one or more of the 4QS manuscripts is excerpted.

One final point: if even one of the *Serekh* manuscripts was excerpted, perhaps for the use of the Maskil (cf. 4QS[d]), it would cast significant light on the purposes of excerpted manuscripts (biblical or otherwise) and also help address questions associated with the possible function(s) of the *Rule of the Community.* These issues are taken up by way of conclusion.

5. Conclusions and Implications

The Question of the Sitz im Leben *of the* Rule of the Community

To take the last mentioned point first, scholars have often wondered about the *Sitz im Leben* of the *Rule of the Community,* especially in the face of multiple and divergent copies. Davies, for example, believes that only one tradition could function as a rule for the Community at any one point in time. The fact that there are *numerous* diverging rules thus creates problems in reconstructing the structure, practice, and belief of the Community.[165] Metso argues similarly, pointing out that the route from the *Serekh*'s textual tradition to the *Sitz* of the composition within the Community may be far more complicated

---

165. Davies, "Redaction and Sectarianism," 156-58.

and far less direct than often thought.[166] While this is undoubtedly true, a few observations can be offered in response. First, it is far from impossible that more than one version of a text was operative at any one time. Multiple literary editions of various compositions existed side-by-side at Qumran, as Ulrich and others have demonstrated. Admittedly, some of these editions did not concern the day-to-day functioning of the Community — that is, they are not halakic texts — but others certainly did relate to the praxis and belief of the Community insofar as they concerned compositions near and dear to the Community's theology and practices (e.g., Torah texts). Second, one should recall the presence of conflicting "rule texts" found in the Old Testament/Hebrew Bible itself, particularly in the Pentateuch. Such contradictory material can be accounted for diachronically, by means of source-critical and/or redaction-critical analyses, but the fact is that these texts now reside together, synchronically, in the final form of their respective compositions (and manuscripts). There are ways of engaging the resulting tensions without — or, perhaps better: *beyond* — standard diachronic analyses.[167] There is no *a priori* reason why the same cannot be true for conflicting rule texts at Qumran.[168] Third, the nature of the legal composition must be assessed. Perhaps the *Rule of the Community*, like other legal corpora in the Hebrew Bible and the ancient Near East, is less a law code than a legal collection. Davies' and Metso's conclusions are already driving toward this latter possibility,[169] with Davies going so far as to say that 1QS is "a rather muddled archive, a receptacle of bits and pieces from different times and authors."[170] But even so, the conclusion

---

166. Metso, *The Textual Development*, 148-49; idem, "The Textual History of the Serek," 2, 5; idem, "The Use of Old Testament Quotations," 228-29; idem, "In Search of the *Sitz im Leben*," *passim;* cf. Davies, "Redaction and Sectarianism," 160; also Bockmuehl, "Redaction and Ideology," 544.

167. See, e.g., Paul D. Hanson, "The Theological Significance of Contradiction within the Book of the Covenant," in *Canon and Authority: Essays in Old Testament Religion and Theology* (ed. George W. Coats and Burke O. Long; Philadelphia: Fortress, 1977), 110-32; James W. Watts, *Reading Law: The Rhetorical Shaping of the Pentateuch* (Biblical Seminar 59; Sheffield: Sheffield Academic Press, 1999), esp. 61-88, 102-7; or more literary-critcial approaches to doublets in the Pentateuch (cf. the next note).

168. Devorah Dimant, "Qumran Sectarian Literature," in *Jewish Writings of the Second Temple Period: Apocrypha, Pseudepigrapha, Qumran Sectarian Writings, Philo, Josephus* (ed. Michael E. Stone; CRINT 2.2; Assen: Van Gorcum, 1984), 501-2, offered a kind of literary explanation for the "doublets" in the *Rule of the Community*. Though Metso (e.g., "The Textual Traditions," 147) has critiqued Dimant, her observations may still have merit.

169. Metso, "In Search of the *Sitz im Leben*," 314; Davies, *Scribes and Schools*, 155. Similar comments are found in Alexander, "The Redaction-History," 439; and Garnet, "Cave 4 MS Parallels," 69.

170. Davies, "Redaction and Sectarianism," 157.

does not follow that "[n]o community could actually function by using this text as a basis for its identity, belief or conduct,"[171] since, in fact, many communities (including Qumran!) have used and continue to use a similarly "muddled archival receptacle" — the Hebrew Bible — as a basis for their identities, beliefs, and conduct. Finally, Davies believes that the continued copying of alternative versions of rule scrolls suggests "that they almost certainly did not function as regulative texts within a community."[172] But the fourth observation — positing excerption for one or more differing rule texts — would prove the exact opposite conclusion. If even one of the divergent *Serekh* scrolls is excerpted, that is, the functional reason for such excerption means that the scroll diverges from its source-text(s) *precisely and exactly because* it was put to some specific (regulative) use and function. Davies is certainly right when he states that the *Serekh* material "is best regarded as a product of individuals or groups, for their own individual or group purposes."[173] He is right to highlight the *purposes* to which manuscripts were put at Qumran (and elsewhere); he has failed to see, however, that the existence of different individuals, groups, and functions can help us understand the problem of textual diversity *synchronically* as well as diachronically.

The Function(s) of Excerpted Manuscripts (Again)

This bring us, once again, to manuscript function(s) — a topic that has been mentioned throughout this essay. The excerpted biblical manuscripts reveal something of their functionality (if not their precise functions) by their very existence. If they were not used for some purpose it is hard to explain their production and unique presentation. Four main options have been offered to explain the purpose(s) of excerpts at Qumran: devotional/personal, liturgical, pedagogical/didactic, or exegetical-ideological.[174] These options are not mutually exclusive; allowance should be made for functional overlap and for the possibility that a particular scroll could have served more than one function at more than one time.[175] Within this range, which purpose would a non-biblical excerpt mostly likely have served?

171. Ibid.

172. Ibid., 158.

173. Ibid.

174. See Tov, "Excerpted and Abbreviated"; Duncan, "Excerpted Texts"; and Strawn, "Excerpted Manuscripts at Qumran."

175. Not unlike biblical compositions today, which at one moment are used for public worship and, at another, for private devotion.

No doubt the answer varies from scroll to scroll.[176] Even so, certain correlations seem probable. Given the genre, an excerpted *Hodayot* text would be best understood as serving a liturgical or devotional purpose. A *Serekh* excerpt would probably fall somewhere in the pedagogical/didactic range, again due to the nature of the composition.[177] This latter correlation is significant since "most classical excerpted texts . . . were made for educational purposes, illustrating a certain topic or idea."[178] On the basis of classical examples, Stanley states that "selections from classical authors were employed for reading and writing exercises in the schools of the Hellenistic period, while anthologies of classical citations arranged according to topic were common fare in the second century rhetorical schools of the Second Sophistic."[179] He traces similar practices in the Latin-speaking world.[180]

This instructional focus of the Greco-Roman excerpts is enlightening. Stanley's own work on *Tanḥumim* shows that this widely-attested practice was also known in Early Judaism, even at Qumran. 4Q176 may even be the record of a note-taking session.[181] Whatever the case, Stanley's data demonstrate "the importance, indeed the sheer ordinariness of note-taking among the more literate members of Greco-Roman society."[182] 4Q176, in turn, demonstrates "that ancient readers were capable of preparing similar anthologies while working their way through a single roll of Scripture" and "should sensitize us to the possibility that other Jewish and Christian authors might have compiled similar collections of verses that somehow struck a chord in the course of their own personal study of Scripture."[183]

If any of the non-biblical manuscripts are excerpted, Stanley's comments lead to two conclusions: (1) the existence of the scroll may be due to

---

176. Cf. Newsom, *The Self as Symbolic Space*, 105, on how each version of the *Rule* would have its own, "somewhat different rhetorical force."

177. But even here, especially given the Maskil's liturgical functions (cf. 1QSa, 1QSb, the *Songs of the Sabbath Sacrifice*, etc.), liturgical functions should not be ruled out. See note 185 below.

178. Tov, "Excerpted and Abbreviated," 598.

179. Stanley, "The Importance," 578; further 578-79 for examples from Xenophon's *Memorabilia* 1.6.14, Aristotle's *Topics* 1.14, Athenaeus' *Deipnosophists* 8.336d, and Plutarch's *Moralia* 464F. See also Chadwick, "Florilegium."

180. Stanley, "The Importance," 579. Note, for example, Cicero (*De Inventione* 2.4), who claims to have excerpted *(excerpsimus)* from previous works in his own textbook on rhetoric; and Pliny the Younger (*Epistles* 3.5), who claims that his uncle, the elder Pliny, took more than 160 volumes of excerpts and notes *(adnotabat excerpebatque)* during the course of his reading.

181. Stanley, "The Importance," 579-80.

182. Ibid., 580.

183. Ibid., 581.

the *didactic function* of the manuscript post-production and/or be the result of *personal study;* and (2) the excerption is an indication, both explicit and implicit, that the source-text is authoritative in some fashion, on communal and, perhaps, personal levels (cf. on 4QD[a] and 4QM1 above). Here again the importance of the Maskil at Qumran and in the *Rule of the Community* must be recalled. If, as Newsom and Alexander and others have argued, the purpose of the *Serekh* as a whole is the formation of the Maskil and that it is "an aide-memoire for someone well versed in the Community's ways,"[184] then it is not only possible but perfectly understandable why a personal copy of this composition might have been made, even one that selectively excerpts from another scroll or that diverges from another manuscript(s) in certain details. The reasons would be preeminently one: the Maskil had need of such a copy, whether it was for his own formation or for his leadership in the Community.[185] Additional pieces of information support such a scenario: the public, didactic, and liturgical functions of the Maskil;[186] the Maskil-rubrics in the *Hodayot* and *Songs of the Sabbath Sacrifice;* and so forth. Even the (possible) use of cryptic A script in 4QS[e], a practice attested especially in calendrical and Maskil-documents,[187] might be related, especially given Stephen Pfann's recent decipherment of nine copies of the *Rule of the Congregation* written in cryptic A (4Q249a-i).[188] The possibility that excerpted copies were made for or by an important person like the Maskil also counters the otherwise cogent argument of Alexander that it is unlikely that ordinary members would have been able to alter an "official" composition like the *Serekh.*[189]

Tov, who first suggested the exegetical-ideological function for excerpted manuscripts, did so on the basis of *Testimonia.* Following his lead, we might ask whether it is possible to shed further light on the purpose(s) of biblical excerpted manuscripts by means of insights gained from the non-

184. Alexander, "The Redaction-History," 439; and see Newsom, *The Self as Symbolic Space,* 102-3.

185. Or even, perhaps, in associated cells. See Newsom, "The Sage," 373, on the Maskil as functionary in "local village communities." Cf. Bockmuehl, "Redaction and Ideology," 545, on "Essenes in outlying or urban communities" maintaining dated versions of the *Serekh.* See also note 163 above on 4Q298.

186. See the important remarks of Newsom, "The Sage," 374-75, 381.

187. Glessmer, "The Otot-Texts," 133; cf. Pfann, "4Q298," 233-34; and Tov, "Letters of the Cryptic A Script," esp. 330-33.

188. Stephen J. Pfann, "249a-i. 4Qpap cryptA 4QSerekh ha-'Edah[a-i]," in DJD 36:534-74. Note that, unlike the 4QS material, all of the 4QSE manuscripts *predate* 1QSa. It is quite likely, then, that the textual differences are related to recensional development.

189. Alexander, "The Redaction-History," 448; cf. Bockmuehl, "Redaction and Ideology," 543.

biblical excerpted manuscripts. In particular, the probable role of the Maskil in excerpts of *Serekh* or *Hodayot* manuscripts (if these existed) might suggest that excerpted biblical manuscripts were also made for and/or used by important Community functionaries. Given the nature of the *Rule* and the *Hodayot,* these functionaries would have probably used excerpts of these texts in liturgical and didactic contexts, whether personal or communal or both. Perhaps the same is true for biblical excerpts, especially those belonging to similar genres.[190] On the one hand, these suggestions regarding function are no more specific than the four options previously mentioned. On the other hand, the suggestions do offer greater specificity insofar as they correlate excerpted scrolls with *specific personages* (the Maskil) and with *particular contexts* — worship and/or instruction especially, perhaps, with new initiates. So, while no drastically new *Sitz* has been determined, greater specificity and context has been added to the four functional options previously posited.

One must beware circularity in the argument — using the excerpted biblical manuscripts to suggest the existence of excerpted non-biblical manuscripts; then, using the importance of the Maskil (or other Community functionary) in the latter to suggest the importance of the Maskil in the former. This is certainly possible, but not yet certain. One thing that does seem certain, however, is that if excerpted non-biblical manuscripts did exist at Qumran, then we have yet another indication that the Community *did* consider some of their "non-biblical" compositions authoritative — indeed, as authoritative as some of their "biblical" compositions. This conclusion would be signaled not just by manuscript *content* but by manuscript *production* and manuscript *function.* That is, both biblical and non-biblical would have served as source-texts for subsequent excerpts. The formal practice of excerption, in turn, would underscore the authoritative nature of the source-texts. Moreover, the functional purpose of the scroll *qua* excerpt would mean that it, too, by its existence, use, and usefulness, belongs to the category of authoritative literature.[191]

In conclusion, the question posed in the title of this paper is not yet definitively answered. The status of any non-biblical manuscript as an excerpted scroll still remains uncertain; but the possibility that a non-biblical manuscript could be an excerpt is just one of many important questions raised by

190. Cf. the Psalm excerpts, esp. those concerning Psalm 119 (Table 1). Charlesworth and Strawn, "Reflections," 408 n. 15, admit that reasons for excerption may never be known.

191. See further Strawn, "Excerpted Manuscripts at Qumran," 148-57. Note also the important remarks of George J. Brooke, "The Rewritten Law, Prophets and Psalms: Issues for Understanding the Text of the Bible," in Herbert and Tov, eds., *The Bible as Book,* 31-40, esp. 35-38.

the excerpted biblical manuscripts. These questions include ones concerning multiple-copy compositions at Qumran, whether "biblical" or not. It may just be the case that one or more of these "copies" is an epitome or an excerpt, not a "copy" in the traditional text-critical understanding of the term. What purpose(s) such manuscripts may have served is another enduring question raised by the excerpted biblical manuscripts. Only time will tell if these questions will be answered to our satisfaction. At present, only one thing is certain: while the jury may still be out, the jurists have more evidence on which to base their verdict.

Tables

The following pages contain the tables referred to earlier in this essay. A pertinent bibliography for each table appears at the foot of its title page. The studies cited in these bibliographies have been rounded out, especially, by the lists in E. Tov, ed., *The Texts from the Judaean Desert: Indices and An Introduction to the* Discoveries in the Judaean Desert *Series* (DJD 39; Oxford: Clarendon, 2002). Even so, it should be stated that the data provided in the tables, as in the case of virtually every listing pertaining to the Scrolls, is provisional and subject to modification (cf., e.g., the tabulations by Rietz in his essay in the present volume).

The following sigla are utilized in the tables:
* * = reconstructed
* Ø = not extant
* ??? = reconstruction not attempted
* (?) = status or identification as excerpted or abbreviated manuscript uncertain.

Table 1
List of Excerpted and Abbreviated Manuscripts at Qumran

Text	Contents	Lines[192]	Date[193]	Remarks
Testimonia (4Q175)	Exod 20:21; Num 24:15-17; Deut 33:8-11; Josh 6:26 from *Apocryphon of Joshua*[b] (4Q379) frg. 22 2.7-14	30 lines	125-75 BCE	For Exod 20:21, cf. SamP and MT Deut 5:28b-29 + 18:18-19[194]
Phylacteries and *mezuzot* (1Q13; 4Q128-155; 5Q8; 8Q3-4; XQPhyl 1-4)	Contents vary	Line counts vary	Dates vary	

192. The line count given for each document is the maximum number of lines extant for that scroll on any preserved fragment or column regardless of editorial reconstructions or the existence of margins (for these latter, cf. E. Tov, "The Dimensions of the Qumran Scrolls," *DSD* 5 [1998]: 69-91). In a few cases, the absolute height of the scroll is given, including margins (see ibid., 77-91).

193. Dates follow B. Webster, "J. Chronological Index of the Texts from the Judaean Desert," in DJD 39:351-446, esp. 371-75.

194. Note E. Ulrich, "The Text of the Hebrew Scriptures at the Time of Hillel and Jesus," in *Congress Volume: Basel 2001* (ed. A. Lemaire; VTSup 92; Leiden: Brill, 2002), 87 n. 2, who points out (*apud* B. J. Pitre) that an expanded form of Exod 20:21, similar to this one, is also found in 4Q158 frg. 6 (4QReworked Pentateuch[a]).

Much of the information in this table follows E. Tov, "Excerpted and Abbreviated Biblical Texts from Qumran," *RevQ* 16 (1995): 581-600, but it has been updated and adjusted by comparison with the editions in DJD; P. W. Flint, *The Dead Sea Psalms Scrolls and the Book of Psalms* (STDJ 17; Leiden: E. J. Brill, 1997); and J. A. Duncan, "Excerpted Texts of Deuteronomy at Qumran," *RevQ* 18 (1997): 43-62. This table also appears in B. A. Strawn, "Excerpted Manuscripts at Qumran: Their Significance for the Textual History of the Hebrew Bible and the Socio-Religious History of the Qumran Community and its Literature," in *The Bible and the Dead Sea Scrolls*, Vol. 2: *The Dead Sea Scrolls and the Qumran Community* (ed. J. H. Charlesworth; Waco: Baylor University Press, 2006), 107-67.

Given some of the theoretical issues raised in the body of the paper, it is possible that more texts could be excerpted or abbreviated. As two examples, I refer to the work of Tov ("Excerpted and Abbreviated," 594-95) who has posited that eight collections manifesting different sequences from and/or additional material to the MT might be excerpted or abbreviated (11QPs[a], also reflected in 4QPs[e], 11QPs[b], and perhaps 4QPs[b] [see above]; 4QPs[a]; 4QPs[d]; 4QPs[f]; 4QPs[k]; 4QPs[n] [see above]; 4QPs[q]; and 11QPsAp[a]); and G. J. Brooke ("Ezekiel in Some Qumran and New Testament Texts," in *The Madrid Qumran Congress: Proceedings of the International Congress on the Dead Sea Scrolls, Madrid 18-21 March, 1991* [2 vols.; eds. J. Trebolle Barrera and L. Vegas Montaner; STDJ 11; Leiden: E. J. Brill, 1992], 1:318) who has raised the possibility that 3Q1 (3QEzek) might be excerpted.

Text	Contents	Lines	Date	Remarks
2QExod[b] (2Q3) esp. frg. 8 (?)[195]	Exod 19:9[196] followed after *vacat*[197] by 34:10	7 lines	30 BCE-68 CE	Note ordering (other frgs. reflect standard order) and writing of divine name in paleo-Hebrew (also in frgs. 2 and 7)[198]
4QExod[d] (4Q15)	Exod 13:15-16 + 15:1	5 lines	250-150 BCE	Abbreviation and ordering; note omission of 13:17–14:31 within one fragment
4QExod[e] (4Q16)	Exod 13:3-5	8 lines (8.2 cm.)	150-100 BCE	Probably not whole biblical book
4QDeut[j] (4Q37)	Deut 5:1-11, 13-15; 5:21–6:3; 8:5-10; 11:6-13; 11:21 (?) + Exod 12:43–13:5; Deut 32:7-8	14 lines (12 cm.)	50 CE	Note the material join between Exodus and Deuteronomy
4QDeut[k1] (4Q38)	Deut 5:28-32; 11:6-13; 32:17-18, 22-23, 25-27	13 lines	30-1 BCE	
4QDeut[n] (4Q41)	Deut 8:5-10 + 5:1–6:1 (with plus of Exod 20:11 after Deut 5:15)	12 lines (6.8 cm.)	30-1 BCE	Different ordering and smaller dimensions; probably not whole biblical book

195. 2QExod[b] is thought to be an excerpted text by A. Steudel, "Testimonia," in *EDSS* 2:938; H. Stegemann, "Weitere Stücke von 4QpPsalm 37, von 4Q Patriarchal Blessings und Hinweis auf eine unedierte Handschrift aus Höhle 4Q mit Exzerpten aus dem Deuteronomium," *RevQ* 6 (1967): 220; and G. J. Brooke, "Torah in the Qumran Scrolls," in *Bibel in jüdischer und christlicher Tradition: Festschrift für Johann Maier zum 60. Geburtstag* (ed. H. Merklein et al.; BBB 88; Frankfort am Main: Anton Hain, 1993), 102. Contrast Tov, "Dimensions," 69; and idem, "Excerpted and Abbreviated," 584, who opts instead for a rewritten Bible text.

196. Tov, "Excerpted and Abbreviated," 584 n. 13, does not think this is Exod 19:9 (so M. Baillet, "3. Exode [deuxième exemplaire]," in *Les 'Petites Grottes' de Qumrân* [by M. Baillet, J. T. Milik, and R. de Vaux; DJD 3; Oxford: Clarendon 1962], 55) but "a nonbiblical addition before 34:10 similar to the additions in 4QRP." Unfortunately, the fragmentary nature of the manuscript precludes certainty, though it should be noted that the text writes the Tetragrammaton in paleo-Hebrew script (see note 198 below). In my judgment, the thematic connections between Exodus 19 and 34, observed by Baillet (DJD 3:55), remain a viable explanation for the arrangement of the text and, hence, its excerption.

197. See M. Baillet (DJD 3:55), who notes that the *vacat* does not correspond to a Masoretic division but that SamP does end a pericope at this point. So, similarly, Exod 34:10 does not begin a new unit in MT but does in SamP.

198. For the latter point, see J. C. VanderKam, "Authoritative Literature in the Dead Sea Scrolls," *DSD* 5 (1998): 385-86, who notes this trait also in 4QIsa[c] and 11QPs[a] though elsewhere it is largely restricted to works that did *not* become part of the Hebrew Bible (e.g., 1QpMic, 1QpHab, 1QpZeph, etc.).

Text	Contents	Lines	Date	Remarks
4QDeut^q (4Q44)	Deut 32:9-10 (?), 37-43	11 lines (11.1 cm.)	50-1 BCE	Limited dimensions; probably only Deut 32
5QDeut (5Q1)	Deut 7:15-24; 8:5–9:2[199]	15 lines	250-150 BCE	Probably not whole biblical book
4QEzek^a (4Q73) (?)	Ezek 10:5-15; 10:17–11:11; 23:14-15, 17-18, 44-47; 41:3-6	21 lines	50-25 BCE	Note possible thematic choice of topics
4QPs^b (4Q84) (?)	Portions of Pss 91-94, 96, 98-100, 102-103, 112-113, 115-118	16 lines (17.5 cm)	30-68 CE	Note minus of Pss 104-111 in frg. 25 col. ii; small dimensions; use of cryptic A in frg. 5
4QPs^g (4Q89)	Portions of Ps 119:37-92	8 lines (8.1 cm.)	50 CE	Probably only Psalm 119 given small dimensions
4QPs^h (4Q90)	Ps 119:10-21	12 lines	30 BCE-68 CE	Probably only Psalm 119 on the scroll (?)
4QPs^n (4Q95)	Pss 135:6-8, 11-12 + 136:23-24	5 lines	30-1 BCE	Note combination of text
4QPs^x (4Q98g olim 4Q236 = 4QPs89)	Ps 89:20-22, 26, 23, 27-28, 31	8 lines	200-100 BCE	Differently ordered and abbreviated text
5QPs (5Q5)	Ps 119:113-120, 138-142	8 lines	1-100 CE	Note only Psalm 119
4QCant^a (4Q106) (?)	Cant 3:4–4:7; 6:11(?)–7:7	14 lines	30-1 BCE	Note abbreviated text
4QCant^b (4Q107) (?)	Cant 2:9–3:5; 3:9–4:3; 4:8–5:1	15 lines	30-1 BCE	
4QDan^e (4Q116) (?)[200]	Dan 9:12-17	6 lines (6.1 cm.)	150-100 (-75) BCE	Probably only a portion of Daniel (9:4b-19?) on the scroll

199. See J. T. Milik, "1. Deutéronome," in DJD 3:171 for frgs. 2-5 of this manuscript, which might come from Deuteronomy 32-33.

200. See the comments by E. Ulrich and C. Niccum, "116. 4QDan^e," in *Qumran Cave 4.11: Psalms to Chronicles* (ed. E. Ulrich et al.; DJD 16; Oxford: Clarendon, 2000), 287.

Table 2
"Non-Biblical" Scrolls of Small Dimensions

Text	Number of Lines	Size (cm.)
4QIncantation (4Q444)	4	???
5QCurses (5Q14)	5	4.5
4QBirth of Noah[b] ar (4Q535)	6	6.4
4QPrEsth[a,b,d] ar (4Q550, 4Q550a, c)	7-8	5.8–6.5
4QDanSus? ar (4Q551)	8	6.6
4QCal. Document B[a] (4Q321)	8-9	9.4
4QToh A (4Q274)	9	5.5
4QApocrDan ar (4Q246)	9	8.5
4QZodiology and Brontology (4Q318)	9	10.1
4QList of False Prophets ar (4Q339)	9	8.5
4QApocrMos[a] (4Q375)	9	7
4QApocr. Psalm and Prayer (4Q448)	9-10	9.5
4QapocrLam B (4Q501)	9	5.8
4QShir[a] (4Q510)	9	10.5
4QS[j] (4Q264)	10	4.4
4QS[f] (4Q260)	10	7.6*
4QcryptA Words of the Maskil (4Q298)	10	8.4
4QAgesCreat A (4Q180)	10	10.5
4QpIsa[b] (4Q162)	10	11
4QAdmonition Based on the Flood (4Q370)	10	12
4QMMT[c] (4Q396)	11	9
4QBarki Nafshi[c] (4Q436)	11	9.7
4QMMT[f] (4Q399)	12 (only 11 inscribed)	7.5
4QH[c] (4Q429)	12	10
4QpNah (4Q169)	12	11.5
4QpapS[a] (4Q255)	12*	11.8+*
4QAgesCreat B (4Q181)	12	???
4QBer[b] (4Q287)	13	8.2
4QTQahat ar (4Q542)	13	9.5
4QBirth of Noah[c] ar (4Q536)	13	11
4QS[d] (4Q258)	13*	12.2
4QS[b] (4Q256)	13	12.5
4QpapTob[a] ar (4Q196)	13, 16	17–18.7
4QapocrLam A (4Q179)	13, 15	8.2

The information in this table follows Tov, "Dimensions," 77-79; and idem, DJD 16:198 n. 4. Cf. the listing in S. Pfann, "4Q298: The Maskil's Address to All Sons of Dawn," *JQR* 85 (1994): 213 n. 14, though some of his data are now out of date. The information has been rounded out by comparison with editions in DJD. Note Tov's somewhat arbitrary definition of what constitutes "small" dimensions: less than 1.5 m and fewer than 13 lines.

Table 3
"Non-Biblical" Scrolls of Medium Size

Text	Number of Lines	Size (cm.)
4QM^c (4Q493)	14	9.5
4QpsJub^a (4Q225)	14	10
5Q11 (5QS)	14*	???
4Qsapiential work (4Q185)	15	12.6
4QMess. Apoc. (4Q521)	15/16	???
4QCat^a (4QMidrEschat^b?) (4Q177)	16	11
4QPs122 (4Q522)	16	13
4QWiles of Wicked Woman (4Q184)	17	13.5
4QJub^a (4Q216)	17	14.5
1QpHab	17	15
4QBarki Nafshi^d (4Q437)	17	12.5
4QS^e (4Q259)	19	14.2
5QNJ ar (5Q15)	19	16
4QpHos^a (4Q166)	19	16.5
4QFlor (4QMidrEschat^a?) (4Q174)	19	18
4QH^e (4Q431)[201]	19-21*	???
4QD^g (4Q272)	20	13.5
4QMMT^a (4Q394)	20	16.6
1QM (1Q33)	20	???
4QpapS^c (4Q257)	20-21	???
4QD^f (4Q271)	21	11.5
4QShirShabb^a (4Q400)	21	12.7
4QD^e (4Q270)	21	13.5
4QInstruction^b (4Q416)	21-22	16.5
4QEn^e ar (4Q206)	21	???
4QBirth of Noah^a ar (4Q534)	21	???
4QCommGen A (4Q252)	22	13
11QT^a (11Q19)	22-29	24-26
4QH^a (4Q427)[202]	23*	???
4QD^a (4Q266)	24-25	18.4–19.2

201. See Eileen Schuller, "4QHodayot^e," in *Qumran Cave 4.20: Poetical and Liturgical Texts, Part 2* (ed. E. Chazon et al.; DJD 29; Oxford: Clarendon, 1999), 200-201, who gives the reconstructed length of the scroll as 4.25 m.

202. See Schuller, "427. 4QHodayot^a," in DJD 29:79-82, who reconstructs the scroll at 3.7 m long.

The listing in this table follows Tov, "Dimensions," 79-81, and his somewhat arbitrary definition of "medium" size (1.5–5 m and between 14 and 24/25 lines).

Table 4
Multiple-Copy "Non-Biblical" Documents from Qumran

Text	Cave I	II	III	Number of Copies per Cave IV	V	VI	XI	Other locales	Total
Commentaries[203]	4		1	17	1				23
Jubilees	2	2	1	15[204]			1	1 (Mas1j)	22
Enoch[205]	2	1		17		1			21
Calendars				12		1			13
Damascus Document				8	1	1		2 (CD MS A and B)	12
Rule of the Community	1			10[206]	1		1[207]		13
Thanksgiving Hymns	2			10[208]					12

203. Following Newsom ("'Sectually Explicit' Literature," 170), note that there are no multiple-copy *peshers,* but insofar as these may be treated as a distinct type (see Robert Williamson, Jr., "Qumran Pesher: A Cognitive Model of the Genre" [*DSD;* forthcoming]), they may be tabulated in this fashion. Also included are the related commentary texts, even if they do not contain the technical term פשר (see PTSDSSP 6B).

204. Including 4Q482-483 (4QpapJub^{i-j}?).

205. The tabulation includes Enoch-like texts or texts with compositions related to the Enoch tradition, especially the Book of Giants, which, admittedly, not all scholars believe belongs to the Enoch materials (see VanderKam, "Authoritative Literature," 398 and n. 33).

206. Alexander and Vermes, DJD 26: 1 n. 1, believe that the fragments of 4QS^h belong to two different scrolls (one which was not a copy of the *Rule of the Community*) and that 4QS^b frg. 1 may also belong to a different scroll, which was also not a copy of the *Rule of the Community.* If this fragment did belong to the *Serekh* (note the correlation with 1QS 1.10), it would constitute an eleventh copy of the *Rule* from cave 4. If both scrolls of 4QS^h were *Serekh* texts, a twelfth might be added.

207. Including 11Q29 (11QFragment Related to Serekh ha-Yahad), though, according to the editors, it is not clear "whether the fragment is part of a copy of *Serekh ha-Yahad,* or from a different composition which relates or refers to it" (F. García Martínez, E. J. C. Tigchelaar, A. S. Van der Woude, *Qumran Cave 11.2: 11Q2-18, 11Q20-31* [DJD 23; Oxford, Clarendon, 1998], 433). Cf. DJD 26:1 n. 1.

208. Including the *Hodayot*-like fragments 4Q433-33a and 4Q440-40a. See the discussion by Schuller, "Classification," 182-93; and idem, "433. 4QHodayot-like Text A," "433a. 4QpapHodayot-like Text B," "440. 4QHodayot-Like Text C," in DJD 29:233-54. Note that 4Q433a was written on the *recto* of 4Q255 (4QpapS^a).

The listing in this table follows C. A. Newsom, "'Sectually Explicit' Literature from Qumran," in *The Hebrew Bible and Its Interpreters* (ed. W. H. Propp, B. Halpern, and D. N. Freedman; BJSUCSD 1; Winona Lake: Eisenbrauns, 1990), 170, but has been revised, extended, and updated with the lists in EDSS 2:1013-56; J. H. Charlesworth et al., eds., *The Dead Sea Scrolls: Hebrew, Aramaic, and Greek Texts with English Translations,* Vol. 6B: *Pesharim, Other Commentaries, and Related Documents* (PTSDSSP 6B; Tübingen: Mohr Siebeck and Louisville: Westminster John Knox, 2002), 379-84; DSSSE 2:1311-61; and, esp., A. Lange with U. Mittmann-Richert, "C. Annotated List of the Texts from the Judaean Desert Classified," in DJD 39:115-64 (see further there). Note that the rather large number of compositions that appear in two copies are not included here. Again, the provisional nature of the present tabulation should be underscored (compare, e.g., the listings, some different, for several of these compositions in Rietz's essay in the present volume). For fuller discussion of several of the main compositions listed above in light of affinities to the *Rule of the Community,* see Newsom, "'Sectually Explicit' Literature," esp. 169-72 and n. 1.

Excerpted "Non-Biblical" Scrolls at Qumran?

Text	Number of Copies per Cave							Other locales	Total
	Cave I	II	III	IV	V	VI	XI		
War Scroll	1			9[209]			1		11
Rule of the Congregation	1			9[210]					10
Songs of the Sabbath Sacrifice				8			1	1 (Mas1k)	10
Instruction	1			7					8
Aramaic Levi	1			6					7
MMT				7					7
New Jerusalem	1	1		3	1		1		7
Visions of Amram				7					7
Apocryphon of Jeremiah C				6					6
Proto-Esther				6					6
Tohorot				6					6
Barki Nafshi				5					5
Berakot				5					5
Pseudo-Ezekiel				5					5
Reworked Pentateuch				5					5
Prayers for Festivals	2			3					5
Tobit				5					5
Temple Scroll				2[211]			3[212]		5
Mysteries	1			3					4
Birth of Noah				3					3
Narrative and Poetic Composition				3					3
Ordinances				3					3
Pseudo-Daniel				3					3
Vision				3					3
Words of the Lights				3					3

209. Including 4Q285, 4Q471, and 4Q497.
210. 4Q249a-i (4Qpap cryptA 4QSerekh ha-ʿEdah[a-i]) as analyzed by S. J. Pfann in *Qumran Cave 4.26: Cryptic Texts and Miscellanea, Part I* (by S. J. Pfann, P. Alexander, et al.; DJD 36; Oxford: Clarendon, 2000), 515-74, esp. 534-46.
211. Including 4Q365a (4QTemple?) along with 4Q524.
212. Including 11Q21 (11QTemple[c]?).

Temporal Shifts from Text to Interpretation: Concerning the Use of the Perfect and Imperfect in the *Habakkuk Pesher* (1QpHab)

LOREN T. STUCKENBRUCK

1. Introduction

Scholarly reconstructions of the "history" behind the Dead Sea texts and, more specifically, the Qumran Community have been derived from various sources of information. With respect to the documents themselves, the *pesharim*, due to the historical allusions they contain, have figured prominently in such studies.[1] The historical allusions found in the *pesharim* from Caves 1 and 4 — in combination with knowledge about the archaeology of the Qumran site, palaeographic analysis of the manuscripts, and comparative studies with contemporary literature such as the Damascus Document and the works of Josephus — have been thought to provide clues that help piece together data about the political, social, and religious circumstances of the Community from the mid-second century B.C.E. until its destruction in June of 68 C.E.[2] In addition to

---

1. So, e.g., much of the literature referred to below. Among the recent publications on this topic, see in particular James H. Charlesworth, *The Pesharim and Qumran History: Chaos or Consensus?* (Grand Rapids: Eerdmans, 2002). Of course, Philip R. Davies attempted to draw more attention to the significance of the *Damascus Document* for discerning the Community's history. See his *The Damascus Covenant: An Interpretation of the "Damascus Document"* (JSOTSup 25; Sheffield: JSOT, 1983).

2. The nature of the discussion below, which focuses on text and language rather than on history, does not require that a precise reconstruction be either undertaken or assumed.

It is an honor to dedicate the following discussion to James H. Charlesworth, whose own research on the Dead Sea materials and Second Temple Jewish literature has been a never-failing source of inspiration. Note that the English translations of Hebrew citations in this essay are my own unless otherwise indicated.

these bodies of data, since the very beginning of Dead Sea Scrolls research, arguments from language, both philological and syntactical, have also been adduced to illuminate the early history of the Qumran group. Though not always regarded as conclusive, evidence based on the uses of the perfect and imperfect forms of verbs in the *pesharim,* and especially in the *Habakkuk Pesher* from Cave 1 (1QpHab), has been appealed to time and time again in this discussion. The focus of the present article is on this latter area of linguistic analysis as it relates to the problem of historical reconstruction.

That the shifts in verb formations in the *Habakkuk Pesher* have been interpreted in a variety of ways goes without saying. It is manifest in the divergent opinions among scholars concerning the identities underlying some of the most prominent sobriquets such as "Wicked Priest," "Man of Lies," "Kittim," and "Righteous Teacher." The following example illustrates the problem. There are five occasions in which the interpretive sections of the *Habakkuk Pesher* refer to the Wicked Priest as the object of an imperfect (prefix conjugation) verb:

10.3-5:[3] יעלנו — "he [God] will raise him up"; ירשיענו — "he will declare him guilty"; ישפטנו — "he will judge him";

11.14: תבלענו — "it [the cup of God's wrath] will swallow him"; and

12.5: ישופטנו — "he [God] will judge him."

Otherwise, 1QpHab refers to the Wicked Priest (as well as the Teacher of Righteousness) by means of perfect (suffix conjugation) verbs. This varied use in itself is neither problematic nor unexpected. However, difficulty for attempts at synthetic reconstructions arises when it is observed that the "Kittim" are *always* referred to with imperfect verbs.[4] The interpretation of these imperfects would therefore be crucial if one wishes to know whether or not the author of the *Habakkuk Pesher* wished to associate the Wicked Priest with the era of the Kittim.

3. In these lines, the object of the imperfect applies to the Wicked Priest if: a) the pronominal suffix does not refer to "the house of judgment" in 10.3; and b) the "pr[iest]," to whom the second "woe" (Hab 2:9) is applied in 10.16, is identified with the Wicked Priest. This identification is strengthened by the fact that the nearest antecedent to 10.16 in a section of commentary is the Wicked Priest (line 9).

4. On this, see already the important early studies by M. H. Segal, "The Habakkuk 'Commentary' and the Damascus Fragments," *JBL* 70 (1951): 131-47; and J. van der Ploeg, "L'usage du parfait et de l'imparfait comme moyen de datation dans le commentaire d'Habacuc," in *Les Manuscrits de la Mer Morte: Colloque de Strasbourg. 25-27 mai 1955* (Paris: Presses Universitaires de France, 1957), 25-35, esp. 32.

Of course, a study of the significance of verb formations used in the commentary portions of 1QpHab must take account of the use of the same in the lemmata, that is, the preceding citations of biblical text. Thus the linguistic question that guides our understanding of what imperfects and perfects may have meant for the author may be formulated as follows: What may we infer when the imperfect or perfect verb forms in the biblical text[5] have been retained or changed in a subsequent commentary on the lemma?

This present investigation offers an analysis of the *Habakkuk Pesher* that focuses on this specific question. The procedure adopted is, firstly, to delineate the linguistic issue that serves as a prerequisite to the discussion (§2); subsequently, to describe the broad results of scholarly analysis (§3); before, finally, offering a systematic consideration of the text of 1QpHab itself (§4).

2. Verbal Formation and Tense

Ascribing precise temporal meanings to the perfect and imperfect Hebrew verbs during the Second Temple period is not a straightforward matter. Numerous scholars have recognized this point. As exemplary, we may make note of two Hebrew grammars that are often cited in relation to the question of verbs and temporality, namely, those by Paul Joüon[6] and M. H. Segal.[7] Joüon's grammar describes the various uses of the imperfect *(yiqtōl)* formation in classical Hebrew. Along the lines of the earlier Hebrew grammar of Gesenius-Kautzsch-Cowley,[8] but in significantly more detail, he describes how in the Old Testament/Hebrew Bible the imperfect was not necessarily equivalent to the future tense. Rather, at a basic level of meaning, the imperfect denotes *aspect* — in this case, *incomplete action* — and therefore can express not only activity in the future but also repeated or continuous action whether in the present or the past. Thus the temporal value of the imperfect,

---

5. This study shall focus primarily on the freestanding forms, though at times it shall be necessary to consider the imperfects with *waw*.

6. P. Joüon, *Grammaire de l'Hebreu Biblique* (Rome: Pontifical Biblical Institute, 1923), 301-2 and 306. See now the English version updated and revised by T. Muraoka, *A Grammar of Biblical Hebrew* (2 vols.; *SubBi* 14; Rome: Pontifical Biblical Institute, 1991), 2:365-73 (§113). On this, see also Bruce K. Waltke and M. O'Connor, *An Introduction to Biblical Hebrew Syntax* (Winona Lake: Eisenbrauns, 1990), 346-47 (§20.2c-h).

7. M. H. Segal, *A Grammar of Mishnaic Hebrew* (Oxford: Clarendon, 1927), 150-65.

8. See GKC, esp. §47 n. 1; also S. R. Driver, *A Treatise on the Use of the Tenses in Hebrew and Some Other Syntactical Questions* (3rd ed.; Oxford: Clarendon, 1892), 27-49. Note the reprint of the latter work by Eerdmans and Dove (1998), in which Driver's study is updated with an extensive introduction by W. Randall Garr.

according to Joüon, was less neatly defined than that of the perfect *(qātal)*, which expresses completed action often (but not exclusively) in the past.[9] Segal's comparative study of biblical and early rabbinic Hebrew noted a clear development towards temporal precision in the later dialect. Concerning both the imperfect and perfect formations, he concluded that "MH [= Mishnaic Hebrew] has attained to a greater preciseness and exactness than BH [= Biblical Hebrew]."[10] This increased precision in Mishnaic Hebrew meant, according to Segal, a simplified time system: the perfect usually coincides with the past tense, the participle to the present, and the imperfect to the future. The conclusions of Joüon and Segal are representative and are generally accepted by Hebraists today. Debate continues, however, when scholars attempt to decide which nuances — classical or Mishnaic — apply to perfects and imperfects in documents composed in Hebrew during the transitional period between biblical and Mishnaic Hebrew. In addition, it is debated whether the Hebrew used at Khirbet Qumran may be taken to reflect some sort of linear development between classical and Mishnaic Hebrew, especially if possible socio-linguistic and historical factors of the Community are taken into consideration.[11]

With regard to 1QpHab, the imperfects applied to the Wicked Priest in the passages cited above have been interpreted in conjunction with varying hypotheses concerning the history of the Qumran group. Consequently, if one espouses a historical reconstruction that distinguishes the era of the Righteous Teacher and his opponents (i.e., the Man of Lies and the Wicked Priest) from the era that involves the invading Kittim (referred to by means of the imperfect), then the imperfects in 1QpHab 10.3-5; 11.14; and 12.5 *cannot* be interpreted as references to future events from the standpoint of the author. On the other hand, if the identification of the Wicked Priest is sought in a person who lived near to or during the time period of the Kittim, then the notion of the imperfect verbs referring to events in the author's future poses no problem. In view of these alternatives, it is imperative to point out that nothing dictates that the perfects or imperfects in 1QpHab *must* have been used consistently with regard to temporal aspect; one needs to be open to the fur-

---

9. See Joüon-Muraoka, *A Grammar of Biblical Hebrew*, 2:372. To be sure, Joüon-Muraoka still refer to the *yiqtōl* formation as generally future, but note departures from this, for example, to the past when the context and/or a foregoing perfect formation demands it. See also GKC §47 n. 1.

10. Segal, *Grammar of Mishnaic Hebrew*, 150. See also Miguel Pérez Fernández, *An Introductory Grammar of Rabbinic Hebrew* (trans. John Elwolde; Leiden: Brill, 1997), 107-8.

11. See esp. W. M. Schniedewind, "Qumran Hebrew as an Antilanguage," *JBL* 118 (1999): 235-52.

ther possibility that, as a whole, the formation may reflect characteristics of both earlier and later Hebrew usage.

3. Four Interpretations of the Imperfect in the *Habakkuk Pesher*

The diverse views of specialists who have discussed the matter of tense in 1QpHab may be placed under four major rubrics. These rubrics are formulated here on the basis of what each has claimed about *imperfect verbs,* since herein lies the primary difficulty for interpretation. The imperfects in the *Habakkuk Pesher* have been explained as references to: (1) *future* events in *human history;* (2) both *future and contemporary* events in *human history;* (3) *future eschatological* events; and, finally, (4) to events in the *past.* Though by no means exhaustive, these four categorizations represent the broad interpretive spectrum and cover most solutions proposed during the past fifty years. I will take up each in order.

Future Events in History

In an article published in 1952, William H. Brownlee insisted that the imperfect verbs in 1QpHab, when applied to the Wicked Priest, referred to future historical events.[12] His formulation of the problem of tense in the document was closely related to ideas being suggested by his contemporaries M. H. Segal[13] and J. van der Ploeg.[14] Segal asserted that although both the Wicked Priest (whom he identified with Alexander Jannaeus) and the Kittim are referred to by means of the imperfect, this does not mean that they are to be considered contemporaries. Whereas the events of the Wicked Priest's life are also described by the perfect, the Kittim are only mentioned in the imperfect. Segal's conclusion was encumbered by a contradiction which he chose not to address:[15] how can one know for certain that the use of the imperfect verbs with these two different subjects, to the extent that the verbs might represent

12. William H. Brownlee, "The Historical Allusions of the Dead Sea Habakkuk Midrash," *BASOR* 126 (1952): 10-20, esp. 11 and 16.

13. Segal, "The Habakkuk 'Commentary' and the Damascus Fragments," 131-47.

14. Van der Ploeg, "L'usage du parfait et de l'imparfait," 33-35.

15. That is, Segal was more concerned with producing an argument on behalf of the view that the Kittim in 1QpHab — who in his view refer to the Romans not yet present in Jerusalem — are not to be identified with the Seleucids.

the same tense, does not in fact place the Wicked Priest and the Kittim within at least the same general period of time? In taking this problem into consideration, van der Ploeg went a step further. While he agreed with Segal that the invasion of the Kittim refers to the near future from the author's point of view, he was not as prepared as Segal to concede that the Wicked Priest belongs to an earlier era. By interpreting the expression נתנו in 1QpHab 9.10[16] as a future perfect, he inferred that from the author's perspective the Wicked Priest had yet to be punished by God through the Community's enemies. For van der Ploeg, this interpretation points toward the possibility that this archrival of the Righteous Teacher was still alive when the *pesher* was composed. The author was, then, living in a time *subsequent* to the hostilities between the Righteous Teacher and the Wicked Priest, but *prior* to the invasion of the Kittim, who, for van der Ploeg, were the Romans.

While Brownlee shared the opinion of van der Ploeg that the *Habakkuk Pesher* holds that the Wicked Priest's chastisement is yet to come,[17] he still maintained with Segal that this does not imply that the Kittim's invasion of Judea occurred during the Wicked Priest's lifetime. As noted for Segal's view above, this involved a contradiction; however, unlike Segal, Brownlee attempted to account for it. Brownlee found his solution by maintaining that the tenses of the *pesher* do not reflect the author's own historical point of view, but rather that of the Righteous Teacher. Therefore, all events that preceded the Teacher's own death were written in the perfect and all that followed were in the imperfect. Thus the future events in the *pesher,* with the exception of the Kittim, had already been fulfilled before the composition of the *pesher* and were conveyed by the author as *vaticinia ex eventu.*[18] If Brownlee was correct in supposing that the *pesher* was fictively composed from the Teacher's point of view, then he had a hypothesis that would have opened the way for allowing the expression "Wicked Priest" to represent more than one

---

16. Cf. 9.9-12: "the [Wi]cked Priest whom, because of (his) wickedness against the Teacher of Righteousness and the men of his council, God delivered [נתנו אל; van der Ploeg: 'will deliver'] into the hand of his enemies in order to humiliate him through punishment to destroy (him) with bitterness of soul [f]or he acted wickedly against his elect."

17. For Brownlee, however, the future punishment is not based on the occurrence of נתנו in 9.10 (which he translated into the past tense, as n. 12 above), but on the imperfects in 11.14 and 12.5. See his "The Wicked Priest, the Man of Lies, and the Righteous Teacher — the Problem of Identity," *JQR* 73 (1982): 1-37, esp. 30, and "The Historical Allusions," 16.

18. See Brownlee, "The Wicked Priest, the Man of Lies, and the Righteous Teacher," 6; and idem, "The Historical Allusions," 20: "my theory reckons with the contradictory evidence which points on the one hand to composition of the book during the reign of Jannaeus, but on the other hand to its composition in early Roman times."

individual, even in one document, as punishments of this figure are related in both the perfect (9.1-2, 10) and the imperfect (9.14 and 12.5).

Jean Carmignac also argued that the conjugations in 1QpHab are to be interpreted strictly temporally, in the sense that the perfect denotes the past and the imperfect represents the future.[19] On this basis he surmised that the *pesher* was written during the time of the Wicked Priest. However, the imperfects for Carmignac, unlike the perfects, do not relate to actual historical events, even though they were intended as such; they are, instead, "simple predictions"[20] that may or may not have come true. Thus Carmignac did not require that the allusions to events conveyed through the imperfect be matched to identifiable events in history. And yet, by identifying the Wicked Priest as Alexander Jannaeus (103-76 B.C.E.), Carmignac is forced to contradict his view of the verbs by translating נתנו in 9.10 as an event yet to happen. The fact that the Kittim invasion lies in the near future led Carmignac to date the *Habakkuk Pesher* to the time of the first warnings of the Romans' coming, that is, to the time of Scylla's campaign against Mithridates in 85-84 B.C.E.

Finally, Frank Moore Cross has, similar to Brownlee, explained the imperfect as referring to the future from the Righteous Teacher's point of view.[21] Cross suggests that certain prophecies may have been worked out during the Teacher's lifetime, but were not actually written down until much later. Thus the future tense, when applied to the Wicked Priest, may be evidence of a tradition *antecedent* to the time of the author. Cross's interpretation of the imperfect is based on his two-fold conviction that the Wicked Priest is Simon (142-134 B.C.E.) and that 1QpHab, probably an autograph, is palaeographically datable to the late Hasmonean era.

---

19. Jean Carmignac, "Interprétations de Prophètes et de Psaumes," in idem, *Les Textes de Qumran: Traduits et annotés* (2 vols.; Paris: Letouzey et Ané, 1961-1963), 2:43-126. Carmignac's view is followed recently by Gregory L. Doudna, *4Q Pesher Nahum: A Critical Edition* (JSPSup 35 and Copenhagen International Series 8; Sheffield: Academic Press, 2001), 620 and n. 712.

20. Carmignac, "Interprétations de Prophètes et de Psaumes," 50: "les châtiments envisagés sont de simples prédictions, qui ont fort bien pu ne pas être vérifées par les événements, et donc qu'ils ne peuvent pas nous servir pour tenter une identification historique" ("The punishments envisioned are simple predictions, which could not have been verified by events and which could never have served us in making a historical identification").

21. Frank Moore Cross, *The Ancient Library of Qumran and Modern Biblical Studies* (3d ed.; The Biblical Seminar 30; Sheffield: Academic Press, 1995 [orig: 1958]), 115.

Both Future and Contemporary Events in History

Three scholars have interpreted the imperfects in 1QpHab as referring to *both* future *and* contemporary events. A. Dupont-Sommer, citing Joüon's grammar, argued that the imperfect, when used in conjunction with the Kittim, does not necessarily denote the future.[22] As described by Joüon, the imperfect may also mark repetition or the continuity of present or even past action. Thus it is the only formation that the author could have used to describe the present manners and characteristics of the Kittim invaders. This argument was strengthened by Dupont-Sommer's appeal to the fact that the author also uses the participle to describe the Kittim (cf. 6.4-6). The imperfects used in relation to the Wicked Priest were, however, understood by him to carry the future tense.[23] The concurrence of different tenses in association with the Wicked Priest suffices as basis for Dupont-Sommer to find in the sobriquet a reference to two high priests: Aristobulus II (67-63 B.C.E.) and Hyrcanus II (63-40 B.C.E.). Consequently, he dated the *pesher* to a time just prior to the Parthian invasion of 40 B.C.E., when Hyrcanus II was taken captive and made incapable of being high priest. Dupont-Sommer explained allusions in the perfect, such as the נתנו in 9.10, as references to Hyrcanus II's predecessor who was taken captive by the Romans when Pompey arrived in Jerusalem in 63 B.C.E.

Karl Elliger likewise took the imperfects in 9.14 and 12.5 as predictions of the downfall of Hyrcanus II.[24] But he departed from Dupont-Sommer when he restricted his identification of the Wicked Priest to Hyrcanus II alone. Thus the perfect tenses are made to refer to the earlier period of Hyrcanus's reign (while נתנו alludes to his capture in 40 B.C.E.). This led Elliger to date the composition of the *Habakkuk Pesher* to just before Herod ransomed Hyrcanus in 37-36 B.C.E. As Dupont-Sommer before him, Elliger understood the Kittim to be present in Palestine during the writing of the *pesher*. In this regard, he appealed to both the continuous action of the imperfect and the vividness of imagery with which the Kittim are described (see, especially, 2.12–4.13).

Finally, the use of the imperfect with *both* present and future sense is evident in Millar Burrows' view.[25] He favors the position that the imperfects in

---

22. A. Dupont-Sommer, *The Jewish Sect of Qumran and the Essenes* (London: Vallentine, Mitchell and Co., 1954), 28.

23. A. Dupont-Sommer, "Le 'Commentaire Habacuc' découvert près de la Mer Morte," *RHR* 137 (1950): 129-71, esp. 165, 169-70.

24. Karl Elliger, *Studien zum Habakkuk-Kommentar vom Toten Meer* (BHT 15; Tübingen: J. C. B. Mohr [Paul Siebeck], 1953), 150-64, 270-74, and 289-92.

25. Millar Burrows, *Burrows on the Dead Sea Scrolls* (Grand Rapids: Baker, 1978), 158.

1QpHab 10.3-5 and 11.14 place the Wicked Priest's punishment in the future as well as in the past. This is, for Burrows, "clear evidence" that the author was referring to events in his own lifetime — that is, that the Wicked Priest was still alive. When the imperfect is considered in relation to the Kittim, Burrows leans in the direction of the arguments of Dupont-Sommer and Elliger, though with less enthusiasm: "the use of the Hebrew tenses may but does not necessarily imply that the Kittim have not arrived."[26]

The strength of the perspectives offered by Dupont-Sommer, Elliger, and Burrows lies in their recognition that the imperfect in 1QpHab may simultaneously share nuances that were common to biblical and Mishnaic Hebrew. One has the impression, however, that they assumed that the imperfect (as related to the Wicked Priest) is to be applied solely within the realm of history. The eschatological coloring of the *Habakkuk Pesher* is thus not given sufficient consideration by these three scholars.[27]

Future Eschatological Events

The work of several scholars has rectified this oversight and offered further insight regarding the imperfects used of the Wicked Priest in 1QpHab. Though many of the scholars already mentioned consider the possibility that the "future" punishments of the Wicked Priest may refer to — or at least include — an ultimate, eschatological reckoning, not many have argued that this is their *primary meaning* in relation to this figure.[28] Some scholars, however, have committed themselves to an eschatological interpretation. One of them is Geza Vermes.[29] According to Vermes, the imperfect, in cases where it is applied to the Wicked Priest, refers to his *eschatological punishment*. This

---

26. Ibid., 141.

27. The same criticism may be levelled at the publications of Brownlee and Carmignac. Cf. William H. Brownlee, *The Midrash Pesher of Habakkuk* (SBLMS 24; Missoula: Scholars Press, 1979), 22; and Carmignac, *Les Textes de Qumran*, 2:49-50: "il oblige à supposer que ces interprétations ont été écrites pendant la vie du Prêtre Impie" ("He is obliged to suppose that these interpretations were written during the lifetime of the Wicked Priest"). Though Carmignac did not think that the imperfects ("simple predictions") were necessarily applicable to subsequent events, he nevertheless argued that they were intended as allusions to events within history and did not entertain the possibility that they could bear an eschatological dimension.

28. For instance, Burrows (*Burrows on the Dead Sea Scrolls,* 158) mentioned this as a mere possibility without exploring the implications of this idea any further.

29. Initially in Geza Vermes, *The Dead Sea Scrolls in Perspective* (Philadelphia: Fortress, 1977), 144.

interpretation makes it possible for Vermes to maintain that the Wicked Priest's identity is to be found in Jonathan (160-142 B.C.E.), since the *pesher* need not have been written during the priest's historical lifetime. Gerd Jeremias[30] has also contended that the imperfects, such as that in 11.14, may be construed as references to the eschaton. Like Vermes, Jeremias is thus able to relegate the figure of the Wicked Priest to the past (that is, to Jonathan) without requiring the imperfects to function as historical allusions.

While considering the use of the imperfect among the other *pesharim* of the Dead Sea Scrolls, Barbara Thiering has advanced a similar view.[31] She draws the distinction between historical and ahistorical allusions on the basis of the imagery being used in any given instance. Therefore, the descriptions of the Wicked Priest's sufferings in 9.1-2, 10-11, couched in the perfect, are offered in such detail that one cannot imagine that these would not have occurred in history. On the other hand, the historical allusions that appear in the imperfect, though definitely pointing towards the future, are more vague and are to be taken as referring to the day of judgment. Thiering argues that the imperfect formation does not automatically involve eschatology, especially since in 4QpPs^a (4Q171) frgs. 1-10 2.17-18 and 4.8-10 the details of the imagery are sufficiently specific as to be regarded as genuine historical allusions. However, in her view, the situation is different in the *Habakkuk Pesher*, in which the imperfects (i.e., in 10.3-5; 11.14; 12.5; and 13.2-3) are all to be regarded as eschatological. For Thiering, imagery detail in effect determines how one, with reference to 1QpHab, may date the Righteous Teacher in relation to the Wicked Priest. Whereas the data in 4QpPs^a seem to refer to a time when both the Teacher and the Wicked Priest were alive as contemporaries, the imperfects of the *Habakkuk Pesher* point exclusively to the final judgment, thus denoting a time when the Teacher's opponent had already died.[32] Without being explicit, Thiering implies that the Teacher, still alive in the Roman period, must have outlived the Wicked Priest. There is, however, no positive evidence for maintaining that the Teacher of Righteousness lived any longer than his opponent, especially as, in contrast to the Wicked Priest, the references to the Teacher occur exclusively in the perfect (cf. 5.8-12; 7.3-5; 9.9-12; 11.4-8).

---

30. Gerd Jeremias, *Der Lehrer der Gerechtigkeit* (SUNT 2; Göttingen: Vandenhoeck & Ruprecht, 1962), 58.

31. See Barbara Thiering, *Redating the Teacher of Righteousness* (Australian and New Zealand Studies in Theology and Religion 1; Sydney: Theological Explorations, 1979), 50-58.

32. Ibid., 53: "On the evidence of the pesharim alone, the simplest hypothesis is that the Teacher was in the Roman period. 4QpPs^a was written while he and the Wicked Priest were still alive; 1QpHab was written subsequently, when the Wicked Priest was dead."

A. S. van der Woude, like Brownlee and Dupont-Sommer, has taken the use of the imperfect (11.14; 12.2,[33] 5-6) and perfect verbs as evidence for multiple persons behind the figure of the Wicked Priest.[34] Commenting on 10.2-5, however, he infers that the imperfect "does not imply that the Priest was still alive at the time of the author."[35] This leads him to regard 10.2-5, which for him refers to a future figure designated the "Wicked Priest," as eschatological. This view requires that the other references to the Wicked Priest in the imperfect (11.14 and 12.5) are historical allusions to another Wicked Priest, since he was still alive when the *pesher* was being composed. Van der Woude's thesis poses a major difficulty in that he does not offer any criteria for differentiating the "historical allusions" in columns 11 and 12 from the final judgment in 10.2-5. The expression "cup of the wrath of God" (11.14)[36] and the phrase "God will judge him to destruction" (לכלה; 12.5)[37] cannot be automatically excluded as bearers of eschatological overtones.

Past Events

Hans Burgmann has offered an interpretation of the imperfect as referring to past events.[38] Arguing against Carmignac's contention that the imperfect used for the Wicked Priest points towards the future, Burgmann cast the spotlight on events surrounding the death of Jonathan (for him, the Wicked Priest). The historical fact that Jonathan suffered a slow death in 142 B.C.E.[39] on account of his imprisonment during the preceding year requires an expression denoting continuous action that the imperfect could satisfy far

---

33. A. S. van der Woude, "Wicked Priest or Wicked Priests? Reflections on the Identification of the Wicked Priest in the Habakkuk Commentary," *JJS* 33 (1982): 351, takes the infinitive לשלם in 12.2 as a future retribution.

34. Ibid., 349-59, esp. 351-57. Van der Woude's view is often referred to as the "Groningen Hypothesis." For a convenient summary, see Florentino García Martínez, "A 'Groningen' Hypothesis of Qumran Origins and Early History," *RevQ* 14 (1989-1990): 521-41; and A. S. van der Woude, "Once Again: The Wicked Priests in the Habakkuk Pesher from Cave 1 of Qumran," *RevQ* 17 (1996): 375-84.

35. Van der Woude, "Wicked Priest or Wicked Priests?" 357.

36. The text is, at the same time, a literary allusion to Isa 51:17 and Jer 25:15.

37. Cf. 13.2-3: "On the day of judgment [יום המשפט] God will destroy [יכלה] all who. . . ."

38. See Hans Burgmann, "Gerichtsherr und Generalankläger: Jonathan und Simon," *RevQ* 9 (1977): 3-72, esp. 52.

39. Accounts of Jonathan's last days are given in 1 Macc 12:39-48, 13:42, and in Josephus, *Ant.* 13.6.

better than the perfect.[40] If it can be shown that the *Habakkuk Pesher* refers to a past event even in the imperfect, what is there to prevent one from likewise regarding the imperfects in 11.14 and 12.5 as historical allusions to a past event, that is, to the Wicked Priest's death?[41] The protasis of this line of reasoning, however, cannot be demonstrated in 1QpHab. Hence it is not surprising that Burgmann provided no examples of a clear use of the imperfect as a past event in the *pesher*. In any case, Burgmann's intention was not so much to prove that the imperfect is a carrier of the past tense in 1QpHab as to undermine the notion that the imperfect has any temporal connotation at all. The possible use of an imperfect as referring to the past with a durative force led him to suspect that the *pesher* has a special affinity to the imperfect, an affinity that he further attempted to explain. Burgmann suggested that the imperfect, when concerned with judgments against the opponents of the Qumran group, is inextricably bound up with events presented as the will of God. On the other hand, the events to which the perfect verbs refer have not been divinely sanctioned or predetermined. Thus the perfect is used to describe the persecutions and animosities that arose among people as they separated themselves from the holiness of God. These grammatical and theological reflections brought Burgmann to the conclusion that the imperfect, under the influence of classical Hebrew, shows no evidence in 1QpHab for any real temporal distinction:

> We believe our analysis has shown that the prefix-conjugation in the [Habakkuk] pesher does not possess any particular force at all, whether it means that the activity has occurred, is occurring, or will occur, respectively, in the past, the present, or the future.[42]

Summary

This survey of the main interpretive views reveals how closely scholars have related the philological issue of interpreting the meanings of verbal forms to rather specific historical reconstructions of events relating to the Qumran Community. It is apparent how interpretations of the imperfect in the

40. Of course, Burgmann's entire argument is based on his view that the Wicked Priest was Jonathan.

41. Burgmann, "Gerichtsherr und Generalankläger: Jonathan und Simon," 51.

42. Ibid., 56: "Wir glauben aber durch unsere Darlegung gezeigt zu haben daß die Präfix-konjugation im Pescher überhaupt keinen Aussagewert besitzt, ob die Handlung in der Vergangenheit, der Gegenwart oder der Zukunft sich abspielte, abspielt, ab-spielen wird."

Habakkuk Pesher have often been made to serve hypotheses that, insofar as they are concerned with the identity of the Wicked Priest, are actually constructed on the basis of a vast quantity of other data. To read and interpret 1QpHab without raising the question of historical allusions to some degree is, of course, unavoidable. But one's interest in the historical allusions should not impede the thoroughgoing study of the world of the text itself, taking its character as literature seriously. The discussion below, therefore, turns to the *Habakkuk Pesher* itself so as to better discern the issues that relate to the use of the perfect and imperfect verb formations there. More specifically, the task is to see how the interpretive sections of the *pesher* have construed the verb tenses when they represent shifts from the verbs cited in the biblical text (lemma). It is hoped that the following discussion will contribute to a way of reading and understanding the *Habbakkuk Pesher* that, unlike the work of the scholars reviewed above, does not depend on the sorts of historical reconstruction that have too often been made decisive in the interpretation of its language.

4. The Imperfect and Perfect Verbal Formations in the *Habakkuk Pesher*

In relation to the biblical text, the following analysis will be less interested in text-critical issues regarding Habakkuk than in the biblical text as cited in 1QpHab.[43] Unless it can be demonstrated that the author's own context has imposed itself on the citation, it is only on the basis of that citation that a study of the relationship between the verb formations in the biblical text and the subsequent interpretation can proceed. Therefore, references to the MT are restricted to cases of lacunae that require the text, for purposes of the discussion, to be restored.

Column One

The first column of the manuscript is rather fragmentary and thus offers little evidence for how finite verbs of the biblical text of Habakkuk have been inter-

---

43. Unless otherwise noted, the text followed in the analysis below is that of Maurya P. Horgan, "Habakkuk Pesher (1QpHab)," in *The Dead Sea Scrolls: Hebrew, Aramaic, and Greek Texts with English Translations*, Vol. 6B: *Pesharim, Other Commentaries, and Related Documents* (ed. J. H. Charlesworth et al.; PTSDSSP 6B; Tübingen: Mohr [Siebeck] and Louisville: Westminster John Knox, 2002), 157-85.

preted. However, in lines 10-11, the author appears to have understood the imperfect verb of Hab 1:4 (תנוג, "[the Torah] grows ineffective") as already fulfilled in his own time. This is suggested perhaps by the end of line 11 which reads, "who rejected [מאשו] the Torah of God." Those whom the pesharist knew to have spurned the Torah were contributing to its growing inefficacy referred to by the biblical prophet.

Column Two

Column 2 begins with an interpretation of Hab 1:5, which was cited at the bottom of 1.16-17 (now lost) and continues into 2.1: "[you will not believe (MT: לוא תאמינו) when] it is told" (יסופר). The author applies the imperfect verb in the expression לוא תאמינו to his own time with two verbs that follow the negative לוֹא, one a perfect (line 4: האמינו) and one an imperfect (line 6: יאמינוא). It would appear that the lack of belief predicted by the prophet Habakkuk has been understood by the author as already fulfilled in his time (as both past and present[44] events). Less clear is whether the imperfect in line 6 could also refer to the future unbelief of those who have opposed the words of the Priest, that is, the Righteous Teacher. Moreover, if the missing verb in line 2 was a perfect (restoring לוֹא האמינו), then we would have to posit that the interpretation distinguished between the time of opposition to the Righteous Teacher and a (later) time when the traitors do (will) not believe in his teachings concerning the end of days (lines 5-6). This suggests that the biblical text has been applied to two interpretive horizons, as the author saw fit:[45] on the one hand, to the life of the Teacher himself; and, on the other, to an era that is later than the Teacher, that is, to the author's own time and beyond. During this latter period, when the Teacher is no longer alive, the pesharist maintains that unfaithfulness manifests itself through a lack of adherence to the Teacher's instructions.

A similar shift from the imperfect to the perfect may be observed in line

44. It is, of course, possible that the imperfect in line 6 denotes a continuous action that includes the past: "they were not believing as they heard." Since such an interpretation cannot, at the same time, exclude the ongoing unbelief of those opposed to the Teacher and the Community (whereas a rendering in the present does not exclude past activity), it is best to render the verb as a present or, possibly, future.

45. So van der Ploeg, "L'usage du parfait et l'imparfait," 30: "L'auteur se croit donc autorié à interpréter les temps des verbes de son texte selon son besoin" ("The author did not consider himself authorized to interpret the *tempus* of the verbs from his text according to his need").

9, which takes its point of departure from the last word of Hab 1:4 (line 1: יסופר). As the prophet does not expect belief to occur even when a special deed, if performed, is reported, so the author regards the unbelief of his day as no surprise since God has already declared (line 9: ספר) through the Priest what is going to happen to his people. The deed of the biblical text is interpreted as the special knowledge God has revealed to the Teacher about what is to happen in the final generation (line 7).

The text of Hab 1:6 and its interpretation offer a subtler shift, from a participle to the use of a perfect and an imperfect. Through the prophet, it is announced that God is raising (line 10: הנני מקים) the Chaldeans. In the interpretation, however, a perfect verb initially describes the activity of the Kittim who have taken possession of lands (line 14: יר[ש]ו[ו]), while an imperfect is used in characterizing them as those who "do not believe [לוא יאמינו] in the statutes of God" (line 14). Since the imperfect verb's primary function is descriptive, it is not simply to be taken as a reference to the author's future. As columns 3-6 show, the Kittim are known to the author as a present force whose activities are predominantly cast in the imperfect formation.

Column Three

The bottom of column 2 is lost, but can be partially restored because it is from the text of Hab 1:6. Therefore, the term ילכו ("they will go") of the *pesher* in 3.1 may be understood as an interpretive reading of the participle in the biblical text — to be restored as ההולך (2.15). The subject of the verb in this case is the Kittim, whose activity the author, near the bottom of column 2, chooses to describe with the imperfect. This shift from participle to imperfect again raises the question whether the imperfect signals that the Kittim are in the future vis-à-vis the author's perspective. A future sense here cannot, however, be taken for granted since activities ascribed to the Kittim (as in 6.4-6) are elsewhere described in the interpretive sections of the *pesher* with the participle. In the remainder of this column, the *pesher* does not deviate from any of the verb forms that are imperfects in the biblical text as cited from Hab 1:7-9.[46] However, the degree to which the pesharist regards

---

46. The consistent use of the imperfect in the interpretation sections of col. 3 does not represent any real temporal shift from the four perfect verbs in the biblical citation. This is because in two cases the perfects from Hab 1:8 bear a stative force (line 6: קלו קול, "they are swift"; חדו, "they are keen"), while the remaining two instances, from 1:7 and 1:8 respectively, do not strictly refer to the past alone (line 3: יצא, "they have arisen/go out"; line 8: חש, "they have hastened/hasten").

the Kittim as contemporary is underscored by the fact that only imperfects are used to describe what they do, whereas the biblical citations contain both imperfects and perfects (though here these do not denote anything in the past).

Column Four

No deviation in tense or formation is apparent in this column. The biblical text, which may be restored from Hab 1:9b (bottom of column 3) and which continues from Hab 1:10a-b on lines 1 and 4, contains verbs in the imperfect formation, except for the participle מְשַׂחֵק ("mocks") in line 1. Since the *pesher* applies the biblical text to the Kittim, there would not be any reason for the author to have adjusted the tense. Thus the perfect forms attached to the conjunction, which occur among a series of imperfects, are each to be understood as perfects + *waw*-consecutive (line 2: וּבֹז; line 3: וְקִלְסוּ; line 8: וְהֶרְסוּם). The next citation, beginning on line 9, is from Hab 1:11, in which a perfect form occurs followed by two imperfect forms with the *waw*-consecutive (i.e., *wayyiqtōl*): "the wind has changed [חָלַף] and it has passed on [וַיַּעֲבֹר], and this one has made [וַיָּשֶׂם] his might as God." The text is interpreted as a reference to the leaders of the Kittim, whose license to raze the land is blamed on the House of Absalom. The pesharist assumes that the advice of the House of Absalom lies in his past, and that the biblical text refers to the resulting threat posed by the Kittim.[47]

Column Five

The column begins with the conclusion of a citation from Hab 1:12-13a (lines 1-2) that began in 4.16. The author of the *pesher* interprets two perfects of the biblical text (line 1: שַׂמְתּוֹ, "you set him,"[48] and יְסַדְתּוֹ, "you established him") with the imperfect verb יִתֵּן (line 4, "he will give"). The biblical text as cited forms part of an affirmation that God will not depart from his decree that the wicked nations will be punished. The *pesher* that follows slips the Community (God's elect, line 4) into the equation as the object ("him") of the perfect

---

47. Hab 1:11b is apparently cited again in line 13, followed by a brief interpretation in lines 14-16. The lacunae-ridden text does not, however, preserve any verb form.

48. In the Habakkuk text, the singular pronominal direct object suffix refers back to the Chaldaeans (cf. 1:6a).

verbs in line 1. Thus the "one who is too pure to look upon evil" (Hab 1:13a) — that is, the one through whom the wicked are to be chastised — is not so much God (as in the MT) as the righteous elect (5.7-8). In choosing to interpret the perfect with imperfect verbs, the author was admitting that God's certain judgment on the nations lies as yet, from his perspective, in the future. He anticipated that this divine justice would be brought about through the assistance of the elect. The contrasting perfect verbs of שמרו (line 5) and זנו (line 7) express what for the author characterized the elect: they "have kept the commandments in their hardship" and "have not whored after their eyes in the age of wickedness."

Several lines later, the *pesher* makes a change in the other direction: the imperfect of the Hab 1:13b at line 8: ותחרוש, "and you are silent," if taken as a verb with the *waw*-consecutive, has been rendered with the perfect נדמו (line 10, "they were silent") and augmented with the phrases עזרוהו (line 11, "they did not help him") and מאס התורה (line 11, "they [collective sg.] rejected the law"). God's silence in the biblical text is applied in the *pesher* to the silence of the House of Absalom and the men of their council. Whereas the texts interpreted in relation to the Kittim in other passages have been altered to or retained in the imperfect (see above), the pesharist has now deliberately chosen three perfect verbs (in lines 10-11) to describe the lack of support for the Righteous Teacher by the House of Absalom before the Man of Lies. God's silence in Habakkuk is correlated to the Community's disappointment at the refusal of another group to come to their aid. In contrast to the Kittim, whose activity is a present reality, the interpretation here refers to specific events of the past known to the author and his Community.

Column Six

The citation of Hab 1:14-16 in 5.12-16 differs from the MT in one apparently significant way. The MT's perfect העלה, "he brought up" (Hab 1:15a), corresponds to the *pesher*'s imperfect יעלה ("he [i.e., humankind = אדם] will bring up") in 5.13. Whether or not this difference resulted from error or deliberate adjustment in scribal transmission, this and other imperfects in the *pesher*'s biblical text (especially ויספהו, "and he gathers it," in 5.14) are interpreted at the top of column 6 with an plural imperfect verb ויסיפו (line 1, "they [i.e., the Kittim] will gather"). Again, the imperfects of Hab 1:16-17 until line 12 of column 6 are all applied to the Kittim. The Kittim gather wealth and are offering sacrifices (lines 3-4: המה זבחים) to their standards, and they will be without pity when they cause death by the sword.

Column Seven

A portion of Hab 2:2 that was lost at the bottom of column 6 is repeated in column 7, line 3: למען ירוץ/ \ירוץ הקורא בו ("so that he who reads it will go quickly"). The participle and the imperfect in this much discussed text are interpreted by the author with a phrase using the Hiphil perfect: "the Righteous Teacher to whom God made known [הודיעו] all the mysteries of the words of his servants the prophets." The interpretation refers directly to the prophet Habakkuk who, identified with the 1st person singular figure in Hab 2:1-2, is acknowledged by the pesharist as the recorder, but not the interpreter, of the vision from God. The alteration of *tempus* to the perfect tense locates the interpretations revealed to the Righteous Teacher in the author's past;[49] nevertheless, the impression is left that the Teacher's interpretations of Habakkuk have a direct bearing on events that the author regards as yet to come: God "will prolong the final age and it will surpass all which the prophets have said" (7.7-8). Despite this openly futuristic language, it is clear that the author remains concerned with potential slackness within his Community in the present. This "delay" is only apparent (7.13); the opening gap between the time of the Teacher and their own day[50] is in fact a divine extension of the final age. Therefore, the "men of truth," also called "doers of the Torah" (7.10-11), are *now* to orient themselves to the *tempus* of God and not become lax in "the service of truth" (7.12-13).

At the bottom of column 7, one perfect and one imperfect verb of Hab 2:4a (line 14: עופלה, "it is swelled," and יושרה, "it is [not] upright," respectively), both with "soul" as their subject, have been interpreted with a phrase containing the imperfect (line 15: יכפלו, "they will double"). This formal shift, however, should not necessarily be understood as a deliberate change of tense on the author's part, because the perfect in the biblical text already bears the stative sense.[51]

Column Eight

The next identifiable shift in tense relates to the citation and interpretation of Hab 2:5-6 in 8.3-13. The relatively lengthy biblical citation in 8.3-8a consists of

49. See above under Column Two.
50. This passage thus militates against the assertion of Doudna (*4Q Pesher Nahum*, 625) that "[n]one of the sobriquet-bearing figures in the Qumran pesharim [including the Teacher of Righteousness] are from a past generation in the world of these texts."
51. Hab 2:4a: "See, his soul in him is swelled within him and is not upright."

imperfects — exceptions are the two *waw*-consecutives in line 5 (ויאספו, "and they have been gathered," and ויקבצו, "and they have been amassed") — which are either free-standing or occur with *waw*-conjunctives (line 3: יבגיד, "it will make faithless"; lines 3-4: לוא ינוה, "he will not abide"; line 4: לוא ישבע, "he will not be satisfied"; line 6: ישאו, "they will lift"; and line 7: ויומרו, "and they will say"). In the interpretation section (lines 8b-13), the verbs without exception take the past tense: the imperfects + *waw*-conjunctive in Habakkuk have been interpreted as imperfects + *waw*-consecutive. The interpretation focuses on the activities that mark the rule of the Wicked Priest: at the beginning he was called by the name of truth (line 9), but, corrupted by wealth, he became a traitor and committed acts of defilement (lines 10-11 and 13, respectively). Clearly, the author has perceived the prophet's words as already fulfilled in the ruling activity of the Wicked Priest.

Column Nine

Habakkuk 2:7-8a, cited in the previous column (8.13-15), contains five verbs. The first three of these, from Hab 2:7, relate to a culpable addressee who is expected to undergo a punishing torture at the hands of tormentors. The first two verbs are imperfects attached to *waw*-conjunctives (lines 1-2: ויקומו, "and they [your biters] shall arise," and ויקיצו, "and they [your torturers] shall make sick"), while the third verb is a perfect with *waw*-consecutive ("and you shall become to them as prey"). That is, these verbs are to be understood in the context of the biblical text as either future or present. The next two verbs in Hab 2:8a, both from the root שלל, are perfect and imperfect respectively. Here, much in the same vein as Hab 2:7, the person/reader who is rhetorically addressed can expect, because of past plundering activities (8.15: שלותה), to be plundered again in the future (8.15: וישלוכה) by all the remaining peoples. The text of Hab 2:7 is regarded by the author as fulfilled in "the priest who "[put as]ide the statutes of [God]"[52] and, as a result, has already had to pay the price with "evil maladies" and "acts of vengeance" on his body (9.1-2).[53] The plundering referred to in Hab 2:8a, however, is interpreted in 9.4-5 as a reference to "the last priests of Jerusalem who shall gather [יקבצו] wealth and spoil by plundering the peoples." Thus, whereas the two references to retribu-

52. The form to be restored, with Brownlee (*Midrash Pesher of Habakkuk*, 148) is ויסי[ר], that is, a *waw*-conjunctive imperfect.

53. The text reads "they inflicted [עשו] evil maladies on him and vengeful acts on the body of his flesh." To emend the verb to יעשו in order to conform to the other uses of the imperfect when the text refers to the Wicked Priest's punishment reaches prematurely to harmonization.

tion envisaged in the biblical text are, as in parallel, concerned with the same event, the pesharist has applied them to acts of divine punishment both past and future. The time of the priest, who is arguably to be identified as the Wicked Priest, is distinguished from the time of the "last priests," whose deeds are deliberately referred to in the imperfect. The shift from the imperfect of Hab 2:7 to the perfect sense in the interpretation seems clear enough. More subtle, however, is the difference between the *pesher* and the biblical text of Hab 2:8a; the contrast comes into sharper focus when the relation between the verbs within each context is recognized. Here, as already observed, the text of Habakkuk contains a perfect and an imperfect verb, the latter of which denotes the reversal of the addressee's fortunes. In the *pesher,* the distinction between the perfect and imperfect is shifted in the interpretation (lines 5-7) to the use of the imperfect (line 5: יקבוצו הון, "they [the last priests] will gather wealth") — to be understood as present or future — in the first instance and another imperfect (line 6: ינתן הונם, "their wealth will be given over"), which clearly denotes the future,[54] in the second.

With respect to the lemma from Hab 2:8b (line 9) and its interpretation (lines 9-12), the author's tendency to associate the Wicked Priest with verbs in the perfect comes again to expression. This is not surprising. The biblical citation, which contains neither a perfect nor an imperfect verb, is interpreted as a reference to the Wicked Priest's punishment by God at the hands of his enemies. The verb used on line 10 is נתנו, that is, "he [God] gave him up" to the power of his enemies,[55] and this contrasts with the imperfect ינתן on line 6, which has been applied to the last priests whose punishment, from the author's perspective, has yet to occur "in the last days" when "their wealth together with their plunder will be handed over to the army of the Kittim" (lines 6-7). There is no internal evidence that the perfect should be read as anything other than a historical allusion, especially if the interpretation builds on the pesharist's comments on the Wicked Priest in lines 1-2 of this column (see above).[56] Thus for the author, at least some of the Wicked

54. The future sense would be hard to dispute, as the verb ינתן follows the phrase "at the end of days" in line 6.

55. The unambiguous perfect in the text should not be emended to יתננו (i.e. "and [God] will give him"), *contra* the harmonizing proposal of Doudna, *4Q Pesher Nahum,* 619: the original author's יתננו was mistakenly copied as נתנו by subsequent scribes.

56. A passage in 4QpPsᵃ (4Q171) frgs. 1-10 4.7-10 may be compared with the present text. Using the perfect tense, the Psalms *pesher* likewise refers to the opposition between the Wicked Priest and the Teacher of Righteousness. However, whereas the Wicked Priest's retribution is expressed with the perfect in 1QpHab, 4QpPsᵃ has the imperfect: "And [God will] pay hi[m] his reward (ולו י שלם [אל את] גמולו), by giving him up into the power of the ruthless ones of the

Priest's punishment for opposition to the Righteous Teacher was made manifest in the past.

Column Ten

The use of the imperfect in both the citation of Hab 2:9-11 (9.12-15) and the interpretation in 9.6–10.5 seems, at first glance, to suggest that no temporal shift has occurred. Upon closer examination of 9.16, however, it appears that the biblical text has been applied to what most scholars have reconstructed as "the p[riest]" ([וֹה]כֹה).[57] If this priest is to be identified as the Wicked Priest mentioned in 9.9, then it is likely that in the commentary on Hab 2:9-11 (esp. v. 10) in 10.3-5 we have a reference to his future judgment: "This is the house of judgment where God will render [יֹתֹ] his judgment in the midst of many peoples, and from there he will raise him for judgment and in their midst he will declare him guilty [יֹרשֹיעֹנוֹ] and judge him [יֹשפֹטֹנוֹ] with the fire of sulphur." Whereas the eschatological overtones of the second and third phrases are unmistakable, there is less certainty about the first phrase. Does the use of the imperfect verb in relation to the "house of judgment"[58] mean that, with respect to the time of the document's composition, the priest was still alive? If so, this would seem to contradict the allusions to his divine punishment in 9.1-2.[59] That being said, it should be observed that 9.1-2 does not refer to the

---

nations to take [vengeance] against him." If both *pesharim* refer to the same event, is one to conclude that the Psalms *pesher*, due to its use of the imperfect, was composed before the *Habakkuk Pesher*, which refers to it in the perfect? A satisfactory answer to this question is not easy to provide. See a recent discussion by Marcus E. M. Wood, "History and Prophecy in the Qumran Pesharim: An Examination of the Key Figures and Groups in the Dead Sea Scrolls by way of Their Prophetic Designations" (Ph.D. diss., University of Durham, 2001), 175-77, who, after discussing some interpretive possibilities for relating the documents and suggesting that the interpretation in 4QpPs[a] is influenced by the imperfect of the psalm, admits that the matter requires further attention.

57. See, e.g., Dupont-Sommer, "Le Commentaire Habacuc," 137; Vermes in all editions of his English translation of the Scrolls (see, most recently, *The Dead Sea Scrolls in English* [4th ed.; London: Penguin, 1997], 483); Maurya B. Horgan, *Pesharim: Qumran Interpretations of Biblical Books* (CBQMS 8; Washington, D.C.: Catholic Biblical Association, 1979), 18 and 45; Brownlee, *The Midrash Pesher of Habakkuk*, 158 and 160 (traces not only of the כ but also of a ו).

58. See Brownlee's discussion of the phrase as a place of infernal punishment in *The Midrash Pesher of Habakkuk*, 162-63, and cf. esp. *Jub.* 10:5, 9 (place of punishment for demonic spirits); 22:22 (of idolaters); and Job 17:13 (place in Sheol reserved for the evil person).

59. It is immaterial whether the pronominal suffix in "his judgment" (line 4) refers to God or the priest. In the former case, the interpretation is still ultimately concerned with divine retribution against the priest.

priest's death as such, and the first phrase here says nothing about it either. Thus perhaps the question of whether the priest was alive or dead at the time of composition is the wrong one to ask, as the text seems to be referring to divine vengeance on a much grander scale. The setting for God's activity against the priest is eschatological,[60] and the three phrases denote a sequence of events. Without making any claims about the status of the priest, the author is more concerned to underscore that an event in the life of the Wicked Priest that he has interpreted as divine retribution (9.1-2 and 10) will be brought to its proper completion in the eschatological future. Thus nothing can be inferred from column 10 alone about the composition of the *Habakkuk Pesher* in relation to the time of the Wicked Priest. However, with the apparently past punishment mentioned in 9.1-2 and 10 in view, it is not unreasonable to infer that for the author the past sins of the Wicked Priest were proleptically followed by divine punishment in the past, while column 10 allows one to infer that these sins will be avenged by God at an undisclosed (eschatological?) point in the future.

In column 10, the participle (line 6: בונה, "who builds") and imperfect with the *waw*-conjunctive (line 6: ויכונן, "and he will establish") in the citation of Hab 2:12-13 have been interpreted with a perfect verb (line 9: התעה, "he caused to go astray") that describes the Man of Lies. The activity of the Man of Lies, which in this case involves building, is regarded as already fulfilled. The punishment of him and his followers, however, has not yet occurred, but lies in the future (line 12: יבואו, "they [i.e., fiery judgements] will come"). The image of "fire" (line 13), as in lines 4-5 of the column (see above), suggests that the punishment being referred to here is eschatological.

Column Eleven

In this column, several participles (line 2: משקה, "giving drink," and מספח, "spilling out"; line 3: שכר, "making drunk") and a perfect (line 3: הבט, "he looked at") from Hab 2:15 have been interpreted in phrases that contain perfects (line 5: רדף, "he pursued"; line 7: הופיע, "he appeared"). The perfect verb of the biblical text, which follows the particle למען ("in order that, so that"), is not, strictly speaking, referring to a past event. However, since the

---

60. I understand the phrase "he will raise him up" as a reference to an afterlife resuscitation, whether spiritual or physical, along the lines of what is foreseen in Dan 12:2 (though there a different, intransitive verb — "they shall awake" — is used). The post-mortem setting for "raising up" — e.g., from Sheol — is already attested in the Old Testament/Hebrew Bible. See Pss 30:4; 40:3; and 1 Sam 2:6.

pesher is making a historical allusion to the well-known confrontation be-tween the Wicked Priest and the Righteous Teacher on the Day of Atonement, there was no reason for the author to use any verb formation other than the perfect.

With respect to the citation of Hab 2:16 and its interpretation at the bot-tom of column 11 (lines 8-15), no alterations of tense are apparent. This in-stance, in which no change has occurred, should not be glossed over because the perfect *and* imperfect forms of the biblical text (so line 8: שבעתה, "you have been sated," and line 10: תסוב עליכה, "will turn against you") are both retained and applied to the Wicked Priest (two perfects: גבר, "prevailed" [line 12]; לוא מל, "he did not circumcise" [line 13]; an imperfect + *waw*-consecutive: וילך, "and he walked"; and one imperfect: תבלענו, "will con-sume him").[61] Up to this point in the document, the imperfects of the biblical text have been regularly changed to perfects when the Wicked Priest's activi-ties have been recounted. The fact that the distinction in tense in the biblical text is upheld in the interpretation here indicates that the author intended תבלענו to denote the future from his perspective. This is an instance, then, in which the author left the tenses of the biblical text alone, since they already provided the tense distinction he wanted to make. The result in the interpre-tation, however, is that the author has intensified the future thrust of the im-perfect. Much as in the retention of the imperfects from the biblical text in column 10, the author underlines the belief that divine retribution will visit the Wicked Priest.

Columns Twelve and Thirteen

Another clear reference in the interpretation to the judgment of the Wicked Priest is found in 12.5. Again, as in 10.4-5 and 11.15, the pesharist has probably retained the imperfect of Hab 2:17 (to be restored at 11.17: יכסך, "it [the viola-tion of Lebanon] will cover/overwhelm you"). The expression ישופטנו אל לכלה (line 5: "God will judge him to destruction") implies an eschatological reckoning; in 13.2-4 the same two roots are combined in a reference to "the day of judgment" (יום המשפט) when God "will destroy [יכלה] all who serve idols and the wicked from the earth."

Since 11.14 (similarly 10.4-5 and 12), the author has associated the imper-

61. The interpretation of Hab 2:16 is applied to "the priest" (line 12), that is, the Wicked Priest who is mentioned in the interpretations immediately preceding (11.4) and following (12.2).

fects with final judgment. 12.14 and 13.2-3 are no exception. In 12.14 the interpretation of Hab 2:18 states that the nations who have fashioned idols will not
be able to save them (יצילם) on "the day of judgment." The imperfect, while
not unexpected, does not correspond in sense to anything in the biblical text,
but rather supplements it as it describes the consequences of the nations'
trust in their idols. These nations are again implicated in 13.2-3. According to
the author's interpretation of Hab 2:19-20, they will be destroyed on the day
of judgment. Again, the reference to eschatological judgment has no direct
correspondence in the biblical text.

5. Concluding Observations on the *Habakkuk Pesher*

Several conclusions are possible following this reading of 1QpHab. Firstly and
generally, it should be noted that the numerous changes and shifts in tense
from the biblical text to the interpretation ought not to be understood as a
lack of respect on the part of the author for the biblical text. The alterations
stem rather from the pesharist's belief that he was living "at the end of days"
(2:5; 9:6: לאחרית הימים), by virtue of which, through the Righteous Teacher,
he (and his Community) possessed a historical perspective that the prophet
Habakkuk did not have.

Secondly, the analysis above reminds us to consider the literary genre to
which the *Habakkuk Pesher* belongs. Though there is some ambiguity, and
hence debate, concerning which exactly among the Qumran documents
ought to be properly labelled as a *"pesher,"* the following definition, offered by
Isaac Rabinowitz, certainly avails here:

> a literary composition which (1) states in ordinary language the realities
> thought to be presaged (i.e., prefigured or portended) by the words of
> some portion of the Hebrew Bible, words regarded whether as already
> fulfilled or as still awaiting fulfilment; and which (2) indicates the person,
> persons, or epochs upon whom the realities of the presaged words had ei-
> ther come, or were yet to come.[62]

However, as the study above suggests, Rabinowitz's definition, while helpful,
needs to be augmented in one area, especially as it relates to 1QpHab: The
uses of the imperfect and perfect in the text should not lead us to highlight

---

62. Isaac Rabinowitz, "Pêsher/Pittârôn," *RevQ* 8 (1973): 219-32, citation from 231. For later
discussions, see George J. Brooke, "Qumran Pesher: Towards the Redefinition of a Genre," *RevQ*
10 (1979-1981): 483-503; and Charlesworth, *The Pesharim and Qumran History*, 68 and 70.

the author's concern with the future and past, respectively. In one sense, we might say that it is not events surrounding the Teacher, the Wicked Priest, and other figures that gave rise to the *pesher,* but rather — and more fundamentally — the author is determined to interpret present circumstances for his Community, circumstances in which the anticipated advent of the Kittim invited contemporary prophetic commentary within the context of the Community's self-understanding. Though allowing for a degree of continuity, the time and particular concerns of the author are, in principle, to be distinguished from the time and concerns with which the Righteous Teacher was faced. Perhaps this explains why so much of the focus is devoted to the activities of the Kittim in columns 3-9 in the document. Since the Teacher's claims about interpretation and his struggle against his opponents provided the frame of reference for this self-understanding, the recalling of events covering selected moments in the Teacher's life, which are seen to have consequences in the future (e.g., for the Wicked Priest), function as a way of reassuring, exhorting, and challenging the Community in the present to adhere to its identity as "men of truth" and "doers of the Torah" (7.10-11).

Thirdly, though the use of the imperfect is not consistent in 1QpHab, a pattern nonetheless comes into focus. There appears to be a linear development within the *Habakkuk Pesher*. From column 3 to column 9, the imperfect verbs in the commentary sections function as references to the Kittim and to "the last priests of Jerusalem." In these instances, the imperfect denotes a historical reality, whether it be events in the author's present or imminent future. This use, however, recedes in columns 10 to 13; it is replaced by an increasing emphasis on the application of the imperfect to eschatological judgment in relation to the Wicked Priest (10.3-5; 11.14; 13.5), to the Man of Lies and his followers (10.12-13), and to the nations (12.14; 13.2-3).

Fourthly and finally, the use of the verb forms appears to have resulted from a deliberate choice by the pesharist. This is already evident at an early stage in the *pesher.* 1.10-11 suggests that the shift from the imperfect of the biblical text to the perfect was prompted by the author's conviction (probably inspired by the Righteous Teacher) that some of the prophet Habakkuk's words had already been fulfilled. In column 2, an imperfect of the cited biblical text (line 1) is rendered in both the perfect (line 4) and imperfect (line 6) in the interpretation. The pesharist's choice of tenses here sets the tone for the remainder of the document. The prophet's message has not only been fulfilled in some recent events, but is also being and will be fulfilled in the future. The use of the tenses throughout the *pesher,* then, is closely related to the author's perception of how the "prophecies" of Habakkuk are being fulfilled in human history and beyond. The claim of the pesharist to have the correct interpretation of Habakkuk is, of course, inspired by his view of the Righteous Teacher "to whom God made known all the mysteries of the words of his servants the prophets" (7.4-5), but whose teachings the author himself has not apparently divulged. However, though the Teacher was pivotal in the Community's self-understanding as God's people in an eschatological age, it is in relation to the composer of the *pesher*, who does not make any specific claim that the interpretations therein derive directly from the Teacher, that the tenses are best understood.

The Temporal Relationship
between the Covenant Renewal Rite
and the Initiation Process in 1QS

MICHAEL A. DAISE

1. Introduction

This essay examines the temporal relationship between two Qumran ritual processes attested in 1QS: the covenant renewal ceremony at 1.18–2.25; and the initiation procedure at 6.13-23 and 5.7-11 (see below).[1] After describing each ritual, I will argue that, on the basis of 1QS, there is no compelling reason to believe their respective times of observance coincided — or, at least, that they coincided by design. The first ritual was to be done once per year, likely at an annual feast, while the latter began and ended at the times inquirers sought membership in the sect, whenever that may have fallen within the liturgical cycle. Though the "indefinite period" (6.14b-15a) of the initiation process could be read as a mechanism created to calibrate the two, evidence from the penal code challenges such an assumption. Penal "redoings" of the initiation

1. The following discussion will be restricted to the *Serekh* recension reflected in 1QS, bracketing the diachronic issues raised by the 4QS/5QS manuscripts. For that discussion, see, e.g., P. S. Alexander, "The Redaction History of *Serekh Ha-Yaḥad:* A Proposal," *RevQ* 17 (1996): 437-38, 448-53; and S. Metso, *The Textual Development of the Qumran Community Rule* (STDJ 21; Leiden: Brill, 1997), 143-49.

It is my delight to dedicate this essay to my *Doktorvater,* James H. Charlesworth. The interest in Jewish ritual that is apparent in this study is in many ways indebted to the premium he consistently placed on Second Temple *halakah* during my graduate studies. An earlier version of this paper was presented in the Qumran Section at the November 2003 national meeting of the Society of Biblical Literature (Atlanta, Georgia). I am thankful for the comments made by participants at that session, though responsibility for the argument remains mine. Note that all translations are my own.

rite likely began and ended from the time offenses were made, and this suggests the same for "first-time" performances of that rite by candidates for membership. They, too, would have begun and would have culminated, more or less, on the date inquiry was made.

2. The Covenant Renewal Ceremony and Initiation Process

The Covenant Renewal Ceremony

As set forth in 1QS 1.18–2.18,[2] the covenant renewal rite consisted of four declarations and affirmations exchanged between the priests and Levites, on one side, and "all who enter the covenant," on the other (1.18-20). In the *first* declaration, the priests and Levites together blessed the God of deliverances and all his faithful deeds (1.19); in the *second,* the priests rehearsed God's works of justice and compassionate favor, after which the Levites recounted Israel's blameworthy transgressions and sins (1.21-24). In the *third,* the priests blessed "all the men of God's lot" and the Levites cursed "all" those "of Belial's lot" (2.1-9). Finally, in the *fourth,* the priests and Levites, again together, cursed any member who, after entering the covenant, would allow himself to be "turned back" into apostasy (2.11-17). To the first, third, and fourth of these pronouncements, those entering the covenant would respond, "Amen, Amen" (1.20; 2.10, 18). To the Levites' declaration of iniquities in the second, they issued a confession of sin, followed by praise for God's mercy:

> We are perverted, [we ha]ve transgressed, [we ha]ve sinned, we have acted wickedly, we [and o]ur fathers before us, in our [wa]lking [. . .] truth. And the [G]od [of Israel] is just, [as are] his judgments on us and [our] fathers. Yet he has dealt out his merciful compassion upon us from age to age. (1QS 1.24–2.1)[3]

2. As J. T. Milik originally suggested, and B. Nitzan has subsequently developed, the rite described at 1QS 1.18–2.25 is likely just one version of a more variegated ritual, also found elsewhere among the Scrolls, most notably 4QBerakhot (4Q286-290). See Milik, "*Milkî-ṣedeq et Milkî-reša'* dans les anciens écrits juifs et chrétiens," *JJS* 23 (1972): 136; Nitzan, "4QBerakhot (4Q286-290): A Covenantal Ceremony in the Light of Related Texts," *RevQ* 16 (1995): 478-506; and idem, "The Benedictions from Qumran for the Annual Covenant Renewal Ceremony," in *The Dead Sea Scrolls Fifty Years After Their Discovery: Proceedings of the Jerusalem Congress, July 20-25, 1997* (ed. L. H. Schiffman, E. Tov, and J. C. VanderKam; Jerusalem: Israel Exploration Society with the Shrine of the Book, Israel Museum, 2000), 263-71.

3. The text is that of E. Qimron and J. H. Charlesworth, "Rule of the Community (1QS)," in *The Dead Sea Scrolls: Hebrew, Aramaic, and Greek Texts with English Translations*, Vol. 1: *Rule*

The passage that immediately follows, 2.19-25, describes an "entrance" of individuals by station. Priests, Levites, then "all the people" — in thousands, hundreds, fifties, and tens[4] — were to enter "into the Rule . . . one after another," so that "every man of Israel may know, each, the place of his station in the Community of God, for an eternal council" (2.22-23). The ceremony was slated to be observed שנה בשנה (2.19), which is usually taken to mean "annually" and identified with a feast — S. Talmon and M. Weise suggested Yom Kippur;[5] J. T. Milik, A. R. C. Leaney, and many following them have preferred Shavuot.[6] A concluding commentary in the scroll casts this array as an emblem of hierarchical harmony:

> And no one shall be lower than the place of his station nor higher than the place of his lot, for all will be in a Community of truth, of benevolent humility, of merciful love and of just purpose, each to his fellow in a holy council — sons of an everlasting assembly. (1QS 2.23-25)

A. Dupont-Sommer took the activity in 2.19-25 to be a separate rite: a "yearly review of the whole sacred militia," distinct from the renewal ceremony of 1.18–2.18.[7] Various clues from the context, however, suggest the two were of a piece. Weise argued for their unity on philological grounds, suggesting that the use of עבר + בסרכ in 2.19-21 is an abbreviation of the fuller formula בברית (א)לפני[8] אל + עבר at 1.16;[9] and one might expand this to in-

---

of the Community and Related Documents (ed. J. H. Charlesworth et al.; PTSDSSP 1; Tübingen: J. C. B. Mohr [Paul Siebeck] and Louisville: Westminster John Knox, 1994), 1-51.

4. On the hypothetical aspect of these groupings, see N. Jastram, "Hierarchy at Qumran," in Legal Texts and Legal Issues: Proceedings of the Second Meeting of the International Organization for Qumran Studies Cambridge 1995 (ed. M. Bernstein, F. García Martínez, and J. Kampen; STDJ 23; Leiden: Brill, 1997), 352-53.

5. Weise also entertained another prominent day of repentance. See S. Talmon, "The 'Manual of Benedictions' of the Sect of the Judaean Desert," RevQ 8 (1960): 498-500; and M. Weise, Kultzeiten und Kultischer Bundesschluss in der "Ordensregel" vom Toten Meer (SPB 3; Leiden: E. J. Brill, 1961), 75-82, 111.

6. See J. T. Milik, Ten Years of Discovery in the Wilderness of Judaea (trans. J. Strugnell; SBT 26; London: SCM, 1959), 101-3, 116-18; and A. R. C. Leaney, The Rule of Qumran and Its Meaning: Introduction, Translation and Commentary (NTL; Philadelphia: Westminster, 1966), 95-107, 135-36.

7. See A. Dupont-Sommer, Observations sur Le Manuel de Discipline découvert près de la Mer Morte (Paris: Librairie Adrien-Masonneuve, 1951), 21-24; and idem, The Jewish Sect of Qumran and the Essenes: New Studies on the Dead Sea Scrolls (trans. R. D. Barnett; New York: Macmillan, 1956), 95-97; quotation from 96.

8. Note the erasure of א with scribal dots.

9. Weise, Kultzeiten und Kultischer Bundesschluss, 69-70, 70 n. 2. M. Delcor, similarly, ap-

clude the interchangeability of עבר with בוא, which, together, span 1.16–2.25.[10] Another consideration is an inference that may be drawn from the broader literary structure of cols. 1-3. The theme of covenant renewal introduced at 1.16 does not, in fact, end at 2.18 or 2.25, but extends further, to 3.12. After 1.16-18a summons all who enter the Rule to enter the covenant, 1.18b–2.25a describes how that is to be done by those who so choose, followed by 2.25b–3.12, which rehearses the fate of "anyone who refuses to enter [the covenant of G]od" (וכול המואס לבוא]בברית א[ל), bidding them, in the end, to rethink their decision. Standing, as it does, in the midst of this larger unit, 2.19-25 would be altogether out of place if it were not itself intimately tied to the idea of "entering the covenant." Given this, and given the language of עבר and בוא that spans 1.16–2.25, it seems best to conclude that the activity described in 2.19-25 was also part and parcel of the covenant renewal ceremony outlined in 1.18–2.18. That is, after the priests, Levites, and all the other members began the "entrance into the covenant" by exchanging the declarations and responses of 1.18–2.18, they concluded this action by "entering" in hierarchical sequence according to 2.19-25 — one by one, each in accordance with his station. And, insofar as the temporal rubric of 2.19 would then apply as much to the first part of this rite as to the last,[11] all of this would have been done regularly, שנה בשנה.

The Initiation Rite

The initiation process at 6.13-23 is well known and much rehearsed. According to its rubrics, when anyone from Israel presented himself to join the Council of the Community, his insight and praxis were first examined by "the man appointed at the head of the רבים" (i.e., the *paqid*), after which, should he "attain the discipline," he was brought into the covenant and further catechized "in all the ordinances of the Community" (6.13-15). After an unspecified period des-

---

pealed to the use of עבר at 2.19-21 and 2.11 (*Religion d'Israël et Proche Orient ancien: des Phéniciens aux Esséniens* [Leiden: E. J. Brill, 1976], 369). But, for the possibility of עבר as עבד in 2.11, see Charlesworth, PTSDSSP 1:11 n. 31.

10. עבר: 1.16, 18, 20, 24; 2.10-11, 19-21 (for 2.11, see previous note); בוא: 1.16; 2.12, 18. On this interchangeability, see Delcor, *Religion d'Israël et Proche Orient ancien*, 368; and S. Pfann, "The Essene Yearly Renewal Ceremony and the Baptism of Repentance," in *The Provo International Conference on the Dead Sea Scrolls: Technological Innovations, New Texts, Reformulated Issues* (ed. D. W. Parry and E. C. Ulrich; STDJ 30; Leiden: E. J. Brill, 1999), 341-42.

11. As noted by Weise and others. See, e.g., Weise, *Kultzeiten und Kultischer Bundesschluss*, 70 n. 2; Delcor, *Religion d'Israël et Proche Orient ancien*, 369.

ignated only as ואחר ("and afterwards"), he was to stand before the רבים, who were questioned about his affairs and decided by lot whether he would "approach" or "depart" their fellowship (6.15-16). If the inquirer was approved, he "came near" (קרב) the Council of the Community and was placed on a two-year probation cycle (with annual reviews). During this time, if his knowledge and behavior proved consistently satisfactory, he was ushered incrementally closer to the core of communal life. In the first year, he was kept from both the טהרת הרבים ("pure-food of the Many," 6.16-17) and the משקה הרבים ("drink of the Many," 6.20-21) and "did not participate in the wealth of the רבים" (6.17). In the second year, if the inquirer was sustained after the first, he became privy to "the Assembly of the Community" (סוד היחד), gained access to the טהרת הרבים (though not yet the משקה הרבים), and had his wealth and goods registered with "the man who examines the goods of the רבים" (i.e., the *měbaqqēr;* see 6.18-21). If approved at the end of that second year, he then reached full membership: he was granted access to the משקה הרבים, his wealth was somehow integrated into the common property of the Community,[12] and he was registered into the Rule along with other members for his particular responsibilities in communal affairs:

> And if the lot goes out for him to draw near the Community, he shall register him into the Rule, according to his rank amidst his brothers, for Torah, for judgment, for (the) purity, and for the integration of his wealth. And his advice and judgment will belong to the Community. (1QS 6.21-23)

Included in this process may have been the oath prescribed at 5.7-11. There it is mandated that everyone who enters the Council of the Community publicly make a two-fold oath, both to return to the Mosaic Torah and to separate from all the unrighteous. For anyone who entered the Council of the Community, "it shall be confirmed upon his soul with a binding oath to return to the Torah of Moses . . . to all that has been revealed of it to the Sons of Zadok" (5.8-9), as well as "to be separated from all the men of unrighteousness, who walk the path of wickedness" (5.10-11). Though possibly the vestige of an earlier initiation rite,[13] this oath may well have been later integrated

---

12. On this "integration" (6.17: יתערב; 6.22: לערב) of goods as access to doing business with Community members (rather than a communal sharing of goods), see C. Rabin, "Private Property in the Qumran Community," in *Qumran Studies* (Scripta Judaica 2; Oxford: Oxford University Press, 1957), 24-31, esp. 30-31.

13. C. Hempel, "Community Structures in the Dead Sea Scrolls: Admission, Organization, Disciplinary Procedures," in *The Dead Sea Scrolls After Fifty Years: A Comprehensive Assessment* (ed. P. W. Flint and J. C. VanderKam; 2 vols.; Leiden: Brill, 1999), 2:71-72.

into the process outlined in column 6. M. Weinfeld and J. Pouilly assumed as much: Weinfeld placing it at the end of that process;[14] Pouilly, after the initial examination by the רבים.[15] But hints in the text suggest a point even earlier, just after the candidate was first examined by the *paqid*. According to 6.14-15, when the *paqid* brought an inquirer into the covenant, it was for a two-fold purpose, described in terms that intimate the two parts of the oath at column 5. Whereas that oath was both "to return [לשוב] to the Torah of Moses" (5.8) and "to separate from all the men of unrighteousness" (5.10: מכול אנשי העול), the *paqid* was to bring a candidate into the covenant "to return [לשוב] to the truth and to depart from all unrighteousness [מכול עול]" (6.15). That the candidate was "to return to the truth" in column 6 appears to echo the oath "to return to the Torah of Moses" in column 5; and that he was "to depart from all unrighteousness" in column 6 seems reminiscent of the oath "to be separated from all the men of unrighteousness" in column 5. In the light of such allusions, there is some justification for positing that the oath at column 5 — perhaps the trace of an earlier and simpler initiation rite — was appropriated into the later, more complex process at column 6 precisely at the point rehearsed in 6.14-15. Upon initial examination and approval by the *paqid*, the candidate was "brought into the covenant," at which time he took up the oath recounted in 5.7-11 — *unto* Torah and *away from* the men of unrighteousness. After further catechism under the *paqid*, the inquirer was then reviewed by the רבים, and, if approved, launched into the two-year probation that would form the lion's share of his initiation.

3. Temporal Coincidence?

Though some have construed the covenant renewal and initiation rites to have been one and the same — or, at least, to have dovetailed in the times of their observance[16] — rubrics in the text say otherwise. The renewal ceremony was to be observed שנה בשנה (2.19), likely at an annual feast, while the initiation process began its cycle at the indeterminable prompting of would-be members — whenever "anyone from Israel presented himself to

14. M. Weinfeld, *The Organizational Pattern and the Penal Code of the Qumran Sect: A Comparison with Guilds and Religious Associations of the Hellenistic-Roman Period* (NTOA 2; Fribourg: Éditions Universitaires and Göttingen: Vandenhoeck & Ruprecht, 1986), 43.

15. J. Pouilly, "L'Évolution de la Législation Pénale dans la Communauté de Qumrân," *RB* 82 (1975): 539.

16. See Milik, *Ten Years of Discovery in the Wilderness of Judaea*, 101-3, 116-18; and B. E. Thiering, "Qumran Initiation and New Testament Baptism," *NTS* 27 (1981): 616-17, 629 n. 11.

join the Council of the Community" (6.13-14), and thus, presumably, at as many different times throughout a year as there were candidates wishing to join. S. Pfann has suggested that this temporal disparity would have been quickly and routinely resolved through the indefinite period of time that occurred at the beginning of the initiation process.[17] The unspecified duration between a candidate's first inquiry and the beginning of his two-year probation, Pfann argues, was deliberately flexible, so as to account for the time needed to calibrate the remainder of the initiation process to the next feast at which the covenant renewal ceremony would be held, no matter how long or short that period might have been for any given candidate.[18] Supporting this hypothesis is the ranking of the candidate that concluded the initiation process. According to 5.20-24, everyone who entered the covenant was to be examined and ranked annually: when they "entered the covenant to act according to all these statutes," they were bidden to "examine their spirits in the Community" and be recorded "in the Rule, each man before his fellow according to his insight and deeds . . . year by year." Inasmuch as the annual covenant renewal ceremony also ends in a sequenced "entry" into the Rule — and this, similarly, according to the very same rank described in column 5 — it is not impossible that the two occurred in tandem. If so, just prior to the yearly ceremony, members would be examined and re-ranked according to their insight and deeds in the prior year. With that done, the ceremony would close with a hierarchical arrangement of each member, queued according to the new ranking each would have for the coming year.[19] Hence, it becomes significant that the initiation rite also closed with the ranking of the initiate: the successful candidate was to be "registered into the Rule, according to his rank [יכתובהו בסרך תכונו] amidst his brothers, for Torah, for judgment, for (the) purity, and for the integration of his wealth," to use the language found in 6.22 (cf. 2.19-25). If such ranking was performed customarily at the yearly renewal ceremony, the review that concluded the initiation process would suggest that it, too, had been temporally aligned with that ceremony.

---

17. Pfann, "The Essene Yearly Renewal Ceremony and the Baptism of Repentance," 339-41.

18. Ibid.

19. The two passages, in fact, share terminology: the examination "of spirit(s)" (5.20-21: לפי רוחותם; 2.20: את רוחום); the registration or entrance "into the Rule" (5.23: וכתבם בסרך; 2.20-21: בסרך). And, though not compelling in itself, it is noteworthy that the phrase used to express the annual character of the rankings at 5.20-24 is שנה בשנה (5.24), used also (and only elsewhere in the *Serekh* documents) for the renewal ceremony. Note 4Q258 (4QS^d) frg. 1 2.3-4; 4Q261 (4QS^g) frg. 1 lines 4-5 (cf. 1QS 5.23-24); and 5Q13 frg. 4 line 4 (cf. 1QS 2.19).

4. The Initiation Process in the Penal Code

The scenario of a temporal alignment between the covenant renewal and initiation rites, however, is challenged by further data from the penal code (6.24–7.25; 8.16b–9.2). As has been noticed by some,[20] and particularly developed by L. H. Schiffman, several penalties in the penal code appear to represent a re-enactment, of sorts, of the initiation process at 6.13-23.[21] At certain junctures, a member under discipline, not unlike an initiate in candidacy, is denied the privileges of טהרת הרבים and משקה הרבים, always for periods of one or two years. In 6.25; 7.2-3, 15-16; and possibly 6.27,[22] an offender is excluded from the הרבים טהרת for one year. In 8.24–9.2, he is banned from the same for two years. And, in 7.18-21, he is removed from the טהרת הרבים — and, one might reasonably infer, the משקה הרבים — for the first year of a two-year probation and from the משקה הרבים for the second year of that probation:

> The person whose spirit vacillates from the foundation of the Community to deal treacherously with the truth and walk in the stubbornness of his heart, if he returns/repents [אם ישוב], he will be punished two years: in the first year he shall not touch the טהרת הרבים and in the second he shall not touch the משקה הרבים;[23] and behind all the men of the Community shall he sit. (1QS 7.18-20)

Moreover, in 7.18-21, as well as at 8.16-19, disciplined members, like new candidates, complete their penalties by being ranked, once again, among the

20. E.g., C.-H. Hunzinger, "Beobachtungen zur Entwicklung der Disziplinarordnung der Gemeinde von Qumran," in *Qumran* (ed. K. E. Grözinger et al.; Wege der Forschung 410; Darmstadt: Wissenschaftliche Buchgesellschaft, 1981), 252; Thiering, "Qumran Initiation and New Testament Baptism," 630 n. 21; F. Avemarie, "'Tohorat Ha-Rabbim' and 'Mashqeh Ha-Rabbim': Jacob Licht Reconsidered," in Bernstein et al., eds., *Legal Texts and Legal Issues*, 215-17.

21. L. H. Schiffman, *Sectarian Law in the Dead Sea Scrolls: Courts, Testimony and the Penal Code* (BJS 33; Chico: Scholars Press, 1983), 161-68; followed by F. García Martínez and J. Trebolle Barrera, *The People of the Dead Sea Scrolls* (trans. W. G. E. Watson; Leiden: E. J. Brill, 1995), 152-54. Cf. also García Martínez, "Les limites de la communauté: pureté et impureté à Qumrân et dans le Nouveau Testament," in *Text and Testimony: Essays on New Testament and Apocryphal Literature in Honour of A. F. J. Klijn* (ed. T. Baarda et al.; Kampen: Uitgeversmaatschappij J. H. Kok, 1988), 118. Pouilly ("L'Évolution de la Législation Pénale dans la Communauté de Qumrân," 528-30) saw the two year probation at 1QS 8.20–9.2 as a re-enactment of an initiation rite he located at 1QS 8.10b-12a.

22. See the discussion (with references) in Schiffman, *Sectarian Law in the Dead Sea Scrolls*, 160, 177 n. 38.

23. The scribe originally wrote בטהרת, then erased טהרת with scribal dots; משקה is written as a supralinear.

other members of the Community. In 7.18-21, the רבים are asked about the offender's affairs (as per 6.15-16, 18, 21), after which, if they "bring him near," he is to be "recorded in his rank":

> Upon his completion of two years of days, the רבים shall be questioned concerning his affairs; and if they bring him near, he shall be recorded in his rank (ונכתב בתכונו); and afterward, he may be questioned regarding judgment. (1QS 7.21)

And, similarly, at 8.16-19. The rubrics for discipline, which include a ban from the טהרת אנשי הקודש for an undefined period of time, direct that the disciplined member be reinstated by being "registered in his rank":

> Let no man from the men of the Community, the covenant of the Community, who, with high hand, turns aside from any commandment it has uttered, touch the טהרה of the men of holiness, nor let him know any of their counsel, until his deeds are pure from all unrighteousness, so as to walk in a path of integrity. Then shall they bring him near the Council on the word of the רבים; and afterward he will be registered in his rank (יכת/ב \ בתכונו).[24] (1QS 8.16-19)

The language of both passages echoes the ranking at the culmination of the initiation rite (see above). Thus, if less so in some passages,[25] certainly in 7.18-21 (and perhaps 8.24–9.2) the penal code seems so to mirror the initiation rite as to suggest it was, at points, a repetition of it.

Significant for the issue at hand is that it is highly unlikely these penal re-doings of the initiation rite would have been delayed very long from the time the offenses were committed — or, in the case of 7.18-21, from the time an erring member "returned" or "repented." That is to say, if, because of some transgression, a member was deemed unworthy to touch the טהרת הרבים and/or the משקה הרבים for one or more years after that act, one is hard pressed to contend he would have been allowed to do so between the time of that transgression and the next renewal ceremony, just so as to calibrate the two in the liturgical year. It is more likely, instead, that the re-initiation cycle required by the penal code would have begun and ended on the date the offense occurred and judgment was made, whenever and how-

---

24. The ב is supralinear.

25. See the critique of Schiffman's evidence in C. Milikowsky, "Law at Qumran: A Critical Reaction to Lawrence H. Schiffman, *Sectarian Law in the Dead Sea Scrolls: Courts, Testimony, and the Penal Code*," *RevQ* 12 (1986): 247.

ever that corresponded to the festal calendar. And, if this was the case for the re-done initiation process prescribed in the penal code, it would be forcing the text to assume anything different for the first initiation process outlined at column 6. Regarding that first initiation process, Hempel has concluded that "it does not seem necessary . . . to suppose that the admission of new members occurred only once a year across the board";[26] and the argument and data presented here would support her statement. The initiation process at 6.13-23, like the re-initiation process within 6.24–7.25 and 8.16b–9.2, would have begun and ended, more or less, when inquiry was made. Since inquiries for membership did not, of necessity, coincide with the feast in which the covenant renewal ceremony was performed, their respective observances, except when they overlapped by chance, would have been temporally disparate.

5. Conclusion

To be sure, additional work, some of it on texts other than 1QS, is needed for more certainty on this issue to be achieved. To cite one example, as part of his model for a delayed and calibrated initiation rite, Pfann has referenced 4Q266 (4QD[a]) frg. 11 lines 5-18 (// 4Q270 [4QD[e]] frg. 7 1.19-21; 2.11-12), where he reads the juxtaposed rubrics for an excommunication ceremony and an annual third-month gathering as evidence that discipline was meted out annually at the covenant renewal ceremony.[27] But, while this argument merits serious consideration, questions nonetheless remain. It is not self-evident, for instance, that the gathering prescribed in 4Q266 frg. 11 lines 17-18 is the *Sitz im Leben* of the excommunication described in the preceding lines (5-16). And, even if so, as Hempel has observed, it is not clear that such an annual expulsion applied to other expulsions and lesser offenses outlined in the *Damascus Document* penal code:

> The formula used to refer to expulsion in the (Damascus Document) penal code "he shall leave and not return" (יצא ולוא ישוב עוד) as well as the lesser penalties for less severe infringements ring of prompt action. It seems unlikely that offenders were punished only once a year in a ceremony in the third month.[28]

26. Hempel, "Community Structures in the Dead Sea Scrolls," 73.

27. Pfann, "The Essene Yearly Renewal Ceremony and the Baptism of Repentance," 342-45.

28. See C. Hempel, *The Laws of the Damascus Document: Sources, Tradition and Redaction*

Here, however, it is enough to observe that a coincidence of the two rites outlined in 1QS 1-2 and 6 — those of covenant renewal and initiation, respectively — is open to question. The covenant renewal ceremony at 1.18–2.25 was to be observed once per year, likely at an annual festival, while the probation period of the initiation process was to begin more or less relative to the time "anyone from Israel presented himself to join the Council of the Community" (6.13-14). The indefinite period at the onset of the initiation rite might have functioned as a temporal mechanism to align the two (so Pfann); but penal repetitions of that same rite render such a reading problematic, if not unnecessary.

(STJD 29; Leiden: Brill, 1998), 180. Hempel's fuller argument turns on the peculiarly severe transgression addressed in 4Q266 frg. 11 lines 5-6 (// 4Q270 frg. 7 1.19-20 = lines 5b-6 in her composite text [ibid., 175]). The specific clause she cites from the *Damascus Document* penal code is 4Q270 frg. 7 1.11, 13 (= lines 24 and 26 in her composite text). יצא in the quotation has been changed, as per the text, from צצא in the original. For Hempel's composite text, see ibid., 141-44.

An Elite Group within the *Yaḥad:*
Revisiting 1QS 8–9

SHANE A. BERG

1. Introduction

It has long been recognized that 1QS 8–9 are in some way distinctive over against the rest of the *Rule of the Community.* Although the requirements and rituals for entering the Community have already been laid out (1.1–3.12) and a slate of regulations governing community life have been set forth (5.1–7.25), in 8.1–9.11 we find references to the formation of a group dedicated to a life of holiness, plans for a sojourn in the wilderness, and further regulations for community life.

In the large amount of secondary literature on 1QS 8.1–9.11, two basic strategies scholars have employed in the attempt to account for the unique features of this section can be discerned. The first is the assertion that the material in 1QS 8.1–9.11 represents a description of some pioneering group in the Community's past. Thus the regulations for community life in 5.1–7.25 are understood as being in force at the time of the compilation of 1QS, while 8.1–9.11 is taken as a remnant of the Community's heroic past that is preserved for posterity.[1]

---

1. The classic example of this approach can be found in Jerome Murphy-O'Connor's "La genèse littéraire de la *Règle de la Communauté*," *RB* 76 (1969): 528-49, in which he built on the arguments of Edmund F. Sutcliffe's "The First Fifteen Members of the Qumran Community," *JSS* 4 (1959): 134-38; other examples of this strategy include: A. R. C. Leaney, *The Rule of Qumran and its Meaning* (Philadelphia: Westminster, 1966), 208-33; J. Pouilly, *La Règle de la Communauté de Qumrân: Son Évolution Littéraire* (Paris: J. Gabalda, 1976).

This essay is offered in honor of James H. Charlesworth, who instilled in me a deep curiosity for the Dead Sea Scrolls and the Community that produced them.

The second strategy is characterized by an attempt to dismiss the significance of the disparities between 8.1–9.11 and 5.1–7.25. The differences are acknowledged but are attributed to the nature of a composite document like the
Rule of the Community, which clearly contains material from a variety of
sources. The goal of such an approach is to assert that 5.1–9.11 applies to the
entire Community.[2]

From time to time, however, attempts have been made to argue that the
two sets of rules (5.1–7.25 and 8.1–9.11) are intended for two different, yet contemporaneous, groups within the Community's pattern of organization. E. P.
Sanders argues that parts, at least, of 8.1–9.26 represent a more rigorous set of
standards that apply to a select group within the Community.[3] John J. Collins
has also recently argued that there are (at least) two distinct groups that are
envisioned in 1QS: (1) the members of the יחד who live throughout the land
and belong to local cells of the group, and (2) an elite group that is commissioned by the larger group to separate itself in order to achieve a higher level
of holiness and in order to perform some atoning function.[4] The primary
goal of this essay is an attempt to build on the insights of Sanders and Collins
by means of a careful analysis of 1QS 8.1–9.21.

The first part of the essay contains the argument that 8.1–9.11 describes
the creation of an elite group within the existing יחד.[5] The second part is concerned with a discussion of 9.12-21, in which a set of precepts for the Maskil
are laid out. Specifically, it will be suggested that there are strong indications
that the Maskil plays an important part in the creation and training of this
elite group.

The result of this study will be a new perception of the relationship between 8.1–9.21 and the rest of 1QS. Rather than preserving a record of the literary evolution of the rules for communal life or reflecting the inconsisten-
cies inherent in a composite document, 1QS 8.1–9.21 will be understood as a

---

2. For examples of this approach see: P. Wernberg-Møller, *The Manual of Discipline*
(STDJ 1; Leiden: Brill, 1957), 122-23; and Sarianna Metso, "In Search of the *Sitz im Leben* of the
Community Rule," in *The Provo International Conference on the Dead Sea Scrolls* (ed. D. W. Parry
and E. Ulrich; STDJ 30; Leiden: Brill, 1999), 306-15.

3. E. P. Sanders, "Appendix 2: 1QS 8.1–9.2," in *Paul and Palestinian Judaism* (Minneapolis:
Fortress, 1977), 323-25. See the discussion of 8.1–9.11 below for the specific passages that Sanders
regards as relevant for the more rigorous group.

4. John J. Collins, "Forms of the Community in the Dead Sea Scrolls," in *Emanuel:
Studies in the Hebrew Bible, the Septuagint, and the Dead Sea Scrolls in Honor of Emanuel Tov* (ed.
S. M. Paul, R. A. Kraft, and L. H. Schiffman; VTSup 94; Leiden: Brill, 2003), 97-111.

5. There is one exception in 1QS 8.16-19, where we find included a penalty for deliberate
Torah transgression that applies to all the members of the larger group.

description of a bold plan for the creation of an elite group within the Community whose life is ordered and described by the material in columns 1–7.[6]

2. An Overview of 1QS 1–7

Before discussing 1QS 8–9, it is necessary to provide a concise overview of 1QS 1–7. Along with most scholars, I take the first major section to comprise 1.1–3.12, consisting of a preamble in 1.1-15, which is followed by a description of the ceremony for the entry into the "covenant" (1.16–2.18) as well as a brief section about the annual covenant renewal ceremony (2.19-25), and then a reflection on the need for genuine repentance when entering the Community (2.25–3.12).

The next major section is the so-called "Two-Spirits Tractate" in 3.13–4.26, where we find the much-discussed dualistic worldview of the group described in detail. Here too is where we learn that the responsibility for instructing members of the sect in this special knowledge falls to the Maskil. This section, like the one before it, bears all the marks of an independent work that has been incorporated into the larger Rule.

Finally, 1QS 5–7 represents a lengthy exposition of communal rules and constitutes a discrete section.[7] It is explicitly stated in 5.1 that the rules apply to the "men of the Community" (אנשי היחד).[8] 5.1-7 is an introduction to this larger unit as well as an affirmation of the authority of the Sons of Zadok and

---

6. A comparison of 1QS 8–9 with the parallel 4QS material will not be carried out in the present essay. Such a comparison would indeed be interesting and potentially quite fruitful, but it lies beyond the scope of the careful analysis of 1QS in its own right that is attempted here.

7. Note that in addition to beginning with a new section heading (5.1: וזה הסרך לאנשי היחד), the manuscript markings provide some indication of the fact that columns 5–7 are a single section. Out in the margin just to the right of וזה הסרך in 5.1 there is a large scribal mark; there is another elaborate scribal mark under the left side of the last line of column 7. Although the precise meanings of these marks in the Scrolls remain largely undeciphered (with the exception of the relatively straightforward *paragraphus* markers that are scattered throughout 1QS), Tov argues that the marks I have mentioned in 1QS can be used to discern how the scribe perceived major divisions in the text. For a general discussion of scribal markings in the Scrolls, see Emanual Tov, "Scribal Markings in the Texts from the Judean Desert," in *Current Research and Technological Developments on the Dead Sea Scrolls* (ed. D. W. Parry and S. D. Ricks; STDJ 20; Leiden: Brill, 1996), 41-77. For the mark at 1QS 5.1, see ibid., 72; for the mark at 7.25, ibid., 75.

8. Unless otherwise noted, all citations of the Hebrew text of 1QS are taken from James H. Charlesworth et al., eds., *The Dead Sea Scrolls: Hebrew, Aramaic, and Greek Texts with English Translations*, Vol. 1: *Rule of the Community and Related Documents* (PTSDSSP 1; Tübingen: J. C. B. Mohr [Paul Siebeck] and Louisville: Westminster John Knox, 1994). All translations are my own.

the multitude of the men of the Community. In 5.7-23 the criteria and procedures for entry into the covenant of the Community are described; stipulations for an annual examination and ranking follow in 5.23-24. Rules for behavior towards one's fellows are found in 5.24–6.3. In 6.3-8, there is a set of
conditions that must be met whenever ten men from the Council of the
Community are present. Beginning in 6.8 is a section denoted as the "rule for
the Session of the Many."[9]

The "Many," הרבים, is an important designation in columns 6–7 for the
Community;[10] it seems to be interchangeable with יחד. The rule for the "Session" (מושב) of the Many continues through 6.23 and deals with a variety of
issues that pertain to the group's communal proceedings. Finally, in 6.24–7.25
we have משפטים (6.24) for a laundry list of violations of the group's rules. Included for each type of case is a description of the transgression and the corresponding penalty that is appropriate.

It would thus appear that 1QS 5–7 constitutes a set of rules that applies
to members of the יחד, also called collectively הרבים, who are located in cells
in various locales. Members in a given cell come together at least for communal meals, for study, and for meetings to address matters pertaining to the
group. Whether members in these small cells[11] lived communally is difficult
to discern from these texts. Within this network of cells, there nevertheless
existed a system of hierarchy. In each cell there were officials such as the מבקר
(6.12, 20) and the פקיד (6.14). The Sons of Zadok also apparently enjoyed a
preeminence in authority, especially as they appear to have been the recipients of divine revelation that was binding on the other members.[12] The figure
of the Maskil is harder to ascertain. Does each cell have its own Maskil, as it
appears to have had its own מבקר and פקיד? This is a difficult question, but
for reasons that are explained below, I think that there was only one Maskil at
any given time in the life of the Community. This Maskil was a charismatic
figure held in great esteem who nonetheless is not an independent agent but
is held to specified standards and prescriptions.

1QS 1–7 thus envisions a group distributed into local cells but whose
overarching ideology bound them rather tightly together, such that the same
rules applied in each of the cells. There is a local hierarchy of authority and

---

9. וזה הסרך למושב הרבים.

10. הרבים or רבים occur in 6.1, 7, 9, 11, 12, 13, 15, 16, 17 (2x), 18, 20 (2x), 21, 25; 7.3, 16 (2x),
19, 20, 21, 25. We have references to the מושב הרבים in 6.8, 11; 7.10 (2x), 13; it is also referred to
obliquely in 7.11.

11. I take the idea of local cells of a group who nonetheless exhibit a translocal identity
from Collins, "Forms of Community," *passim.*

12. See 5.9.

esteem, but at the same time there appears to be some translocal authority resident in the Sons of Zadok and quite likely in the person of the Maskil.

3. The Elite Group in 1QS 8.1–9.11

8.1-16a: The Formation and Training of the Elite Group

With an overview of 1QS 1–7 now in place, we can turn to columns 8–9 and the central question concerning them: How does the material found in 8.1–9.11 relate to what precedes it in columns 1–7? Any attempt to answer this question is beset with difficulty. To name one example, the number and diversity of epithets for the Community and its members found throughout 1QS tend to defy systematic categorization; this fact has made the task of identifying the group(s) discussed in 8.1–9.11 problematic. The difficulty of analyzing this material is also compounded by shortcomings in the manuscript itself. To be more specific, in 8.7-13 we encounter several lacunae, multiple erasures, and a substantial amount of supralinear writing. It is no wonder, given these and other problems, that scholars have struggled long and hard with this section in their attempt to make sense of it.

Despite these very real problems, it can be shown that the whole of 8.1–9.11 (and, in fact, 8.1–9.21) can be interpreted as a coherent body of material that is not superfluous to, or in tension with, 1QS 1–7. A careful line-by-line analysis will demonstrate that the best way to make sense of 8.1–9.11 (and the related material in 9.12-21) is to read it *as a description of the creation of a special group,* not yet formed, that is to serve in a unique role in the life of the larger Community.

In 8.1, it is stated that "in the Council of the Community"[13] there are to be 12 men and 3 priests[14] who are "perfect in everything that has been revealed from the Torah."[15] The first step in a proper understanding of columns 8–9 is the identification of this עצת היחד. A review of this phrase in 1QS clearly shows that it does not refer to a distinct group within the יחד, but rather is indistinguishable from the יחד itself: the two terms are used

---

13. בעצת היחד.

14. It is unclear whether a group of 15 men is meant here (12 men + 3 priests) or 12 men (3 of whom are priests). For the purpose of my argument a definitive answer to this question is unnecessary. However, I find it more likely that a group of 15 men is meant: 12 "lay" members representing the 12 tribes of Israel and 3 additional members drawn from the priests, who were held in high esteem in the Community and exercised at least some degree of oversight.

15. 8.1-2: תמימים בכול הנגלה מכול התורה.

interchangeably throughout the whole of 1QS.[16] On the basis of this fact it is logical to conclude that the 12 men and 3 priests are a sub-group within the larger עצת היחד. Additional evidence from this section will support this claim.

One of the difficulties in the identification of the עצת היחד is the ambiguity of the preposition -ב in the phrase בעצת היחד. As is true for most prepositions in Hebrew, -ב can be ambiguous, and this is no less true when it is used to express the relationship of members to a group. In this sense, -ב is comparable to the following equally ambiguous uses of "in" in English: (1) "*In* the United States Senate there are 51 Democrats and 49 Republicans" means that these members *compose the entire Senate.* However, (2) "*In* the United States Senate there are 97 men" means that the 97 men are *a subset of the larger whole.* In each case, the meaning of "in" must be inferred from context. In these examples, the context that must be known is that the United States Senate consists of 100 members; only this knowledge permits one to interpret the meaning of "in" correctly. Likewise, in order to know whether the 15 men who are בעצת היחד constitute the עצת היחד or are members of a smaller group within it requires some knowledge of the composition of the עצת היחד that is *external* to the phrase itself insofar as the preposition itself is ambiguous with respect to this information. Since, as I have argued, it is clear from the rest of the document that עצת היחד refers to the entire Community in the same way that יחד does, it follows that in 1QS 8.1 the preposition -ב must mean that "within" the עצת היחד there is a distinct group of 12 men and 3 priests — that is to say, an elite group.

The role and function of this elite group is described in three parallel clauses that follow in 8.2-4.[17] The group is to keep perfect Torah observance (1) in order to exhibit exemplary behavior within the group and to represent a faithful presence in the land (8.2-3), (2) in order to pay for iniquity via just works and refining anxiety (8.3-4), and (3) in order to walk truthfully in accord with the regulation of the time (8.4). The mission of the elite group is thus linked with Torah observance, strict regulations for behavior, and an awareness of what is required "by the regulation of the time" (8.4).

At the end of this list in 8.4, we find a reference to the time when "these"

---

16. In many cases עצת היחד is used just like יחד to refer to the entire group. See 3.2; 5.7; 6.3, 10, 12-13, 14, 16; 7.2, 22, 24; 8.5, 11 (עצת אנשי היחד), 22; and 11.8. This fact is noted by Collins, "Forms of Community," 103-4.

17. לעשות . . . ולרצת . . . ולהתהלך. Contra Wernberg-Møller, who simply asserts without argument that despite the reference to the group of 15 in 8.1, everything that follows after refers to the whole Community (*Manual of Discipline,* 122). Sanders rightly notes that the smaller group in 8.1 must be the subject of the three infinitives that follow ("Appendix 3," 327).

come into being in Israel (בהיות אלה בישראל).[18] The antecedent of אלה must be determined from context, and the two options seem to be either the elite group of 15 ("when *these ones* come into being in Israel") or, more generally, the larger situation described in 8.1-4 ("when *these things* happen in Israel"). The meaning of the phrase, however, does not vary significantly if one antecedent is chosen over the other.

Following this temporal phrase are the results of the formation of this group (8.5-10). The "Council of the Community[19] will be established[20] in truth" (8.5: עצת היחד (ה)נכונה) באמת) as "an eternal planting, a house of holiness for Israel and an assembly of utmost holiness for Aaron, witnesses of the truth for judgment, and chosen ones of (God's) will in order to atone for the land and to repay the wicked their reward" (8.5-7). Furthermore, "it" (note the 3fs pronoun, היאה, referring back to the עצת היחד) will then be "the tested wall" and the "very expensive cornerstone" (8.7) whose "foundation walls" shall be unable to be disturbed (8.8).[21] It will be a Community with "eternal[22] knowledge of the covenant of justice" that "establishes the covenant according to eternal precepts" (8.8-10). Finally, written in supralinear script, is the declaration that the Community will "atone for the land" and "fix the judgment for the wicked." Finally, a concluding phrase asserts that "there will be no more evil" (8.10).

In short, the text is indicating that the elite group will act as a catalyst that will result in the larger יחד taking on an atoning and judging role within Israel. The creation of the elite group thus represents an attempt on the part of the יחד to press forward toward their eschatological goals vis-à-vis Israel.

In 8.10 the discussion shifts back to the elite group: in this instance, when "these ones are established" (בהכון אלה) in the "foundation of the community" for two years in "perfect behavior" (בתמים דרך), they will "be separated"[23] as "holy" in "the midst of the Council of the men of the Community" (8.11). This line raises serious difficulty for any theory that asserts

---

18. This phrase recurs in 8.12 and 9.3, both times referring to this same group of 15.

19. עצת היחד, again referring to the whole group.

20. As the argument progresses, the reason for my rendering the predicative niphal participle נכונה as a future will become clearer. I take the clause that precedes it (בהיות אלה בישראל) as circumstantial; the two phrases together should then be translated: "when these (ones) come into being in Israel, the Council of the Community will be established in truth as an eternal planting. . . ."

21. Note here the use of imperfects: יודעזעו, יחישו (8.8).

22. With most commentators, I read עולם for כולם here.

23. יבדלו (niphal). Note once again the use of the imperfect, which in context here clearly implies an event in the future.

that columns 8–9 simply refer to the whole יחד. If the entire Community is in view, how could it be "set apart as holy *in the midst* of the Council of the men of the Community" (8.11)? In this case, אלה must refer to a group that is distinct from the עצת אנשי היחד.

This segregated group, then, will undergo a two-year period of training in the midst of the larger Community in preparation for its special mission. It is further asserted that the "Interpreter" will not conceal from this group (מאלה, "from these") any revealed thing that has been hidden from Israel — they are thus privy to the full scope of the Interpreter's special knowledge (8.11-12).

After the reference to the training period, we find in 8.12 a repetition of the phrase found in 8.4, בהיות אלה בישראל.[24] (It would seem, then, that this phrase, in both instances, refers to the time *after* the completion of the initial two-year training period and not to the initial mustering of the elite group.)[25] After this training, and within the confines of the larger Community, the elite group is to "be separated"[26] from the "midst of the session of the men of deceit"[27] in order to go into the wilderness and "to prepare there the way of him" (8.13). The segregation of this elite group is thus understood to be related to the well-known prophecy of Deutero-Isaiah (40:3) in which the preparing of the way of the Lord is a prelude to the revelation of God's glory. In creating, training, and consecrating the elite group, the members of the יחד anticipate a similar setting-in-motion of eschatological events that will result in vindication for the just and judgment for the wicked. Moreover, as the text proceeds to explain, this preparation in the wilderness is specifically understood to entail the study of Torah, particularly as its proper observance has been revealed to the sect (8.15-16).

24. A second hand has added above the line here \ליחד/ ("for a/the Community"). It is unclear what was intended by such an addition.

25. Thus the point at which the eschatological effects of the elite group described in 8.5-10 will be realized is *after* the training period and not in the preliminary selection of the group.

26. Note the use here once again of the niphal imperfect after a temporal clause (ובהיות . . . + יבדלו). What is being described is in the future.

27. While it is true that the charge to separate from the men of deceit is incumbent upon all members of the group (see, e.g., 5.1, 10), a supralinear correction to 8.13 further specifies the imperative to separate from the men of deceit by asserting that the separation is to be "according to these regulations" (\בתכונים האלה/) — that is, in accord with the particular conditions just laid out in the first part of column 8.

8.16b-19: The Penalty for Deliberate Torah Transgression
by Members of the יחד

So far I have argued that 1QS 8.1-16a has in view the elite group or the immediate effects of that group. At this point, however, 8.16-19 rather abruptly
provides the penalty and conditions for reinstatement for any member of
the larger group (יחד) who deliberately transgresses any Torah regulation.
To say that it is abrupt or intrusive is not necessarily to say that it is random,
for the text has just referred to the study of Torah incumbent upon the elite
group. But why would an editor insert a penalty concerning Torah observance in the midst of a discussion of the study of Torah on the part of the
elite group?

It seems plausible that the editor(s) of the tradition preserved in 1QS
wanted to avoid any possible inference that the existence of an elite group
that practiced an elevated level of holiness might indicate a relaxation of the
rules for Torah observance for members of the larger community. Although
any attempt to explain the digression in 8.16b-19 is necessarily uncertain, the
editor(s) does seem to acknowledge that the flow of thought has been inter-
rupted in a potentially confusing way. The concluding phrase of 8.19 ("and
this משפט applies to everyone who joins the יחד") is unnecessary unless at
least two groups are in view. Otherwise, why would there be any need to make
clear to whom the rule applies? Moreover, additional evidence for the fact
that two groups are in view is found in the section that immediately follows,
which contains *another, different* penalty for deliberate Torah transgression,
despite the fact that such an offense and its penalty is already presented in this
section (see further below).

8.17–9.2: The Penalties for Torah Transgressions
by Members of the Elite Group

In 8.20–9.3, the elite group is again the focus of the discussion. That this
group is in view again is not immediately apparent due to some shifts in terminology, but the penalties and stipulations for reinstatement laid out in this
section make the most sense if understood as carrying on the discussion of
the elite group found in 8.1-16a.

8.20–9.3 contains משפטים for the "men of perfect holiness."[28] In the
immediately preceding section, the penalty for deliberate Torah transgression

---

28. אנשי התמים קודש; cf. 6.24, where we find the משפטים for cases among the Many.

is exclusion for the offender until his behavior is once again perfect (8.17-18); this stipulation, as we have noted, applies to every person who enters the יחד (8.19). However, in 8.21-23 it is stated that a member of "the Council of Holiness, the ones who behave perfectly,"[29] who transgresses Torah deliberately or through negligence is banished from the עצת היחד with no chance of reinstatement. One way of making sense of such a discrepancy is to postulate two different groups to whom different standards of behavior apply.[30] When one then takes into consideration that an elite group is in view in 8.1-16a, the differences in the penalty for deliberate Torah transgression are made comprehensible by understanding the first penalty as applicable to all members of the יחד (as is obvious from 8.19) and the more stringent regulation as applicable to the elite group.

The more rigorous Torah observance regulation continues in 8.24-27 with the provision that if a person transgresses Torah inadvertently, he is excluded from the pure-meal and from participation in the עצה[31] — that is, he is excluded from the whole Community, and not just the elite group, but has a chance for later reinstatement. In such cases, a special משפט is applied whereby although the transgressor cannot judge any person or be asked for his counsel for two years (8.25), he can return to some participation *among the Many* during this probationary period if his behavior is "perfect among them,"[32] and provided that he commit no further inadvertent offenses (8.26-27). Thus if a member of the elite group commits an inadvertent error, his probationary period is spent among the larger group, the רבים.

The distinction between the penalties for deliberate and inadvertent violations is reiterated in 9.1-2, where an important new piece of information is given. While 8.24-27 does not clearly indicate that an inadvertent Torah offender is restored to the elite group after a successful probationary period, 9.2 strongly suggests that this is, in fact, the case. After the two years of testing among the Many, "afterwards he shall be enrolled in his rank for the Commu-

---

29. 8.21: עצת הקודש ההולכים בתמים דרך.

30. Sanders argues that the two sets of penalties for the same infraction is the clearest indication that two distinct groups are in view here ("Appendix 2," 324-25).

31. For a discussion of this occurrence of עצה, see further below.

32. I arrive at this rendering of the text by reading the במושב at the beginning of 8.26 as בם ישב (whether the verb is construed as a Qal imperfect or a Qal jussive does not greatly affect the meaning). In this reading, the בם goes with the preceding conditional clause אם תתם דרכו (8.25), resulting in the following translation: "If his behavior is perfect among them." This protasis is then completed by the apodosis "he shall return (or: let him return) to study and the Council under the authority of the Many" (8.26). This phrase is then finally qualified further by the condition that he commit no further inadvertent offenses for a two-year period (8:26-27: אם לוא שגג עוד).

nity of Holiness."[33] The question is which group is referred to here by יחד קודש: the larger community or the elite group? In order to answer this question, the larger issue of epithets modified by the language of "holiness" as well as "perfection" in 1QS 8–9 needs to be examined.

The noun (ה)קודש is used as the absolute in a construct chain in quite a number of instances throughout 1QS in epithets describing the Community and its members.[34] One could certainly not conclude, then, that the mere description as "holy" is a unique marker of the elite group, for it seems to have been a quality associated with all members of the יחד. The language of "perfection" permeates the document in much the same way as "holiness."[35] Similarly, then, one cannot look to "perfection" as a defining characteristic of the elite group over against the יחד.

This being said, it is significant that the collocation of "holiness" and "perfection" occurs only four times in 1QS — all of which are in columns 8–9 and all of which refer to the elite group. The first occurrence is in 8.20, the opening line of the section containing the precepts for the אנשי התמים קודש. The second is in the very next line, 8.21, where these "men" are described as the "ones who enter the Council of Holiness, the ones who behave perfectly . . ." (הבא בעצת הקודש ההולכים בתמים דרך).[36] It has already been argued above that the more stringent penalties for Torah transgression in 8.20-27 apply to members of the elite group. It follows that members of the elite group are held to a standard of "perfect holiness," in contrast to the rest of 1QS where these two qualities are *never* conjoined in describing the Community or its members.

With this data, we may return to the question of the referent of יחד קודש in 9.2, as well as to עצת הקודש in 8.21. As was argued earlier, throughout 1QS עצה, יחד, and עצת היחד are used interchangeably to refer to the entire Community. It seems necessary to regard the occurrence of עצת הקודש in 8.21, however, as a reference to the elite group given its context in the section containing the more rigorous penalty for Torah offense. Another impor-

---

33. 9.2: ואחר יכתוב בתכונו ליחד קודש. Note that the probationary period of two years corresponds to the number of years of initial training in the midst of the Community which members of the elite group undergo (see 8.10).

34. אנשי הקודש: 5.13, 18 (sg.); 8.17, 23; 9.8; יחד קודש: 9.2; היחד קודש קודשים: 9.6; עדת קודש: 11.8; מבנית קודש: 8.5-6; סוד קודש קודשים: 8.21; עצת הקודש: 8.5-6; עצת קודש: 2.25; בית קודש: 8.5; 9.6.

35. להלכת תמים: 3.9; תמימים תמים: 2.2; 9.6, 8; תמימים: 3.3; ההולכים תמים: 1.8; להתהלך לפניו תמים: תמימים בכול הנגלה מכול: 4.22; תום דרכו: 5.24; תמים דרך: 8.10, 18, 21; 9.5, 9; תמימי דרך התורה: 8.1-2.

36. The other two occurrences come in 9.6 and 9.8; see the discussion below.

tant consideration is that עצת הקודש is a *hapax legomenon* in 1QS that collocates "holiness" and "perfection." The context and uniqueness of the phrase suggest that we have here an instance of an epithet for the elite group. This in turn makes more likely the possibility that יחד קודש in 9.2 (also a *hapax legomenon*) is also a reference to the elite group and that to which the chastened Torah transgressor is reinstated.[37]

Because "holiness" and "perfection" are commonly-used attributes of the members of the יחד, it is possible that the combination of the two attributes was an attempt to distinguish the characteristics of the elite group in some way. As conceptually problematic as the modifier "perfectly holy" might appear to many today, it has a certain logic when imagined against the backdrop of an attempt to describe an elite group in the midst of a larger group whose self-understanding already included the qualities of "holiness" and "perfection." In other words, one way to distinguish an elite group with a "house of holiness" comprising "the perfect of the Way" is to describe that group as "perfectly holy." Be that as it may, what can be said with more than a fair degree of certainty is that 8.20–9.2 refers to a distinct group within the יחד, and this group is described as "perfectly holy."

9.3-11: Concluding Reflections on the Role of the Elite Group

In 9.3 we have a new section that begins with בהיות אלה בישראל, which by now appears to be something of a catch-phrase for the commissioning of the elite group.[38] This reference to the elite group's formation is modified by the phrase "according to all these norms" (9.3: ככול התכונים האלה), which is certainly a reference to the program and rules outlined in 8.1–9.2. The atoning function of this group that results from its "coming into existence in Israel" is described in 9.3-5. In 8.4-10 it is asserted that it is the whole Community that takes on an atoning role, while here it is the elite group. But this should come as no surprise: if the elite group results in an atoning function for the entire

---

37. It seems that the degree of certainty with respect to the identification of עצת הקודש with the elite group is higher than the case of יחד קודש. The context of עצת הקודש in 8.21 essentially necessitates taking it as a reference to the elite group. By analogy יחד קודש in 9.2 may very well refer to the elite group as well, but the contextual evidence is not as strong. We might just as well take it as a reference to the Community as a whole, which would imply that the chastened Torah-offender from the elite group is not reinstated to the elite group after his probationary period but rather regains some formal ranking in the larger group.

38. Not only is 9.3 indented, but in the right margin there is yet another elaborate scribal mark of some kind. See Tov, "Scribal Markings," 75.

Community, then the elite group itself can also be described as playing an atoning role.[39]

Near the end of 9.5-6 we find that "in that time," the אנשי היחד will "cause to be separated"[40] a house of holiness for Aaron, a Community of the holy of holies (or "of utmost holiness"), and a house of the Community for Israel. The "men of the Community" are the subject of יבדילו in 9.5, so again we see that there must be some other group that is the object of this separation, regardless of how one construes the nature of the separation. We are told that these who are separated off as a holy Community are "the ones who walk perfectly." A distinct group within the יחד that can be simultaneously described as both "holy" and "perfect" would fit perfectly with the elite group of 8.1-16a and 8.27–9.2.

In 9.7-8 there is a stipulation that addresses those areas in which the jurisdiction and authority of the Sons of Aaron is affirmed with respect to the elite group. We learn that it is only the Sons of Aaron who "shall rule over משפט and הון" (9.7). This general statement is qualified in the next clause; the Sons of Aaron have authority over "every norm of the אנשי היחד," but only over the property of "the men of holiness who walk perfectly."[41] The purpose of this statement seems to be to make it clear that the elite group still falls, to some degree at least, under the authority of the hierarchy of the larger group; its property is under the jurisdiction of the Sons of Aaron. From this we can deduce that the elite group does not represent the leadership of the whole group, but is rather commissioned with a special mandate by those in authority in the larger group. But if it is *only the property* of the members of the elite group that falls under the control of the Sons of Aaron, to whom are they accountable, if anyone, in other matters? Below a case is made that an answer to this question is found in the figure of the Maskil who plays an important role in the training of the elite group.

Finally, in 9.9-11 we find one last set of rules for these "men of holiness who walk perfectly" (9.8). Their property is to remain distinct from that of the men of deceit (9.9-10), they are not to walk in the stubbornness of their hearts (9.10), and finally and most interestingly, they are to "be judged in the first judgments" in which the men of the Community began to be instructed.[42] This last assertion would seem to indicate that the one of the goals for creating the elite group is to *reenact some dimension of the early experience*

---

39. Note also the atoning function of the elite group as described in 8.2-4.

40. Here again a future reference seems to make the best sense of the grammar: a temporal clause (בעת ההיאה) followed by an imperfect verb (יבדילו, hiphil).

41. 9.8: אנשי הקודש ההולכים בתמים.

42. 9.10: ונשפטו במשפטים הרשונים אשר החלו אנשי היחד לתיסר בם.

of the larger group. This return to the roots of the Community by the elite group will continue until the coming of the prophet and the messiahs of Aaron and Israel.

4. The Maskil and the Elite Group

We must now ask whether the החוקים למשכיל that begin in 9.12 are in any way connected to the elite group that is in view in 8.1–9.12. First, however, several cursory observations about the figure of the Maskil must be made on the basis of the evidence of 1QS and 1QSb.[43]

In these two documents, the term "Maskil" refers to a formal office, and is not simply a reference to a "sage" or "wise" man (√ שכל). The reasons supporting this statement are several. First, the Maskil occupies a prominent role in the public ceremonies of the Community. For instance, in 1QSb the Maskil is the figure who delivers the blessings to the various members of the group.[44] Second, the Maskil is clearly an important teacher. In 1QS 3.13 we learn that he is the steward of the Community's pronounced dualistic worldview and is responsible for instructing the members of the group in it. As we shall see, teaching is also part of the Maskil's duties as articulated in 9.12-21. Finally, insofar as the hymn appended to 1QS is put in the mouth of the Maskil, this figure is imbued with a distinct personality in a way that is absent from descriptions of other office holders in 1QS.[45]

This evidence points to the fact that the Maskil is an important office within the Community; moreover, it indicates that there is only a single Maskil at any given time within the communal hierarchy. The fact that in

43. Although 1QSb (like 1QSa) is an independent document, it is nonetheless valuable for distilling information about a figure like the Maskil on the assumption that, since this document was included on the same scroll as 1QS, the role and function of the Maskil attested in it was regarded as valid in the sect at the time of the production of the scroll. For an overview of the role of the Maskil in the Dead Sea Scrolls, see Carol Newsom, "The Sage in the Literature of Qumran: The Functions of the *Maskîl*," in *The Sage in Israel and the Ancient Near East* (ed. J. G. Gammie and L. G. Purdue; Winona Lake: Eisenbrauns, 1990), 373-82.

44. See 1QSb 1.1; 3.22; and 5.20. Many scholars have speculated that 1QS originally opened with למשכיל] ל in 1.1, which would represent once again the public role of the Maskil in the covenant entry ceremony. However, since 1QS is so fragmentary at this point and there is no comparative material from Cave 4, this possibility remains unproveable. Note also that in the Songs of the Sabbath Sacrifice and in 4Q510-4Q511 *(Songs of the Master)* we find the Maskil portrayed as leading the Community's liturgy.

45. In fact, the only figure among the Scrolls who provides any sort of appropriate analogy for the Maskil's role in the group is the Righteous Teacher.

1QSb the blessings of the Sons of Zadok and the Prince of the Congregation, for instance, all fall to the Maskil implies a solitary officer and not simply one of any number of *Maskilim* from local cells. The uniqueness of the office of the Maskil becomes even clearer through an analysis of 9.12-21.

The opening line of the "statutes for the Maskil" makes it quite obvious that the Maskil's dealings with every member of the Community are in view, for it is asserted that these statutes apply to his conduct "with every living being" (9.12: עם כול חי). Even so, there are a number of indications in this section that suggest that the Maskil is described here as having a special role in training the members of the elite group. First among such indicators is the context of 1QS: 9.12-21 follows immediately on the heels of the outline of the elite group.[46] Second, in 9.17-19, it is said that the Maskil is to instruct the "chosen of the way"[47] in the "midst of the men of the Community" (בתוך אנשי היחד) so that they can achieve "perfect behavior." This reference to a group being trained *within* the Community bears marked similarity to what is encountered in 8.1–9.11. This impression is strengthened in the next two sentences: "This is the time to prepare the way to wilderness. He [i.e., the Maskil] should instruct them in everything that has been found to do at that time" (9.19-20).[48] Given that the preparation to go into the wilderness is associated with the elite group in 8.12-16, it is reasonable to conclude that the mention of a distinct group being trained within the Community in anticipation for a journey to the wilderness here in 9.18-21 refers to the same group. If this is indeed the case, it constitutes further evidence that the Maskil is a solitary official within the Community, and that one of his tasks is to train the elite group for their special task.

In light of the preceding analysis, the opening reference to the Maskil's dealings with "every living thing" should be reconsidered. Perhaps that statement does not serve to signal the scope of the statutes but emphasizes, instead, how the Maskil's interaction with every person is characterized by strict proportionality. In other words, the Maskil is charged always to treat people in a manner that is precisely proportional to their degree of merit or malice.

---

46. Although there is an indentation of the beginning of 9.12 and a *paragraphus* marker out in the right margin, there is not an elaborate scribal marking of the type we have seen elsewhere that indicates major transitions in the document.

47. לביחרי דרך. This is probably a transcriptional error for an intended לבחירי דרך (cf. 9.14: ובבחירי). However, if we allow the text to stand as is (לביחרי דרך, "to the ones who choose the way"), the meaning for our purposes remains the same.

48. The sentence immediately following is a reference to separating from the men of deceit (9.20-21). As I noted earlier, this was an injunction for the whole Community, but in the context of the elite group it seems to have taken on a more stringent and literal meaning.

By way of example, in 9.12 the Maskil's "behavior with every living thing" is to be conducted in accord with "the regulation of every time and the weight of every man." Continuing in this vein, the Maskil is to "perform God's will according to everything that has been revealed from time to time" (9.13) and "to measure out all the understanding that has been discovered according to the times and according to the statute of the time" (9.13-14). It appears that the Maskil is charged with knowing what particular duties are dictated by a particular time, and to instruct and deal with persons in a manner appropriate to the prevailing mandates of the time or age. That the section opens with such an assertion, then, does not rule out a shift to the elite group midway through the section.[49]

So, at least in 9.18-21, the role of the Maskil is described in relation to the elite group and not the whole Community. Not only does this analysis point once again to the existence of an elite group, but also to the fact that the Maskil is a singular official whose duties fall into the spheres both of the larger Community and the elite group.

5. Conclusion

The present essay has attempted to offer a coherent reading of 1QS 8.1–9.21 in its present form — one that does not need to appeal exclusively to theories of source or redaction criticism to account for the relationship of this unit to the surrounding material. If this reading is correct, significant implications for the reconstruction of the Community's history follow. An assessment of those implications is the work of another time and is contingent on at least two tasks: (1) a thorough comparison of 1QS with the parallel 4QS material,

---

49. A puzzling and tantalizing reference to the Maskil's "separating" and "weighing" of the בני הצדוק is found in 9.14. Should this be translated "Sons of Zadok" or "Sons of Righteousness"? The definite article on the absolute in the construct chain would lead one to prefer "Sons of Righteousness" (as is the case with the parallel text in 4QSᵉ frg. 1 3.10: בני הצדק), but the *waw* would seem to signal the proper name "Zadok" (see 5.2, 9). Robert Kugler argues that the presence of the *waw,* which he thinks is not likely to be the result of scribal error, must be taken as indicating the name "Zadok" ("A Note on 1QS 9.14: The Sons of Righteousness or the Sons of Zadok?" *DSD* 3 [1996]: 315-20). What is especially interesting is the fact that the Maskil "separates" these individuals — an idea that in columns 8–9 is associated with the elite group. Are the Sons of Zadok somehow associated with the elite group? (Note the mention of the atoning function of the Sons of Zadok in 1QSa 1.2-3 and the suggestions of their distinct status and holiness within the Community in 1QSb 3.22-28.) Ought we to understand that the Maskil has the authority to rank and evaluate the Sons of Zadok? While possible, given the lack of data, these are unfortunately only speculations built on conjectures, and nothing certain can be concluded.

followed by a reevaluation of the relationship between 1QS and CD; and (2) a thorough comparison of 8.1–9.21 with 1QSa and the forms of Community envisioned there.

Again, such avenues of inquiry are secondary to the thesis I have attempted to advance here. That thesis can be stated simply: 1QS 8–9 reflect a plan to muster an elite group that would act in a manner consistent with the Community's practices and beliefs, but whose rigor and segregation would result in new dimensions for the Community's role and function in Israel.[50] For the framers of 1QS, this elite group represented an important step forward in the Community's quest to right the wrongs that existed in Israel.

50. This point is articulated by Collins, "Forms of Community," 103.

The Prince of the Congregation:
Qumran "Messianism" in the Context of *Milḥāmâ*

C. D. ELLEDGE

Recent studies of Qumran Messianism illustrate a methodological conundrum that pervades Dead Sea Scrolls research as a whole: whether to harmonize similar terms and phrases from different documents into a comprehensive portrait of Qumran theology or to treat such terms and phrases on a document-by-document basis that recognizes important differences among the traditions that the Community preserved over the span of approximately two centuries. This conundrum is well illustrated by contrasting the following quotations from two of the foremost specialists in the study of Second Temple literature. Each epitomizes two conflicting methodological approaches to the classification of Messianic titles and terms in the Dead Sea Scrolls.

- Morton Smith: "Though unjustified, the tacit presupposition of uniformity is common. Witness the many articles which take for granted that

---

Much of the research for this article was undertaken during my doctoral studies at Princeton Theological Seminary and completed while I was on a grant provided by the U.S. Student Fulbright Program. I wish to express my appreciation to the Israel Antiquities Authority for permission to view several of the fragments discussed in this essay, and to Émile Puech and Jean Duhaime of the École Biblique de Jérusalem for their many fine lectures and studies regarding these materials. Most importantly, the basic methods of research employed in this study were learned first hand at Princeton Theological Seminary (1996-2001), while assisting Prof. James H. Charlesworth in the production of PTSDSSP 4A, 4B, and 6B. To the Seminary, President Thomas W. Gillespie (emeritus), Dean James F. Armstrong (emeritus), and especially Prof. Charlesworth, goes my enduring gratitude. Translations generally follow those of PTSDSSP 1, 2, and 6B, unless otherwise indicated.

the data are to be harmonized. . . . But the manifest diversity of the material requires us first to make complete and distinct accounts of each separate title, and not to impose on any document any concept it does not clearly contain."[1]

- John J. Collins: "[T]he correlation of various epithets and titles that may be applied to the same figure is an essential step in the interpretation of the Scrolls."[2]

Whether one ought to provide "distinct accounts of each separate title" (so Smith) or a "correlation of various epithets and titles" (so Collins) remains among the most important methodological problems in Qumran Messianology.

In the last decade or so, studies of Qumran Messianism have favored by far a harmonizing methodology. This is especially the case when one considers recent critical assessments of the "Prince of the Congregation" (*Nāśî̕ Ha-̕Ēdâ;* נשיא העדה), a figure who is mentioned in at least the following six passages preserved at Qumran:

> *Damascus Document:* CD MS A 7.20//4Q266 (4QD^a) frg. 3 3.20-22
> *Rule of Blessings* (1QSb) 5.23-28[3]
> *War Scroll:* 1QM 5.1-2 (cf. 3.15-16 and 4Q496 [4QM6] frg. 10)
> *Commentary on Isaiah^a* (4Q161 [4QpIsa^a]) frgs. 2-6 2.18-19 and frgs. 8-10 3.15-29
> *Rule of War* (4Q285 [4QSMil]) frg. 4 and frg. 7 (cf. 11Q14)[4]
> *Moses Apocryphon^b* (4Q376 [4QapocrMoses^b]) frg. 1 3.1-3

---

1. Morton Smith, "What is Implied by the Variety of Messianic Figures?" *JBL* 78 (1959): 66-72, esp. 71. On this quotation, see Kenneth E. Pomykala, *The Davidic Dynasty Tradition in Early Judaism: Its History and Significance for Messianism* (SBLEJL 7; Atlanta: Scholars Press, 1995), 231-32.

2. John J. Collins, *The Scepter and the Star: The Messiahs of the Dead Sea Scrolls and Other Ancient Literature* (ABRL; New York: Doubleday, 1995), 60. Note the context of the full quotation: "The Branch of David (צמח דויד, mentioned clearly in the third line of the fragment) cannot be other than an anointed eschatological king, and is in fact explicitly identified as 'the righteous messiah' (משיח הצדק) in another Qumran pesher, 4QpGen (= 4QPatriarchal Blessings, 4Q252). In fact, the correlation of various epithets and titles that may be applied to the same figure is an essential step in the interpretation of the Scrolls."

3. Supplemented by Schøyen Collection MS 1990; see Phillip S. Alexander and Geza Vermes, *Qumran Cave 4.19: 4QSerekh Ha-Yaḥad* (DJD 24; Oxford: Clarendon, 1998), 231.

4. Numbering follows the reconstructions proposed by Phillip S. Alexander, "A Reconstruction and Reading of 4Q285 (4QSefer ha-Milhama)," *RevQ* 19 (2000): 333-48.

Among these very different documents, the *Nāśî'* consistently appears in military contexts. Twice, he receives the epithet "Branch of David" (צמח דויד). He is never, however, directly called either "Messiah" (משיח) or "king" (מלך). Despite this striking omission, a number of scholars have classified this figure as, in fact, "the Davidic Messiah." Milik, Ringgren, van der Woude, Brown, Vermes, Abegg, VanderKam, Puech, Nitzan, Collins, Brooke, Tigchelaar, Evans, Lichtenberger, and Pomykala are among those who refer to the "Prince" as a royal or Davidic Messiah.[5]

5. Note the following: J. T. Milik, "28*b*. Recueil de Bénédictions (1QSb)," in *Qumran Cave I* (by D. Barthélemy and J. T. Milik; DJD 1; Oxford: Clarendon, 1955), 128: "Ce personage est sans doute eschatologique, identique au נשיא כל העדה de CD vii 20 et probablement au Messie d'Israël"; Helmer Ringgren, *The Faith of Qumran: Theology of the Dead Sea Scrolls* (ed. J. H. Charlesworth; exp. ed.; Christian Origins Library; New York: Crossroad, 1995), 181: "this prince is the messianic king"; A. S. van der Woude, *Die Messianischen Vorstellungen der Gemeinde von Qumran* (SSN 3; Assen: Van Gorcum, 1957), 115: "Es unterliegt demnach keinem Zweifel, dass 1Q Sb V, 20ff ein Segens-wunsch für den erwarteten Messias-König vorliegt, der auch hier als Davidide betrachtet sein muss"; Raymond E. Brown, "J. Starcky's Theory of Qumran Messianic Development," *CBQ* 28 (1966): 51-57, esp. 55: "'the Prince of the whole congregation' can be the Davidic messiah"; Geza Vermes, "The Oxford Forum for Qumran Research Seminar on the Rule of War from Cave 4 (4Q285)," *JJS* 43 (1992): 85-94; esp. 89: "the triumphant Messiah son of David"; Martin G. Abegg, Jr., "Messianic Hope and 4Q285: A Reassessment," *JBL* 113 (1994): 81-91, esp. 86: "though he is nowhere directly equated with the Messiah, the son of David, the connection can be supposed in such passages as CD 7:19-20 (4Q266 frg. 3 4.9)" (see also idem, "The Messiah at Qumran: Still Seeing Double?" *DSD* 2 [1995]: 145-64); James VanderKam, "Messianism in the Scrolls," in *The Community of the Renewed Covenant: The Notre Dame Symposium on the Dead Sea Scrolls* (ed. E. Ulrich and J. VanderKam; Christianity and Judaism in Antiquity 10; Notre Dame: University of Notre Dame Press, 1994), 210-34, esp. 219: "[Messiah, Branch of David, and Prince of the Congregation] are the three principal messianic titles for the Davidic messiah, and . . . the three are equated with one another"; Émile Puech, "Messianism, Resurrection, and Eschatology," in *The Community of the Renewed Covenant*, 235-56, esp. 238: "The title נשיא, 'Prince' — an Ezekielian designation of the Davidic Messiah . . . refers to the king Messiah"; Bilhah Nitzan, *Qumran Prayer and Religious Poetry* (STDJ 12; Leiden: Brill, 1994), 164: "the King Messiah"; Collins, *Scepter and the Star*, 60 (see also note 2 above and cf. Collins' superior treatment in "'He Shall Not Judge by What His Eyes See': Messianic Authority in the Dead Sea Scrolls," *DSD* 2 [1995]: 145-64); George J. Brooke, "Kingship and Messianism in the Dead Sea Scrolls," in *King and Messiah in Israel and the Ancient Near East: Proceedings of the Oxford Old Testament Seminar* (ed. J. Day; JSOTSup 270; Sheffield: Sheffield Academic Press, 1998), 434-55, esp. 447: "several compositions are implying an increased interest in the expectation of an eschatological king, specifically to a Davidic figure (4Q161; 4Q174; 4Q252; 4Q285)"; Eibert J. C. Tigchelaar, "Working with Few Data: The Relation between 4Q285 and 11Q14," *DSD* 7 (2000): 49-56, esp. 50: "it seems safe to assume that the 'Prince of the Congregation' is a messianic figure"; Craig A. Evans, "Prince of the Congregation," in *EDSS* 2:694: "it seems clear that Qumran's Prince of the Congregation is none other than the Davidic Messiah"; Hermann Lichtenberger, "Messianic Expectations and Messianic Figures in the Second Temple Period," in *Qumran-Messianism: Studies on the Messianic Expectations in the Dead Sea*

Such an assessment assumes a "correlation of . . . epithets and titles" and seems to reflect the following logic: since (A) the "Prince" is called "the Branch of David" in two texts, and since (B) "the Branch of David" is called "the Righteous Messiah" (משיח הצדק) in 4Q252 (4QCommGen A), then (C) the "Prince" must be "the Davidic Messiah."[6] To use an algebraic analogy, A = B and B = C; therefore, A = C, and the Prince of the Congregation is the Davidic Messiah — notwithstanding the differences in genre and terminology that may exist among the manuscripts in question. There is no doubt that Davidic Messianism is attested in the scrolls, especially in 4Q174 (4QFlor) and 4Q252, two Qumran manuscripts which may be safely numbered among the quintessential expressions of Davidic Messianism in Palestinian Judaism of the Second Temple Period.[7] The methodological problem, however, is when varying titles and terms are synthesized into a picture of Davidic Messianism at Qumran that is larger than any single literary expression of these writings. Morton Smith and J. A. Fitzmyer warned long ago of the dangers of harmonization, and contemporary assessments would do well to take their words of admonition seriously.[8] Moreover, as Schiffman and Charlesworth have each noted through their work on the "Rule" documents, "divergent ideas were held at Qumran at different times during the same period of occupation and even at the same time" in the Community's history.[9]

Scrolls (ed. J. H. Charlesworth, H. Lichtenberger, and G. Oegema; Tübingen: Mohr-Siebeck, 1998), 9-20, esp. 12: The Prince in 1QSb carries "all the features of the Davidic King-Messiah"; Pomykala, *The Davidic Dynasty Tradition*, 212: "at least for the stage of Qumran thought represented by these documents, a reasonably coherent notion about a Davidic messiah emerges." But note Pomykala's reserve concerning 1QSb, 1QM, and CD: "the Prince is not understood as a Davidic messiah . . . it seems the Prince of the Congregation was only interpreted as a Davidic messiah in the Herodian period and not before" (ibid., 243).

6. Collins, *Scepter and the Star*, 60.

7. See especially George J. Brooke, *Exegesis at Qumran: 4QFlorilegium in Its Jewish Context* (JSOTSup 29; Sheffield: JSOT Press, 1985), 202; idem, "252. 4QCommentary on Genesis A," in *Qumran Cave 4.17: Parabiblical Texts, Part 3* (ed. G. J. Brooke et al.; DJD 22; Oxford: Clarendon, 1996); and the editions of both documents by Jacob Milgrom and Joseph L. Trafton, respectively, in *The Dead Sea Scrolls: Hebrew, Aramaic, and Greek Texts with English Translations* Vol. 6B: *Pesharim, Other Commentaries and Related Documents* (ed. J. H. Charlesworth et al.; PTSDSSP 6B; Tübingen: Mohr Siebeck, 2002).

8. See Smith, "What is Implied," 71; and J. A. Fitzmyer, "The Aramaic 'Elect of God' Text," *CBQ* 27 (1965): 348-72, esp. 355-56.

9. See Lawrence H. Schiffman, "The Messianic Idea," in idem, *Reclaiming the Dead Sea Scrolls* (Philadelphia: Jewish Publication Society, 1994), 317-27, esp. 326; and James H. Charlesworth, "Challenging the Consensus Communis Regarding Qumran Messianism (1QS, 4QS MSS)," in Charlesworth et al., eds., *Qumran-Messianism*, 120-34; the citation above is from ibid., 120-21.

If this is the case, then a harmonizing approach to Qumran Messianism would obscure what are clear differences in terminology and emphasis among individual documents.

As the foregoing comments betray, in my judgment, the current assessments of the title "the Prince of the Congregation" that have christened this figure (into) "the Davidic Messiah" may be unwarranted. This harmonizing approach may be criticized by methods of research that recognize and maintain differences in emphasis and terminology among and between individual manuscripts. Though ancient readers of these titles at Qumran may well have harmonized them through their own practices of study,[10] more careful attention should be devoted to analyzing the content of the individual manuscripts themselves, *in isolation,* before assigning them automatically to the domain of Davidic Messianism.

The present study will argue that a more adequate understanding of the Prince of the Congregation would be "the Qumran latter-day warrior"; such a classification more precisely reflects this figure's emergence in the latter-day conflict with Israel's enemies and his function as a primarily militaristic figure.[11] Moreover, the texts that mention the Prince of the Congregation are somewhat ambivalent. On the one hand, he is a necessary military figure within the Community's restorationist hopes for the reclamation of the land; on the other, his future role in the Community is primarily limited to the latter-day war, and he is ultimately peripheral to the predominance of priestly authority within the Community's ideology. Notions of a "Davidic Messiah," thus, prove misleading when assessing the nature and function of this figure

---

10. This may have been the case especially with the relationships among titles preserved in 1QS, 1QSa, and 1QSb, since all three documents were included on the same manuscript from Cave 1 and because all three appear to have been originally copied by the same hand. See further James H. Charlesworth and Loren T. Stuckenbruck, "Blessings (1QSb)," in *The Dead Sea Scrolls: Hebrew, Aramaic, and Greek Texts with English Translations,* Vol. 1: *Rule of the Community and Related Documents* (ed. J. H. Charlesworth et al.; PTSDSSP 1; Tübingen: J. C. B. Mohr [Paul Siebeck], 1994), 121.

11. Or, perhaps, as Jean Duhaime describes him, "the secular head of the entire congregation" (see Duhaime, "The War Scroll [1QM, 1Q33]," in *The Dead Sea Scrolls: Hebrew, Aramaic, and Greek Texts with English Translations,* Vol. 2: *Damascus Document, War Scroll, and Related Documents* (ed. J. H. Charlesworth et al.; PTSDSSP 2; Tübingen: J. C. B. Mohr [Paul Siebeck], 1995), 107. Note also Schiffman's reserve in his "Messianic Figures and Ideas in the Qumran Scrolls," in *The Messiah: Developments in Earliest Judaism and Christianity: The First Princeton Symposium on Judaism and Christian Origins* (ed. J. H. Charlesworth et al.; Minneapolis: Fortress, 1992), 116-29, esp. 124: "[Authors of the Isaiah *pesharim*] clearly expected to be led in the end of days by the prince of the congregation and/or the Davidic Messiah." In Schiffman's "and/or" one senses the possibility of distinguishing between the two figures.

within the Community's hopes for the future. Four observations support the argument presented here.

1. First Observation

The *Nāśî' Ha-'Ēdâ* is never called משיח or מלך in any extant manuscript among the Dead Sea Scrolls.

This terminological omission should not be overlooked, since 1QS, 1QSa, and 4Q252 (4QCommGen A) all indicate that the title משיח is well within the Community's vocabulary for naming messianic figures.[12] Neither משיח nor מלך, however, appear in reference to the *Nāśî'*. Thus, the two most important titular designations in Davidic royal ideology are simply not applied to the *Nāśî'*.[13] Though it is theoretically possible that this is simply a coincidence of language or due to the circumstances of manuscript survival, the fact that the lack is total suggests a consistent reticence to use these terms in relation to the *Nāśî'*. That fact, consequently, should be taken seriously as an important feature of Qumran usage of this title. This is especially true due to the sustained sensitivity to symbolic *termini technici,* cryptograms, and epithets that runs throughout the corpus of Qumran sectarian literature.[14]

Damascus Document: CD MS A 7.20//4Q266 (4QDᵃ) frg. 3 3.20-22

Perhaps the earliest reference to the *Nāśî'* to be found at Qumran occurs in the *Damascus Document* tradition, which was influential upon numerous aspects of the sectarian ideology of the Community.[15] 4Q266 is the earliest copy

---

12. Note 1QS 9.11: ומשיחי אהרון וישראל ("the Messiahs of Aaron and Israel"); 1QSa 2.12: המשיח ("the Messiah"), 2.14: [מש]יח ישראל ("[the Mess]iah of Israel"), 2.20: משיח ישראל ("the Messiah of Israel"); and 4Q252 (4QCommGen A) frg 6 5.3-4: משיח הצדק צמח דויד ("the Righteous Messiah, the Branch of David").

13. On the centrality of these titles for Davidic royal ideology, see the classic studies by Sigmund Mowinckel, *He That Cometh: The Messiah Concept in the Old Testament and Later Judaism* (Oxford: Blackwell, 1956), 62-69; and Tryggve N. D. Mettinger, *King and Messiah: The Civil and Sacral Legitimation of the Israelite Kings* (ConBOT 8; Lund: Gleerup, 1976), 185-232.

14. Devorah Dimant, "Qumran Sectarian Literature," in *Jewish Writings of the Second Temple Period: Apocrypha, Pseudepigrapha, Qumran Sectarian Writings, Philo, Josephus* (ed. M. Stone; CRINT 2.2; Philadelphia: Fortress, 1984), 483-550, esp. 503-4.

15. Joseph M. Baumgarten and Daniel R. Schwartz, "Damascus Document (CD)," in PTSDSSP 2:6-7. Here, I share the assumptions of Baumgarten and Schwartz that the *Damascus*

among the 4QD fragments, and attests a Hasmonean semi-cursive hand, paleographically dated to "the first half or to the middle of the first century" BCE.[16] Here, the נשיא כול העדה is mentioned in conjunction with "the interpreter of the Law," both of whom are prophesied in Num 24:17:

4Q266 frg. 3 col. 3

[כאש]ר כתוב דרך [כוכב מיעקוב]   20
[וקם שב]ט מישראל השבט ה[וא נ]שי[17] [כו]ל [העדה ובעומדו]   21
[וקרקר א]ת כול בני שית   22

20 ... [a]s it is written, "A star moves out [of Jacob,
21 and a ro[d] arises out of Israel." The rod is the [P]rince [of the who]le
   congregation. And when he takes his stand,
22 he will destroy] all the sons of Seth.[18]

In this case, the *Nāśî'* is equated with the "rod" (שבט) of the biblical citation, an equation that probably plays upon the use of שבט to denote an instrument of physical violence (cf. 1QSb 5.23-28 below),[19] since the commentary explicitly states that he will "destroy all the sons of Seth," according to the prophecy of Num 24:17. Thus, at the earliest stage in the traditions mentioning the Prince, he is primarily associated with victory in battle. Nowhere, however, is he called "Messiah."[20] Nor is the *Nāśî'* called "David" or "King." In fact, where מלך is used just a few lines earlier in the same column, it refers to "the assembly" (הקהל) of the covenanters, not to the *Nāśî'*. Furthermore, though the previous line (CD 7.16) quotes Amos 9:11 ("I will lift up the fallen Booth of Da-

---

Document was "a product of the same general movement" that produced other Qumran writings, but was probably not the literary creation of the Qumran Community *sensu stricto*. Note that 4Q376 (4QapocrMoses[b]) may be roughly contemporaneous with the *Nāśî'* tradition in the *Damascus Document,* if Strugnell is right about its date and provenience. See the treatment of 4Q376 below.

16. Joseph M. Baumgarten, *Qumran Cave 4.13: The Damascus Document (4Q266-273)* (DJD 18; Oxford: Clarendon, 1996), 30.

17. On the orthography, see Baumgarten, DJD 18:30.

18. Text restored following CD MS A, as presented in Baumgarten and Schwartz in PTSDSSP 2. Throughout this article, biblical citations appear in bold type.

19. See Exod 21:20; 2 Sam 7:14; 18:14; 23:21; 1 Chr 11:23; Job 9:34; 21:9; 37:13; Ps 89:33; Prov 10:13; 22:15; Isa 10:5, 15, 24; 14:29; 30:31; Lam 3:1; Micah 4:14. Note, however, that Collins translates "scepter" here and in 1QSb 5.23-28 (*Scepter and the Star,* 61).

20. This is the case even in CD. Though the term משיח (or משוח) appears there three times in the recurrent temporal phrase, עד עמוד משיח מאהרון ומישראל (CD MS A 19.33–20.1; cf. the pars. in 12.23–13.1; 14.18-19; 19.10-11), it is *not* used of the *Nāśî'*, despite the fact that both titles appear in the very same document.

vid"), the Davidic language of the passage seems to be a collective designation for the entire people of Judah, and their accession over Ephraim. Nowhere is the Davidic language applied to the *Nāśî'*. Even in CD 5.1-2, which directly cites the biblical legislation regarding the מלך (see Deut 17:17), the term נשיא has been used in direct substitution for the biblical title מלך.[21]

Rule of Blessings (1QSb) 5.23-28

Another document from the earliest period of the Qumran Community that refers to the Nāśî' is the *Rule of Blessings,* which is paleographically dated to the Hasmonean period c. 125-75 BCE.[22] This document records a series of eschatological blessings that the Instructor is to confer upon approximately eight persons or groups.[23] The Nāśî' is, thus, envisioned in the blessings as participating in an eschatological scenario in which his role is organically related to that of numerous other figures, including the members of the sect and the "Sons of Zadok." The first four lines of the column mentioning the Nāśî' are frustratingly fragmentary and list a number of directives which the Nāśî' will accomplish in the future: he will renew the covenant of the Community in order to establish the kingdom of his people forever and to judge the poor with righteousness; and he will establish his holy covenant amid the anguish of those who are seeking it.

The remaining lines of the column contain a blessing for the Nāśî', which is characterized by the kind of idealized poetical language one finds in other Qumran liturgies. Many of these include militaristic imagery. The blessing is as follows:

1QSb col. 5

י[ש]אכ[ה אדוני לרום עולים[24] וכמגדל עו[ז] בחומה	23
ארץ וברוח שפתיכה בעז[פי]כה בשבטכה תחריב [ ] נשגבה וה]ייתה כ[25]	24

---

21. Baumgarten and Schwartz, PTSDSSP 2:21; Yigael Yadin, *The Scroll of the War of the Sons of Light against the Sons of Darkness* (London: Oxford University Press, 1962), 278.

22. G. J. Brooke, "1Q28b. 1QSerekh ha-Yaḥad b (fragment)," in DJD 26:229.

23. I follow the divisions of the text proposed by J. Licht, "The Benedictions (Recueil des Bénédictions, 1QSb)," in *The Rule Scroll — A Scroll from the Wilderness of Judaea: 1QS, 1QSa, 1QSb — Text, Introduction and Commentary* (Jerusalem: Magnes, 1965), 274-75 (Hebrew); defended more recently by L. H. Schiffman, *The Eschatological Community of the Dead Sea Scrolls: A Study of the Rule of the Congregation* (SBLMS 38; Atlanta: Scholars, 1989), 72-76; and further employed by Charlesworth and Stuckenbruck, PTSDSSP 1:119-31.

24. Read עולם, following Milik and PTSDSSP 1:128; cf. the proper spelling of עולם two lines below.

25. Restored following Schøyen Collection MS 1990 (Brooke, DJD 26:231).

25 תמית רשע[יתן לכה[27 רוח עצ]ה וגבורת עולם רוח   דעת ויראת אל והיה[26

26 צדק אזור[מותניכה   [° אזור ח[ ] °°° [ו]ישם קרניכה ברזל ופרסותיכה נחושה

27 תנכח כפ]ר עמים רבים ותרמוס גוי]ים28 כטיט חוצות כיא אל הקימכה לשבט

28 למושלים לפ]ניכה   וכול לא]ומים יעובדוכה ובשם קודשו יגברכה

23 [. . .] (May) the Lord [r]a[ise yo]u[29] to eternal heights, and (make you) like a mighty tower on an inaccessible wall

24 and m[ay you be like . . .] with might of your [mouth], with your rod may you devastate (the) land, and by the breath of your lips

25 may you kill the wicked. [May he grant you a spirit of couns]el and everlasting strength,
a spirit of the knowledge and fear of God. May

26 righteousness (be) the belt of [your loins . . .]° belt of ḥ[. . .]°°°, [and] may he make your horns iron and your hooves bronze.

27 May you gore like a young b[ull many peoples and may you trample the nati]ons like mud of the streets. For God raised you up as a rod

28 against the rulers bef[ore you. . . . And may all the na]tions serve you. And may he strengthen you with his holy name.[30]

Most of these blessings assume at least two functions for the *Nāśî'* in the latter days: *First,* there are blessings that pray for his strength and military might. As in the *Damascus Document,* the *Nāśî'* is a "rod" (שבט) who will strike the enemies of Israel, physically killing the wicked.[31] The liturgy prays that he will be endowed with might (גבר, גבורה) in the latter days, a characteristic of the great warriors (גבורים) that had fought against Israel's enemies in days gone by.[32] The term גבורה even appears inscribed upon the standards, trumpets, and lances of the faithful in the *War Scroll,* and generally describes the might with which the "Sons of Light" face the Kittim in the *milḥāmâ.*[33]

Second, the blessings include a few brief prayers that the *Nāśî'* may be endowed by spiritual attributes — "[couns]el . . . a spirit of the knowledge

26. Note that this word was not adequately transcribed in Brooke, DJD 26:231.

27. Restored following Schøyen Collection MS 1990 (Brooke, DJD 26:231).

28. Restoration follows Brooke, DJD 26:233.

29. The liturgy employs a sophisticated paronomasia here. It prays that the Lord "raise" (√ נשא) the נשיא as a high tower upon a wall.

30. Text and translation generally follow Charlesworth and Stuckenbruck, in PTSDSSP 1:128-31.

31. Charlesworth and Stuckenbruck, PTSDSSP 1:120.

32. Kosmala, "גבר," *TDOT* 2:373-75.

33. See 1QM 3.5; 4.4, 12; 6.2; and cf. 1.14; 6.6; 11.4, 9; 13.13; 16.1; 18.11, 13. On these texts, see Roland E. Murphy, "GBR and GBWRH in the Qumran Writings," in *Lex tua veritas: Festschrift für Hubert Junker* (ed. H. Groß and F. Mußner; Trier: Paulinus, 1961), 137-43, esp. 140.

and fear of God" and by righteousness and faithfulness. These spiritual at-tributes probably assume the earlier description of the *Nāśî'* as one who will judge the poor in righteousness. The liturgy thus prays that the *Nāśî'* will be endowed with the divine aid necessary for doing his job in the latter days: exe-cuting just judgment and destroying Israel's enemies.

The picture of the *Nāśî'* that emerges from the *Rule of Blessings* is thus that of a charismatically-endowed military leader who will subject the nations to his authority and judge the poor righteously. Despite the exalted poetic lan-guage used to describe his work, however, the *Nāśî'* is nowhere termed Messiah or King.[34] Nor is he associated with David anywhere in the passage, despite the fact that the spiritual attributes ascribed to the *Nāśî'* probably derive from Isa 11:2-5,[35] the famous "stump of Jesse" passage, to which I shall return below.

War Scroll: 1QM 5.1-2 (cf. 3.15-16 and 4Q496 [4QM6] frg. 10)

As the title to this article indicates, the *Nāśî'* frequently appears in those doc-uments of the Qumran library that accentuate its *milḥāmâ* or "holy war" ide-ology. This is the case with the *War Scroll* manuscripts, as well as other docu-ments pervaded by the *milḥāmâ* ideology, such as the *Commentary on Isaiahᵃ* (4Q161) and the *Rule of War* (4Q285).

Two manuscripts of the *War Scroll* mention the *Nāśî'*. First of all, 1QM, dated paleographically to "the last part of the first century B.C.E.,"[36] attests an enigmatic passage in which the names of Israel, Levi, Aaron, the other twelve tribes of Israel, and the twelve commanders (שרים) of the individual tribes shall be written "upon the sh[ie]ld of the Prince of the whole congregation."

1QM col. 5

1   ועל מ[ג]ן נשיא כול העדה יכתובו שמו[ו]שם ישראל ולוי ואהרון ושמות שנים
עשר שבטי ישראל כתולדותם

2   ושמות שנים עשר שרי שבטיהם   *Vacat*

And upon the sh[ie]ld of the Prince of the Whole Congregation shall be written his
name, [and] the name of Israel, and of Levi and Aaron, and the names of the
twelve tribes of Israel, according to their generations,
and the names of the twelve commanders of their tribes.[37]

34. Charlesworth and Stuckenbruck, PTSDSSP 1:120.
35. Ibid.
36. Duhaime, PTSDSSP 2:80.
37. Text generally follows Duhaime in PTSDSSP 2:106; I have supplemented Duhaime with readings from Yadin, *Scroll of the War*.

This passage is far too brief to make sweeping assumptions about the role of the *Nāśî'* in the conflict. Davies even suspects that the passage represents a secondary insertion.[38] Nevertheless, a few observations may be made. First, the writers apparently envision a figure who is armed for military conflict and who holds a shield. Second, the figure may well serve as a kind of representative champion for all Israel in the battle, since the names of all the tribes are symbolically written upon his shield. Third, the *Nāśî'* is to be distinguished here from the שרים, who are the individual commanders of the twelve tribes. Apparently, his command incorporates that of the tribal leaders into a single office, but the *War Scroll* is completely silent on his further role in the conflict. Immediately prior to this section of the *War Scroll*, the title *Nāśî'* is also mentioned in the "Rule of Standards" (סרך אתות), where reference is made to the "Prince of the Tr[ibe]" ([ט]נשי השבט) and the "Prince of the Myriad" (נשיא הרבוא) (3.15-16). These titles probably do not refer to the "Prince of the Whole Congregation" (5.1), but rather to chieftains over tribes and larger hosts of soldiers.[39] These uses of the title *Nāśî'* do, however, indicate that it may be used of military chieftains over both smaller and larger companies of troops, and that the "Prince of the Whole Congregation" is imagined to be the highest ranking military commander of this kind.

References to the title *Nāśî'* in the (paleographically) pre-Herodian 4Q496 (4QM6) are written exclusively in supralinear corrections to frg. 10 lines 3-4, a text that roughly corresponds to the "Rule of Standards" in 1QM.[40] Here, in line 3, is a reference to "the Prince who is at the head of" though the text unfortunately breaks off at this point.[41] This use of the title may refer either to "the Prince who is at the head of [the whole congregation]" or to "the Prince who is at the head of [a tribe]" (see lines 5-6).

Once again, the *Nāśî'* is not called "Messiah" or "King" in any of these references, nor is he associated with David. Instead, he serves as a kind of military captain for the entire people, with subsidiary divisions and their respective officers under his command. The *Nāśî'*'s military activity is thus especially pronounced in the *War Scroll*. He is imagined, quite graphically, as a military commander who holds a shield and commands subordinate officers

---

38. Phillip R. Davies, *1QM, The War Scroll from Qumran: Its Structure and History* (BibOr 32; Rome: Biblical Institute Press, 1977), 35-36.

39. Yadin, *Scroll of the War*, 47-48.

40. On the paleography, see Maurice Baillet, *Qumrân grotte 4.3 (4Q482-4Q520)* (DJD 7; Oxford: Clarendon, 1982), 56-58.

41. As the *apparatus criticus* to PTSDSSP 2:184 n. 61 points out, this correction does not appear within the corresponding passage of 1QM.

in a ritually orchestrated war. Correspondingly, the more mythological and poetic language of the *Rule of Blessings* is lacking here.

Commentary on Isaiah[a] (4Q161 [4QpIsa[a]]) frgs. 2-6 2.18-19 and frgs. 8-10 3.15-29

The most exalted view of the *Nāśî'* in the Scrolls is clearly to be found in 4Q161 (4QpIsa[a]), a *pesher* on Isa 10:20–11:5 dating paleographically to the Herodian period.[42] This *pesher* is highly charged with the Community's *milḥāmâ* ideology, and interprets the Isaianic references to Assyria's destruction in terms of the Community's latter-day conflict with the Kittim. Once again, the text is frustratingly fragmentary:

4Q161 frgs. 2-6, col. 2

18]בשובם ממדבר הע[][מי[][מ]‎[43] ב[

19]נשיא‎[44] העדה ואחר יס[][ו][ר מעלי]הם

[. . .] when they return from the wilderness (of) the pe[ople]s *b*[
[. . .] the Prince of the Congregation. And afterwards, he will de[part] from [them][45]

Though the Prince is clearly mentioned in line 19, the only conclusion that can be drawn is that he was discussed at this point in the *pesher,* probably in an exegetical reflection upon Yahweh's wrath against Assyria found in Isa 10:24-27 (see frgs. 2-6 2.10-15).

A more extensive reference emerges in frgs. 8-10 3.15-29, which contains a *pesher* on Isa 11:1-5. This section of the *pesher* seems to describe the works of the *Nāśî'*, though direct reference to him is not actually preserved in the extant remains. The citation from Isaiah contains a highly idealized description of a shoot that will emerge from the stump of Jesse. This shoot will bear the spirit of the Lord, including a spirit of wisdom, perception, counsel, and might, the spirit of the knowledge and fear of the Lord. He will judge the poor with righteousness, and destroy the earth with the rod of his mouth including all of its wickedness.

42. Maurya P. Horgan, "Isaiah Pesher 4 (4Q161 = 4QpIsa[a])," in PTSDSSP 6B:83.

43. As in PTSDSSP, the symbols "[[ ]]" mark joins between frg. 5 (right) and frg. 6 (left) of 4Q161. See John M. Allegro with Arnold A. Anderson, *Qumrân Cave 4.1: (4Q158-4Q186)* (DJD 5; Oxford: Clarendon, 1968), Pl. 4.

44. According to the textual reconstruction of Horgan, the *Nāśî'* is viewed as "the rod," or (less likely) "the whip," of Isa 10:24-27 (PTSDSSP 6B:88-89).

45. Text and translation generally follow Horgan, PTSDSSP 6B:88-89.

Hardly as concerned with the spiritual qualities enumerated in the Isaiah quotation,[46] the actual commentary upon this citation deals primarily with the *Nāśî'*'s military might and his righteous judgment:

4Q161 frgs. 8-10, col. 3

[דויד העומד באח]רית הימים[47]	22
או]יבו ואל יסומכנו ב[רוח ג]בורה [	23
כ]סא כבוד נזר ק[ודש]ובגדי ריקמו[ת]	24
[בידו ובכול הג]ואי[ם ימשול ומגוג	25
כו]ל העמים תשפוט חרבו ואשר אמר לוא	26
[למראה עיניו ישפוט]ולוא למשמע אוזניו יוכיח פשרו אשר	27
[וכאשר יורוהו כן ישפוט ועל פיהם	28
[עמו יצא אחד מכוהני השם ובידו בגדי[48]	29

22 [. . .] David, who will take (his) stand in the lat[ter days . . .]
23 [. . .] his [ene]my. And God will sustain him with [a mi]ghty [spirit . . .]
24 [. . . th]rone of glory, a h[oly] crown, and garments of variegated stu[ff . . .]
25 [. . .] in his hand, and over all the n[ation]s[49] he will rule, and Magog
26 [. . . al]l the peoples will his sword judge. And as for what it says, "**Neither**
27 [**will he judge by what his eyes see**] **nor will he decide on what his ears hear**," its interpretation (is) that
28 [. . .] and as they teach him, so will he judge, and according to their (command)
29 [. . .] with him. One of the priests of renown will go out, and in his hand the garments of[50]

There is explicit reference to David in the commentary, probably as the "Branch of David," though the text must be restored to render this epithet. Still, the actual relationship between David and the *Nāśî'* remains obscure. Nowhere is there even the slightest hint of a genealogical relationship, nor is the title "son of David" used as in *Pss. Sol.* 17:21. What is more certain is that military power is an important attribute of this figure. God will sustain him with the spirit of military might (רוח גבורה). He bears a sword that will judge Magog and all the nations. Furthermore, this figure will serve as a just

46. As Pomykala rightly notes (*The Davidic Dynasty Tradition*, 201).
47. On the restoration, see Collins, *Scepter and the Star*, 57.
48. Cf. בגדי in the third line of this citation.
49. Or, "Gentiles."
50. Text and translation follow Horgan, PTSDSSP 6B:96-97.

judge over the people. This is highlighted especially in the remains of lines 27-29. Here, it is claimed that he will judge the people in accordance with what an undisclosed group will teach him. Though the text is fragmentary, the most logical restoration to the text is that the "priests of renown," mentioned in the very next line, will teach this figure how he is to judge the peoples.[51] If this restoration is correct, then it clarifies what "righteous judgment" means to the pesherist — it means judgment as executed according to priestly command.[52] Nowhere, however, is this figure called "Messiah" or "King."

Rule of War (4Q285) frg. 4 and frg. 7 (cf. 11Q14)

The *Nāśî'* is mentioned twice in the controversial 4Q285, which was released amid some hysteria in the early 1990s. Though press releases originally suggested that the text proclaimed a slain Messiah, most Qumran scholars now recognize that the *Nāśî'* in this text is the aggressor, not the victim, in the eschatological war,[53] with only Eisenman and Wise[54] and Tabor[55] reserving the possibility that the Prince is slain in this text. Though Milik originally proposed that this document was the lost ending to the *War Scroll*,[56] it is more likely that 4Q285 represents an independent document, which, though heavily influenced by the *War Scroll*, provides a distinctive rendition of the eschatological battle.[57] Cave 11 preserves an additional copy (11Q14 [11QSMil]). Both copies date paleographically to the latter Herodian period

---

51. Cf. 11Q19 57.11-15. See also van der Woude, *Vorstellungen*, 181-82; Pomykala, *The Davidic Dynasty Tradition*, 202.

52. Furthermore, if the "garments" in the priest's hands are those that clothe the *Nāśî'* in line 17, this manuscript may have gone on to describe the sacral institution of the *Nāśî'* as an authority based upon priestly appointment.

53. Schiffman, *Reclaiming the Dead Sea Scrolls*, 344.

54. Robert Eisenman and Michael O. Wise, *The Dead Sea Scrolls Uncovered: The First Complete Translation and Interpretation of 50 Key Documents Withheld for Over 35 Years* (Rockport: Element, 1992), 24-27.

55. James D. Tabor, "A Pierced or Piercing Messiah? — The Verdict is Still Out," *BAR* 18/6 (November-December 1992): 58-59.

56. J. T. Milik, "*Milkî-ṣedeq* et *Milkî-reša'* dans les anciens écrits juifs et chretiens," *JJS* 23 (1992): 95-144, esp. 143.

57. Alexander, "Reconstruction and Reading of 4Q285," 348. Among the most convincing arguments that can be offered in support of this assessment is the total absence of the *termini technici* בני חושך and בני אור in 4Q285 and 11Q14. These terms are, by contrast, central to the ideology of the *War Scroll*.

(c. 30-50 CE).[58] The ideas contained therein post-date the composition of the *War Scroll*.

In the first reference to the *Nāśî*, the figure is mentioned in a fragmentary context that alludes to wickedness being struck down.

4Q285 frg. 4

1   ת תנגף רשעה]

2   נשי]א העדה וכול ישר]אל עמו

3   ההיאה העת אשר הי]ה כתוב] עליה[59]

4   לשבר אשור בארצי ו]על הרי א]בוסנו[60]

5   ה]כתיים[61]   ]°

6   נ]שיא העדה עד הים ה]גדול

---

58. Florentino García Martínez, Eibert J. C. Tigchelaar, and A. S. van der Woude, *Qumran Cave 11.2: 11Q2-18, 11Q20-31* (DJD 23; Oxford: Clarendon, 1998), 244.

59. The full citation formula is restored following CD MS A 1.13 (ה]הי אשר העת היא). (כתוב] עליה) and 4Q266 frg. 2 1.16-17. For additional alternatives, see C. D. Elledge, "Appendix: A Graphic Index of Citation and Commentary Formulae in the Dead Sea Scrolls," in PTSDSSP 6B:367-77. One might well argue that since the phrase בעת ההיאה appears twice in the following lines, the full citation formula may justifiably be restored. For similar conjectures on the formula, see P. Alexander and G. Vermes, "285. 4QSefer ha-Milḥamah," in *Qumran Cave 4.26: Cryptic Texts and Miscellanea, Part I* (by S. J. Pfann et al.; DJD 36; Oxford: Clarendon, 2000), 236.

60. After the word כתוב, 4Q285 probably contained a citation of Isa 14:24-25. Verse 25a is restored following the MT. Since this fragment of 4Q285 contains neither a right nor a left margin, it is virtually impossible to determine precisely the original placement of the individual words on the lines. At least some part of the biblical quotation probably began in the previous line, though it is impossible to determine how much. Based upon Alexander's proposal that the scroll originally contained 50-55 letter spaces per line ("Reconstruction and Reading of 4Q285," 342), it is probable that the citation contained at least v. 24b and it is possible that portions of v. 24a may have appeared in the previous line. It also appears that the citation ended either with v. 25a or immediately thereafter, since the following line precludes the continuation of the citation. One may imagine that an isolated *pesher* followed the citation, though this remains purely conjectural. Though virtually impossible to identify in most photographs, examination of the manuscript in person revealed a space after הרי and the illegible traces of an additional letter, which I have transcribed as א based upon Isa 14:25a. As Alexander and Vermes note (DJD 36:236), the traces of the consonant are visible in PAM 42.260. They themselves prefer to restore a citation of Ezek 39:3-4 (על הרי י]שראל) under the assumption that the following lines of the fragment are influenced by the wars with Gog and Magog from that chapter of Ezekiel. Émile Puech rejects this reading on epigraphic grounds, since the downstroke of the scribe's י is remarkably straight and would have left more than a mere speck of ink at the top of the letter. Thus, Puech prefers my own reading (private communication), since an א would require a more diagonal mark at the top of the consonant.

61. Alexander and Vermes suggest that a "King of the] Kittim" is mentioned here, but this is far from certain (DJD 36:236).

ונס[ו מפני ישראל בעת ההיאה]   7

[יעמוד עליהם ונעכרו עליהם]   8

[°ושבו אל היבשה בעת הה]יאה   9

ו[הביאוהו לפני נשיא] העדה   10

1 [. . .]*t* wickedness shall be struck down [. . .]
2 [. . . Prin]ce of the Congregation and all Isr[ael with him . . .]
3 [. . . this is the time concerning which it i]s written [. . .]
4 [(I shall) **break Assyria in my land and**]**upon my mountain I**[**shall trample him**[62] . . .]
5 [. . . the]Kittim [. . .]
6 [. . . P]rince of the Congregation as far as the [great] sea [. . .]
7 [. . . and they shall fle]e from before Israel at that time [. . .]
8 [. . .] he shall stand before them, and they shall be stirred up before them [. . .]
9 [. . .]? and they shall turn back to the dry land at th[at] time [. . .]
10 [. . . and] they shall bring him before the Prince[of the Congregation . . .][63]

In this text, the *Nāśî'* is grouped together with all Israel. The Kittim are mentioned, and the context suggests that lines 6-10 describe the exploits of the *Nāśî'* and all Israel in the latter-day conflict, including their movements along the Mediterranean coast.[64] Given the word כתוב, it is probable that these events emerge according to scriptural prophecy. That prophecy may well have been Isa 14:25, where Yahweh vows to tread down the Assyrians upon his mountain. The application of Yahweh's treatment of the Assyrians to the Kittim would be consistent with the interpretation of Isa 10:34 in 4Q161 and 4Q285 frg. 7 (see below). Indeed, the "Kittim of Assyria" (כתיי אשור) are directly cited in the prologue to the *War Scroll* as the enemies of God, with the promise, "Ashur shall fall and there will be none to help him."[65]

The second reference is the controversial one. Though not a *pesher* in the technical sense, 4Q285 frg. 7 cites Isa 10:34–11:1 and interprets the passage in terms of the conflict with the Kittim. It shares this characteristic with 4Q161, though 4Q285 seems much more directly concerned with the conflict

---

62. Isa 14:25a; perhaps portions of v. 24 originally preceded this.

63. Cf. the edition by Alexander and Vermes (DJD 36:235-37).

64. Alexander envisions a "sea-battle," but this is unlikely (as he himself notes); "Reconstruction and Reading of 4Q285," 344. The references to the sea are probably used directionally here.

65. 1QM 1.6: ונפל אשור ואין עוזר לו. See Davies, *1QM,* 59.

between the cedar of Lebanon and the shoot of Jesse in the biblical citation. Its scriptural citation is, therefore, strategically limited to Isa 10:34–11:1, which accentuates this very conflict.

4Q285 frg. 7

כאשר כתוב בספר [ישעיהו הנביא⁶⁷ וניקפ]⁶⁶ סבכי היער בברזל   1

והלבנון באדיר י[פול ויצא חוטר⁶⁹ מגזע ישי [ונצר משרשיו יפרה⁶⁸   2

צמח⁷⁰ דויד ונשפטו את]   3

[והמיתו נשיא העדה צמ]ח דויד   4

[ם ובמחוללות וצוה כוהן ⁷¹]   5

ה]לל[י⁷² כתיי[ם]ל[]   6

1 [. . . as it is written in the book]of Isaiah the prophet, "**And there shall be cut dow[n the massive (trees) of the forest with iron,**]

2 [**and Lebanon in (its) majesty shall**]**fall; and there shall come forth a shoot from the stump of Jesse** [**and the sprout of his roots shall bear fruit**"⁷³ . . .]

3 [. . .] the Branch of David. And they shall be brought into judgment with [. . .]

4 [. . .] and the Prince of the Congregation, the Bran[ch of David] will kill him [. . .]

5 [. . .]*m* and with woundings. And the priest shall command [. . .]

6 [. . . sl]ain of the Kitti[m . . .]*l*[. . .]⁷⁴

66. Or וניקפ]ו, as in 4Q161 frgs. 8-10 lines 5-6.

67. For the restoration of the citation formula, see 4Q163 (4QpIsaᶜ) frgs. 8-10 line 8; 4Q174 frgs. 1-2 1.15; frg. 15 line 1; 4Q265 (4QSD) frg. 1 line 3; and Elledge, "Graphic Index of Citation and Commentary Formulae."

68. Restoration of the biblical citation in these lines is only approximate, since neither the left nor right hand margin of the column is extant. Alexander and Vermes conjecture that frg. 7 preserves the left hand portion of a column, but this is hardly certain.

69. 11Q14 (11QSMil) frg. 1 1.10: חו[טר.

70. 11Q14 frg. 1 1.11: צמ]ח. 11Q14 frg. 1 1.7 apparently preserves an additional reference to the צמח ד[ויד that is not preserved in 4Q285.

71. Perhaps restore כוהן [הרואש, as Florentino García Martínez and Eibert J. C. Tigchelaar, *The Dead Sea Scrolls Study Edition* (2 vols.; Leiden: Brill, 1998), 2:642-43. Cf. similar terminology in 1QM 2.1-2; 15.4; 18.5; 19.11; and 4Q492 (4QM2) frg. 1 line 4, which describe the duties of the "High Priest," amid the war with the Kittim. The end of the *War Scroll* portrays the "High Priest" leading in prayers among the slain of the Kittim.

72. 11Q14 frg. 1 1.15: חללי [ ]פ°[. 11Q14 and 1QM 19.11 suggest the possible restoration, נפול ח]ללי.

73. Isa 10:34–11:1.

74. Cf. Alexander and Vermes, DJD 36:238-41.

In the commentary, the *Nāśî'* apparently receives the epithet "branch of David" (on this title, see below). There are cryptic references to an unknown group being judged. The Prince of the Congregation, the Branch of David, will kill an unknown foe. Finally, the priest will issue an unknown command in the presence of the slain Kittim. What is "Davidic" about this figure remains unclear, as in 4Q161. Nowhere is the *Nāśî'* called "son of David." Nor is he called "Messiah" or "King."[75]

Moses Apocryphon[b] (4Q376 [4QapocrMoses[b]]) frg. 1 3.1-3

Finally, the *Nāśî'* surfaces once again in the fragmentary remains of what was originally a piece of apocryphal legislation, dating paleographically to the late Hasmonean or early Herodian period.[76] This manuscript is practically ignored in most critical treatments of the *Nāśî'*, yet it remains important for studying the legal perspectives that may have influenced Qumran usage of the title. John Strugnell is of the opinion that the work pre-dated the Community and was, thus, not composed at Qumran.[77] Nevertheless, like the *Damascus Document*, this legal pseudepigraphon reinforced the Community's expectations regarding the *Nāśî'* and further defined his proper relationship to Torah when waging wars. Fragment 1 preserves brief reference to the "Urim," which the priests employ as instruments of divination.[78] Fragment 2 presumably describes the supernatural signs that the Urim may display under various circumstances. Fragment 3 then provides additional legislation regarding the *Nāśî'*'s military strategies under various circumstances. In light of the Temple Scroll's legislation on kingship (11Q19 58.18-21),[79] it is likely that these three

75. E.g., James H. Charlesworth, "Sense or Sensationalism? The Dead Sea Scrolls Controversy," *The Christian Century* (1992): 92-98, esp. 97: "It is obvious, therefore, that the term 'Messiah' and its cognates do not appear in the Hebrew fragment [4Q285]. It is also clear that the fragment may not be messianic at all."

76. John Strugnell, "Moses-Pseudepigrapha at Qumran," in *Archaeology and History in the Dead Sea Scrolls: The New York University Conference in Honor of Yigael Yadin* (ed. L. H. Schiffman; JSPSup 8; Sheffield: JSOT, 1990), 221-56, esp. 235-36.

77. Strugnell, "Moses-Pseudepigrapha at Qumran," 247-48.

78. See especially Num 27:21. Cf. 4Q175 (4QTestim) line 14; 4Q164 (4QpIsa[d]) frg. 1 line 5; 4Q174 (4QFlor) frgs. 6-7 lines 3-7; and 4Q522 (4QapocrJos[c]) frg. 9 2.10-11.

79. E.g., 11Q19 58.18-21: "And he shall not go forth until he comes before the high priest and inquires of him by the judgment of the Urim and Thummim. According to his command shall he go out and concerning his command shall he come in, he and all the children of Israel who are with him. He shall not go out according to any counsel of his own heart, until he inquires by the judgment of the Urim and Thummim. Then he shall have success in all his ways, when he goes out according to the judgment that. . . ." See also Strugnell's comments on

fragments of 4Q376 preserve a scenario in which priestly divination, through the Urim and Thummim, grants instructions to the *Nāśî'* regarding appropriate military strategy.[80]

4Q376 frg. 1, col. 3

1 ‏[ ]○נ העדה לכול אשר הנשיא יהיה במחנה ואם הזה המשפט ככול‏

                                                ‏ו‏

2 ‏[אשר] דבר לכול או עליה לצור לעיר ילכו כי או עמו וישראל איבו‏

3 ‏רחוקה] השדה [ ]ל[ ]כ ד[ ]ל[ ]ל[ ] לנשיא‏

1 according to all this judgment. And if there shall be in the camp the Prince who is (over) the whole congregation (and) *n○*[. . .]
2 his enemy and Israel with him, or when they march to a city to besiege it, or for any matter that [. . .]
3 for the Prince [. . .]*l*[. . .]*d k*[. . .]*l*[. . .] the field is distant [. . .][81]

This casuistic legislation[82] requires various actions by the *Nāśî'* under circumstances of battle that no longer remain extant. There is reference to his being in the camp. He is coupled with "Israel." There is reference to the besieging of cities and to his enemy. Once again, the context is clearly militaristic. He is not, however, described as Messiah or King. Nor is there any Davidic epithet.

Summation

Without "harmonizing" these texts too heavily, we may summarize the following basic features of the *Nāśî'*. The *Nāśî'* is an exalted military leader, equipped with supernatural might. He is also endowed with shield *(War Scroll)* and sword *(Commentary on Isaiah*ᵃ*)*. He does battle against the "sons of Seth" *(Damascus Document);* destroys the earth, the wicked, and the rulers *(Rule of Blessings);* and does battle against the Kittim *(War Scroll, Commen-*

Josephus, *Ant.* 3.216-218 in "Moses-Pseudepigrapha at Qumran," 243; and 4Q164 (4QpIsaᵈ) frg. 1 line 5; and 4Q175 (4QTestim) lines 16-20.

    80. On the Temple Scroll's legislation, see Yigael Yadin, *The Temple Scroll* (3 vols; Jerusalem: Israel Antiquities Authority, 1983), 2:264-65; and C. D. Elledge, *The Statutes of the King: The Temple Scroll's Legislation on Kingship (11Q19 LVI 12–LIX 21)* (CahRB 56; Paris: Gabalda, 2004), 188-95.

    81. Text and translation generally follow J. Strugnell, "376. 4QApocryphon of Mosesᵇ?," in *Qumran Cave 4.14: Parabiblical Texts, Part 2* (by M. Broshi et al.; DJD 19; Oxford: Clarendon, 1995), 126-27; idem, "Moses-Pseudepigrapha at Qumran," 247-48.

    82. Note the structural formula: ‏ואם‏ . . . ‏או‏ . . . ‏או‏ . . .

tary on Isaiah[a], *Rule of War)*, Magog, and the nations *(Commentary on Isaiah*[a]*)*. At least two of the six texts envision his righteous judgment for the poor and afflicted *(Rule of Blessings, Commentary on Isaiah*[a]*)*. He is twice associated with David in exegetical reflection upon Isa 11:1-5 *(Commentary on Isaiah*[a], *Rule of War)*, and once with the "rod from Jacob" in Num 24:17 *(Damascus Document)*. Nowhere, however, is he called "Messiah" or "King." Certainly, the Prince may be classified as a quasi-messianic figure who is expected to emerge in the latter days. His precise function within Qumran ideology, however, is overstated when he is too easily designated "the Davidic Messiah." The *Nāśî'* not only lacks the quintessential titles of Davidic Messianism, he also generally lacks the royal dominion traditionally reserved for David and his offspring in royal ideology. This leads directly to the second observation.

2. Second Observation

> Lacking the genuine office of King, the *Nāśî'* has little or no abiding political kingdom or reign beyond his military conflict with Israel's enemies.

Among the six traditions in which he is mentioned, only 4Q161 seems to envision an abiding political role for the *Nāśî'* beyond his military service. In this text, the *Nāśî'* is expected to rule over all the nations (or Gentiles; see frgs. 8-10 3.25: ‏ובכול הג[וא]י[ם ימשול‎). Furthermore, he is associated with a "throne of glory," a "holy crown," and "garments" (frgs. 8-10 3.24). At first glance, the *Nāśî'* seems virtually a king in this passage, and it is possible that the author of 4Q161 employed certain aspects of royal symbolism when describing his latter-day mission. Nevertheless, his "rule" is completely subverted to the institution of the priesthood, since the remaining lines of 4Q161 probably describe the nature of this reign as administering justice according to the teachings of the priests of renown (see above). Thus, even where his power and influence are described in their most exalted terms, the *Nāśî'* remains the executor of priestly commands.

This also appears to be the case in the final line of 4Q285 frg. 7,[83] and in the apocryphal legislation of 4Q376.[84] Furthermore, though 1QSb can use

---

83. Brooke, "Kingship and Messianism," 450.

84. See especially the following text in which various figures must consult priestly oracles before going out into battle (Judg 1:1; 18:5; 20:18, 23-27; 1 Sam 10:22; 14:37; 22:10-15; 23:2-4; 28:6; 30:8; 2 Sam 2:1; 5:19-23; 1 Chr 14:10).

the terminology of "kingdom" in describing the work of the *Nāśî'*, the term is immediately qualified as "the kingdom of his people," not the kingdom of the *Nāśî'*[85] or of his royal "house."[86] The remaining traditions that mention the *Nāśî'* provide no abiding political kingdom or reign for this figure beyond his military duties. After the battle, he simply rides off into the sunset, as it were, and gradually fades from view. The traditions are much more interested in the re-establishment of a righteous rule through military victory than they are with the ongoing nature of perpetual Davidic kingship. In this sense, the *Nāśî'*'s role is typical for Qumran eschatology, which often circumscribes eschatological figures within particular events and functions, without having a more comprehensive interest in their individuality or status. The *Nāśî'* is primarily a figure whose role is circumscribed within the eschatological time of military conflict with the Kittim. This is hardly an enthusiastic hope in an ideal Davidic ruler *per se*. This leads to the third observation.

3. Third Observation

The *Nāśî'*'s associations with David are preserved in only two of these six texts, and even here the *Nāśî'*'s actual relations to David are unclear.

As Pomykala notes in his study of the Davidic Dynasty Tradition, the earliest *Nāśî'* traditions preserved at Qumran do not use title "Branch of David" (צמח דויד). In both the *Damascus Document* tradition and in 1QSb, David is not named in association with the *Nāśî'*. The ascription of the title "Branch of David" to the *Nāśî'* in 4Q161 and 4Q285, thus, seems to be a secondary ascription added to the title *Nāśî'*, perhaps sometime during the late Hasmonean or early Herodian periods. This ascription of the title "Branch of David," of course, does not appear in 1QM or 4Q376. Thus, out of six documents mentioning the *Nāśî'*, only two actually use a Davidic title in reference to him. This should raise serious questions about the ultimate adequacy of the Davidic model for assessing the functions of this figure.

Furthermore, even in those texts that do associate the *Nāśî'* with David, the nature of those associations remains uncertain. The closest biblical prece-

---

85. It should be noted, in fact, that the language of "kingdom" appears elsewhere in the document with reference to other groups, apart from any mention of the *Nāśî'*. Cf. 3.5 and 4.26.

86. Cf. בית in 2 Samuel 7.

dents for the epithet appear in Jer 23:5-6,[87] 33:14-16,[88] and Ps 132:17-18.[89] None of these passages, however, can account for the militaristic contexts in which the Qumran epithet appears. The epithet צמח דויד appears in 4Q285 in the context of the *Nāśî*'s conflict with his enemies. The use of the title "Branch of David" in 4Q285 emerges after a selective citation of Isa 10:34–11:1, which emphasizes the conflict between the "cedar of Lebanon" and the "shoot from the stump of Jesse." In the interpretation, which employs aspects of allegorical reading and symbolism, the *Nāśî* is called the "Branch of David," who will supercede his enemy the "cedar of Lebanon." The epithet in this context seems to convey a sense of divinely sanctioned military might, the branching forth of God's chosen against the enemies of Israel. There is nothing in the passage that would suggest that the title functions as an exclusively royal designation. Davidic terminology may as easily refer to David the warrior who killed Goliath and who slew his tens of thousands, as to David the royal Israelite monarch. When David is referred to in the supernumerary Psalm (11Q5 [11QPs^a] 28.3-14) and the *War Scroll* (1QM 11.1-5) from Qumran, it is precisely his victory over Goliath and the Philistines that is recounted. In the *War Scroll*, especially, this victory has become the typological precedent for Israel's eschatological triumph over the Kittim.[90] It is possible that the "Branch of David" terminology carried similar connotations of military power and typological fulfillment when applied to the *Nāśî*.[91]

The use of the title as restored in 4Q161 presents a more exalted picture of the "Branch of David." As in 4Q285, the "Branch" is a designation expressing militancy. Immediately after the reference to the "Branch," the commentary probably makes reference to "his enemy." Thus, in the two texts that employ the Davidic epithet for the *Nāśî*, military victory over the enemy is the

87. Note: "And I will raise up for David a Righteous Branch" (והקמתי לדוד צמח צדק).

88. Note: "I shall cause to branch forth for David a Righteous Branch" (אצמיח לדוד צמח צדקה).

89. Note: "I shall cause a horn to grow for David, I shall prepare a lamp for my Anointed, his enemies I shall clothe with shame, and upon him his crown shall flourish" (שם אצמיח קרן לדוד ערכתי נר למשיחי אויביו אלביש בשת ועליו יציץ נזרו).

90. Or one may prefer the position of Marvin A. Sweeney who states that "[h]ere, the Davidic typology is present, but a Davidic Messiah is not. The author of the War Scroll sees God as the leader of the Sons of Light, not a Davidic figure" ("Davidic Typology in the Forty Year War between the Sons of Light and the Sons of Darkness," in *Proceedings of the Tenth World Congress of Jewish Studies, Division A: The Bible and Its World* (Jerusalem: World Union of Jewish Studies, 1990), 213-20; citation from 220.

91. Cf. also Sir 47:2-11. In praise of David, Sirach notes both his militaristic and cultic functions. Cf. Josephus, *Ant.* 7.389-390. In this concluding encomium to his treatment of David, Josephus summarizes both his military and ethical characteristics.

most common element. This would suggest that the epithet itself is primarily a militaristic designation, not unlike the term שבט in the *Damascus Document* and 1QSb.[92] 4Q161, of course, is unique in ascribing to the "Branch" a continuing role of governance beyond military conquest. It is possible that the author(s) of this tradition expanded earlier *Nāśî'* traditions, in ways that ensured this figure would remain the executor of priestly teachings beyond the military conflict. Messianism may even have been an underlying influence in such a process.[93] It is vital to remember, however, that this figure remains a *Nāśî'*, not a מלך or משיח. The traditions about David in 4Q504 (4QDibHam), in fact, can refer to his everlasting kingdom as a divine promise for the entire people of Israel, void of any genuine messianic expectations.[94] Only 4Q252 (4QCommGen A) expands the "Branch" terminology into full-blown Davidic Messianism. But this document uses the title משיח הצדק, *not* the title *Nāśî'*. This raises the important question of what the title *Nāśî'* might have meant as the preferred designation for this militant figure. This question leads to the fourth and final observation.

4. Fourth Observation

The title *Nāśî'* as used in the scrolls adapts biblical usage, where the *Něśî'îm* are portrayed as tribal intermediaries between the priestly classes and the whole congregation of Israel.

Biblical uses of the title *Nāśî'* are diverse, ranging from references to the leaders of foreign tribes,[95] to Abraham (Gen 23:6),[96] Solomon (1 Kgs 11:34),[97] and Sheshbazzar (Ezra 1:8).[98] The most important references, however, are to the

---

92. Even in 4Q174, which may contain a genuine expression of Davidic Messianism, the epithet occurs in the general context of Israel's victory over the enemy (see esp. frg. 1 1.1-5).

93. Note that the reference here is only to 4Q161.

94. See 4Q504 (4QDibHam) frg. 2 4.1-13.

95. Gen 17:20; 25:16; 34:2; Num 25:28; Josh 9:15-21; 13:21; Ezek 26:16; 27:21; 32:29-30; 38:2-3. Baruch Halpern accentuates the antiquity of Josh 9:15-21, where the *Naśî'îm* have "a special role in the sealing and enforcing of covenants" (*The Constitution of the Monarchy in Israel* [HSM 25; Atlanta: Scholars Press, 1981], 212).

96. The use of the title in reference to Abraham probably occurs on analogy with its ascription to the leader of a tribe. Cf. the previous note.

97. After the secession of the Northern Kingdom, Solomon is called *Nāśî'*, probably in recognition of the fact that he is now primarily the chief of Judah, not the king of all tribes.

98. Sheshbazzar provides an interesting analogy to Ezekielian and Qumran usage, especially in his duties to priest and Temple.

chieftains who preside over the tribes of Israel. Two sources are the most interesting in light of Qumran usage.

Pentateuchal Legislation (especially Priestly)

First, in the legislation of the book of Numbers, the twelve tribes each have a *Nāśî'*, who performs a number of functions that implement the laws of Moses among the people. One man of every tribe from the house of his fathers is appointed as a *Nāśî'* (see Num 1:16, 44). There are thus twelve *Něśî'îm* for all Israel. The *Něśî'îm* bring offerings to the altar on behalf of their respective tribes (Numbers 7), and are responsible for the apportioning of territories in Canaan (Numbers 34). The social functions of these figures are best described as representative and intermediate: they represent their individual tribes before other tribes, the cult, and Moses; they also serve to implement the commands of Moses and the Torah before the people. A variety of other uses in Exodus, Leviticus, the Deuteronomistic History, and Chronicles refer to similar functions for these figures.[99] Noth's classic treatment of this terminology accentuated its origins in early amphictyonic traditions.[100] More recently, Levenson has shown that more than half of the pentateuchal uses of the term are of Priestly (P) origin and place the rule of the *Nāśî'* directly under the Sinai theocracy.[101] Speiser, in fact, once complained that the common English translation, "prince," inadequately described the functions of these figures within the theocracy. He preferred the LXX ἄρχων, the Targumic paraphrase רב,[102] and En-

99. A number of additional references may also use the title *Nāśî'* to refer to these tribal leaders. In Exodus, these figures hear the commands of Moses (Exod 16:22; 35:21), apparently so as to implement them among the tribes; and they contribute resources for the crafting of priestly vestments (35:27). Leviticus attests a single instance in which the *Něśî'îm* provide sacrifices on behalf of the people (Lev 4:22). In Joshua, the *Něśî'îm* play a fairly active role in negotiating with foreign tribes (Num 9:15, 18-21), they hear cases and pass judgment together with Eleazar and Joshua (17:4), and they help to negotiate intertribal disputes (22:14, 30, 32). In 1 Kings, they attend Solomon in the processional of the ark (1 Kgs 8:1). Finally, Chronicles is especially interested in the genealogies of the *Něśî'îm* and also presents them as attending the court of Solomon (1 Chr 2:10; 4:38; 5:6; 7:40; 2 Chr 1:2; 5:2).

100. Martin Noth, *Das System der Zwölf Stämme Israels* (Stuttgart: Kohlhammer, 1930), 151-62. See also E. A. Speiser, "Background and Functions of the Biblical Naśî'," *CBQ* 25 (1963): 111-17.

101. Jon Douglas Levenson, *Theology of the Program of Restoration of Ezekiel 40-48* (HSM 10; Missoula: Scholars Press, 1976), 62, 69.

102. One might add to Speiser the Syriac ܪܘܪܒܐ or the Latin (Vulgate) *princeps,* as used in Numbers 7.

glish terms such as "Leader," "Chieftain," or even "President."[103] Halpern has called specific attention to the military functions of the *Něśî'îm* within P's terminology (see Num 34:16-19); this is an especially important feature given the usage of the term נשיא at Qumran. Halpern summarizes the functions of the *Něśî'îm* within the old Israelite polity as "military, civil, and sacral."[104]

Ezekiel 34–37 and 40–48

Second, and most importantly, Ezekiel describes a future Davidic *Nāśî'* who emerges as a significant figure within his Temple restoration program. As Puech, Evans, Collins, and Pomykala have noted, Ezekiel 34–37 and 40–48 provide the most likely biblical sources for Qumran usage of the title *Nāśî'*.[105] In contrast to the passages in Numbers, Ezekiel's restoration prophecies present only a single figure entitled *Nāśî'*. The antithesis to the false shepherds whom Ezekiel upbraids in 34:1-22 emerges in his prophecy concerning a true shepherd that is to come:

> I will set up one shepherd over them, and he shall feed them, even my servant David. . . . And I the LORD will be their God, and my servant David a prince among them; I the LORD have spoken it. (34:23-24)

A second prophecy reinforces this expectation:

> My servant David shall be king over them; and they all shall have one shepherd: they shall also walk in my judgments, and observe my statutes, and do them. And they shall dwell in the land that I have given unto Jacob my servant, wherein your fathers have dwelt . . . and my servant David shall be their prince forever. (37:24-25)

These prophecies are almost euphoric in the status that they ascribe to the *Nāśî'*: perpetual Davidic kingship. Yet they take a more tangible form of implementation in chapters 40–48, where the role of the *Nāśî'* is more clearly defined, especially in his duties to the Temple and to the people. As Levenson's study demonstrates, the juxtaposition of the royal prophecies of

103. Speiser, "Background and Functions," 111, 115-16.
104. Halpern, *Constitution of the Monarchy*, 214.
105. Puech, "Messianism," 238; Evans, "Prince of the Congregation," 2:693-94; John J. Collins, "The Nature of Messianism in Light of the Dead Sea Scrolls," in *The Dead Sea Scrolls in Their Historical Context* (ed. T. Lim; Edinburgh: T&T Clark, 2000), 199-217, esp. 209; and Pomykala, *The Davidic Dynasty Tradition*, 241.

Ezekiel 34–37 with the more sober legislation of Ezekiel 40–48 has remained an enduring problem in biblical research.[106] Chapters 40–48 have also radically re-defined the nature of kingship as servanthood to the cult and the people; and in this portion of Ezekiel, the title "king" has apparently been avoided. This modification of Israelite royal ideology is achieved *(mutatis mutandis)* through the use of the older tribal terminology *Nāśî'*, a more intermediate and representative figure ultimately subservient to cult and Torah. As Levenson himself summarizes, he is "a denizen of Zion defined by Sinai."[107]

The implications of this terminological nuance are indicated in the legislation itself. In his vision of the restored Temple, Ezekiel foresees an eastern gate, where the *Nāśî'* will enter in to eat bread before the LORD (44:1-3), leading a procession of the people for sacrifice (46:1-15). A portion of land surrounding the Temple city is reserved for the Prince in 44:7 (cf. 48:21). The purpose of assigning the *Nāśî'* this specific portion seems clear in the very next verse: "my princes shall no more oppress my people; and the rest of the land shall they give to the house of Israel according to their tribes" (44:8). The prince is further charged with preparing numerous offerings on behalf of the people (45:17, 22-25) — legislation that shares much with the role of the *Něśî'îm* in Numbers 7. The prince may leave his inheritance only for his sons (see 46:16-17), but he may not seize the inheritance of his people (46:18). These legal mechanisms detract from the *Nāśî'*'s ability to amass a large and perpetual administrative bureaucracy in the land, a key prerequisite for the development of monarchy.[108] Through this legislation, the exalted status of the Davidic prince is restricted, as it were, and put to cultic service. It is no coincidence that Ezekiel thus calls him "my servant" David.[109] He is, in essence, not an absolute monarch, but rather the cultic patron of Ezekiel's restored Temple. An ambivalence thus surrounds the *Nāśî'* in Ezekiel: in a positive sense, the Davidic prince will be the antithesis of the false shepherds who have exploited the people, and will instead judge the people righteously; in a more negative sense, Ezekiel is well aware of what royal power can do unchecked — hence he includes commands that will keep the prince the servant of the theocracy.[110]

106. Levenson, *Theology of the Program of Restoration,* 57-73.

107. Ibid., 75.

108. Ibid., 114-15.

109. As Paul M. Joyce notes, Ezekiel's use of the term probably "represents a downgrading of royal language" ("King and Messiah in Ezekiel," in *King and Messiah,* 232-37; citation from 331). Baumgarten and Schwartz also describe the title as "a deflated substitute for 'king'" (PTSDSSP 2:21). Halpern insightfully adds that in Ezek 7:26-27 the title *Nāśî'* is actually understood in contradistinction from that of king (*Constitution of the Monarchy,* 212).

110. The Temple Scroll's laws on kingship (56.12–59.21) provide their own distinctive

Qumran Usage

Like both the Priestly and Ezekielian traditions,[111] Qumran preference for the title *Nāśî'* may well reflect priestly attempts to submit non-priestly rule under the larger auspices of its own superior authority. Seven points of comparison follow in regard to Qumran usage of the title *Nāśî'*.

1. Like the Priestly traditions of the Pentateuch, as described by Halpern,[112] but unlike Ezekiel's "Prince," the Qumran *Nāśî'* performs an important military function in the eschatological scenarios envisioned by the *Damascus Document*, 1QSb, 1QM, 4Q161, and 4Q285. In the presumably non-eschatological legal context of 4Q376, the *Nāśî'* is also militaristic. If Qumran traditions make recourse to Ezekiel's Prince, they have also fully modified him to fit within the Community's war-ideology. Such thorough modification of Ezekiel's usage, otherwise quite in line with Qumran's, indicates the fervency of the war-ideology in the Community's distinctive adaptation of this biblical term.

2. Qumran usage, like that of Ezekiel, envisions only one *Nāśî'* for the whole people. Though both traditions revert to the archaic terminology of the tribal federation, a harmonization of the office into a single figure has taken place, though the *War Scroll* clearly envisions additional נשיאים under his command.

3. The passages of Ezekiel provide the best terminological link between the title *Nāśî'* and the person of David, a connection that is assumed in the exegeses of 4Q161 and 4Q285. It is possible that the authors of these documents had inherited earlier uses of the title in the Community[113] and made a clearer connection with references to David, as they searched the oracles of Ezekiel and Isaiah.

4. Though Ezekiel calls this figure "King" once (37:24), the traditions

---

counterpart to this legislation. Like Ezekiel, it formulates a sophisticated program that reforms kingship from the perspective of theocracy. See also the source for the Temple Scroll's legislation in Deut 17:14-20, which also attempts to bring the role of the king under the auspices of Torah. See N. Lohfink, "Distribution of the Functions of Power: The Laws Concerning Public Offices in Deut 16:18–18:22," in *A Song of Power and the Power of Song* (ed. D. L. Christensen; Winona Lake: Eisenbrauns, 1993), 336-52; J. G. McConville, "King and Messiah in Deuteronomy and the Deuteronomistic History," in *King and Messiah*, 271-95; Collins, "Messianic Authority," 152-53; and, more recently, Elledge, *Statutes of the King*.

111. See Speiser ("Background and Functions," 117) for a discussion of the apparent relationship between these two "priestly" uses of the *Nāśî'* terminology.

112. Halpern, *Constitution of the Monarchy*, 213-14.

113. E.g., from compositions such as the *Damascus Document*, the *Rule of Blessings*, the *Apocryphon of Moses*[b], and perhaps the *War Scroll*.

mentioning the *Nāśî'* in the scrolls never use this language, despite the designation in Ezekiel. If Ezekiel has subdued earlier notions of Davidic kingship through the use of the term *Nāśî'*, then Qumran traditions have subdued them even further by completely omitting the title מלך. In this sense, Qumran usage bears a striking resemblance to Ezekiel 40–48, which also avoids the title "king."

5. The scrolls are absolutely silent about the role of a *Nāśî'* in the ministrations of the Temple. This defies both Priestly and Ezekielian usage. The total absence of a cultic role for the *Nāśî'* cannot be overlooked in light of the Hasmonean centralization of cultic and civil authority from 152 to 76 BCE. The Qumran *Nāśî'* is a very different kind of political leader than those who presided over Israel and the Temple during the formative era of the Qumran Community.[114] The polemical and reformist nature of this aspect of the Qumran *Nāśî'* should not escape notice.

6. Ezekiel's emphasis upon the uprightness of the Davidic Prince as one who will not oppress the people may be shared with the traditions preserved in 1QSb and 4Q161, where the *Nāśî's* just judgment is accentuated.

7. Finally, Ezekiel's priestly ambivalence concerning the office of the *Nāśî'* should not be overlooked in relation to Qumran descriptions of the *Nāśî'*: Both in Ezekiel and Qumran usage, the Prince is given exalted description, yet he is ultimately peripheral to the centrality of priest and Temple in the restored Israel. Both Ezekiel and the Qumran writings seem dependent upon such a figure to fulfill certain specific political objectives, yet are simultaneously reticent to ascribe a larger function to him within the divine plan.

In this sense, the title *Nāśî'* is a safe one for Qumran ideology, since its biblical precedents already assume that the one who holds this title is the faithful servant of priest and Temple. Starcky and Van der Woude, in fact, once proposed that the term *Nāśî'*, not מלך, appears in the scrolls to distinguish the coming ruler of the people, polemically, from the Hasmonean priest-kings, who bore the title of "King" beginning with Aristobulus I.[115] Indeed, one may sense a clear hint of political subversion in Qumran's use of

114. See the growing military power among the Hasmonean high priests in 1 Macc 10:6; 13:7-11, 36; 14:9-10, 32-44; 15:7; Josephus, *Ant.* 13.201-2, 223-24, 249, 254-57, 275-81, 348-97; *J.W.* 1.61, 85-106.

115. See J. Starcky, "Les Quatre Étapes du Messianisme à Qumran," *RB* 70 (1963): 488; and van der Woude, *Vorstellungen*, 116. Jonathan A. Goldstein has made similar proposals about the use of Davidic terminology ("The Hasmonean Revolt and the Hasmonean Dynasty," in *CHJ* 2:292-351. He finds the use of Davidic ideology in the *Psalms of Solomon*, especially, to be polemical and anti-Hasmonean in character. It is possible that the Davidic language applied to the *Nāśî'* may have had a similar polemical orientation.

the title. In contrast to the prevailing "kings" of their day, both Hasmonean and Gentile, the Community creatively envisioned the advent of a holy warrior and judge who would secure the interests of theocracy in a land where priest and Temple had finally triumphed.

5. Conclusion

In sum, these observations demonstrate that greater care should be used in the ascription of Davidic Messianism to documents mentioning the title *Nāśî'*. He is not called "Messiah" or "King." Only twice is he associated with David, and even then the relationship remains somewhat unclear. Biblical precedents for the title *Nāśî'* present an intermediate tribal figure whose authority is subordinate to that of the priests and the Torah. This figure has little or no abiding political reign beyond his military function. He should not be harmonized too easily with the "Messiahs" of 1QS, 1QSa, 4Q174, or 4Q252. These figures never fight; the *Nāśî'* always does. Moreover, never are the two terminologies משיח (משיחים) and נשיא used together in clear reference to a single figure. *It is even possible that the Community may have understood them as two different eschatological figures with differing roles in the latter days.*

Given the consistent differences in terminology, a broader critical taxonomy for messianic beliefs seems appropriate, one that recognizes the following:

1. The vast majority of Qumran traditions mentioned no Messiah.[116]
2. Some traditions attest belief in a coming Messiah (4Q252, 1QSa).
3. Others expected coming Messiahs (1QS; cf. CD).
4. Others expected various non-messianic figures, such as the Prophet (1QS).
5. Still others expected a *Nāśî'*.
6. Davidic description may or may not be associated with items 2, 3, and 5.

Stated simply, Qumran usage of the title *Nāśî'* resists simplification to the model of "Davidic Messianism." This is especially the case if we may compare the more active Davidic Messianism of *Pss. Sol.* 17–18. Here all the classic terms of Davidic Messianism are in full flower. This figure is "Messiah," "King," and "Son of David." In comparison, Qumran description of the *Nāśî'* is, at best, quasi- or proto-messianic. It is very possible that Messianism has

---

116. Collins, *Scepter and the Star*, 56: The corpus of messianic texts "is still modest in proportion to the entire corpus of the Scrolls."

influenced the most exalted portrayal of the *Nāśî'* in 4Q161, but to harmonize these scattered references into a larger portrait of Davidic Messianism at Qumran is precarious due to the absence of clearly messianic terminology in reference to the *Nāśî'*.

All of this is not to underestimate the significance of the *Nāśî'* within the war ideology of the Community. On the contrary, within that ideology he remains one of the most prominently featured eschatological figures that the Community envisioned on the horizon of future history. His emergence in the conflict with the Kittim will mark an important stage in the reclamation of the land, after which, the priests of the Community will re-institute true worship — all according to the prophecies of Numbers and Isaiah. When these documents employ the title *Nāśî'*, therefore, they indicate the Community's hopes in a charismatic warrior who will lead the whole congregation toward victory in battle and execute just administration of priestly teachings, *without re-establishing the royal Davidic dynasty in the process.*

Certainly, specialists in this field will continue to refer, casually, to the *Nāśî'* as "the Davidic Messiah," in spite of the four observations presented above. It is clear, however, that specialized treatments of this figure demand a more discriminating assessment.[117] The Qumran fragments present the modern scholar with some of the earliest literary evidence for the emergence of Jewish Messianism. The accurate assessment of the various figures that the Community expected to emerge in the latter days thus remains a critical task of the utmost importance for both history and theology.[118]

117. Indeed, more recent publications may well indicate that such a process is already under way. See Pomykala, *The Davidic Dynasty Tradition;* note also Collins's more recent qualifications in "Nature of Messianism," 199-217.

118. The reverberations of the present discussion, for example, will be felt by specialists in Christian Origins and by those considering the importance of the title נשיא ישראל as employed by Bar Kochba.

4Q521: The Works of the Messiah or the Signs of the Messianic Time?

LIDIJA NOVAKOVIC

1. Introduction

Since its publication in 1992[1] under the name "Une apocalypse messian-ique,"[2] 4Q521 has stirred much controversy regarding the relationship between the end-time miracles described in frg. 2 2.5-8, 11-13 and the messianic figure mentioned in line 1. In the original publication of this document, Émile Puech described it as "an exhortation based on the blessings or

1. Even though J. Starcky described this document already in 1956 ("Le travail d'édition des fragments manuscrits de Qumrân," *RB* 63 [1956]: 66), 4Q521 was published for the first time by É. Puech in 1992 ("Une apocalypse messianique [4Q521]," *RevQ* 15 [1992]: 475-519 [and pls. 1-3, pp. 520-22]; see also idem, *La croyance des Esséniens en la vie future: Immortalité, résurrection, vie éternelle? Histoire d'une croyance dans le Judaïsme Ancien* [2 vols.; EtB.NS 21-22; Paris: Lecoffre/Gabalda, 1993], 2:627-92). A photograph and English translation of one fragment was published by R. H. Eisenman in the previous year ("A Messianic Vision," *BAR* 17.6 [1991]: 65). The first English translations of the document were offered by G. Vermes ("Qumran Forum Miscellanea I," *JJS* 43 [1992]: 303-5) and by R. H. Eisenman and M. O. Wise (*The Dead Sea Scrolls Uncovered: The First Complete Translation and Interpretation of 50 Key Documents Withheld for Over 35 Years* [Shaftesbury/Rockport/Brisbane: Element, 1992], 17-23). A complete transcription and translation of all the fragments may now be found in Puech, *Qumrân grotte 4.18: Textes Hebreux* (DJD 25; Oxford: Clarendon Press, 1998), 1-38 and pls. I-III.

2. Other names given to this document were "On Resurrection" (E. Tov, "The Unpublished Qumran Texts from Caves 4 and 11," *JJS* 43 [1992]: 126) and "The Messiah of Heaven and Earth" (Eisenman and Wise, *The Dead Sea Scrolls Uncovered*, 19).

This essay is dedicated to James H. Charlesworth in appreciation of his enthusiastic and expert supervision of my work in the Princeton Theological Seminary Dead Sea Scrolls Project. Note that all translations of the original texts are mine, unless indicated otherwise.

chastisements which God will bring about through or in the days of his Messiah."[3] Much of the subsequent discussion, however, focused on the first part of Puech's formulation ("which God will bring about *through . . . his Messiah*"). The issues that were predominantly considered included the question whether God performs the eschatological miracles through the agency of the Messiah, and, if so, whether the latter should be understood in royal, prophetic, or priestly categories. The interest in these questions was reinforced by the observation that there is an astonishing similarity between the description of future blessings (healing of the wounded, giving life to the dead, and preaching the good news to the poor) and Jesus' answer to the question of John the Baptist in Matt 11:5 and Luke 7:22.[4]

In contrast to the proposals offered so far, the present essay calls attention to the other, typically-neglected aspect of Puech's formulation ("which God will bring about . . . *in the days of his Messiah*"). In the first part (§2), I will show that any conclusion regarding the function and the character of the Messiah in the end-time events described in 4Q521 is destined to be inconclusive because the text of this fragment neither ascribes the execution of these miracles directly to the Messiah nor, more fundamentally, clarifies the

---

3. Puech, "Une apocalypse messianique," 514.

4. Scholarly interest in the relation between 4Q521 and the Q-material found in Matt 11:4 and Luke 7:22 was initially provoked through an erroneous transcription and translation of line 11 offered by Eisenman and Wise (ונכ\ב\דות שלוא היו מעשה אדני: "And as for the wonders that are not the work of the Lord"), with the implication that the grammatical subject of line 12 is the Messiah. Some of the first interpretations of 4Q521 are made under this assumption; see for example M. O. Wise and J. D. Tabor, "The Messiah at Qumran," *BAR* 18.6 (1992): 60-65; J. D. Tabor and M. O. Wise, "4Q521 'On Resurrection' and the Synoptic Gospel Tradition: A Preliminary Study," *JSP* 10 (1992): 149-62 (repr. in *Qumran Questions* [ed. J. H. Charlesworth; BibSem 36; Sheffield: Sheffield Academic Press, 1995], 151-63); O. Betz and R. Riesner, *Jesus, Qumran und der Vatikan: Klarstellungen* (Giessen: Brunnen Verlag, 1993), 111-15; and P. Stuhlmacher, *Wie treibt man biblische Theologie* (BThSt 24; Neukirchen-Vluyn: Neukirchener Verlag, 1995), 32. Even after the superiority of Puech's transcription had been generally recognized, the interest in the relation between 4Q521 and Q continued to capture scholarly attention. See, e.g., J. J. Collins, "The Works of the Messiah," *DSD* 1 (1994): 98-112; idem, *The Scepter and the Star: The Messiahs of the Dead Sea Scrolls and Other Ancient Literature* (ABRL; New York: Doubleday, 1995), 117-23; idem, "A Herald of Good Tidings: Isaiah 61:1-3 and its Actualization in the Dead Sea Scrolls," in *The Quest for Context and Meaning: Studies in Biblical Intertextuality in Honor of James A. Sanders* (ed. C. A. Evans and S. Talmon; BIS 28; Leiden: Brill, 1997), 225-40; M. Becker, "4Q521 und die Gesalbten," *RevQ* 18 (1997): 73-96; K.-W. Niebuhr, "Die Werke des eschatologischen Freudenboten (4Q521 und die Jesusüberlieferung)," in *The Scriptures in the Gospels* (ed. C. M. Tuckett; BETL 131; Leuven: University Press, 1997), 637-46; and H. Kvalbein, "The Wonders of the End-Time: Metaphoric Language in 4Q521 and the Interpretation of Matt 11.5 par.," *JSP* 18 (1998): 87-110.

Messiah's identity in the first place. In the second part (§3), I will demonstrate that 4Q521 emphasizes, instead, *the temporal aspect* of the expected miracles by presenting them as *the signs of the messianic time* rather than manifesting an interest in the specific manner of their actual execution. 4Q521 thus reflects a tradition also found elsewhere in Early Jewish documents — namely, that in the messianic time the primary object of human perception will not be the person of the Messiah per se, but the wonderful state of affairs that is going to take place then due to God's initiative. I will conclude the essay, finally, by comparing 4Q521 with the Gospel material in the New Testament (§4) with the purpose of showing that the similarity between these texts lies not in the personal but the temporal aspect of the eschatological blessings. Although these conclusions may not appear, on the face of it, to directly advance our understanding of the identity of the messianic figure mentioned in 4Q521 frg. 2 2.1, they will nevertheless diminish the ambiguity of the text by anchoring it within a clearly discernable messianic tradition and point the way forward for future research on this and related messianic documents.

2. Eschatological Blessings as Messianic Deeds

4Q521 was most likely copied in the first quarter of the first century BCE.[5] A precise dating of the composition is impossible, however, because 4Q521 is a copy, not the autograph.[6] According to most scholarly estimations of its

---

5. This dating is based on the paleographical examination of the script. Cf. Puech, DJD 25:5.

6. According to Puech (*La croyance*, 664-69; and idem, "Some Remarks on 4Q246 and 4Q521 and Qumran Messianism," in *The Provo International Conference on the Dead Sea Scrolls: Technological Innovations, New Texts, and Reformulated Issues* [ed. D. W. Parry and E. Ulrich; STDJ 30; Leiden: Brill, 1999], 552), the original Hebrew composition was most likely created in the second half of the second century BCE by the members of the Essene community. He supports this conclusion by the following observations: the suppression of the Tetragrammaton in the quotations of Psalm 146, the constant use of אדני, the appearance of medial letters in the final positions, the use of the relative -ש alongside אשר, and so forth. Puech presumes the Qumran origin of the document on the basis of the terms צדיקים, ענוים, חסידים, and קדושים. He also notes certain similarities in vocabulary with the *Hodayot* and several other Qumran documents. R. Bergmeier ("Beobachtungen zu 4Q521 f 2, II, 1-13," *ZDMG* 145 [1995]: 44-45), however, contends that 4Q521 does not contain the characteristic features of Qumran theology, but rather of other Early Jewish psalms. Similarly, Collins ("The Works of the Messiah," 106) notes the absence of the typical sectarian terminology and believes that it is not very likely that this document was composed at Qumran. Collins also notes the presence of ideas that are rarely documented in the sectarian literature, such as the resurrection.

genre, the document is an eschatological psalm[7] and not an apocalypse.[8] It consists of 16 fragments, the largest and best preserved of which is fragment 2. The first line of column 2 in this fragment mentions the Messiah in the following fashion: "[hea]ven and earth will listen to his Messiah"[9] (הש[מים] והארץ ישמעו למשיחו). Even though the grammatical subject of this clause is "heaven and earth," God's Anointed is the presupposed speaker to whose words the heaven and earth will listen (obey).[10] A problem is immediately encountered, however: is משיחו singular or plural?[11] Contextually, the next line could be understood as parallel to the first:

7. Cf. K.-W. Niebuhr, "4Q521, 2 II — Ein eschatologischer Psalm," in *Mogilany 1995: Papers on the Dead Sea Scrolls Offered in Memory of Aleksy Klawek* (ed. Z. J. Kapera; Kraków: The Enigma Press, 1996), 151-68; Bergmeier, "Beobachtungen," 41; Collins, "A Herald of Good Tidings," 234.

8. See, however, Puech's defense of this designation in his essay "Some Remarks on 4Q246 and 4Q521," 551-52.

9. The translation of this and other phrases from 4Q521 incorporates the modifications proposed by Puech, "Some Remarks on 4Q246 and 4Q521," 553; for the Hebrew text of 4Q521 and restorations of this and other phrases, see Puech, DJD 25:10. A translation of the entire column may be found in L. Novakovic, *Messiah, the Healer of the Sick: A Study of Jesus as the Son of David in the Gospel of Matthew* (WUNT 2.170; Tübingen: Mohr Siebeck, 2003), 170-71.

10. It is difficult to discover the background of this statement. In none of the extant Jewish writings can we find a claim that both heaven and earth will listen to (obey) the Messiah. Some interpreters see here an allusion to Isa 1:2a, even though this is an invitation to listen to God (Puech, "Une apocalypse messianique," 487; Bergmeier, "Beobachtungen," 39; Becker, "4Q521 und die Gesalbten," 84); Deut 32:2, where Moses asks heaven and earth to listen to his words (Puech, "Une apocalypse messianique," 487; Becker, "4Q521 und die Gesalbten," 84); Psalm 2, which speaks about the universal reign of God's Anointed (Bergmeier, "Beobachtungen," 39, 43); or Sir 48:3, which recounts Elijah's famous command of the heavens (Collins, *Scepter and the Star*, 120). M. Philonenko, "Les cieux et la terre obéront à Son Messie," *RHPR* 82 (2002): 115-22, argued that 4Q521 frg. 2 2.1 depends on an apocalyptic piece originally written in Hebrew and preserved in some MSS of the Latin *Life of Adam and Eve*, which in 29:8 contains the clause, "Heaven and earth, night and day, and all creatures will obey him and will not transgress his commandment, nor will they alter his works" (translation from G. A. Anderson and M. E. Stone, eds., *A Synopsis of the Books of Adam and Eve* [2d rev. ed.; Atlanta: Scholars Press, 1999], 32E). How far these references can elucidate the understanding of 4Q521 frg. 2 2.1 is far from clear. There is no compelling reason to prefer one over the other, because we either do not find the idea of anointing in them, or, if we do (as in Psalm 2), we do not find a clear reference to heaven and earth.

11. למשיחו can be read either as singular (לְמְשִׁיחוֹ) or defective plural (לְמְשִׁיחָו). The plural משיחיה in 4Q521 frg. 8 line 9 is of no help here, because that form is plural with a feminine pronominal suffix, whereas למשיחו has the masculine suffix, which, according to Qumran orthography, can have two forms (see E. Qimron, *The Hebrew of the Dead Sea Scrolls* [HSS 29; Atlanta: Scholars Press, 1986], 59; and Puech, "Some Remarks on 4Q246 and 4Q521," 557). M. Becker ("4Q521 und die Gesalbten," 78) insists that למשיחו must be plural because משיחיה in 4Q521 frg. 8 line 9 is clearly plural, and there is no reason to suppose a conceptual change in a

‫[וכל א]שר בם לוא יסוג ממצות קדושים‬

"[and] no[ne w]ho is in them will turn away from the commandments of holy ones."

Such an assumption, however, does not necessarily imply that ‫ משיחו‬should be read as plural in order to match the plural ‫קדושים‬.[12] There are, after all, numerous examples of *parallelismus membrorum* in which the nouns in the lines do not correspond to each other in number. Note, for example, *Pss. Sol.* 11:1: "Sound in Zion the trumpet to summon the saints. Proclaim in Jerusalem the voice of him who brings good tidings" (σαλπίσατε ἐν Σιων ἐν σάλπιγγι σημασίας ἁγίων, κηρύξατε ἐν Ιερουσαλημ φωνὴν εὐαγγελιζομένου). Another telling example is found in *Pss. Sol.* 17:43c, which likens the words of the Messiah to the words of the Holy Ones: οἱ λόγοι αὐτοῦ ὡς λόγοι ἁγίων. In these cases we do not have identical or synonymous parallelism but comparisons. Puech has suggested that it is lines 2 and 3, not 1 and 2, that are parallel. If so, ‫ קדושים‬corresponds to ‫מבקשי אדני‬, and has no direct impact on ‫ משיחו‬in line 1.[13] Despite these uncertainties surrounding ‫משיחו‬, and in anticipation of the thesis that will be developed below, which argues that 4Q521 resembles certain messianic expectations that are also discernible in other Early Jewish documents, ‫ משיחו‬is best understood as singular.

In the rest of the fragment, the Messiah is not mentioned. The actions described in lines 5-8, which have the form of a list — including renewing the faithful ones by his might, glorifying the devout on the throne of an eternal

---

single document. But, as Puech notes, "it is difficult to use these examples [i.e. the plural ‫ משיחיה‬in frg. 8 line 9 and the partially preserved form [ ]‫ משיח‬in frg. 9 line 3, because they are] far from the columns under investigation and may be in another context" ("Some Remarks on 4Q246 and 4Q521," 557). The reasoning of F. García-Martínez ("Messianic Hopes in the Qumran Writings," in *The People of the Dead Sea Scrolls: Their Writings, Beliefs, and Practices* [ed. F. García Martínez and J. Trebolle Barrerra; Leiden: Brill, 1995], 168) that ‫ למשיחו‬must be singular because the parallel expressions in line 6 with pronominal suffixes, ‫ רוחו‬and ‫בכחו‬, are also singular, cannot be sustained because lines 1 and 6 cannot be brought in any direct relationship. Cf. Puech, "Some Remarks on 4Q246 and 4Q521," 556-57; Becker, "4Q521 und die Gesalbten," 76. A decision here can be made only on the basis of the context, but the fragmentary nature of the text does not allow much certainty at this point. If Isa 61:1 can be taken as a hermeneutical key of this passage, then the singular seems to be more appropriate than the plural.

12. For the plural reading of ‫ משיחו‬on the basis of ‫ קדושים‬see Niebuhr, "4Q521, 2 II," 153; idem, "Die Werke des eschatologischen Freudenboten," 638; H. Stegemann, *Die Essener, Qumran, Johannes der Täufer und Jesus: Ein Sachbuch* (Freiburg: Herder, 1994), 49-51. R. Bergmeier, on the other hand, argues that *parallelismus membrorum* between the first two lines suggests that ‫ קדושים‬in line 2 should be understood as singular ("Beobachtungen," 39).

13. Puech, "Some Remarks on 4Q246 and 4Q521," 555.

kingdom, releasing captives, giving sight to the blind, and raising up those who are bowed down — are all ascribed to the Lord.[14] The same applies to lines 12-13, which declare that "he [the Lord] will heal the wounded" (ירפא חללים), "give life to the dead" (ומתים יחיה), "preach good news to the poor" (ענוים יבשר), "[sat]isfy the [weak]" (ו[דלי]ם ישב[ע]), "lead those who have been cast out" (נתושים ינהל), and "enrich the hungry" (ורעבים יעשר).[15]

The rather clear grammar and syntax of these clauses have not, however, prevented scholarly speculations regarding the role and the character of the Messiah mentioned in line 1, namely that the Messiah, rather than the Lord, is somehow involved in these actions. Such positions are based on the assumption that there is an internal coherence between the lines 1-2(3) and the rest of the fragment.[16] Even though the *vacat* at the end of line 3 would seem to separate the first three lines from the text that follows, it is, in this scholarly perspective, more likely that the latter explicates the exhortation in line 3: "You who are seeking the Lord, strengthen yourselves in his service." This request is supported by a series of eschatological promises, some of which are introduced by the particle כי (lines 5 and 7). The resolution of the speaker to "cling [to those who] hope" (line 9) is followed by another series of promises that enumerate "the glorious things that have not taken place" (line 11). Within this progression, the promise in line 12 that "he [the Lord] will preach good news to the poor," which echoes Isa 61:1, serves as an additional cohesive factor that provides a link between the description of the eschatological blessings and God's Anointed in line 1.[17]

In addition to these considerations, the argument that is most frequently advanced in favor of the claim that God will perform these actions through the agency of his Anointed is that it is nowhere else ever said that God will preach good news to the poor. This is the task of a herald or messenger. This suggests, in turn, that the other actions might also be performed through human agency. Thus, despite the fact that God is the grammatical

---

14. Lines 5-8 contain many expressions from Ps 146:5-8; line 8 even quotes Ps 146:7b-8a verbatim with the omission of יהוה. The subject of these actions is אדני from line 5.

15. The second list of eschatological promises found in lines 12-13 contains allusions to several biblical passages, such as Deut 32:39a; Isa 26:19; 61:1; and Ps 146:7a-b, but none of them is directly quoted despite the introduction at the end of line 11, "the Lord will do as he s[aid]" (יעשה אדני כאשר ד[בר]).

16. Differently, Bergmeier ("Beobachtungen," 43), who believes that the first two lines mark the end of a psalm, followed by another beginning in line 3.

17. Cf. Collins, "A Herald of Good Tidings," 235. In Collins' view, the internal cohesion is provided by a string of allusions to Psalm 146 in lines 1-9. See, however, the critique by Puech, who contends that "the quotation of Psalm 146:7b-8a in line 8 does not authorize seeing a pseudoquotation of Psalm 146:6 in lines 1-2" ("Some Remarks on 4Q246 and 4Q521," 554).

subject of line 12 (continued from line 11: אדני), God cannot be the immediate logical subject but requires an agent.[18] And, since no other human figure is mentioned in the text except God's Anointed, he must be the one who will actually execute these deeds on God's behalf.[19]

Once this assumption is made, further speculation about the character of the Messiah in this text follows logically. The dominant hypotheses are that he is either (1) a royal figure, (2) a prophet like Elijah, or (3) an anointed priest:

1. The strongest case for *a Davidic Messiah* was principally based on an erroneous transcription and translation of the document that took the grammatical subject of lines 12-13 to be the Messiah.[20] 4Q521 was thus understood as a direct precursor of the Christian understanding of Jesus as the Messiah.[21] The word שבט[ו], "[his] scepter," which appears in frg. 2 3.6, is also sometimes taken as an argument in favor of a Davidic Messiah.[22] However, not only are the reading[23] and transla-

18. See Collins, "The Works of the Messiah," 100; "A Herald of Good Tidings," 235-36. In a rejoinder to those who insist on the fact that only God is the grammatical subject of these clauses (so, e.g., Bergmeier, "Beobachtungen," 44), Collins reemphasizes the anomalous use of the verb יבשר, which implies human agency ("A Herald of Good Tidings," 236). The counterexample from Gal 3:8, mentioned by Puech ("Some Remarks on 4Q246 and 4Q521," 558), where Paul says that Scripture proclaimed the good news beforehand to Abraham, does not invalidate Collins' reasoning, because it is quite apparent that Paul here personifies Scripture. Thus neither 4Q521 nor Gal 3:8 make sense on a purely literal/grammatical level concerning the actual execution of proclamation.

19. Such a conclusion is not meant to deny that God is the ultimate doer of these acts because, as Collins aptly notes, "works performed through an agent would, of course, be nonetheless the works of God" ("A Herald of Good Tidings," 235).

20. See note 4 above.

21. Thus, e.g., Wise and Tabor assert that "our Qumran text, 4Q521, is, astonishingly, quite close to this Christian concept of the messiah [i.e. the messiah who is David's descendant and who is God's cosmic agent]. Our text speaks not only of a single messianic figure ('[the hea]vens and the earth will obey His Messiah, [the sea and all th]at is in them'), but it also describes him in extremely exalted terms, quite like the Christian view of Jesus as a cosmic agent" ("The Messiah at Qumran," 60). Another argument for a Davidic Messiah has been suggested by García Martínez ("Messianic Hopes in the Qumran Writings," 169), who understands the text as a description of the eschatological blessings limited to the members of the Qumran Community, and concludes from this that the simple title "Messiah" could be a reference to the Prince of the Congregation along the lines of 1QSb.

22. Puech, "Une apocalypse messianique," 498-99; cf. DJD 25:18-19. In Puech's view, the scriptural basis for this interpretation can be found in Num 24:15-17. This biblical text plays a significant role in CD MS A 7.19-20, which identifies the scepter as the Prince of the Congregation; 1QM 11.6; 4Q161 frgs. 2-6 2.19; and 4Q175 lines 12-13.

23. It is questionable whether the second letter should be read as ב or מ. Moreover, the

tion[24] of this word uncertain, it also appears in a context in which the Messiah is *not* mentioned, at least in the presently-extant text of the fragment.

2. The most elaborate argument for *a prophetic Messiah* is presented by John J. Collins. He discusses the role of the Messiah in 4Q521 and claims that "he most probably serves as God's agent in raising the dead."[25] Because such a role is nowhere else attributed to the royal Messiah in Jewish literature, Collins argues that "the messianic activity envisaged in this text is appropriate to an eschatological prophet rather than to a king."[26] The force of the argument that Collins presents thus depends on two important claims: a) that the resurrection of the dead is never attributed to the royal Messiah; and b) that the term "Messiah" in the Dead Sea Scrolls can refer to a prophet. The first claim can be quite easily defended because the Early Jewish documents[27] and rabbinic writings[28] that associate the resurrection with the messianic age do not attribute the agency of this event to the Davidic Messiah. The second claim, however, is more difficult to sustain. First of all, it is true that Isa 61:1, which forms the background of 4Q521 frg. 2 2.12, is also alluded to in 11Q13, but "the anointed of the spir[it]" ([ח]רוח משיח; 11Q13 2.18) is not necessarily "a prophetic figure."[29] The quotation from Dan 9:25, which most likely followed the introductory clause ("about whom Dan[iel] said," [יאל]אשר אמר דנ) suggests that he is "a leader/ruler/prince" (נגיד). To interpret this character as a prophetic figure on the

---

third letter is hardly visible. Cf. García Martínez, "Messianic Hopes in the Qumran Writings," 169; Collins, "The Works of the Messiah," 103.

24. שבט can also be translated as "tribe." Cf. Collins, "The Works of the Messiah," 103.

25. Ibid., 98.

26. Ibid., 99.

27. *2 Bar.* 30:1, e.g., describes the events following the earthly career of the Messiah and claims that when he returns in glory "all who sleep in hope of him will rise" (*OTP* 1:631). *4 Ezra* 7:29-32 speaks about the death of the Messiah followed by the resurrection, which occurs after seven days of primeval silence.

28. Collins objects that in his book *Messiah in Context: Israel's History and Destiny in Formative Judaism* (Philadelphia: Fortress, 1984), 86-98, J. Neusner only "claims that there was a 'prevalent notion that the Messiah would raise the dead' but cites no evidence in support of this view" ("The Works of the Messiah," 101 n. 12). This critique is probably too harsh because Neusner does offer several examples in support of his claim, but they only demonstrate the association between the Davidic Messiah and the time of his appearance and not his agency in the resurrection: "[i]t was like what someone says, 'Until the dead will live!' . . . 'until David's son will come'" (*y. Qidd.* 4:1 II/I); "[i]t is the land in which the dead will first come to life in the time of the Messiah" (*y. Ketub.* 12:3 VIII H).

29. Collins, "The Works of the Messiah," 101; see also Bergmeier, "Beobachtungen," 44.

basis of a similar expression in CD MS A 2.12 (משיחי רוח קדשו)[30] is questionable in view of the very diverse character of Qumran documents. Also, the references to the prophets as "anointed ones" in CD MS A 2.12; 6.1; and 1QM 11.7 are all constructed in the plural, not the singular. All of this hinders a positive identification of "his Messiah/Anointed" in 4Q521 as a prophetic figure.[31]

3. The notion of *a priestly Messiah* has been advocated by several authors,[32] who emphasize that anointing did not characterize Israel's prophets,[33] but only kings and priests. In view of the untenable nature of the hypothesis for a royal Messiah, this third possibility focuses on the evidence for anointed priests. There is no doubt that numerous biblical passages show that anointing was a common characteristic of Israel's priesthood.[34] Clear references to priestly anointing can be also found in the Dead Sea Scrolls,[35] even though some examples mentioned by K.-W. Niebuhr, such as CD MS A 2.12 and 6.1,[36] are highly debatable. Collins offers an accurate critique, then, when he states that "Niebuhr is unable to cite a single case where either term [i.e. 'anointed' and 'holy'] is used substantively as a noun with clear reference to priests in plural."[37]

The work of Puech falls into this third possibility but contains

---

30. Cf. Collins, "A Herald of Good Tidings," 230.

31. The questionable aspect of Collins' argument is his thesis that the agent of God's glorious acts is the *messianic* eschatological prophet. Collins presents quite a strong case for the Elijah typology in 4Q521 ("The Works of the Messiah, 101-6; "A Herald of Good Tidings," 235-36). Also, it cannot be denied that "Elijah's command of the heavens was legendary" ("A Herald of Good Tidings," 235; cf. 1 Kgs 17:1; Sir 48:3), or that Elijah is traditionally associated with raising the dead. What is lacking is the evidence that such a figure can be called "the Anointed." A conjecture on the basis of 4Q521 is in itself inconclusive.

32. Niebuhr, "4Q521, 2 II," 151-68; idem, "Die Werke des eschatologischen Freudenboten," 637-46; Puech, "Some Remarks on 4Q246 and 4Q521," 551-58.

33. Puech thinks that the command given to Elijah to anoint Elisha (1 Kgs 19:16) is an error; due to the parallelism with the king. Accordingly, he regards the examples in CD MS A 2.12; 6.1; and 1QM 11.7 as figurative, not literal, descriptions of the prophets ("Some Remarks on 4Q246 and 4Q521," 556). Even Collins, in whose argument for a prophetic Messiah 1 Kgs 19:16 plays an important role, has to admit that the actual anointing of Elisha is never reported in the Bible. Collins suggests, therefore, that one ought to understand the command given to Elijah metaphorically as a reference to appointing ("A Herald of Good Tidings," 227).

34. Exod 28:41; 29:7; 30:30-31; 40:14-15; Lev 4:3, 5, 16; 7:36; 8:12; 21:10; Num 3:3; 35:25; Sir 45:15; etc.

35. 1QM 9.6-9; 4Q375 2.9; 4Q376 1.1; 1QS 9.11.

36. Niebuhr, "4Q521, 2 II," 156.

37. Collins, "A Herald of Good Tidings," 236.

further nuance. His inclination to understand למשיחו in 4Q521 in priestly categories is primarily based on his interpretation of Isa 61:1, which he reads as "the speech of the (new) high priest to his brethren the priests, and the assembly."[38] He recognizes a similar structure in the second paragraph of 4Q521 frg. 2 col. 2, and identifies the "I" of line 9 as belonging to the high priest who addresses the members of his community. Puech also believes that in 11Q13 2.15-20, "the messenger of good news that announces salvation" from Isa 52:7 refers to Melchizedek, the high priest, who is referred to in the *pesher* that follows. For him, it is highly significant that only this part of the citation of Isa 52:7 has been interpreted by way of a direct quotation of Isa 61:2-3, because it gives additional support to the hypothesis of priestly implications of this biblical passage.

It is interesting to note that the interpretation of Isa 61:1 plays a central role in both of the latter two arguments, in support of the notion of a prophetic or priestly messianic figure. And yet, given the diverse evidence at our disposal, this should come as no surprise. A final determination will depend to no small degree on one's view of the use of Scripture in Early Jewish literature and the nature of scribal exegetical traditions. It is appropriate now, then, to briefly review the history of the interpretation of Isa 61:1 in biblical and extra-biblical literature so as to see whether any definite conclusion can be reached on this basis.[39]

In the Hebrew Bible, Isa 61:1-3 might have functioned as a midrash on the servants songs in Deutero-Isaiah, especially Isa 42:1-4, 7 and 49:8-9,[40] even though form-critically it represents a prophetic self-description.[41] It is clearly

38. Puech, "Some Remarks on 4Q246 and 4Q521," 557. Puech follows P. Grelot, who argued that the speaker in Isa 61:1 is a high priest after the exile ("Sur Isaïe LXI: La Première Consécration du Grand-Prêtre," *RB* 97 [1990]: 414-31).

39. For a succinct sketch of "a history of function of Isa 61:1-3 from its appearance in the Tanak to its role in the Lukan account of Jesus' appearance and sermon in the Nazareth synagogue," see J. A. Sanders, "From Isaiah 61 to Luke 4," in *Christianity, Judaism, and Other Greco-Roman Cults: Studies for Morton Smith at Sixty* (ed. J. Neusner; 4 vols.; SJLA 12; Leiden: E. J. Brill, 1975), 1:73-106; the quotation is from the opening sentence on p. 75.

40. Cf. D. Michel, "Zur Eigenart Tritojesajas," *ThViat* 10 (1966): 213-30; W. A. M. Beuken, "Servant and Herald of Good Tidings: Isaiah 61 as an Interpretation of Isaiah 40–55," in *The Book of Isaiah: Le livre d'Isaïe* (ed. J. Vermeylen; BETL 81; Leuven: Peeters and Leuven University Press, 1989), 411-42; P. D. Hanson, *The Dawn of Apocalyptic: The Historical and Sociological Roots of Jewish Apocalyptic Eschatology* (rev. ed.; Philadelphia: Fortress, 1979), 65-68; Sanders, "From Isaiah 61 to Luke 4," 83.

41. Cf. K. Elliger, "Der Prophet Tritojesaja," *ZAW* 49 (1931): 112-41; C. Westermann, *Isaiah*

understood in the latter sense in the Targum Isaiah, which introduces 61:1 with the clause "the prophet said" (אמר נביא), which indicates that, for the targumist, this passage is a reflection of a prophet on his prophetic vocation. Moreover, instead of רוח אדני יהוה עלי ("the spirit of the Lord GOD is upon me") the Targum has רוח נבואה מן קדם יהוה אלהים עלי ("the spirit of prophecy from before the LORD God is upon me"), a reading that interprets the spirit of God from the biblical text as the spirit of prophecy. Also, instead of יען משח יהוה אתי ("because the LORD has anointed me"), the Targum has חלף דרבי יהוה יתי ("because the LORD has appointed me"). The idea of anointing is thus eliminated and replaced with the idea of appointing.

Among various allusions to Isa 61:1-3 in the Dead Sea Scrolls,[42] the use of Isa 61:1-3 in 1QH and 11Q13 is especially interesting. In 1QH^a 23.14-15,[43] the speaker apparently takes up the role of the herald from Isaiah 61. He sees himself as a bearer of God's goodness, sent to proclaim to the poor the abundance of God's mercies. Even on the basis of this relatively short passage some scholars have pondered that the poet might be the Righteous Teacher.[44] Happily, the allusions to Isaiah 61 in 11Q13 are more explicit; indeed, they play a significant role in this document.[45] The text relates various scriptural quotations (Lev 25:13; Deut 15:2; Pss 82:1-2 and 7:8-9; Isa 52:7; and Dan 9:25) to Isa 61:1, which is interwoven into the text of the interpretation.[46] Melchizedek, a priestly figure mentioned in Gen 14:18 and Ps 110:4, is the main character in the eschatological scenario described in the document. He is called אל and אלוהים and is pictured as a heavenly deliverer who proclaims the year of Jubilee in which the captives — in this case, the members of the Community — will be released from the burden of their sins. He is also a judge of Belial and

---

40–66: A Commentary (trans. D. M. G. Stalker; OTL; Philadelphia: Westminster, 1969), 366; Collins, "A Herald of Good Tidings," 226-27.

42. 4Q171 (4QpPs^a) 37 2.9-10; 1QS 9.21-23; 1QM 7.4-5.

43. The lines and column numbers follow the reconstruction of the Hodayot by H. Stegemann, "Rekonstruktion der Hodajot: Ursprüngliche Gestalt und kritisch bearbeiteter Text der Hymnenrolle aus Höhle 1 von Qumran" (Ph.D. diss.; University of Heidelberg, 1963); cf. also É. Puech, "Quelques aspects de la restauration du Rouleau des Hymnes (1QH)," JJS 39 (1988): 38-55.

44. D. Flusser, "Blessed are the Poor in Spirit . . ." IEJ 10 (1960): 10; Collins, "A Herald of Good Tidings," 231.

45. Cf. P. J. Kobelski, Melchizedek and Melchireša' (CBQMS 10; Washington: Catholic Biblical Association, 1981), 3-23; J. T. Milik, "Milkî-sedeq et Milkî-reša' dans les anciens écrits juifs et chrétiens," JJS 23 (1972): 95-144; A. S. van der Woude, "Melchisedek als himmlische Erlösergestalt in den neugefundenen eschatologischen Midraschim aus Qumran Höhle XI," OTS 14 (1965): 354-73.

46. See M. P. Miller, "The Function of Isa 61:1-2 in 11Q Melchizedek," JBL 88 (1969): 467-69.

his followers. This description of the end-time events is supplemented in 2.15-16 by the quotation of Isa 52:7 followed by its interpretation. In 2.18, the text identifies "the messenger" (המבשר) from the scriptural text as "the anointed of the spir[it]" (משיח הרו[ח]) about whom Daniel spoke. The designation משיח הרוח is not taken from the biblical text, but is most likely construed under the influence of Isa 61:1. It serves as a link between Isa 52:7 and Dan 9:25b. Since the latter contains the reference to the "anointed one," it is very likely that this verse was quoted after the introductory clause אשר אמר [דני]אל. If so, then, as most scholars assume, "the anointed of the spirit" should be identified with "the anointed prince" of Dan 9:25. The fragmentary state of the text, however, prevents any certainty regarding the identity of משיח הרוח in 11Q13, so that other interpretations remain possible. Proposals include that this figure is Melchizedek himself,[47] a prophetic figure other than Melchizedek,[48] the Prince of Light,[49] the Danielic "one like a son of man,"[50] or even the Righteous Teacher.[51] Whatever the case, the interpretation of Isa 52:7 that continues in lines 18-19 apparently takes up the next term that appears in that text: "[the messenger] of good news that announ[ces salvation]" (ומבשר] טוב משמי[ע ישועה]). But, given the broken context and paucity of extant text, it is difficult to say anything conclusive except that this designation seems to have been explained by a direct quotation of Isa 61:2-3.

In none of these appropriations of Isaiah 61 is the herald of good news identified as the Messiah. Even in 4Q521, the tasks that the biblical text assigns to this figure are detached from his personality and presented in a wider context of the eschatological blessings whose ultimate executor is God himself. Yet the fact that within this context God's Anointed is mentioned gives a messianic flavor to the entire passage. This is, however, *all that can be said* with any certainty. A review of the history of interpretation of Isa 61:1-3 has shown that the actualizations of this text were diverse, even within a distinct religious group such as the Qumran Community. The anointed messenger of the good news from Isa 61:1 could be interpreted as a prophet; the Righteous Teacher; the anointed prince of Dan 9:25a; Melchizedek, a biblical priest who

---

47. Sanders, "From Isaiah 61 to Luke 4," 91; P. Stuhlmacher, "Das paulinische Evangelium," in *Das Evangelium und die Evangelien: Vorträge vom Tübinger Symposium 1982* (ed. P. Stuhlmacher; WUNT 28; Tübingen: Mohr Siebeck, 1983), 171, 173; idem, *Biblische Theologie des Neuen Testaments* (2 vols.; Göttingen: Vandenhoeck & Ruprecht, 1992), 1:112.

48. Collins, "A Herald of Good Tidings," 230; M. de Jonge and A. S. van der Woude, "11QMelchizedek and the New Testament," *NTS* 12 (1965/1966): 306.

49. Kobelski, *Melchizedek and Melchireša'*, 36.

50. Puech, *La croyance*, 554-58.

51. Milik, "*Milkî-sedeq et Milkî-reša'*," 126.

takes the role of the heavenly deliverer; and so forth. The exegetical traditions of Isa 61:1-3 are far from uniform and evidence some of the most common characteristics of midrashic interpretation. A text could be understood in a variety of ways, depending on a given situation and the interests of the group for which the interpretation was made. There can be no doubt that Isa 61:1-3 has a latent potential for a messianic reading, especially since that is readily available through the concept of anointing. But, if and when necessary, such a messianic idea could be filtered out or completely reformulated, as the Targum shows. It seems that among the reviewed texts, only 4Q521 uses the messianic potential of Isaiah 61 by alluding to, though not quoting, vv. 1-3 within a messianic framework.

To summarize to this point: we can conclude that it is virtually impossible to clarify with greater precision the role and character of God's Messiah in 4Q521 frg. 2 2.1, because the text does not specify the relationship between God and his Anointed. To use S. Talmon's phrase, "the conjunction between the state of salvation and the Anointed who brings about salvation"[52] has not yet taken place in 4Q521. As the next section will demonstrate, such a situation is quite similar to other Early Jewish documents that treat the same topic. They, too, generally ascribe the main role in the end-time events to God, not God's Messiah. If within that framework they mention the Messiah, they never specify whether these events will take place through his agency or not.

3. Eschatological Blessings as Signs of the Messianic Time

H. L. Strack and P. Billerbeck's claim that "the healing of all illnesses was expected in the messianic end-time"[53] has found a wide acceptance among New Testament interpreters,[54] even though their correlative assertion that the es-

---

52. The German original is: "Konfluenz von Heilssituation und heilbringendem (oder: heilbringender) Gesalbten." See S. Talmon, "Biblische und frühnachbiblische Messias- und Heilserwartungen," in *Juden und Christen im Gespräch: Gesammelte Aufsätze II* (Information Judentum 11; Neukirchen-Vluyn: Neukirchener, 1992), 103.

53. H. L. Strack and P. Billerbeck. *Kommentar zum Neuen Testament aus Talmud und Midrasch* (6 vols.; München: C. H. Beck, 1924-1956), 1:593.

54. J. Schniewind, *Das Evangelium nach Matthäus* (11th ed.; NTD 2; Göttingen: Vandenhoeck & Ruprecht, 1956), 139-40; D. A. Hagner, *Matthew 1–13* (WBC 33A; Dallas: Word 1993), 301; U. Luz, *Das Evangelium nach Matthäus* (3 vols.; EKKNT 1; Zürich: Benziger, 1985-1997), 2:169; A. Richardson, *The Miracle-Stories of the Gospels* (London: SCM Press, 1941), 43; J. Becker, *Jesus von Nazareth* (Berlin/New York: W. Gruyter, 1996), 220; W. J. Bittner, *Jesu Zeichen im Johannesevangelium: Die Messias-Erkenntnis im Johannesevangelium vor ihrem jüdischen Hintergrund* (WUNT 2.26; Tübingen: J. C. B. Mohr, 1987), 136.

chatological blessings were expected to take place through the agency of the Messiah[55] has been universally rejected.[56] Still, even the first claim is occasionally questioned. E. P. Sanders, for example, notes that "subsequent Jewish literature does not indicate that Jews habitually looked for miracles as a sign of the coming end."[57] In an article published several years ago, Hans Kvalbein challenged the claim made by Strack and Billerbeck by reviewing the entire evidence provided in their commentary.[58] In his view, these "texts speak quite generally about a coming time of salvation without illness, pain and distress. The salvation is described in collective terms referring to the people as a whole. God himself is the redeemer. The Messiah has no function as healer or physician in these texts, and they do not even mention healing miracles."[59] Despite the overall accuracy of Kvalbein's conclusions, they are too general and need to be explicated with greater precision. In what follows, I will reexamine several Early Jewish texts with the purpose of showing that, like 4Q521, some of them describe, not only the future time of salvation generally, but the messianic time specifically, in terms of general health, including even miracles of healing. Special attention will be given to the question of the relationship between the end-time blessings and the Messiah.

The oldest passage relevant for the topic under investigation can be found in *Jub.* 23:26-30. It describes the future age of salvation in terms of peace, spiritual renewal, the gradual prolongation of the life span, the slowing down and eventual disappearance of aging, and the restoration of health. It is quite clear that the context "points to a life in this world and not to a life after death or after a resurrection of the dead,"[60] but Kvalbein pushes his thesis too far when he says that "no individual miracles of healing are mentioned."[61] This is true only to the extent that the text does not speak about *specific* diseases or *particular* afflicted individuals that are going to be healed, but the claim that "all of their days will be days of blessing and healing" (23:29) and

---

55. "Man nahm an, dass der Messias seinem Volk Israel alle jene Güter widerbringen werde, die durch Adams Fall verloren gegangen waren; dazu gehörte natürlich auch die Beseitigung von Krankheit und Tod" (Strack-Billerbeck, *Kommentar*, 1:593).

56. There is a broad consensus among contemporary biblical scholars that "there is not one pre-70 Jewish writing that depicts the Messiah as one who will come and heal the sick or give sight to the blind" (J. H. Charlesworth, "Solomon and Jesus: The Son of David in Ante-Markan Traditions [Mk 10:47]," in *Biblical and Humane: A Festschrift for John F. Priest* [ed. L. B. Elder, D. L. Barr, and E. S. Malbon; Atlanta: Scholars Press, 1996], 150).

57. E. P. Sanders, *Jesus and Judaism* (Philadelphia: Fortress, 1985), 163.

58. Kvalbein, "The Wonders of the End-Time," 101-6.

59. Ibid., 101-2.

60. Ibid., 103.

61. Ibid.

the expectation that "the Lord will heal his servants" (23:30)[62] seem to imply individual healings. This understanding of the statements related to healing is also supported by the context, which presumes a gradual and not a sudden change of all life conditions. Even so, the text does not mention any messianic figure and clearly ascribes all improvements concerning the length and quality of life to God.

In *1 En.* 96:3, a healing medicine is promised to those who have previously suffered. Since there is no indication that this suffering comes from physical illnesses, it is possible to understand the reference to healing more generally. However, if the first line of the contrasting passage in *1 En.* 95:4 refers to "magical practices for healing purposes,"[63] which are rejected in the second line by a warning that the healing medicine will not be available to those who engage in such activities, then the reference to healing in 96:3 could also be understood more specifically, as a promise of the recovery of physical health given to the righteous and denied to the sinners.[64]

The text in *4 Ezra* 7:120-126, which speaks of "safe and healthful habitations" (7:121), the glory of the Most High (7:122), a paradise with unspoiled fruit "in which are abundance and healing" (7:123), and the shining of the faces of those who practiced self-control (7:125), evidently refers to a life after death. Despite the somewhat puzzling reference to healing in 7:123, the text does *not* presume that in the afterlife people will still suffer from sicknesses that need to be healed through the fruit of paradise. *Fourth Ezra* 8:51-53 confirms this by specifying that illness will be banished from paradise. It is certainly true, as Kvalbein notes, that "in this life of resurrection, healing from sickness and pain has no function."[65]

Unlike the texts considered so far, *2 Bar.* 73:1-7 describes the messianic reign that will begin after the Messiah completes the annihilation of Israel's enemies. His reign is presented as a paradise *redivivus*, characterized by peace,

---

62. *OTP* 2:102. In its present context, v. 30 expands and further develops the idea found in v. 29; see G. L. Davenport, *The Eschatology of the Book of Jubilees* (SPB 20; Leiden: E. J. Brill, 1971), 33 n. 3.

63. G. W. E. Nickelsburg, *1 Enoch: A Commentary on the Book of 1 Enoch* (ed. K. Baltzer; Hermeneia; Minneapolis: Fortress, 2001), 464; cf. M. Black, *The Book of Enoch or I Enoch: A New English Edition with Commentary and Textual Notes* (SVTP 7; Leiden: E. J. Brill, 1985), 297.

64. Two additional passages from *1 Enoch* are mentioned in Strack-Billerbeck's commentary, *1 En.* 5:8 and *1 En.* 25:5-7 (the reading in manuscripts B and C), but despite the fact that they refer to prolonged life expectations due to the disappearance of ailments, they do not mention healings in the sense of recovery of health by those who were previously ill. Cf. Kvalbein, "The Wonders of the End-Time," 103.

65. Kvalbein, "The Wonders of the End-Time," 104.

joy, rest, the absence of illness, fear, tribulation, premature death, and child-birth pains. The expected changes in the behavior of wild animals (wild beasts will serve humans, and asps and dragons will be subjected to children) resemble similar motifs found in the description of the messianic time in Isa 11:6-9 and elsewhere. It should be kept in mind, however, that this is not a de-scription of the afterlife but of life on earth.[66] The expected blessings charac-terize the messianic time, not the person of the Messiah. However, since 2 *Bar.* 73:2 does not present the dew of health as a reoccurring event and even adds that illness will vanish, there is no reason to assume that this passage envis-ages healing miracles or individual healings.[67]

Second Baruch 29:3–30:1 describes the messianic time before the resur-rection of the dead. This period starts with the appearance of the Anointed One, who "will begin to be revealed" (2 *Bar.* 29:3).[68] The days of the Messiah are characterized by constant marvels, such as the abundance of food, the dis-appearance of hunger, and the dew of health. Since these marvels will take place every day (29:6), the text does not presuppose a state of universal satis-faction or universal health. None of these wonders are ascribed to the agency of the Messiah. Even though it is not explicitly specified, the text presumes that they will take place through a divine intervention into the laws of nature.[69] Yet it is important to recognize that these events nevertheless play a significant role in the process of the revelation of the Messiah. Even though the text does not clarify the nature of this relationship, it does permit a few conclusions:

1. both the miracles and the process of revealing the Messiah are the result of divine initiative;
2. there is a direct link between the wonders and the messianic time — the marvels partake in the fulfillment of "the time of the appearance of the Anointed One" (2 *Bar.* 30:1)[70] and thus verify that the latter is taking place; and
3. the marvels point to the presence of the Messiah and participate, though in an unspecified way, in the process of the revelation of his person.

Two additional passages depict a similar relationship between God's marvelous acts, the time of the Messiah, and the revelation of his identity,

---

66. Ibid., 105.

67. Ibid.

68. *OTP* 1:630.

69. Kvalbein notices the similarity with the exodus wonders, especially the manna in the desert ("The Wonders of the End-Time," 105).

70. *OTP* 1:631.

even though they do not contain explicit references to healings. The first text is found in *4 Ezra* 7:26-28, which speaks about the "signs" [*signa*] (v. 26) and "wonders" [*mirabilia*] (v. 27) of the messianic time. Although the content of the end-time wonders is not specified, the text ascribes them the status of visibility. Since everyone shall see them, they are *observable events*. They are intrinsically linked to the revelation of the Messiah, even though the text does not specify the character of this connection.

The second reference can be found in chapters 17 and 18 of the *Psalms of Solomon*, a document written most probably after Pompey's conquest of Jerusalem in 63 BCE. The text claims that the time of the Messiah's appearance has been decided upon by a divine decree known only to God.[71] Yet in the messianic time, the object of seeing and thus perception will not be the Messiah himself, but the wonderful state of affairs that is going to take place upon God's initiative. Thus *Pss. Sol.* 17:44 declares that "blessed are those born in those days to see the good fortunes of Israel which God will bring to pass" (μακάριοι οἱ γενόμενοι ἐν ταῖς ἡμέραις ἐκείναις ἰδεῖν τὰ ἀγαθὰ Ισραηλ . . . ἃ ποιήσει ὁ θεός). *Psalms of Solomon* 18:6 repeats this almost verbatim: "blessed are those born in those days, to see the good fortunes of the Lord which he will do for the coming generation" (μακάριοι οἱ γενόμενοι ἐν ταῖς ἡμέραις ἐκείναις ἰδεῖν τὰ ἀγαθὰ κυρίου ἃ ποιήσει γενεᾷ τῇ ἐρχομένῃ). This conclusion is not undermined by the fact that in *Psalms of Solomon* 17 and 18, the content of "the good fortunes" is not expressed in terms of the improvement of health and life expectancy but of political and social conditions. What matters is that God's wonderful acts confirm the advent of the messianic time and fortify the human perception of its arrival.

The relevant passages in Early Jewish writings reviewed above show that the expectations regarding the improvement of health in the future were far too diverse to allow a general conclusion that "we have no evidence at all for the assumption that the Jews in the Hellenistic and Early Roman period expected healing miracles for individual Israelites in the time of salvation."[72] Two texts, *Jub.* 23:26-30 and *2 Bar.* 29:3–30:1, speak about the improvement of health of people in the time of salvation, and in both cases this improvement is envisioned for life in this world and not the afterlife. Those texts that associate the recovery of health (*2 Bar.* 29:3–30:1) or a complete disappearance of illness (*2 Bar.* 73:1-7) with the appearance of the Anointed One present these

---

71. *Pss. Sol.* 17:21: "See, Lord, and raise up for them their king, the son of David, to rule over your servant Israel in the time known to you, O God"; *Pss. Sol.* 18:5: "May God cleanse Israel for the day of mercy in blessing, for the appointed day when his Messiah will reign."

72. Kvalbein, "The Wonders of the End-Time," 106.

blessings as the characteristics of the messianic time, not of the person of the Messiah *per se,* and regard them completely as God's own acts.

4Q521 shares with these documents several important features. First, there is a heavy emphasis on the uniqueness of the events that are going to happen. Thus, for example, *4 Ezra* 7:27 speaks about "wonders" *(mirabilia)* and *Ps. Sol.* 17:44 and 18:6 about "the good fortunes" (τὰ ἀγαθά), whereas 4Q521 frg. 2 2.11 mentions "the glorious things that have not taken place" (**ונכבדות שלוא היו**). Second, these marvels are the result of divine activity. Thus in *4 Ezra* a divine voice calls them "my wonders" *(mirabilia mea),* *Pss. Sol.* 17:44 explicitly says that it is God who will bring to pass the good fortunes of Israel (ἃ ποιήσει ὁ θεός), and 4Q521 frg. 2 2.11 asserts that "the Lord will do" (**אדני יעשה**) the glorious things that have not yet taken place. Finally, these wonders can testify or point to the presence of the Messiah. The relationship between the Messiah and the wonders is, however, never fully explained. *2 Baruch* 29 and *4 Ezra* 7 speak about the "revelation" of the Messiah, whereas *Pss. Sol.* 17 and 18 and 4Q521 simply assume his presence when these events begin to take place.

4. The Relationship between 4Q521 and Matt 11:2-6//Luke 7:18-23 (Q)

In contrast to the other texts mentioned above that are only thematically related to 4Q521, the Q passage preserved in Matt 11:2-6 and Luke 7:18-23 contains the closest known parallel to this document, because both texts go beyond their common scriptural basis in Isa 61:1 by adding the reference to the resurrection of the dead prior to the reference to preaching good news to the poor. Direct dependence between the Q material and 4Q521, whichever direction such might run, cannot be established, however. It is instead probable that both texts go back to a common tradition.

It is true that much interest in 4Q521 has been spurred because of its notable similarity to the Gospel passages. But, again, the comparison between the texts has, heretofore, been predominantly based on the inference that God acts through the agency of the Messiah in 4Q521. As a result, the temporal component that is actually quite dominant in these documents has gone largely ignored.[73] This common temporal aspect of the messianic time must now be explored more fully.

---

73. This does not mean that this aspect was completely overlooked. Thus, for example, F. Neirynck proposes that "in defining the genre of the logion itself, the parallel in 4Q521 can be

The Gospel Materials

The question of John the Baptist, "Are you he who is to come or should we wait for another?" (Matt 11:2//Luke 7:19) expresses his genuine astonishment and demonstrates his inability to relate the reports about Jesus' miracles to the question of Jesus' messianic identity. It confirms the general impression that we get from other Early Jewish literature that miracles are, in themselves, not necessarily messianic signs. They are not able to authenticate a messianic claim in any clear fashion because the Messiah was not expected to be a wonder-worker. Yet on the other hand, the question demonstrates that the miracles *could* give rise to the query of one's possibly messianic identity. The text presupposes a certain correlation between the two, but the exact relationship remains ambiguous and unspecified.

The most interesting but often-neglected aspect of John's question is actually the alternative that he mentions. That alternative is not to dismiss the hope that Jesus is the Messiah, though that is certainly implied, but to "wait for another." August Strobel has demonstrated that this alternative reflects a dilemma that was created by the experience of the delay of the expected end-time events, the scriptural basis of which can be found in Hab 2:3.[74] This text offers an assurance to readers that even if the end seems to be delayed, they should continue to wait for it:

כי עוד חזון למועד ויפח לקץ ולא יכזב
אם־יתמהמה חכה־לו כי־בא יבא לא יאחר

> For there is still a vision for the appointed time; it speaks of the end, and does not fail. If it seems to tarry, wait for it; for it will surely come, it will not delay.

It can be shown that one stream of Early Jewish tradition that goes back to Hab 2:3[75] reinterpreted an eventual delay of the end-time events as the de-

---

helpful as an example of the *topos* of a description of the time of salvation" ("Q 6,20b-21; 7,22 and Isaiah 61," in *The Scriptures in the Gospels* [ed. C. M. Tuckett; BETL 131; Leuven: University Press, 1997], 62). Also, Puech generally characterizes 4Q521 frg. 2 as speaking "about eschatological benefits that God will enact for his faithful in the last days and about marks which will show them the coming of the days of the messiah" ("Some Remarks on 4Q246 and 4Q521," 553).

74. A. Strobel, *Untersuchungen zum eschatologischen Verzögerungsproblem* (NovTSup 2; Leiden/Köln: E. J. Brill, 1961), 265-77.

75. Among them, 1QpHab 7.5-14 contains probably the most explicit reference to Hab 2:3. Hab 2:3a is quoted in lines 5-6 followed by a *pesher* in lines 7-8. Hab 2:3b is quoted in lines 9-10 followed by a *pesher* in lines 10-14. The *pesher* on Hab 2:3a relates the prophecy concerning the

lay of the advent of the Messiah.[76] Texts reflecting this tradition are found in *4 Ezra:*

- 12:32: "This is the Messiah whom the Most High has kept until the end of days";[77]
- 13:26-27: "As for your seeing a man come up from the heart of the sea, this is he whom the Most High has been keeping for many ages";[78] and
- 13:52: "just as no one can explore or know what is in the depths of the sea, so no one on earth can see my Son or those who are with him, except in the time of his day."[79]

A distinction between the period of the hiddenness of the Messiah and the time of his visible appearance can also be found in the *Similitudes of Enoch.* According to *1 En.* 48:6b, the messianic figure, who in chapter 48 is called the Son of Man (48:2) and the Elect One (48:6a), "was concealed in the presence of (the Lord of the Spirits) prior to the creation of the world, and for eternity."[80] This idea is even more elaborated in *1 En.* 62:7: "For the Son of

---

appointed time and the assurance that "it will not fail" (ולוא יכזב) to the prolongation of the last end-time (יארוך הקץ האחרון). Since the verb in question is either Qal imperfect (יארוך) or Hiphil imperfect (יאריך) from ארך, it can be translated either as "will be prolonged" (M. P. Horgan, "Habakkuk Pesher," in *The Dead Sea Scrolls: Hebrew, Aramaic, and Greek Texts with English Translations,* vol. 6B: *Pesharim, Other Commentaries, and Related Documents* [ed. J. H. Charlesworth et al.; PTSDSSP 6B; Tübingen: Mohr Siebeck, 2002], 173) or "will be delayed in coming" (S. Talmon, "Notes on the Habakkuk Scroll," *VT* 1 [1951]: 35). The *pesher* on Hab 2:3b addresses the problem that the men of truth might encounter "when the last end-time is drawn out for them" (בהמשך עליהם הקץ האחרון) by offering an assurance that "all of God's end-times will come according to their fixed order, as he decreed for them in the mysteries of his prudence" (1QpHab 7.13-14). With this, the objectivity of the delay is denied by treating it as a mere, indeed erroneous human impression that is contrasted to the firm belief that everything is going to take place according to the divine decree. The targumic reading of Hab 2:3 betrays a similar conviction that the end has been predetermined by God, and affirms that despite the reader's impression of a delay, the end will occur when the time set up by the divine decree arrives: "For the prophecy is ready for a time and the end [קץ] is fixed, nor shall it fail; if there is delay [ארכא] in the matter wait for it, for it shall come in its time and shall not be deferred [ולא יתעכב]."

76. The messianic interpretation of Hab 2:3 is most apparent in the rabbinic writings, especially in *b. Sanh.* 97b, which addresses the problem of the delay of the coming of the Messiah. The solution to this problem is found in the idea of waiting, for which Hab 2:3 offers scriptural justification. The passages from *4 Ezra* and *1 Enoch* discussed above demonstrate that we are dealing here with a very old tradition.

77. *OTP* 1:550.

78. *OTP* 1:552.

79. *OTP* 1:553.

80. *OTP* 1:35.

Man was concealed from the beginning, and the Most High One preserved him in the presence of his power; then he revealed him to the holy and the elect ones."[81] Various phrases that express the duration of time, such as "until the end of days" (*4 Ezra* 12:32) or "for many ages" (*4 Ezra* 13:27), and the verbs that denote keeping and preserving (*4 Ezra* 12:32; 13:27; *1 En.* 62:7) link these texts to the subject matter of Hab 2:3.[82] These texts, then, like 1QpHab 7.5-14,[83] ascribe the reasons for the (seeming) delay to God and his predetermined design of the end-time events. By doing so, the reality of the delay is *de facto* denied (because in actuality there is no delay at all), and the entire problem is attributed to human inability to perceive the actual events and the lack of patience to wait.

If this is correct, the question of John the Baptist appears in a new light. It betrays the puzzlement caused by an apparent delay of the expected messianic time. In that sense, it reflects a discernable *temporal aspect,* which refers to human incapability to recognize either the appearance or the closeness of the end-time. On the other hand, the temporal aspect has been supplemented, or rather suppressed, by a *personal aspect.* John's question in fact does not ask about the recognition of the messianic time, but about the recognition of the Messiah himself.

Interestingly enough, Jesus does not answer this question with a simple affirmation or denial, but with a recapitulation of the events that are currently taking place. His answer thus consciously neglects the personal aspect of the inquiry and responds only to its implied temporal component. By alluding to the salvation oracles from Isaiah, especially Isa 35:5-6 and 61:1,[84] Jesus enumerates the end-time blessings, some of which[85] are explicitly associated with the appearance of the Messiah in 4Q521.[86] Jesus' answer thus

---

81. *OTP* 1:43.

82. This link was first noted by Strobel, who criticized the previous research on this topic, especially the work of E. Sjöberg (*Der verborgene Menschensohn in den Evangelien* [Lund: C. W. K. Gleerup, 1955], 41-98), because "die Nähe zur eschatologischen Verzögerungsterminologie (s. die '*langen Zeiten*') wird allgemein nicht gewürdigt" (*Untersuchungen zum eschatologischen Verzögerungsproblem*, 25).

83. See note 75.

84. Other texts to which Jesus' answer alludes are Isa 26:19 and 29:18.

85. Namely, giving sight to the blind, raising the dead, and preaching good news to the poor.

86. Before the publication of 4Q521, it was difficult to show that Isaianic texts refer to the blessings of the messianic time. Thus for example, W. D. Davies and D. C. Allison assert that "Jesus is the Coming One of John's preaching, the Messiah of prophecy who, through his proclamation to the poor and his miraculous and compassionate deeds, brings to fulfillment the messianic oracles uttered so long ago by Isaiah the prophet" (*The Gospel According to Saint Matthew*

points to the observable signs of the messianic time and *not* to the person of the Messiah himself.[87] In this way, Jesus makes a somewhat vague link between his miracles and his messianic identity. This ambiguity is clearly reflected in the concluding sentence: "And blessed is he who takes no offense at me" (Matt 11:6//Luke 7:23).

The redactional activity of Matthew and Luke shows that both evangelists tried to remove the ambiguity between Jesus' miracles and his messiahship. Matthew refers to Jesus' miracles in this passage as "the deeds of the Messiah" (τὰ ἔργα τοῦ χριστοῦ; Matt 11:2), whereas Luke adds that Jesus was curing many diseases at the time of the encounter with John's disciples (Luke 7:21). It is easy to understand the Evangelists' apologetic interest. They wanted to demonstrate that a historical person, Jesus of Nazareth, was indeed the expected Messiah.

Qumran

In contrast to the Gospel writers, neither the Qumran covenanters who copied and preserved 4Q521 in their library nor the original author(s) of this document, if these differed from the former, had such an interest or apologetic tendency. If 4Q521 frg. 2 2.10, which claims that "the fru[it of a] good [wor]k will not be delayed for anyone" can serve as an indicator of their concern, they wanted to be assured that the end-time blessings, here understood as a reward for their service of the Lord,[88] would certainly take place. The need for

---

[3 vols.; ICC; Edinburgh: T&T Clark, 1988-1997], 2:242). A. Strobel (*Untersuchungen zum eschatologischen Verzögerungsproblem*, 274) also regards Isaianic salvation oracles as "messianic." The problem is that Isa 26:19; 29:18; 35:5-6; and 61:1 describe the blessings of the future age, but the latter is nowhere associated with the coming of the Messiah. 4Q521 now shows that in the postbiblical period at least Isa 61:1 was interpreted messianically.

87. H. Frankemölle believes that this feature of the Q-text speaks in favor of its high age: "Nicht ein 'Ich-bin-es' is Zielpunkt der Aussage, vielmehr die messianische Praxis. . . . Endzeitliches Heil Gottes bricht an, dahinter tritt auch der Bote Jesus zurück. Vielleicht könnte gerade diese implizite Christologie ein Zeichen für ein hoher Alter für das hinter dem Text liegende Verständnis sein" ("Jesus als deuterojesajanischer Freudenbote? Zur Rezeption von Jes 52,7 und 61,1 im Neuen Testament, durch Jesus und in den Targumim," in *Vom Urchristentum zu Jesus: Für Joachim Gnilka* [ed. H. Frankemölle and K. Kertelge; Freiburg: Herder, 1989], 53). Collins also points out that "insofar as Isaiah 61 and the texts that allude to it emphasize the eschatological liberation rather than the person of the messenger, they provide a paradigm of messianic action that would seem to fit well the career of the historical Jesus as it is described in the Synoptics" ("A Herald of Good Tidings," 239-40).

88. Cf. line 3: "You who seek the Lord, strengthen yourselves in his service."

such a reassurance might have come from the experience of the delay of the eschatological recompense. This interpretation is supported by the relationship between the phrase in 4Q521 frg. 2 2.10 (לוא יתאחר) and that used in Hab 2:3 (לא יאחר). In both instances, we have the negative particle followed by the imperfect of the verb אחר,[89] and in both instances the phrases refer to future (eschatological) events. This similarity suggests that the function of the subsequent lines in 4Q521 frg. 2 col. 2, which enumerate various "glorious things that have not taken place" that "the Lord will do as he said," might be comparable to the function of Jesus' answer to the implied temporal component in the question of John the Baptist. Both would point to the individual blessings, which, according to the author of 4Q521 who introduces them with the clause כאשר ד[בר], have a scriptural basis. The main difference between 4Q521 and the Q material is that the former expects these events to occur in the future, whereas the latter maintains that they are already taking place in the present, associated with a specific messianic individual.

5. Conclusion

The elaborate description of the eschatological blessings found in 4Q521 frg. 2 col. 2 can be related to the messianic figure mentioned in line 1 only indirectly. This conclusion is supported by both the grammar and inner logic of the text. Although it may be true that God will use human agency for the execution of some or even all of the end-time wonders, the text is strangely silent in regard to the implications of human involvement in the divine design. A comparison with other Early Jewish documents that deal with the same topic has shown that this reticence is not an isolated phenomenon. In a number of passages that describe the blissful future and that also mention the Messiah, the main interest clearly falls on the eschatological marvels, whereas the messianic figure appears somewhat in the background. And yet, by their very character, these events signal that the expected messianic time has arrived. Such miracles participate, therefore, but in an unspecified way, in the revelation of the person of the Messiah.

The startling similarity between 4Q521 and the Q passage (Matt 11:2-6// Luke 7:18-23), which is best attributed to a common tradition, casts additional light on the relationship of end-time marvels and the person of the Messiah. Both texts share not only the unusual combination of the references to the resurrection of the dead and preaching good news to the poor, but also the

---

89. The main difference is Piel in Hab 2:3 and Hithpael in 4Q521.

reference to possible waiting, whose scriptural basis can be found in Hab 2:3. This biblical verse addresses the problem of a seeming delay of the end-time events and advises the reader to trust God's designs and wait. In 4Q521, the allusion to Hab 2:3 appears in the form of a reassurance that the eschatological reward will not be delayed for anyone. In Q, the allusion to Hab 2:3 appears in the question of John the Baptist, who offers an alternative, "or should we wait for another?" The personal aspect of John's formulation represents a further, specifically Christian development of the problem of the delay of the end-time happenings, which is completely absent from 4Q521. It should come as no surprise, therefore, to see that the extant text preserved in frg. 2 col. 2 of 4Q521 focuses almost exclusively on the *events* that will indicate the arrival of the expected time of eschatological blessings and offers very little with regard to the identity and the role of God's Anointed mentioned in line 1.

The Concept of Unity at Qumran

CARSTEN CLAUSSEN AND MICHAEL THOMAS DAVIS

It has long been recognized that various works found among the Dead Sea Scrolls employ a range of characteristic, and sometimes unique, Hebrew terminology.[1] This is especially the case in such "sectarian" works as the *Rule of the Community*,[2] but many other Qumran scrolls employ a number of *termini technici* with rather specific meanings. Some of the best known of these terms relate to the identity or self-identification of the members of the Qumran Community. These sectarians call themselves the "Sons of Light" (בני אור),[3] the "Sons of Truth" (בני אמת),[4] or the "Sons of Righteousness" (בני הצדוק)[5] while all others in the world are called "Sons of Darkness" (בני חושך).[6] The more advanced members of the Qumran Community are called "Men of Ho-

---

1. See also (and for further literature) the excellent study by E. Qimron, *The Hebrew of the Dead Sea Scrolls* (HSS 29; Atlanta: Scholars Press, 1986); idem, "The Nature of DSS Hebrew and Its Relation to BH and MH," in *Diggers at the Well: Proceedings of a Third International Symposium on the Hebrew of the Dead Sea Scrolls and Ben Sira* (ed. Takamitsu Muraoka and John F. Elwolde; STDJ 36; Leiden: Brill, 2000), 232-44.

2. See J. H. Charlesworth, "Community Organization in the Rule of the Community," in *EDSS* 1:133-36.

3. See 1QS 2.16; 3.13, 24-25; 1QM 1.1, 3; 4Q280 frg. 2 line 1.

4. See 1QS 4.5-6; cf. בני אמתו in 4Q266 frg. 11 line 7.

5. See 1QS 9.14; 4Q259 3.10; 4Q286 frg. 1 2.7.

6. See 1QM 1.1, 10, 16; 4Q496 frg. 3 line 7.

We would like to take this opportunity to dedicate this essay to James H. Charlesworth, whose support and encouragement of students and younger colleagues is well known and deeply appreciated by those who have benefited greatly from his generosity.

liness" (אנשי הקודש).[7] The whole Community is either called "the Many" (הרבים),[8] the "House of Holiness" (בית קודש),[9] or, most frequently, just "(the) Community" (יחד or היחד; see below). This use of specific, technical, and self-descriptive terminology replete with a complex skein of meanings peculiar to the group indicates the existence of a "sociolect" or "in-house" jargon characteristic of the Qumran Community and its culture. A study of the terminology found in this "sociolect," therefore, can obviously provide insights into the self-understanding, internal organization, and "worldview" of the Community.

In this essay, we shall argue that the self-designation of the Qumranites offers significant insight into their concept of unity — in both the institutional and "spiritual" sense. The obvious starting point for such an investigation is, of course, the frequently used term (ה)יחד.[10] This important term of self-designation figures prominently in the *Rule of the Community,* occurring some 60 times, but it also appears in the *Rule of the Congregation* (1QSa) about seven times, as well as in some of the *pesharim*[11] and other texts.[12] The

7. See 1QS 5.13.

8. See 1QS 8.26.

9. See 1QS 8.5.

10. For bibliography, see S. Talmon, "The Sectarian יחד — A Biblical Noun," *VT* 3 (1953): 133-40; J. Maier, "Zum Begriff יחד in den Texten vom Toten Meer," *ZAW* 72 (1960): 148-66, reprinted in *Qumran* (ed. K. E. Grözinger et al.; Wege der Forschung 410; Darmstadt: Wissenschaftliche Buchgesellschaft, 1981), 225-48; A. Neher, "Échos de la secte de Qumran dans la littérature talmudique," in *Les manuscrits de la mer Morte: Colloque de Strasbourg 25-27 mai 1955* (Bibliothèque des Centres d'Études Supérieures Spécialisés; Travaux du Centre d'Études Supérieures Spécialisé d'Histoire des Religions de Strasbourg; Paris: Presses universitaires de France, 1957), 49-55, esp. 49-54; E. Koffmann, "Rechtsstellung und Hierarchische Struktur des יחד von Qumran," *Bib* 42 (1961): 433-42; B. W. Dombrowski, "היהד and τὸ κοινόν: An Instance of Early Greek and Jewish Synthesis," *HTR* 59 (1966): 293-307; P. Wernberg-Møller, "The Nature of the Yaḥad According to the Manual of Discipline and Related Documents," *ALUOS* 6 (1969): 56-81; H. Bardtke, "Literaturbericht über Qumrân; V. Teil," *TRu* 35 (1970): 196-230, esp. 224-25; M. Hengel, "Qumran und der Hellenismus," in *Qumrân, sa piété, sa théologie et son milieu* (ed. M. Delcor; BETL 46; Paris: Duculot, 1978), 333-72, esp. 348-49, reprinted in M. Hengel, *Judaica et Hellenica: Kleine Schriften I* (WUNT 90; Tübingen: J. C. B. Mohr/Paul Siebeck, 1996), 258-94, esp. 272-74; and H. Stegemann, "The Qumran Essenes — Local Members of the Main Jewish Union in Late Second Temple Times," in *The Madrid Qumran Congress: Proceedings of the International Congress on the Dead Sea Scrolls: Madrid 18-21 March, 1991* (ed. J. Trebolle Barrera and L. Vegas Montaner; 2 vols.; STDJ 11; Leiden: Brill, 1992), 83-166, esp. 155-56.

11. See 1QpHab 12.4; 4QpPs^a (4Q171) frgs. 1-10 2.15, 18, 19; frg. 11 line 1; 4Q252 (4QCommGen A) 6.5; 4Q174 (4QFlor) 3.17; 22.2; 4Q177 (4QCat^a) 5.16; 14.5.

12. It must be admitted that it is sometimes not possible to distinguish whether יחד represents the noun ("Community") or the adverb ("together"). Cf. 1QH^a 11.23; 12.25. Numbering of 1QH^a follows Stegemann. See his "The Material Reconstruction of 1QHodayot," in *The Dead*

term has been variously translated — "togetherness," "unity," "C/community," or even the German neologism "Einung" are among the many options put forth.[13] While these translations reveal crucial aspects of the concept of the יחד, the semantic history and development of the word, to which we shall now turn, sheds even more light on why this term could become such an ideal expression of the Qumran Community's self-understanding. Further, it will be shown that, when viewed in socio-historical perspective, Qumran terminology of "unity" essentially mirrors the consequences and experience of its break from the other branches of contemporary Judaism.

To begin our discussion, we first turn to a brief survey of the biblical and general Semitic backgrounds of the root יחד and then the Greek terminology used by Greco-Roman sources that is pertinent to understanding the Qumran sectarians and their Community.

1. The Term יחד: Semitic and Biblical Background

yḥd *in Semitic*

The earliest occurrences of the root *yḥd* in the Ugaritic texts stand for "alone," "sole," or "community."[14] This extra-biblical material is somewhat helpful in gaining a sense of the general semantic background of the term. But, like all Judaisms of the time, the religious belief-system of the Qumranites, as well as the terminology through which it was expressed, was derived primarily (and more immediately) from the Hebrew scriptures. It makes sense, then, to look for certain passages in those scriptures in which יחד occurs in order to determine whether such passages influenced the terminology used at Qumran to express the Community's identity.

Sea Scrolls Fifty Years After Their Discovery: Proceedings of the Jerusalem Congress, July 20-25, 1997 (ed. Lawrence H. Schiffman, Emanuel Tov, and James C. VanderKam; Jerusalem: Israel Exploration Society, 2000), 272-84, and esp. 280 for a comparison between his system and that of Sukenik.

13. The last translation goes back especially to the publications of L. Rost and H. Bardtke, "Die Rechtsstellung der Qumran," *TLZ* 86 (1961): 93-104.

14. H.-J. Fabry, "יחד," *TDOT* 6:41. Fabry is dependent upon *UT* 19.1087 which refers to text 1056:7 (= *KTU*² 4.224:7) where we find the phrase *pqr yḥd*, which Dahood took to mean "the overseer of the (ecclesiastical) community." However, note Gregorio del Olmo Lete and Joaquín Sanmartín, *A Dictionary of the Ugaritic Language in the Alphabetic Tradition* (trans. W. G. E. Watson; 2 vols.; HdO 1/67; Leiden: Brill, 2003), 2:960: "*pqr yḥd* PN: special/unique (use) (?)."

yḥd *in the Hebrew Bible*

When we turn to the biblical material we find that, while not particularly common, the root יחד occurs in verbal, adjectival, adverbial, and possibly nominal forms. The verb יחד is rare and seems to occur, at the most, three times in the Hebrew Bible:

- Gen 49:6: בקהלם אל־תחד כבדי, "my glory *will not be associated* with their congregation"[15]
- Isa 14:20: לא־תחד אתם בקבורה, "you will *not be united* with them in the grave" (i.e., "you will not lie in the royal family's tomb along with your ancestors")
- Ps 86:11: יחד לבבי ליראה שמך, "my heart *fixes* upon the fear of your name."

The adjective/substantive (ה)יחיד is more frequent and can have the sense of "only," "unique," or "alone." This range of meaning is well illustrated in the following examples:

In Gen 22:2, God commands Abraham קח־נא את־בנך את־יחידך, "take your son, *your only one*." In Pss 22:21-22a and 35:17 we find the feminine form of the substantive in parallel to נפש as apparently meaning a person's *life*, possibly indicating its unique and irreplaceable nature:

הצילה מחרב נפשי
מיד־כלב יחידתי
הושיעני מפי אריה

Rescue my soul from the sword,
My very life from the dog's strength,
Save me from the lion's jaws! (Ps 22:21-22a)

In Ps 25:16 we find יחיד used to convey the sense of isolation: כי־יחיד ועני אני, "for I am *alone* and suffering." Likewise, in Ps 68:7: אלהים מושיב יחידים ביתה, "God brings the *abandoned* home."

The adverb יחד/יחדו is very interesting in that, as opposed to the partitive sense of the adjective/substantive (ה)יחיד, the adverb is, like the verbal root, clearly associative. Note the following examples:

---

15. Unless otherwise indicated, translations are our own. In the case of the Scrolls, translations follow the PTSDSSP.

- Gen 22:6: וילכו שניהם יחדו, "and the two of them went on *together*"
- Ps 34:4: ונרוממה שמו יחדו, "and *together* let us praise his name"
- Ps 71:10: כי־אמרו אויבי לי ושמרי נפשי נועצו יחדו, "for my enemies speak about me, those who watch my every move conspire *together*"
- Job 38:7: ברן־יחד כוכבי בקר ויריעו כל־בני אלהים, "when *together* the stars of the morning raised a cry, and all the Sons of God shouted in triumph."

Surprisingly, when we look for nominal forms of יחד we find them in only two passages: Deut 33:5 and 1 Chr 12:18. Each deserves some discussion.

1. *Deuteronomy 33:5*

The so-called "Blessing of Moses" (Deuteronomy 33) opens with the following passage:

תורה צוה־לנו משה
מורשה קהלת יעקב
ויהי בישרון מלך
בהתאסף ראשי עם
יחד שבטי ישראל

Moses gave instruction to us,
The assembly of Jacob, His possession.
He was king in "Yeshrun"
When the heads of the people gathered,
The full community of the tribes of Israel.

(Deut 33:4-5)

As with the whole of Deuteronomy 33, this passage is riddled with difficulties that render the text not only difficult to interpret, but, in places, even difficult to read coherently. Yet the overall sense of the action and structure of vv. 2-5 is reasonably clear. The passage opens with a theophany involving Yahweh's arrival as Divine Warrior from his holy mountain in order to lead, defend, and instruct his people during the wilderness wandering. In vv. 4-5, we find a string of group designations characterizing Israel. Israel is: מורשה, "His (God's) possession"; קהלת יעקב, "the assembly of Jacob"; and ישרון, which seems to be a special designation of Israel as Yahweh's "darling" or "favorite." Then the heads of the people are gathered before their king at which point we find the phrase, יחד שבטי ישראל. Given the development of the scene — the whole nation being led, instructed, and ruled — and the chain of various characterizations of Israel as ישרון/קהלת יעקב/מורשה, as well as the mention of the gathering of the leaders of Israel, it seems natural to take the phrase יחד שבטי ישראל as a continuation, indeed, the climax of the sequence, referring to the *entire* community gathered together by and before Yahweh, its ruler and protector. The phrase is sometimes translated "the united tribes of Israel" (cf. NRSV), but it seems more natural to take יחד here as a noun in construct, as we find so often in the Qumran scrolls. If so, the phrase יחד שבטי ישראל should be understood in apposition to ראשי עם בהתאסף, equating the "gathering" with "the full community of the tribes of Israel."[16]

2. 1 Chronicles 12:18

In this text, David addresses some men from the tribes of Judah and Benjamin who have proposed joining his band of soldiers:

ויצא דויד לפניהם ויען ויאמר להם אם־לשלום באתם אלי לעזרני
יהיה־לי עליכם לבב ליחד

And David went out to meet them and answered them saying, "If you have come in friendship in order to aid me, I shall consider you *as allies.* . . ."

The phrase ליחד could also be rendered "as part of (my) band, troops, or alliance," emphasizing David's willingness to *incorporate* these new volunteers into his military force.

Summary

From this brief survey, two observations may be made. First, the semantic range of the root יחד is distinctly "bipolar." That is, in its adjectival and substantive forms it has a partitive sense — it indicates something that is "separated out" or "made distinct from" — characterizing that thing as "isolated," "alone," or "unique." Yet, the rare instances of the verb indicate it had associa-

---

16. This gathering has sometimes been interpreted in terms of "the Ancient Hebrew Parliament." See M. Sulzberger, *The Am Ha-Aretz, the Ancient Hebrew Parliament: A Chapter in the Constitutional History of Ancient Israel* (Philadelphia: J. H. Greenstone, 1910). Cf. Talmon, "The Sectarian יחד," 134; Fabry, "יַחַד," 44. Martin Rose translates accordingly: "als die Häupter des Volkes sich versammelten, die *Vereinigung* der Stämme Israels" (*5. Mose 1–11 u. 26–34: Rahmenstücke zum Gesetzeskorpus* [ZBK 5/2; Zürich: Theologischer Verlag, 1994], 575, 578; emphasis ours).

tive senses of "concentration/focusing," "associating/uniting," or "bringing together." The adverbial use of the root also emphasizes actions that occur at the same time or that are performed together. Likewise, the rare nominal uses seem to refer to a larger group of integrated or united individuals. Therefore, we can say that the root has a semantic range that embraces both the sense of "unity" and "association" as well as "isolation" and "separation."

Second, while the root יחד does appear in the Hebrew Bible in verbal, adjectival, adverbial, and nominal forms, it is most common as an adverb or adjective. The rarity of verbal and nominal occurrences is quite striking. Given the pervasiveness of communal terminology in the Qumran literature involving the noun יחד, one might have expected more extensive use of the noun in the Bible, which would have served as a model for this Qumranic usage. In fact, this lack of convergence with biblical usage leads us to conclude that the Community at Qumran coined this terminology *without* a precedent grounded in scriptural language. If this is the case, we may ask where the Qumranites came up with this term and why it was so attractive to them. This question leads us to look for analogies and parallels in the context of other types of communities and/or voluntary associations in the ancient world.

2. Greco-Roman Backgrounds or
Parallels to the Qumran Use of יחד?

One source that might provide a clue to the origins of the terminology of community in the Qumran literature is the terminology used in the Greco-Roman period describing associations, corporations, or communities.[17]

---

17. Bardtke, "Die Rechtsstellung der Qumran," 93-104, was the first one to compare the organization of the Qumran Community to those of contemporary hellenistic associations. He concludes: "Unter dem Gesichtspunkt des hellenistischen Vereins zeigt die Qumrān-Gemeinde die typische hellenistische Vereinsorganisation und die privatrechtliche Stellung eines solchen innerhalb der Umwelt und gegenüber den einzelnen Mitgliedern. Sie würde deshalb ein hervorragendes Beispiel der Aneignung des hellenistischen Vereinsgedankens mit allen Rechtskonsequenzen durch den jüdischen Geist des 2. Jahrhunderts v. Chr. sein" (104). A more cautious view is expressed by E. Koffmahn, "Rechtsstellung und Hierarchische Struktur," 433-42, who stressed the uniqueness of the Qumran Community: "יחד war aber auch der Terminus, der den Sinn von 'Einzigkeit' vermittelte. Die Qumrangemeinde betrachtete sich als die allein seligmachende Gemeinschaft des damaligen Judentums" (441). See also Koffmahn's "Die staatsrechtliche Stellung der essenischen Vereinigungen in der griechisch-römischen Epoche," *Bib* 44 (1963): 46-61. The closeness of the Qumran organizational pattern and that of hellenistic associations was also stressed by Dombrowski, "היחד," 293-307. However, M. Weinfeld, *The Or-*

Though a comprehensive review of such terminology is impossible here, a brief overview will prove useful. It has been long recognized that looking at "groups and sects, which were prevalent in the Hellenistic world" is instructive in the attempt to understand the nature and organization of the Qumran Community.[18]

The use of Greek terms related to κοινός and κοινωνία was quite common in describing civic, social, and religious associations of the period.[19]

---

ganizational Pattern and the Penal Code of the Qumran Sect: A Comparison with Guilds and Religious Associations of the Hellenistic-Roman Period (NTOA 2; Fribourg: Éditions Universitaires and Göttingen: Vandenhoeck & Ruprecht, 1986), 8, argues that "although the external form and structure of this sect is similar to that of the Hellenistic associations, the basic ideology of the sect is in its nature unique." Cf. also M. Klinghardt, "The Manual of Discipline in the Light of Statutes of Hellenistic Associations," in *Methods of Investigation of the Dead Sea Scrolls and the Khirbet Qumran Site: Present Realities and Future Prospects* (ed. M. O. Wise, N. Golb, J. J. Collins, and D. G. Pardee; Annals of the New York Academy of Sciences 722; New York: New York Academy of Sciences, 1994), 251-70. Klinghardt explicitly builds his argument on Weinfeld's earlier work; cf. also Klinghardt, *Gemeinschaftsmahl und Mahlgemeinschaft: Soziologie und Liturgie frühchristlicher Mahlfeiern* (TANZ 13; Tübingen and Basel: Francke, 1996), esp. 227-49. H. Stegemann, "The Qumran Essenes — Local Members of the Main Jewish Union in Late Second Temple Times," in *The Madrid Qumran Congress*, 83-166, argues in a different direction: "The new organizational term created by the Teacher for his unification of all Israel as far as he could reach it was *ha-yaḥad*. This was a new term, inaugurated neither from the past nor from the hellenistic term *to koinon*, which mainly designated local societies, or single communities. The Teacher's term *ha-yaḥad* basically had other connotations" (155). This understanding is highly influenced by Stegemann's overall picture of "*ha-yaḥad* as a confederation of all existing Jewish groups, their union in a new religious body, which had never existed before" (ibid.). His sharp distinction between the organizational pattern of hellenistic associations and the Qumran Community becomes even clearer in his book, *Die Essener, Qumran, Johannes der Täufer und Jesus: Ein Sachbuch* (5th ed.; Freiburg: Herder, 1996), 230: "Wichtig ist vor allem, daß sie [the overall organizational and administrative structure of the Essenes] durchgängig auf Maßgaben der Tora basierte und gesamtisraelitisch orientiert war, nicht hingegen einer Vereinsordnung. Die Essener waren ihrem Selbstverständnis nach kein besonderer *Verein im Rahmen Israel,* sondern repräsentierten schlicht *Gesamtisrael.*"

18. See Weinfeld, *The Organizational Pattern*, 13-14.

19. F. Poland, *Geschichte des griechischen Vereinswesens* (Preisschriften der Fürstlich Jablonowski'schen Gesellschaft 38; Historisch-Nationalökonomische Section 23; Leipzig: Teubner, 1909), 163-67; E. Ziebarth, *Das griechische Vereinswesen* (Preisschriften der Fürstlich Jablonowski'schen Gesellschaft 34; Historisch-Nationalökonomische Section 21; Leipzig, 1896), 136; Hengel, "Qumran und der Hellenismus," 333-72, esp. 348-49, reprinted in idem, *Judaica et Hellenica*, 258-94, esp. 273-74; Marcus Niebuhr Tod and Simon Hornblower, "clubs, Greek" in *OCD* 351-52; George Hope Stevenson and Andrew William Lintott, "clubs, Roman," in *OCD* 352-53; P. Foucart, *Des associations religieuses chez les Grecs* (Paris: Klincksieck, 1873); and J.-P. Waltzing, *Étude historique sur les corporations professionnelles chez les Romains depuis les origines jusqu'à la chute de l'Empire d'Occident* (Louvain: Charles Peeters, 1895).

Therefore it is not at all surprising that Philo and Josephus use this terminology to describe the communal life of the Essenes.[20] Two examples are particularly instructive:

> They treat wealth with disdain and their association (κοινωνικόν) is quite admirable; one does not find anyone rising over the others in status because of property.[21]

> First of all, then, no one exclusively owns his own house; so that it cannot be shared in common (εἶναι κοινὴν συμβέβηκε) by all. For this reason they live together in communities (κατὰ θιάσους συνοικεῖν), and these are open to those likeminded visitors who come from the outside. And so for all there is a single treasury and a common distribution of funds (δαπάναι [κοιναὶ]). Their clothes are provided communally as is their food in common meals (συσσίτια).[22]

This second text comes from the end of a long passage in which Philo describes the virtues found among the Essenes. Philo opens this description with the assertion that these virtues are the "myriad" proofs of the Essene's love of God.[23] Indeed, Philo reduces the ethos of the community to their adoption of three basic principles: love of God, love of virtue, love of humankind.[24] For Philo, the last virtue, φιλανθρώπον, is perhaps the Essene's greatest. At the climax of his list, Philo links φιλανθρώπον with the virtue of κοινωνία and writes of the Essene's "love of humankind through a sense of humility, equality, and a fellowship (κοινωνία) which goes beyond any expression."[25] Note that Philo uses the term κοινωνία to represent a common ideal characteristic of *general* community, a principle and spirit of coopera-

---

20. Philo, *Prob.* 84, 91; Josephus, *J.W.* 2.122-23 have, of course, been central to these discussions as they are to ours. The connection between יחד and *koinon* was emphasized by Dombrowski, "היחד," 293-307.

21. Καταφρονηταὶ δὲ πλούτου, καὶ θαυμάσιον αὐτοῖς τὸ κοινωνικόν, οὐδὲ ἔστιν εὑρεῖν κτήσει τινὰ παρ' αὐτοῖς ὑπερέχοντα (Josephus, *B.J.* 2.122).

22. Πρῶτον μὲν τοίνυν οὐδενὸς οἰκία τίς ἐστιν ἰδία, ἣν οὐχὶ πάντων εἶναι κοινὴν συμβέβηκε· πρὸς γὰρ τῷ κατὰ θιάσους συνοικεῖν ἀναπέπταται καὶ τοῖς ἑτέρωθεν ἀφικνουμένοις τῶν ὁμοζήλων. εἶτ' ἐστὶ ταμεῖον ἐν πάντων καὶ δαπάναι κοιναί, καὶ κοιναὶ μὲν ἐσθῆτες, κοιναὶ δὲ τροφαὶ συσσίτια πεποιημένων (Philo, *Prob* 85-86). Cf. also the parallel material in Josephus, *J.W.* 2.124-27.

23. Τοῦ μὲν οὖν φιλοθέου δείγματα παρέχονται μυρία (Philo, *Prob.* 84).

24. ὅροις καὶ κανόσι τριττοῖς χρώμενοί τῷ τε φιλοθέῳ καὶ φιλαρέτῳ καὶ φιλανθρώπῳ (Philo, *Prob.* 83-84).

25. Τοῦ δὲ φιλανθρώπου εὔνοιαν, ἰσότητα, τὴν παντὸς λόγου κρείττονα κοινωνίαν (Philo, *Prob.* 84).

tion and unity which may to some degree be necessary for any kind of group identity.[26]

While Philo's use of κοινωνία does not appear to be related to a concrete description of the institutional structure of community, it is evident that it does denote a guiding principle of institutional formation. This is evident in Philo's praise that no other group translates its philosophy of κοινωνία so completely into its life style of living in community (ὁμοδίαιτος), sharing living quarters (ὁμωρόφιος), and sharing meals (ὁμοτράπεζος). Philo's use of these terms, all nouns prefixed with ὁμο-, certainly makes clear that the communal organization values its unity and egalitarianism — and this certainly resonates with the notion of (ה)יחד. Yet it must be said again that this terminology refers to the "spirit" of the Community and not to its concert, institutional structure.

Indeed it is interesting that when Philo *does* refer to the Essene "communities" as such in this passage, he uses the term θίασος. Philo also reports that these communities maintain "synagogues"[27] to which they go to gather on the Sabbath.[28] These are technical, institutional terms, but they are "nonsectarian" in nature — that is, they reflect a type of terminology not confined to the Essenes and their institutions, but applicable also to other Jewish or Greco-Roman institutions. θίασος, as is well known, is a common term often used in the Greco-Roman world to refer to a religious association — among those, Bacchic/Dionysian cult-associations.[29]

In a particularly suggestive monograph, Moshe Weinfeld has discussed in detail a number of comparisons between a wide range of religious and voluntary associations from the Roman and Hellenistic period and the penal code found primarily in 1QS but also to a certain extent in the *Damascus Document*. For his comparative purposes, Weinfeld draws upon a wide array of material, including papyri from the Ptolemaic period, rabbinic literature, and epigraphic materials. One inscription in particular is of considerable interest

26. Cf. κοινωνία in Acts 2:42; 1 Cor 10:16; etc. While in Rabbinic texts Greek words appear frequently as "Lehnwörter," this is not the case in any Qumran text.

27. See C. Claussen, *Versammlung, Gemeinde, Synagoge: Das hellenistisch-jüdische Umfeld der frühchristlichen Gemeinden* (SUNT 27; Göttingen: Vandenhoeck & Ruprecht, 2002), 60, 120 and nn. 55, 144, 179.

28. εἰς ἱεροὺς ἀφικνούμενοι τόπους, οἳ καλοῦνται συναγωγαί (Philo, *Prob.* 81).

29. See M. P. Nilsson, *The Dionysiac Mysteries of the Hellenistic and Roman Age* (Lund: Gleerup, 1957); but note P. McGinty, *Interpretation and Dionysos: Method in the Study of a God* (Religion and Reason 16; New York: Mouton, 1978), esp. 104-40; and R. L. Wilken, *The Christians as the Romans Saw Them* (New Haven: Yale University Press, 1984), 41-47. See further Albert Henrichs, "Changing Dionysiac Identities," in *Jewish and Christian Self-Definition* (ed. E. P. Sanders et al.; 3 vols.; Philadelphia: Fortress, 1980-1983), 3:137-60, 213-36.

and is treated at length. This is a very well preserved and rather lengthy Greek inscription dating from 178 CE relating to a Dionysian association that had existed for some time in Athens. This inscription, which Weinfeld calls "The Statutes of the Iobacchi," is a transcription of the minutes of an important meeting of the association.[30]

The group was undergoing a change of priestly leadership, and this occasion was used to confirm the rules governing the association — a confirmation that was recorded in stone, listing the renewed statutes governing the association. Hence we have a perfect opportunity to compare this Roman religious association's regulatory and organizational structure with that of Qumran. That such a comparison might be fruitful is indicated by the very opening of the inscription where the statutes for the Dionysic society are renewed:

> Nicomachus, nominated by Herodes as vice-priest, read aloud the statutes drawn up by the ex-priests . . . and after the priest and the archbacchus and the patron had expressed their approval there were shouts of "These are what we always observe," "Hurrah for the Priest!," "Revive the statutes: you ought to," "Long life to the Bacchic Society, and good order!"[31]

This does, in a way, remind one of the opening of 1QS and the covenant renewal ceremony, which is described at length there (1QS 1.18–2.22). This is especially the case in the affirmations made by the Community and presumably new initiates:

> When they cross over into the covenant the priests and the Levites shall praise the God of salvation and all his true works, and all those who cross over into the covenant shall say after them: "Amen, Amen!" (1QS 1.18-20)

Clearly the ceremony involved in the covenant renewal is more involved than that in the Bacchic renewal of its statutes, involving admissions of guilt, and priestly blessings and curses, but the basic *form* of the procedure is basically the same. A priestly authority reads or proclaims the basic principles and the conditions of the association, and those who are to be bound by them show their agreement by communal acclaim.

---

30. The text used here is *IG* no. 1368. The translation quoted in this essay is from Weinfeld, *The Organizational Pattern*, 51-54; another may be found in M. N. Tod, *Sidelights on Greek History* (Blackwell: Oxford, 1932), 86-91.

31. *IG* no. 1368 lines 5-16; Weinfeld, *The Organizational Pattern*, 51.

Weinfeld is able to point to parallels that are far more striking than the loose analogy above and that involve initiation into a sect and the maintenance of order during meetings and communal banquets. To take but one example, we find in regard to initiation into the association:

> No one may be a Iobacchus [a member of the association] unless he is first registered in the usual manner with the priest and is approved by the vote of the Iobacchi as being clearly worthy and fit to be a member of the Bacchic society.[32]

Weinfeld compares this with 1QS 6.13-16:

> And (regarding) each one who freely offers himself from Israel to join the Counsel of the Community, the overseer at the head of the Many shall examine him with respect to his insight and his works. If he is suited to the discipline he shall be permitted to enter into the covenant and turn to the truth and depart from all deceit; he shall instruct him in all the precepts of the Community. And later, when he enters to stand before the Many; then they shall be asked concerning his affairs, and as the lot comes out according to the counsel of the Many, he shall approach or withdraw.

Therefore, there were broad structural markers that would have led an ancient observer from outside the Community to associate the Qumranites with other religious associations of the day. These "markers" would have included the following: (1) initiation procedures,[33] (2) the maintenance of a common treasury,[34] (3) concern for at least some aspects of the material welfare of the members of the group,[35] (4) the central role of a banquet or common meal in the life of the Community,[36] (5) the establishment of bylaws governing the initiation and defining the responsibilities of the members of the group,[37] (6) the definition of penalties for violating the bylaws of the group,[38] and (7) a strong religious affiliation and identity.

It is apparent, then, that while the Qumran Community differed greatly in its purpose, ideology, details of organization, and exclusivity from Greco-Roman societies and associations of the time, *outsiders* would probably nev-

---

32. *IG* no. 1368 lines 32-36.
33. 1QS 6.13-20.
34. 1QS 1.11-13; 6.19; cf. Josephus, *Ant.* 18.20, 22; *J.W.* 2.122.
35. CD MS A 14.12-17.
36. 1QS 6.4-5; cf. Josephus, *J.W.* 2.129-131.
37. 1QS 5.8-10; 9.10.
38. 1QS 6.24-27.

ertheless have noted a sufficient number of similarities so as to use terminology in describing the Community that applied to contemporary societies and associations in general.

The terminology used by Philo and Josephus to describe the Qumran Community, therefore, marks out only what it had *in common* with other voluntary or religious associations found in the Greco-Roman world, and can contribute little to the understanding of the Community's self designation as היחד — especially since this is clearly an *insider* designation. Consequently, we turn now to an examination of just how the term appears and is used within the Qumran literature itself.

3. The Term יחד in Qumran

Probably the earliest instance in which we find יחד in the sense of a call to form a community is in the apocryphal Psalm 154 (11Q5 18.1-3):[39]

> Your souls with the good ones and with the perfect ones to glorify the Most High. Form a community (החבירו יחד) to make known his salvation, and be not lax in making his might and his glorious-beauty to all the simple ones.

This early text, which may date from the third or second century BCE, clearly outlines a mission that would resonate with the ideology of the Qumran Community (cf., e.g., 1QS 1.1-17).

How central the term יחד is for the self-understanding of the Qumran Community can be easily seen by the wide variety of constructions where it serves as *nomen rectum*:[40]

> אנשי היחד — "the men of the *yaḥad*": CD MS B 20.32; 1QS 5.1, 3, 16; 6.21; 7.20, 24; 8.16; 9.6, 7, 8, 10, 19; 1Q31 1.1; 4Q165 (= 4QpIsaᵉ) frg. 9 line 3; 4Q174 frgs. 1-2 1.17; 4Q177 frgs. 5-6 line 1; 4Q252 5.5; 4Q254 frg. 4 line 4; 4Q256 9.8; 4Q258 1.7, 8; 6.5; 8.3; 4Q259 2.7; 4Q284a frg. 2 line 4; 4Q286 frg. 20 line 4
>
> סרך היחד — "the rule of the *yaḥad*": 1QS 1.1, 16; 4Q255 frg. 1 line 1; 4Q256 2.1

---

39. Hengel, "Qumran und der Hellenismus," 348, believes this psalm is from a pre-Qumranic milieu.

40. See further Fabry, "יַחַד," 40-48. Some of the instances in the following list are partly reconstructed.

עצת היחד — "the council of the *yaḥad*": 1QS 3.2, 6; 5.7; 6.3, 10, 12-13, 14, 16; 7.2, 22, 24; 8.1, 5, 22; 11.8; 1Q14 frgs. 8-10 line 8; 1QSa 1.26, 27; 2.2, 11; 1QSb 4.26; 1QpHab 12.4; 1Q14 (1QpMic) frgs. 8-10 line 8; 4Q164 (= 4QpIsa^d) frg. 1 line 2; 4Q171 frgs. 1-2 2.14; 4Q174 frgs. 1-2 1.17; 4Q177 frg. 14 line 5; 4Q256 9.6; 4Q257 3.3; 4Q258 1.6; 4Q259 2.5, 13; 4Q265 frg. 4 2.3; frg. 7 lines 7-8; 4Q286 frg. 7 2.1; 4Q288 frg. 1 line 1

סוד היחד — "the assembly of the *yaḥad*": 1QS 6.19; 8.10; 4Q259 3.17-18

משפטי היחד — "the laws of the *yaḥad*": 1QS 6.15; 4Q270 frg. 3 3.19

ברית היחד — "the covenant of the *yaḥad*": 1QS 3.12; 8.16-17; 1QSb 5.21; 4Q255 2.9

הון היחד — "the property of the *yaḥad*": 1QS 7.6

יסוד היחד — "the authority/foundation of the *yaḥad*": 1QS 7.17, 18; 8.10; 4Q261 frgs. 6a-e line 4; 4Q258 6.4

עצת אנשי היחד — "the council of the men of the *yaḥad*": 1QS 8.11

שולחן היחד — "the table of the *yaḥad*": 1QSa 2.17-18

עדת היחד — "the congregation of the *yaḥad*": 1QSa 2.21; 4Q171 frgs. 3-10 4.19; 4Q427 frg. 7 2.9

מדרש יחד — "the examination/inquiry of the *yaḥad*": 1QS 6.24

ממשלת יחד — "the dominion of the *yaḥad*": 4Q511 frg. 2 1.9

The broad use of the term יחד, as indicated by the evidence above, makes it clear that when the Community deals with issues of membership, governance, "legal" or disciplinary matters, communal meals and table etiquette, as well as institutional or organizational structures, it expresses itself in terms of the Qumranites' deeply rooted understanding of their unity. Yet, it is quite striking that when one examines the terminology above, one finds that יחד seems to be largely devoid of obvious "theological" content and seems to refer most frequently to elements of the Community's social and organizational structure.

Also important for the self-understanding of the group are a number of additional phrases where יחד serves as the *nomen regens* associated with vocabulary that does manifest obvious religious significance:

יחד אל — "the *yaḥad* of God": 1QS 1.12; 2.22

יחד עצתו — "the *yaḥad* of his (God's) counsel/council": 1QS 3.6

יחד כול אנשי סודי — "the *yaḥad* of all the men of my (God's?) council": 1QH^a 6.18

רוח יחד — "the spirit of the *yaḥad*": 4Q477 frg. 2 2.6

יחד ברית עולם — "the *yaḥad* of the eternal covenant": 1QS 5.5-6

יחד אמת — "the *yaḥad* of truth": 1QS 2.24, 26; 4Q257 3.1

יחד קודש — "the *yaḥad* of holiness": 1QS 9.2; 4Q258 7.3

יחד בתורה ובהון — "(the) *yaḥad* in/with Torah and property": 1QS 5.2;
4Q258 1.2

Several observations should be made concerning the use of the word
יחד in these passages: First, it is interesting to note that, compared with the
first group of citations, instances of יחד used in phrases employing moral/re-
ligious terminology are relatively few. That is, יחד is most often used to refer
to the Qumran Community in its "horizontal" or "human" dimension, not its
"vertical" or "theological" dimension. And yet, the terminology belonging to
the second type does provide evidence for the latter dimension in Qumran's
self-definition — which is to say the Community's relation to God and God's
eternal covenant with them.

Particularly significant in this respect is the mention of the יחד אל in
1QS 1.12 and 2.22. In 1QS 1.11-12 we read of "all those devoting themselves to
his truth bringing all their knowledge and their strength and their property
into the Community of God" (הנדבים לאמתו יביאו כול דעתם וכוחם והונם
ביחד אל). Likewise, in 2.22 we find, "so that every single Israelite may know
his standing place in the Community of God" (לדעת כול איש ישראל איש
בית מעמדו ביחד אל). Here the Qumran Community is seen not only in its
human dimension as an institution whose members "held all things in common and were devoted in oneness to all responsibilities."[41] Rather, the Community seems to be identified with the *divine* יחד, the *heavenly* community
with which the earthly יחד identified. This is most evident, as we shall see, in
the Community's liturgical life.

In the next two sections we will examine in detail both of these dimensions — the "horizontal," human dimension of communal cohesiveness and
institutional structure as well as the "vertical" dimension as it pertains to the
Community's religious and moral self-definition.

4. The Social and Organizational Significance of יחד

Many characteristics of יחד come to life when one looks at the organizational
pattern of the Community. The priests occupy the highest ranks within the
Community.[42] They have priority in all organizational matters such as taking
up the first seats in the "session of the Many" (1QS 6.8), or offering the first

41. Charlesworth, "Community Organization," 133.
42. See 1QS 1.18-19; 2.19-20; 6.8.

blessings over bread and wine (1QS 6.4-5) at communal meals. These "sons of Aaron" rule over questions of judgment and of property affecting the Community as a whole (1QS 9.7). Wherever a group of ten people comes together a priest shall be its leader (1QS 6.3-4; CD 13.2).

At the annual covenant ceremony the priests are at the head of the ceremonial procession (1QS 2.19-20). In connection with this, and just after the new members have "cross(ed) over into the covenant" (1QS 1.18), it is the priests' task to "report the righteousness of God along with its wondrous works and recount all (his) merciful acts of love towards Israel" (1QS 1.21-22). Second-rank in the hierarchy are the Levites. At the covenant ceremony it is the Levites' task "to praise the God of salvation and all his true works" (1QS 1.19). Later, they "enumerate the inequities of the sons of Israel and all their guilty transgressions and their sins during the dominion of Belial" (1QS 1.22-24).

This ceremony is very much reminiscent of Israel's "crossing over" the Jordan,[43] followed by Moses' and the Levites' proclamation: "This very day you have become the people of the LORD our God. Therefore obey the LORD your God, observing his commandments and his statutes that I am commanding you today" (Deut 27:9b-10; NRSV). This ceremony, as described in Deuteronomy, is followed by curses delivered by the Levites (27:14-26) and blessings (28:1-14) and more curses (28:15-46) pronounced by Moses. But even more important for the Qumran covenantal ceremony is the convocation of Israel in Exodus 19. Otto Betz has argued for a significant connection between the Israelites at Mount Sinai and the Qumranites. He writes:

> The "standing of Israel" in Exodus 19 served as a kind of model for the life of the Qumran community and justified their attempt to apply the rules of priestly purity to the lay members as well. Everyone had to be as holy as the priests serving before God. The organization of Israel at Mount Sinai — the division of elders (Ex 19:7; cf. 1QS 6.8), priests, and laymen (Ex 19:21-22) in groups of ten, fifty, and one hundred (Ex 18:21); living in camps (Ex 19:2); and the necessary ritual purity and abstinence from sexual intercourse (Ex 19:14-15) — was followed at Qumran and instituted as a permanent order of the life of the community in expectation of the second coming of God. Hence, the ideal of becoming a kingdom of priests and a holy people (Ex 19:6) was pursued at Qumran.[44]

---

43. Cf. Deut 27:2-4, 12 with 1QS 1.18. Cf. also 1QH[a] 6.19-33, which may have been used at the Qumran ceremony. See H. Ringgren, *The Faith of Qumran: Theology of the Dead Sea Scrolls* (ed. J. H. Charlesworth; rev. ed.; New York: Crossroad, 1995), 211.

44. O. Betz, "Jesus and the Temple Scroll," in *Jesus and the Dead Sea Scrolls* (ed. J. H.

The data presented above underscores yet again what has long been known: the Qumranites were organized in terms of a strictly hierarchical pattern. This provided every member with a very clear idea of his standing inside the Community: "the lesser one shall obey the greater with respect to work and money" (1QS 6.2). And yet, despite the hierarchy, daily life in the יחד provided the members with concrete experiences of unity: "And they shall eat (in) unity (ויחד), say benedictions (in) unity (ויחד), and give counsel (in) unity (ויחד)" (1QS 6.2-3). In fact, a clearly defined hierarchy with well-defined roles and positions for both groups and individuals could actually *increase* the sense of belonging to a tightly knit, relationally coherent social whole.

The high degree of integration of the members into the Community, regardless of the hierarchy, seems to have taken shape especially in the common possession of goods (1QS 6.19). Upon entry into the Community, the new member not only transferred his belongings to the group (1QS 6.22), he also gained a share in the property of the יחד (cf. 1QS 6.17). The importance of these shared belongings can be seen in the naming of the Community as "the *yaḥad* with Torah and property" (יחד בתורה ובהון; 1QS 5.2).

The unity of the יחד was also, and perhaps ultimately, stressed through the hate and the reproach offered to those outside the Community (see 1QS 5.1, 10; 8.13; 9.9, 20). Consequently, the men of the יחד needed to separate themselves from those who are called "the congregation of deceit" (1QS 5.1-2). This rigorous separation from all those who do not belong to the Community is crucial for the establishment of the יחד (1QS 5.2). The application of "t[ru]th, humility, and merciful love to another" (1QS 5.25) applies *only to fellow members* of the Community. The guidelines are set out clearly in the *Rule of the Community*: "For they shall all be in the Community of truth (יחד אמת), of virtuous humility, of merciful love, and of righteous intention [towa]rds one another, in a holy council, and members of an eternal assembly" (1QS 2.24-25; cf. 1.9-10).

The social and organizational features of the יחד are thus obvious. But further questions must be asked. In particular, what values and beliefs can be identified as the backbone of these specific features of the יחד? It is to this question that we now turn.

Charlesworth; ABRL; New York: Doubleday, 1992), 94. Already in 1855, A. Ritschl believed that the Essenes were trying to fulfill Exod 19:6 ("Über die Essener," *Theologische Jahrbücher* 14 [1855]: 315-56, esp. 348; cf. J. VanderKam and P. Flint, *The Meaning of the Dead Sea Scrolls: Their Significance for Understanding the Bible, Judaism, Jesus, and Christianity* [New York: HarperSanFrancisco, 2002], 263).

5. The Moral and Religious Significance of the יחד

As striking as the unity of the Qumranites and their strict separation from the world may be *prima facie,* it is actually firmly rooted in their understanding of God's own action. God is portrayed in the *Rule of the Community* as the creator of both the spirits of light and of darkness (1QS 3.25). As for the former, God takes "pleasure in all its doings forever," but God "hates forever . . . the other" (1QS 4.1).

This dualism is also reflected in the strict distinction between the "Sons of Light" and "Sons of Darkness" (see above). All those outside the Community were subject to God's wrath and curse (1QS 2.17; 5.12). They were under the rule of the Angel of Darkness (1QS 3.20). The antithesis between the יחד and the world could thus hardly have been any stronger. Without going into further detail of what has rightly been called a "complex pattern of dualism,"[45] it must be observed that this is certainly what lies behind the Qumranites' rigorous application of the categories of love and hate (1QS 1.9-10).

What defines Qumran's ethical system on the inside? At the center of the matter lies the Qumranites' self-understanding and their belief that God had made a new covenant with them.[46] As already noted, they called themselves "the יחד of the eternal covenant" (1QS 5.6). While Israel's sin had made the earlier covenant invalid (CD MS A 6.19; MS B 20.12), the יחד became virtually synonymous with God's covenant: Thus volunteers (see הנדבים in 1QS 1.7, 11; 5.21, 22) who wanted to enter the יחד were, after a three-year period of testing, invited to "cross over *into the covenant* before God by the Rule of the Community, in order to act according to everything which he has commanded" (1QS 1.16; emphasis added).

The invocation of covenant terminology raises the issue of Torah. It cannot be overstressed that Torah is the integrating center of the יחד (1QS 5.2).[47] Unity was therefore achieved through the integration of every member into the Community with its hierarchical order and through the orientation of each member towards the Torah. Whoever failed to comply with the group's regulations (read: Torah) would be expelled:

45. Jörg Frey, "Different Patterns of Dualistic Thought in the Qumran Library: Reflections on Their Background and History," in *Legal Texts and Legal Issues: Proceedings of the Second Meeting of the International Organization for Qumran Studies, Cambridge, 1995 Published in Honour of Joseph M. Baumgarten* (ed. Moshe J. Bernstein, Florentino García Martínez, and John Kampen; STDJ 23; Leiden: Brill, 1997), 289.

46. CD MS A 6.19; 8.21; 20.12; 1QpHab 2.3-4.

47. So M. Appold, *The Oneness Motif in the Fourth Gospel: Motif Analysis and Exegetical Probe into the Theology of John* (WUNT 2/1; Tübingen: J. C. B. Mohr [Paul Siebeck], 1976), 184.

> The Levites and those who live in the camps shall convene on the third month and curse those who stray from the Law to the right [or to the left].[48]

This being the case, it is nevertheless important to point out that the Qumranites, precisely because of their self-understanding as the יחד, were not concerned only with unity among themselves as those living on earth in the end time. They also believed that their priestly courses and their calendar were in tune with *heaven,* with the way the angels were worshiping God in heaven. This can be seen clearly in the *Songs of the Sabbath Sacrifice,* which demonstrate that the Qumran Community had a highly developed understanding of heavenly worship that is depicted in glorious detail.[49] Other texts, too, indicate that the members of the Community thought themselves to be united with the angels in their worship:

> The perverse spirit You have cleansed from great transgression, that he might take his stand with the host of the holy ones, and enter together (or in the *yahad*) with the congregation of the sons of heaven. And for man, You have allotted an eternal destiny with the spirits of knowledge, to praise Your name together.[50]

Unity with the angels in worship is the clearest and most developed notion of heavenly unity that is found in the Qumran literature. It should be noted that this language of oneness is limited almost entirely to the description of the Community centered on Torah and organized in strict, hierarchical fashion. The expressions of oneness are not used therefore to describe any relationship of the Community to messianic figures or even to the Teacher of Righteousness. There is also not the slightest mention of any concept of immanence or oneness between the יחד and God. Thus, the Qumranite belief in unity with the "divine" יחד nowhere exceeds or cancels their mundane existence — the Community is definitely "in the world." The only exception to

---

48. 4Q266 frg. 11 lines 16-18.

49. See, e.g., Carol A. Newsom, "Angelic Liturgy: Songs of the Sabbath Sacrifice (4Q400-4Q407, 11Q17, Masık)," in *The Dead Sea Scrolls: Hebrew, Aramaic, and Greek Texts with English Translations,* Vol. 4B: *Angelic Liturgy: Songs of the Sabbath Sacrifice* (ed. J. H. Charlesworth, C. A. Newsom, et al.; PTSDSSP 4B; Tübingen: Mohr Siebeck and Louisville: Westminster John Knox, 1999), esp. 6-12. Cf. also 1QSb 3.25-26; 4.24-26; 1QH[a] 3.21-22; 11.7-13.

50. 1QH[a] 11.22-24; the translation follows M. O. Wise, M. G. Abegg, and E. M. Cook, *The Dead Sea Scrolls: A New English Translation* (New York: HarperCollins Publishers, 1996). Cf. also 1QH[a] 14.15-16; 19.16-17.

this is the Community's participation in the liturgical celebrations in the heavenly temple with the angelic hosts.

A search for the reasons that lay behind these beliefs leads one to investigate the history of the Qumran Community and how that history may have influenced the Qumranites' longing for unity.

6. The Search for Communal Origins

One cannot understand the Qumranic emphasis on and appreciation of being יחד(ה) without going back to the very origins of the movement. From the very beginning of research on the Scrolls the identification of the Qumranites as a part of the larger Essene movement has received the lion's share of support. Eleazar Sukenik was the first to publish this hypothesis, and many have followed in his footsteps.[51] The *Rule of the Community* (1QS), which provides the most significant evidence regarding the usage of the term יחד(ה), has long played a central role in the Essene identification. Although Josephus provides us with a description of the Essenes,[52] he offers us almost no information regarding their origins or their historical development. In the absence of extensive, external confirming evidence, scholars have been forced to base their historical reconstructions of the Essene movement on the Qumran writings themselves. The archaeology of Qumran indicates that the origins of the group that lived there lie in the earlier decades of the second century BCE. Their earliest roots probably go back to the Hellenistic crisis that led to the persecution launched by Antiochus IV Epiphanes (175-164 BCE).[53] The Teacher of Righteousness appeared about twenty years later.[54] He was a priest of high Zadokite lineage[55] and must be seen as the founder and early organizer of the Community at Qumran.

Why did the Righteous Teacher and his followers withdraw to the desert? The most plausible reconstruction rests on the identification of the founder's main enemy: the Wicked Priest. 1QpHab 8.8-13 portrays him as follows:

---

51. See VanderKam and Flint, *The Meaning of the Dead Sea Scrolls*, 239-50, for a recent summary of the evidence. See also E. Schürer, *The History of the Jewish People in the Age of Jesus Christ (175 B.C.-A.D. 135)* (ed. G. Vermes, F. Millar, M. Black, and M. Goodman; 3 vols.; rev. ed.; Edinburgh: T&T Clark, 1979-1987), 2:555-90.

52. Josephus, *J.W.* 2.119-161; *Ant.* 18.11, 18-22.

53. Cf. CD 1.5.

54. CD 1.10-11.

55. 4Q171 (4QpPs 37) 2.19; 3.15.

the Wicked Priest, who was called by the true name at the beginning of his standing, but when he ruled in Israel, his heart became large, and he abandoned God, and betrayed the statutes for the sake of wealth. And he stole and amassed the wealth of the men of violence who had rebelled against God, and he took the wealth of peoples to add to himself guilty iniquity. And the abominable ways he pursued with every sort of unclean impurity.

The most likely figure behind this description seems to be Jonathan Maccabeus.[56] He had been the leader of the Jewish people beginning in 160 BCE. In 152 BCE, he took upon himself the high priesthood. When Josephus retells this story, known from 1 Maccabees, he adds some interesting information:

> Now at this time there were three schools of thought among the Jews, which held different opinions concerning human affairs; the first being that of the Pharisees, the second that of the Sadducees, and the third that of the Essenes.[57]

Although he does not give us any further details about their origins it is certainly noteworthy that he places them in this period of Jewish history, that is, during Jonathan's rule. The Teacher of Righteousness and his adherents may well have fled from Jerusalem when Jonathan became high priest. It is obvious from the Scrolls that they strongly detested the Wicked Priest's priesthood. However, the hostility was mutual: Once, on the day when the Qumran Community celebrated their Day of Atonement, the Wicked Priest visited the Community in order to "swallow up" the Teacher of Righteousness and his followers.[58]

For the present discussion of the meaning and significance of (ה)יחד as Qumran's self-designation, it is crucial to notice that the Community was very likely forced out of — expelled from — their original location within that branch of Judaism represented by the Jerusalem Temple and its priesthood. Although we can only partially reconstruct the circumstances and the Qumranites' interpretation thereof, the Scrolls provide ample evidence that they strongly disagreed with the priestly authorities in charge. They therefore had no other choice than to leave their surroundings and, in their perspective,

56. Another less likely identification would be Simon, who became high priest when his brother Jonathan died in 142 BCE, or even a series of Maccabean and Hasmonean rulers. See VanderKam and Flint, *The Meaning of the Dead Sea Scrolls*, 290-91, for a discussion.

57. Josephus, *Ant.* 13.171. Cf. *Ant.* 18.11. The translation follows R. Marcus in LCL.

58. See 1QpHab 11.4-8.

replace an institution and way that had become obsolete. So it was that their יחד became the "new covenant."[59]

7. Conclusion

To sum up, the present study has described the significance of the Qumran-ites' concept of (ה)יחד and its relationship to their self-understanding. It must be recognized that the term has a "bipolar" nature, which can be traced back to the semantics of its basic root sense. While, on the one hand, a con-cept of togetherness is stressed by יחד, it also implies, on the other hand, be-ing set apart and being alone. Accordingly, the essential character of the Qumran Community can be seen in their tight fellowship as well as in their separation from the rest of Judaism — not to mention the rest of the world. Thus, in whichever of these two directions one looks, renderings of the word יחד may include not only "Comm*unity*" (cf. *Gemein*schaft) but also "sect" (cf. *Abspalt*ung).

Another important conclusion of this study is that the use of the term (ה)יחד is unique to the Community's literature and has not been simply (or simplistically) derived from parallels or analogies in the Semitic or Greco-Roman worlds. Equally unique is the concept of their identity as marked by love among themselves and hatred toward outsiders. On one side, the יחד forms a Community in unity with the angels and the Torah. Thus they pre-pare the way for God's final judgment and for the coming of the two Messiahs of Aaron and Israel. But, on the other side, and in this very process, they strictly separate themselves from all people outside their Community includ-ing the other branches of contemporary Judaism. The Qumran literature gives the impression that the Qumranites did not want any contact with the outside world. The reason for this strict separation may in part be a reaction to the expulsion of the founders of the Community at the time of its origins. Thus they form a very different type of "society of contrast" *(Kontrast-gesellschaft)*[60] and do not see themselves as being sent to love their neighbors *and* their enemies as well.

---

59. הברית החדשה in CD MS A 6.19; 8.21; CD MS B 19.33; 20.12.
60. Gerhard Lohfink, *Wie hat Jesus Gemeinde gewollt?* (Freiburg: Herder, 1982), 188 and *passim.*

Identity and Resistance:
The Varieties of Competing Models
in Early Judaism

LOREN L. JOHNS

Much of the literature of Second Temple Judaism depicts violent conflict — conflict in the form of contemporary, historical battles against ruling imperial powers *and* in the form of the final eschatological battle that will bring to an end the present evil era and inaugurate the unending reign of God. Both involve varying conceptions of human and divine violence. In this essay, I intend to focus on what one can learn from this literature about the ethical propriety of *human* violence in these conflicts and to reconsider the main categories used by contemporary scholars in characterizing the various models present in this literature.[1]

One cannot assume any linear or monolithic development in the ethical theology of Early Judaism from the Maccabean Revolt to the First Jewish Re-

---

1. I am not attempting to compare "Jewish" literature with "Christian" literature in this essay. The categories themselves are problematic and anachronistic with regard to Second Temple Judaism. Rather, I am comparing various writings that grew out of the period and heritage of Second Temple Judaism, including the Apocalypse of John, which likely was written after the destruction of Jerusalem by the Romans in 70 CE.

I write this essay conscious of the fact that *essay* derives from a Middle French word meaning "initial tentative effort." I dedicate the present "effort" to Dr. James H. Charlesworth, who encouraged me to take Early Judaism seriously — not only as a resource for understanding early Christianity, but also for its own sake. Charlesworth's own work on the redefinitions of power at work in the Apocalypse of John lies behind my interest in this essay on the intersection of identity and models of resistance in Early Judaism. See his, "The Apocalypse of John: Its Theology and Impact on Subsequent Apocalypses," in James H. Charlesworth, *The New Testament Apocrypha and Pseudepigrapha: A Guide to Publications, with Excursuses on Apocalypses* (Metuchen: The American Theological Library Association and London: Scarecrow, 1987), 19-51.

volt. Various conceptions or models of resistance emerged in response to the Hellenizing efforts of Antiochus IV Epiphanes in Judea — conceptions and models that continued to develop through the Roman period down to the First Jewish Revolt. How did these conceptions or models of resistance reflect differing opinions concerning the efficacy and ethical propriety of human violence in resisting Greco-Roman cultural, political, and military power and influence? The primary texts I will examine in response to this question are 1, 2, and 4 Maccabees, Daniel, the *Assumption of Moses,* the Apocalypse of John, and the *War Scroll* (1QM) from Qumran.

Humanity's capacity to derive biblical precedent for the legitimation of violence has been adequately demonstrated over centuries by all adherents of three of the Abrahamic monotheistic religions. At the same time, both the Bible itself and subsequent history have born witness to ways in which the biblical witness has served to delegitimate human violence.[2] As I have noted elsewhere, religion is dangerous business.[3] Arguably, more people have been murdered in the name of religion than for any other reason in the history of humanity. Religion has inspired humanity's most profound acts of benevolence *and* its most horrifying acts of violence. One particular issue in the second century BCE proved particularly significant in this debate and spurred theological reflection on the subject of human participation in violent conflict. That issue was the intensified Hellenization that took place under Antiochus IV Ephiphanes.[4] It is here, therefore, that our investigation begins.

2. Among the many articles and books that could be cited as evidence, see, e.g., the essay by John J. Collins, "The Zeal of Phinehas: The Bible and the Legitimation of Violence," *JBL* 122 (2003): 3-21. With regard specifically to those Dead Sea Scrolls that bear witness to the Qumran Community, see Raija Sollamo, "War and Violence in the Ideology of the Qumran Community," in *Verbum et Calamus: Semitic and Related Studies in Honour of the Sixtieth Birthday of Professor Tapani Harviainen* (ed. Hannu Juusola et al.; Studia Orientalia 99; Helsinki: Finnish Oriental Society, 2004), 341-52. At the broader level, see Wes Avram, *Anxious About Empire: Theological Essays on the New Global Realities* (Grand Rapids: Brazos, 2004); and Jack Nelson-Pallmeyer, *Saving Christianity from Empire* (New York: Continuum, 2005). It is worth noting that President George W. Bush exegeted the Fourth Gospel in legitimating America's military responses. On the anniversary of the September 11 attacks, he addressed U.S. citizens in front of the Statue of Liberty with these words: "Ours is the cause of human dignity: freedom guided by conscience and guarded by peace. This ideal of America is the hope of all mankind. That hope drew millions to this harbor. That hope still lights our way. And the light shines in the darkness. And the darkness will not overcome it. May God bless America" (quotation from Avram, *Anxious About Empire,* 91).

3. Loren L. Johns, *The Lamb Christology of the Apocalypse of John: An Investigation Into Its Origins and Rhetorical Force* (WUNT 2/167; Tübingen: Mohr Siebeck, 2003), 1.

4. The Hellenizing program of Antiochus IV Epiphanes was not simply a new crisis within Early Judaism imposed from without. Although I speak of this "program" in the singu-

1. Antiochus IV Epiphanes and the Books of the Maccabees

The Hellenizing program of Antiochus IV led to a watershed in the history of Early Judaism. The effects of internal debates in response to that program were far-reaching and did much to define the character of Early Judaism for the next 250 years. The origins of the Qumran Community — and indeed, the relation of the Qumran Community to the broader Essene community — remain a matter of debate. Be that as it may, the majority of historical reconstructions of those origins see the Hellenizing program of Antiochus IV and the Maccabean Revolt as significant for the formation of the Essenes or of the Qumran Community, or both.[5]

---

lar, I use the term loosely and broadly to refer to a complex of conversations and actions that included various mutually exclusive theological and ethical responses, the variety of which elicited secondary responses in the history and theology of Early Judaism, one of which was likely the formation of the Essene movement.

There are clearly significant methodological and historiographical questions here, including whether the mid-century Hellenizing program of Antiochus IV Epiphanes can properly be seen as precipitating a "crisis" within Early Judaism. My description of the aggressive actions of Antiochus IV derives largely from 1 Maccabees. However, such aggressive tactics were otherwise unknown among the successors of Alexander the Great. See Uriel Rappaport, "Maccabean Revolt," in *ABD* 4:433-39, for a discussion of the historical questions surrounding the characterization of the Hellenizing threat by the author of 1 Maccabees. Elias Joseph Bickerman and Avigdor Tcherikover have variously argued that the primary threat represented by the Hellenizing project came more from within Judaism than from an external source like Antiochus IV Epiphanes. Certainly this theory fits with some of the harsh intra-Jewish invective known from the literature at the time, including the Dead Sea Scrolls. See Elias Joseph Bickerman, *From Ezra to the Last of the Maccabees: Foundations of Postbiblical Judaism* (New York: Schocken, 1962); and Avigdor Tcherikover, *Hellenistic Civilization and the Jews* (New York: Atheneum, 1982). See also Emil Schürer et al., *History of the Jewish People in the Age of Jesus Christ (175 B.C.-A.D. 135)* (rev. ed.; 4 vols.; Edinburgh: T&T Clark, 1997), 1:137-63.

Martin Hengel's *Judaism and Hellenism: Studies in Their Encounter in Palestine during the Early Hellenistic Period* is important here (2 vols.; Philadelphia: Fortress, 1974), but cf. also Louis H. Feldman's pointed response to Hengel: "Hengel's *Judaism and Hellenism* in Retrospect," *JBL* 96 (1977): 377-82. In his *Heritage and Hellenism: The Reinvention of Jewish Tradition* (Hellenistic Culture and Society 30; Berkeley: University of California Press, 1998), Erich S. Gruen argues that the Maccabean revolt was not against Hellenism as such — or even against the Seleucids as such — but rather against indigenous Gentiles in areas around Judea. Indeed, as kings, the Hasmoneans themselves became remarkably Hellenistic in character almost immediately. The mid-second century BCE was, in any case, a remarkably creative time in which identity and resistance issues were paramount.

5. See the summary statements in Adam S. van der Woude, "Fifty Years of Qumran Research," in *The Dead Sea Scrolls After Fifty Years: A Comprehensive Assessment* (ed. Peter W. Flint and James C. VanderKam; 2 vols.; Leiden: Brill, 1998), 1:30. See also the comments by Martin Hengel, who suggests that "the whole rich and neglected subject 'Qumran and Hellenism,' or

Almost immediately, then, literature was produced that characterized the struggles of the 170s and 160s BCE and its ensuing effects as the final eschatological battle between good and evil. Daniel is usually dated in the 160s, and the work of Jason of Cyrene was probably completed by 160. The epitome of Jason's work, 2 Maccabees, was completed some years later, and 1 Maccabees was likely completed before the end of the reign of John Hyrcanus in 104.[6]

First Maccabees is *not* among those writings that characterized the struggle of the 170s and 160s BCE and its ensuing effects as the final eschatological battle between good and evil. Nevertheless, it recounts some of the responses within Early Judaism to the Hellenizing efforts of Antiochus. And it does have a very specific message or ideology concerning how the faithful are to maintain their identity as God's people: they must resist the evil Gentiles *and* the unfaithful Jews in league with them!

The book begins, perceptively enough, by placing the Hellenizing efforts of the Seleucid dynasty in the context of the triumph of Alexander the Great over the Mediterranean world. When Antiochus IV Epiphanes accelerated his program of Hellenization within Israel, responses among the faithful varied. Some counseled cooperation with the Seleucids and compromise with the cultural and religious demands of the occupiers. They eagerly approached the Hellenistic rulers and "made a covenant" with them (1 Macc 1:11, 43b; Dan 9:27). They joined the Hellenizers, even though Antiochus had desecrated the Temple (cf. Dan 9:27; 11:31; 12:11; 1 Macc 1:20-28; Josephus, *Ant.* 12.237).[7] They built a gymnasium in Jerusalem and removed the marks of circumcision (1 Macc 1:14-15). The assessment of the author of 1 Maccabees

---

more precisely 'Essenism and Hellenistic civilization,' would deserve a monographic treatment" ("Qumran and Hellenism," in *Religion in the Dead Sea Scrolls* [ed. John J. Collins and Robert A. Kugler; SDSSRL; Grand Rapids: Eerdmans, 2000], 55).

6. The fact that Esther's tale parallels 1 and 2 Maccabees so closely has suggested to some that, like Daniel, Esther was either written or canonized in the mid–second century BCE in response to the Hellenizers. In both Esther and Maccabees the Jews are threatened with annihilation (cf. 1 Macc 7:26 with Esther 3:6), a threatened massacre occurs on the thirteenth of the month of Adar (cf. 1 Macc 7:43 with Esther 3:7-13), the defense of the Jewish people was miraculously successful (cf. 2 Macc 15:25-34 with Esther 9:1-19), and a new holiday is established to celebrate the deliverance (cf. the day associated with Mordecai in 2 Macc 15:36 and 1 Macc 7:48 with "Purim" in Esther 9:20-26). See, e.g., John W. Miller, *How the Bible Came to Be: Exploring the Narrative and Message* (New York: Paulist, 2004), 13-14.

7. One might also include the reference to "those who violate the covenant" in 1QM 1.2 (מרשיעי ברית) as referring to such collaborators. Although the point is debated, the phrase likely refers to some group of Jews whom the author considers so wrong that they are among the "sons of darkness" who will be destroyed in the eschatological conflict. Cf. references to the ἄνομοι in 1 Macc 2:44; 3:5-6; 7:5; 9:23; 11:25; 14:14. For the παράνομοι, see 1 Macc 1:11; 4:11, 14; 2 Macc 13:7; cf. also 2 Macc 6:21; 8:4.

regarding those who took this response to the Hellenizing pressures of Antiochus is clear enough: they "abandoned the holy covenant . . . and sold themselves to do evil" (1 Macc 1:15) and were guilty of "apostasy" (ἀποστασία; 1 Macc 2:15).

This Hellenizing foreign influence was felt in a variety of ways, and it was not obvious to many how one should respond. *Language* was one issue. While seemingly innocuous at one level, each language has its own thought structure, and even one who works hard at rendering concepts faithfully in translation finds it nearly impossible to render some things faithfully enough to evoke the same meaning.[8] *Cultural innovations* represented another broad challenge. It is impossible and anachronistic to separate culture from religion in this respect. Something as benign in our day as eating or exercising patterns suddenly became significant religious and social identity issues in the context of second-century Early Judaism — and rightly so.

The first response of many of the Jews who could not go along with the pragmatic solution of compromise was simply to lament (cf. 1 Macc 1:24b-28, 36-40). Israel had had reason to lament before, and it had the spiritual and scriptural resources needed to engage in that process again. But in the midst of their mourning and lamentation came an even sharper challenge: In an effort to establish unity among his subjects, Antiochus required Israel to abandon her faith. Specifically, the Jews were required to:

1. adopt foreign cultural practices;
2. abandon all observance of feasts and holy days, including the Sabbath;
3. abandon all sacrifice and offering at the Temple;
4. discontinue circumcision, that central rite that defined the Jewish male's identity as a son of Abraham;
5. abandon the practice of purity, that crucial distinction between what is holy and what is profane, maintained in ritual observance;
6. adopt another religion and actively participate in the worship of other gods through sacrifice and other means; and
7. destroy any and all Jewish Scriptures ("the books of the Law").[9]

---

8. Cf., e.g., the prologue to Sirach.

9. Antiochus's destruction of the books of the Law subsequently required a systematic rediscovery and collection of the sacred books once the Maccabeans had regained control (2 Macc 2:14). The author of 2 Maccabees notes that Judas re-gathered "all" of them (ἐπισυνήγαγεν πάντα). This could suggest the existence of at least one proto-canon at the time. Some have claimed that the Hellenizers played a role in bringing the Hebrew Scriptures to their final form (e.g., see Miller, *How the Bible Came to Be*, 9). Philip R. Davies states that "the fixing of a canonical list was almost certainly the achievement of the Hasmonean dynasty" ("The Jewish Scrip-

Those found to be secretly preserving written copies of the Law were given the death penalty (1 Macc 1:57). The Temple was transformed into a Temple to Zeus (or Baal-Shamem)[10] and the Jews were forced to participate in a festival in honor of Dionysus. In short, the Jews were required to forget the Law and to abandon their religion. This was not a matter of persuasion or encouragement or even pressure. This was *law* with the force of the death penalty behind it: anyone who defied it was to be executed.

Antiochus followed up with a thorough-going and systematic effort to enforce this initiative and to establish new patterns of religious devotion in Israel. Scores of inspectors were dispatched to ensure compliance. The result was chaos and violence. Many resisted — some violently and some in secret defiance. Even over the issue of "unclean food" many of the Jews resisted . . . and faced the death penalty.[11] "They chose to die rather than to be defiled by food or to profane the holy covenant; and they *did* die. Very great wrath came upon Israel" (1 Macc 1:63-64).[12]

In his first chapter, the author of 1 Maccabees sets up the historical context in which his heroes, the Maccabees, took action. Beginning with the father, Mattathias, then proceeding through the narratives of three successive brothers, the book clearly shows its pro-Maccabean bias. Without arguing for it as such, the book declares the superiority of the "resistance" option. As Lester Grabbe has put it, "The persuasive strength of the book lies in its apparent ingenuousness: it seems straightforward and honest. But this is a part of its rhetoric of persuasion. A simple narrative . . . allows the writer's own

---

tural Canon in Cultural Perspective," in *The Canon Debate* [ed. Lee Martin McDonald and James A. Sanders; Peabody: Hendrickson, 2002], 50). Caution is warranted here, however, since canonization itself is community-specific. That is, canon is always defined in relation to one or more specific communities. There is little doubt about the pluriformity of the biblical text at the turn of the Common Era.

10. The "translation" of the names of gods from one language and religious culture to another is itself a fascinating and complex matter. Baal-Shamem was usually "translated" as "Zeus" in Hellenistic contexts. The phrase "abomination of desolation" (KJV), "abomination that desolates," or "abomination that makes desolate" (NRSV) — השקוץ משומם — occurs (with variations in spelling) in Dan 9:27; 11:31; and 12:11, with משומם serving as a word play on the name of the god Baal-Shamem (cf. John E. Goldingay, *Daniel* [WBC; Dallas: Word, 1989], 212; Paul M. Lederach, *Daniel* [Believers Church Bible Commentary; Scottdale, Pa.: Herald Press, 1994], 276).

11. Debate over the propriety of "unclean food" in the second century is likely an important part of the *Sitz im Leben* for Daniel 1.

12. The "wrath" (ὀργή) spoken of here in 1 Macc 1:64 does not seem to be a hint that God was punishing Israel through Antiochus, unlike the theology of 2 Maccabees (e.g., 2 Macc 6:12). Rather, it is an impersonal word expressing grief and tragedy.

perspective to prevail without intrusion on the reader's consciousness. The book is very pro-Maccabean."[13]

Much has been made about the differences of perspective between 1 Maccabees and 2 Maccabees: the former may *seem* to be a more straightforward history of events, but as Evans has noted, the straightforwardness of that history is disingenuous at best. The author of 2 Maccabees shows interest in the theological and religious issues involved. The author of 1 Maccabees praises the Hasmonean family as a whole, while the author of 2 Maccabees focuses on the role of Judas.

The habit of some to ignore or underplay the religious "tendency" of 1 Maccabees may be due in part to a lack of precision regarding the political and religious options regarding resistance to foreign influence. The author of 1 Maccabees is highly tendentious in his criticism of Antiochus IV and of the entire Hellenistic challenge. Specifically, the author applauds resistance to the Hellenizing challenge, supporting one particular approach to resistance — the option of active, violent resistance. Regardless of the connections (or lack of connections) between the "zeal of Phineas" (cf. Num 25:1-15) exhibited by Mattathias in 1 Macc 2:26 (cf. also 1 Macc 2:50, 54; 2 Macc 4:2; 4 Macc 18:12) and the possible existence of a "Zealot" party in the years between the Maccabean revolt and the Jewish revolt against Rome, it is clear that the option of active, violent resistance inspired by Phineas and executed by the Maccabees was the right and faithful option in the mind of the author of 1 Maccabees.[14]

---

13. Lester L. Grabbe, "1 and 2 Maccabees," in *Dictionary of New Testament Background* (ed. Craig A. Evans and Stanley E. Porter; Downers Grove: InterVarsity, 2000), 658.

14. The "fourth philosophy" of which Josephus speaks in *Ant.* 18.1.6 has often been identified with a so-called Zealot party. Richard Horsley has called that identification into question (see Richard A. Horsley and John S. Hanson, *Bandits, Prophets, and Messiahs: Popular Movements in the Time of Jesus* [New Voices in Biblical Studies; San Francisco: Harper & Row, 1988]). Josephus's own words could suggest that the "fourth philosophy," if such a thing existed in the second century BCE, may have begun as a party of active resistance to the Seleucids, though not necessarily a violent one, even if it became so later. On this matter, see Warren J. Heard Jr. and Craig A. Evans, "Revolutionary Movements," in *Dictionary of Jesus and the Gospels* (ed. Joel B. Green and Scot McKnight; Downers Grove: InterVarsity, 1992), 693:

> This resistance . . . is never stated by Josephus as armed rebellion. In fact they seem instead to be willing sufferers: "They shrug off submitting to unusual forms of death and stand firm in the face of torture of relatives and friends, all for refusing to call any person master" (*Ant.* 18.1.6 §23). Instead of armed resistance, proponents of the Fourth Philosophy felt that if they remained firm and resisted Rome through obedience to the Torah, "God would eagerly join in promoting the success of their plans, especially if they did not shrink from the slaughter that might come upon them" (*Ant.* 18.1.1 §5). If this under-

There is no question about the author's religious viewpoint: Mattathias's murder of a fellow Jew at Modein is expressly linked with his "zeal for the Law" as well as with the example of Phinehas in his own murderous zeal for the Law (1 Macc 1:24, 26). Furthermore, such actions are expressly linked with upholding the covenant (1 Macc 1:27; 2:50). The last testament of Mattathias in 1 Macc 2:49-68 is a rousing rehearsal of Israel's history precisely in support of the connection between courage, zeal for the law, and violence. It concludes with praise for Judas Maccabeas: "leader of an army, and he will fight a war of the people" (ἄρχων στρατιᾶς καὶ πολεμήσει πόλεμον λαῶν, 1 Macc 2:66). The testament ends with a call to arms that twice more connects observance of the Law to revenge against the Gentiles (1 Macc 2:67-68).

In contrast to 1 Maccabees, the author of 4 Maccabees cites the zeal of Phinehas only in the final soliloquy, in which the mother recounts Israel's history as a series of contrasts between those who take lives into their own hands (including Cain and Phinehas) and those who entrust their lives into the hands of God (including Abel [?], Isaac, Joseph, Hananiah, Azariah, Mishael, and Daniel. Then she appeals to Isaiah, David, Solomon, Ezekiel, and Moses in support of quietistic trust in God and of the resurrection, which makes nonviolent resistance to the point of death thinkable. She concludes with the implication that the Song of Moses supports the idea that life and the taking of life belongs to God alone (4 Macc 18:19).

2. "Active" Resistance, "Passive" Resistance, and Active Nonviolent Resistance

In an important article on the political perspective of the Revelation to John published in 1977, Adela Yarbro Collins considered the Hellenizing program and persecution of Antiochus IV.[15] She stated that behind the two primary options of accommodation and resistance were two different kinds of resistance: active resistance and passive resistance.[16] The ideology of the Mac-

---

standing of the Fourth Philosophy is correct, this group traced its lineage to the martyrs under Antiochus Epiphanes IV.

15. Adela Yarbro Collins, "The Political Perspective of the Revelation to John," *JBL* 96 (1977): 241-56. As a student of the Apocalypse of John, I will refer repeatedly in this essay to the Apocalypse as one voice in the chorus of voices within Early Judaism regarding the propriety of human violence in service to God's reign. In so doing, I am attempting to read the Apocalypse through the lenses provided by the history and theological categories of Early Judaism.

16. The categories "active resistance" and "passive resistance" have a long history. Yarbro Collins' contribution in this article was to offer a further distinction between two different

cabeans favored active resistance through armed rebellion. Yarbro Collins' primary contribution in the article is to demonstrate that "passive resistance" actually has two subcategories or forms. One form of passive resistance is the "pure" passive resistance advocated by Daniel.[17] In this model the faithful do not participate in the final battle, but rather endure and wait. A second form of passive resistance is a kind of synergistic passive resistance. As with the so-called "pure" passive model, the faithful do not participate directly in the final battle in a physical manner. However, the martyrdom of the faithful actually plays a synergistic role in the final battle. She cites the *Assumption of Moses* as an example of this second type of passive resistance in which the faithful play a passive, though synergistic role.

In contrast to the accommodationist approach, all three of the resistance models were characterized by a readiness to die. The Maccabees were ready to die in their armed resistance to the foreigners. The (pure) passive resisters were ready to die whether God saved them or not (see, e.g., Dan 3:16). And the synergistic passive resisters were ready to die as a contribution to the final battle of God with evil. When Pilate placed a golden eagle over the great gate of the Temple in the first century CE, the Jews protested boldly, though nonviolently. A crowd took to the streets of Caesarea and exposed their necks in defiance, showing that they were prepared to die rather than to tolerate such a blasphemy in violation of the Law. They even offered the necks of their wives and children to the sword.[18]

Yarbro Collins calls this kind of resistance "open," but "passive," since it was not violent. But this seems to be an odd and obfuscating use of terms, since rushing out into the streets to bare one's neck in defiant resistance to Pilate's decree is hardly "passive," even if it is nonviolent. In the *Assumption of Moses,* the martyrdom of Taxo and his seven sons seems to play a role in the

---

kinds of "passive" resistance. Use of the broader terms "active resistance" and "passive resistance" are attested widely. See, e.g., Theodore Hiebert, "Warrior, Divine," in *ABD* 6:879; Paul M. Lederach, *Daniel,* 280; John R. Yeatts, *Revelation* (Believers Church Bible Commentary; Scottdale: Herald, 2003), 24; William G. Bixler, "How the Early Church Viewed Martyrs," *Christian History: Persecution in the Early Church* 27 (1990): 28-33; M. Eugene Boring, *Revelation* (Interpretation; Louisville: John Knox, 1989), 22, 61. However, John B. Toews refers to Paul's admonition in Rom 12:1 not to be conformed to the world as an invitation for believers to engage in "active resistance" to the socialization of the "dominant social groups, the culture, and institutions of this age" (John E. Toews, *Romans* [Believers Church Bible Commentary; Scottdale: Herald, 2004], 299).

17. As we shall see, even Daniel is a call to "active" resistance, so it cannot serve as an example of passive resistance, whether purely or "impurely." The very concept of "passive resistance" may indeed be an oxymoron, since passivity and resistance do not easily coexist.

18. See Josephus, *J.W.* 2.169-174; 2.195-198; *Ant.* 18.53-59.

appearance of the kingdom. This kind of synergistic "passive" resistance actually was seen as contributing to the coming of the kingdom, even through one's own death. Similarly, the remarkably courageous stories of martyrdom in 2 and 4 Maccabees can hardly be called examples of "passive resistance."

Yarbro Collins is not alone in using such terminology. Loveday C. A. Alexander has used the same categories:

> Martyrdom may be described as "passive resistance" . . . apocalyptic perhaps as "theoretical resistance"; but there is no trace in these Diaspora texts of any active resistance to the domination of the world empires. For that we have to turn to the land of Israel and to the literature of the Maccabean period, which produced not only martyrs *(2, 4 Macc)* but also freedom fighters willing and able to take up arms in the cause of independence *(1, 2 Macc)*.[19]

Steven D. Fraade uses similar terms when he writes, "[f]or those who rejected the Hellenizing reforms forced upon them from within and without, there were essentially two alternatives: armed revolt against the Hellenizers and Syrian forces (emphasized in 1 Maccabees), or passive resistance and martyrdom in the face of their edicts (emphasized in 2 Maccabees)."[20] Here again we see "armed revolt" as an implied equivalent to "active resistance" and martyrdom as an implied equivalent to "passive resistance." Fraade goes on to say that "both responses presumed that *divine* intervention would be required to bring the events to their redemptive consummation; the question was the required *human* role in a sacred history that was rapidly approaching its long-anticipated climax."[21]

Fraade is right to emphasize that both responses expected and depended upon *divine* intervention, but he is not clear about what, exactly, is in question regarding the human role. Is it a matter of *whether* a human role is envisioned? Presumably not. Is it a question of whether that human role is "active" or "passive"? Here I would say, "No." The question, rather, is whether the human role consists of *accommodation* or *resistance*, and if the latter is the case, then whether that resistance is to be *violent* or *nonviolent*. The message of Daniel, at least, is that the "active" (cf. Dan 11:32) resistance of the faithful is to be *nonviolent*.

The author of 4 Maccabees sees the courageous resistance of the martyrs as a matter of warfare. The author invokes the language and mythology of holy

---

19. Loveday C. A. Alexander, "Early Christian Attitudes Toward Rome," in *ABD* 5:836.
20. Steven D. Fraade, "Palestinian Judaism," in *ABD* 3:1060.
21. Ibid.

war to advocate for a certain kind of active nonviolent resistance. They are to "fight zealously" in active resistance to the tyrants.[22] In fact, they nullify violence through their own nonviolent suffering.[23] As Warren Heard puts it:

> In most of the passages commenting on the effect of the martyrs' deaths, the martyrs themselves are the agents of victory. Thus, the contribution of the martyrs is the cardinal contribution in the war effort. . . . Without them victory would have been impossible. In the author's opinion the martyrs single-handedly defeat Antiochus and his evil forces. They accomplish his downfall by clinging to their Law, not compromising and giving clear testimony to their faith. Righteousness is the lethal weapon in their struggle. They fight by persevering in their righteousness and patiently enduring torture and martyrdom; these are the martyrs' only weapons.[24]

The language of warfare occurs throughout 4 Maccabees as the author applies the mythology and categories of holy war to the nonviolent resistance of martyrdom. The mother says, "My sons, noble is the contest to which you are called to bear witness for the nation. Fight zealously for our ancestral law."[25] Later the author editorializes, "Truly the contest in which they were engaged was divine,"[26] implying that it was a "holy war." The author praises the mother, calling her a warrior of God in the cause of religion (δὶ εὐσέβειαν θεοῦ στρατιῶτι, 4 Macc 16:14).

When Yarbro Collins applies these models to the book of Revelation, she concludes that the book advocates a "passive" type of resistance. The story in Revelation 12 "does not advocate or reinforce a program of active resistance or even self-defense, but awakens trust in the power of heaven to protect and rescue. . . . No major role is taken by the elect in the final stage of the eschatological conflict; rather the adversaries are defeated by the risen Christ and other heavenly beings."[27] Within its historical context, and given the categories with which Yarbro Collins is working, Revelation "advocates passive resistance of the second type" in that the martyrdom it lauds plays a positive synergistic, though still "passive," role in the eschatological battle.

But John the seer took up the tradition of holy war in Second Temple

---

22. Cf. 4 Macc 16:16; 17:11.

23. 4 Macc 9:30; 17:2.

24. Heard and Evans, "Revolutionary Movements," 695.

25. ῏Ω παῖδες, γενναῖος ὁ ἀγών, ἐφ' ὃν κληθέντες ὑπὲρ τῆς διαμαρτυρίας τοῦ ἔθνους ἐναγωνίσασθε προθύμως ὑπὲρ τοῦ πατρῴου νόμου (4 Macc 16:16).

26. Ἀληθῶς γὰρ ἦν ἀγὼν θεῖος ὁ δι' αὐτῶν γεγενημένος (4 Macc 17:11).

27. Yarbro Collins, "The Political Perspective of the Revelation to John," 247.

Judaism as a way of encouraging *active* resistance to the idolatries of the Roman Empire, an active resistance characterized by martyrdom — not the martyrdom that results from literal warfare, but rather the martyrdom that results from faithful, nonviolent witness. Such a purpose required John to appeal to certain well-established traditions on the one hand, while simultaneously engaging in thoroughgoing redefinitions on the other hand.[28] It entailed the *redefinition of "holy war" or "Yahweh war"* itself, from a literal battle between righteous and unrighteous armies on earth, to a semi-literal but nonviolent "battle" between good and evil waged in the streets of the Roman Empire through the everyday demands of political and religious allegiances. It required a *redefinition of "victory" itself* — to which John's Apocalypse amply witnesses — from victory as physical conquering through violence to spiritual conquering through faithful witness, sealed through martyrdom. It required a *redefinition of power,* from military and civil power whose pinnacle was the state-sanctioned death penalty, to "consistent resistance" to evil, whose pinnacle, ironically, was the consistent resistance that was sealed in the death penalty. Thus the very meaning, or value, of *death itself* was redefined.

The basic ethical stance called for by the author of the Apocalypse was that of ὑπομονή. Commentators of Revelation have too often read into ὑπομονή a quietistic — indeed, *passive* — ethical vision. However, the word has a more *active* sense. In his treatment of ὑπομονή in the *Theological Dictionary of the New Testament,* Friedrich Hauch writes

> as ὑπομονή later came to hold a prominent place in the list of Greek virtues, so there predominates in ὑπομένειν the concept of the courageous endurance which manfully defies evil. Unlike patience, *it thus has an active content. It includes active and energetic resistance to hostile power,* though with no assertion of the success of this resistance.[29]

In keeping with Hauch's comments, Elisabeth Schüssler Fiorenza has aptly translated ὑπομονή as "consistent resistance" instead of "patient endurance."[30] M. Eugene Boring agrees:

28. Appealing to well-established traditions while simultaneously engaging in thoroughgoing redefinitions is fraught with opportunity for miscommunication and misinterpretation, as the history of the interpretation of the Apocalypse amply testifies. It is not easy to determine when or where the appeal to tradition is meant to recall and support the cultural and religious associations that pertain to that tradition and when or where the author is recalling the tradition in order to subvert it or to redefine it on the basis of his Christology.

29. Gerhard Hauck, "ὑπομένω, ὑπομονή," in *TDNT* 4:581.

30. Elisabeth Schüssler Fiorenza, *The Book of Revelation: Justice and Judgment* (Philadelphia: Fortress, 1985), 4.

The quality of Christian action it expresses is not *passive* resignation; it is an *active* holding firm "for the sake of my name" (2:3, 13; 3:8), having courage in the face of interrogation by the Roman officials. . . . In settings other than oppression and persecution, "patient endurance" as the essence of Christian responsibility in the world can be misunderstood as all too *passive*.[31]

Yarbro Collins' attempt to probe distinctions among the various "passive" responses to the Hellenistic program is helpful and should be lauded. However, her consistent application of "active" to models of violent resistance and "passive" to models of nonviolent resistance is problematic. Her use of words like "bold" and "open" to characterize some expressions of "passive" resistance does little to mitigate the situation. What the literature bears witness to is the presence of an *active*, though *nonviolent*, form of resistance.

I agree with Yarbro Collins that Daniel is the prototypical advocate of the nonviolent model of resistance.[32] But as John J. Collins has noted,[33] this nonviolent resistance is nevertheless an *active nonviolent resistance*, not a *passive resistance*. Daniel 11:32 declares that, in the face of the king's challenge,

MT: ועם ידעי אלהיו יחזקו ועשו

Theodotion: λαὸς γινώσκοντες θεὸν αὐτοῦ κατισχύσουσιν καὶ ποιήσουσιν.

Old Greek: ὁ δῆμος ὁ γινώσκων ταῦτα κατισχύσουσι καὶ ποιήσουσι.

"The people who are loyal to their God shall *stand firm and take action*."[34]

Again, this is hardly "passive." The context here is that the king will attempt to "seduce" (רשע, "cause to act wickedly") those who violate the covenant, but in resistance to such seduction, the faithful will *stand firm* and *act* or *take action*. Both חזק and κατισχύω are strong, active verbs. The former carries con-

---

31. Boring, *Revelation*, 96 (emphasis mine).

32. See also John J. Collins, *The Apocalyptic Vision of the Book of Daniel* (HSM 16; Missoula: Scholars Press, 1977), esp. 191-218. Collins calls Daniel an example of "resistance literature" and a "political manifesto." He states that "[t]he mythical symbolism of the visions of Daniel is designed to inspire *active* but *non-militant* resistance" (ibid., 208; emphasis mine). Similarly, "the manifesto which we find in Daniel is one of resistance. . . . However, the resistance evoked is not military action, but the non-violent assertion of their religious loyalty and submission to martyrdom if necessary. . . . The visions of Daniel . . . demand a specific reaction to the existing political state" (ibid., 213).

33. Ibid., 208.

34. NRSV (emphasis mine).

notations of being strong, prevailing, and having courage. The latter is a synonym of νικάω and, much like חזק, connotes strength, overpowering, and overcoming. Furthermore, *active* nonviolent resistance is a more accurate and straightforward description of a model of resistance that calls the people to "act" (עשה). Thus, the kind of nonviolent resistance to evil that is advocated by Daniel is better called an *active nonviolent resistance,* based on confidence in the monergistic triumph of God in the final battle.[35]

In a book on the New Testament theology of peace, Willard Swartley takes issue with the categories of "active" and "passive" that Yarbro Collins uses in her article. He writes:

> I agree with Collins that Revelation depicts passive resistance of the second type, with the martyrs seeing their faithful endurance and death as participating in the eschatological coming of the kingdom. But more must be said: their role is not really passive. It has a fervent active component in the prayers of the saints and in their worship and praise of God.[36]

Yarbro Collins is certainly right that John's understanding of the final battle calls the saints to play a more synergistic, though nonviolent, role. To cite one example, the prayers of the saints have an active and effective function. They call for and even help to bring about the final victory of God (see Rev 5:8; 6:9-11; 8:3-4). Thus, these two types of "passive" resistance would better be referred to as two different types of *active nonviolent* resistance, a *monergistic* active nonviolent resistance and a *synergistic* active nonviolent resistance. Even the opening blessing on those who hear and who "keep" (τηρέω) what is written in the words of prophecy in this book suggests that John expects his

---

35. *Monergism* refers to the acting of God alone in war, with God's people playing no role in the battle, while *synergism* refers to the action of God's people along with God in war. The Hebrew Bible reflects ample evidence of and embraces both theologies. Millard C. Lind has argued that the monergistic theology derived from the paradigmatic Exodus event and that it was that event, with its monergistic divine warfare, that remained the ideal or theological benchmark (cf. Exod 14:14) even later in Israel's history when Israel went to war and articulated a theology of synergism (see *Yahweh is a Warrior: The Theology of Warfare in Ancient Israel* [Scottdale: Herald, 1980]). Even with the theology of synergistic divine/human warfare, the Israelites are called to play down the significance of their own role and actions and to recognize God's help (see, e.g., Deut 1:30; 3:22; 20:4; 32:30; Josh 10:42; 23:10; 2 Chr 32:7-8; Ps 144:1-2). The terms *monergism* and *synergism* are elucidated in and play a central role in Albert Curry Winn's introduction to Israel's theology of war. See Albert Curry Winn, *Ain't Gonna Study War No More: Biblical Ambiguity and the Abolition of War* (Louisville: Westminster/John Knox, 1993).

36. Willard M. Swartley, *Covenant of Peace: The Missing Peace in New Testament Theology and Ethics* (Grand Rapids: Eerdmans, 2006), 330.

readers to play some kind of active role. While the role of the saints in the Apocalypse is clearly nonviolent, it is not a "passive" but "active" role. In fact, one of the difficulties the author is addressing is the problematic *passiveness* of the seven churches in the face of various compromises with Greco-Roman religion and culture that the author equates with idolatry.[37] Passivity in the face of spiritual crisis is part of the problem, not the answer.

Thankfully, there is some evidence that the tide is beginning to turn on the use of phrases like *active resistance* and *passive resistance*. Brian K. Blount has written recently that, in the Apocalypse, "the language of witness commends civil disobedience in the form of active, nonviolent resistance."[38] However, Peter Flint, following David Aune, obscures the matter when he says that "the eschatological holy war tradition takes two forms: the *passive* model, in which the victory is won by God alone or with his heavenly armies; and the *active* model, in which the people of God physically participate in the warfare against their enemies (this is the model found in the *War Rule*)."[39] While Aune and Flint see the *War Scroll* as a relatively straightforward example of the "active" model of eschatological warfare, they see the Apocalypse of John as "more complex," even "contradictory." Complexity and contradiction are no doubt features of Revelation,[40] but such an assessment could also be caused by the inadequacy of the categories with which previous scholars have been working.

3. The *War Scroll* and the Apocalypse of John

In 1988 Richard Bauckham's article on the Apocalypse of John as a "Christian War Scroll" appeared.[41] Although Bauckham does not directly engage Yarbro Collins on the adequacy of her categories of "active" and "passive" resistance,

37. Cf. Mitchell G. Reddish, who clearly sees the role of the saints as active, rather than passive, but also nonviolent (Mitchell G. Reddish, *Revelation* [Smyth & Helwys Bible Commentary; Macon: Smyth & Helwys, 2001], 25, 331-32).

38. Brian K. Blount, "Reading Revelation Today: Witness as Active Resistance," *Interpretation* 54 (2000): 398.

39. Peter Flint, "The Dead Sea Scrolls and the Book of Revelation," in Peter Flint and James VanderKam, *The Meaning of the Dead Sea Scrolls: Their Significance for Understanding the Bible, Judaism, Jesus, and Christianity* (San Francisco: HarperSanFrancisco, 2002), 368. Flint is following David E. Aune, "Qumran and the Book of Revelation," in Flint and VanderKam, eds., *The Dead Sea Scrolls After Fifty Years*, 2:622-48, esp. 645-47.

40. See n. 27 above.

41. Richard Bauckham, "The Book of Revelation as a Christian War Scroll," *Neot* 22 (1988): 17-40, reprinted as chap. 8 in idem, *The Climax of Prophecy: Studies on the Book of Revelation* (Edinburgh: T&T Clark, 1993), 210-37.

he does so indirectly. He says that the author is convinced of "the need for God's people to engage in the conflict with evil by active resistance to the religio-political claims of Rome and pagan society."[42] There is no hint in Revelation that John or his readers were tempted to take up arms against Rome. Nevertheless, John writes

> to alert the readers to the fact that what is going on around them, in the social and political life of their own cities, is part of a conflict of cosmic proportions, the eschatological war of good and evil, the conflict of sovereignty between God and the devil, in which they are called to take sides, to take a firm stand, and by faithful witness to the truth to play their part in resisting the pagan state and pagan society. The message is not, 'Do not resist!', so much as, 'Resist — but by witness and suffering, not by violence'. The active metaphor of warfare serves this purpose better than the language of passive resistance.[43]

This suggests at minimum that John writes to encourage his readers to be active in their resistance to Greco-Roman idolatry. He wants them to take up their positions in this cosmic war — not through violent rebellion against Rome, but through active nonviolent resistance to its idolatrous demands.

The basic thesis of Bauckham's article is that along with many other pieces of literature from Early Judaism, some of which are now lost to us, both the *War Scroll* and the Apocalypse of John draw from a well-established tradition of eschatological "holy war" in Early Judaism.[44] Both compositions make use of the categories of monergism and synergism to express their respective understanding of the faithful community's role in that war. However, central to Bauckham's essay is his insistence that John "takes up and reinterprets specific traditions about the messianic war" in such a way as to transfer "its meaning to non-military means of triumph over evil."[45]

Bauckham's reading of the Apocalypse with regard to its ethic of partic-

---

42. Bauckham, *Climax of Prophecy*, 234.

43. Ibid.

44. The term "holy war," which was an important concept for Gerhard von Rad (see *Holy War in Ancient Israel* [Grand Rapids: Eerdmans, 1991 (German orig.: 1952)]), does not appear in the Hebrew Bible. In response to von Rad, Rudolf Smend argued that we should *not* speak of "holy war," since Israel's wars were not cultic, but rather of "Yahweh war." See Smend, *Yahweh War and Tribal Confederation: Reflections Upon Israel's Earliest History* (Nashville: Abingdon, 1970). This distinction is significant for the canonical material, but perhaps not for the *War Scroll*, since the eschatological war choreographed in 1QM clearly *is* cultic.

45. Bauckham, *Climax of Prophecy*, 213, 233.

ipation in the Lamb's eschatological battle is both clear and compelling. Many scholars have accepted his basic thesis — namely, that John has taken up and reinterpreted specific traditions about the messianic war in such a way as to apply the metaphor of warfare to witness and martyrdom, while precluding the participation of the faithful in any literal eschatological war. That said, Bauckham's use of the *War Scroll* as a foil against which to elucidate the ethics of the Apocalypse is somewhat problematic. He recognizes at least two of the problems himself.

The first problem is the difference in genre: even if the *War Scroll* is apocalyptic in the more general sense of the term, it is not technically an apocalypse. What it *is* has been a matter of debate. Many consider it a "rule," based in part on the common restoration of סרך ("rule") in 1.1.[46] Jean Duhaime calls the composition a "tactical treatise."[47] Geza Vermes, however, states that it "should not be mistaken for a manual of military warfare pure and simple. It is a theological writing . . . [that] symbolizes the eternal struggle between the spirits of Light and Darkness."[48] In Lester Grabbe's words, "The data may at times be those of a military manual, but the message is a theological one."[49] That is, if the *War Scroll* can legitimately be called a "military manual," it must by definition be a different kind of military manual, certainly not one with a secular, nonreligious purpose.

Second, Bauckham assumes a tradition of militant messianism in Early Judaism. The evidence for such a tradition, however, is rather slim. Bauckham writes that he hopes to show "that John shows detailed knowledge of a kind of military messianism which must have been common in some Jewish circles of his time, of which we have only hints, for the most part, but for which 1QM provides our best evidence."[50] Bauckham admits that the best evidence for

---

46. Or is it the other way around? Is the restoration based on the assumption that it is a "rule"? Although Florentino García Martínez restores סרך in 1QM 1.1, he lists the book in his section of "literature with eschatological content" rather than with the other "rules" of Qumran (*The Dead Sea Scrolls Translated: The Qumran Texts in English* [2d ed.; Leiden: E. J. Brill, 1994]). James C. VanderKam also categorizes 1QM as an "eschatological work" (*The Dead Sea Scrolls Today* [Grand Rapids: Eerdmans, 1994], 64-65).

47. Jean Duhaime, "War Scroll," in *The Dead Sea Scrolls: Hebrew, Aramaic, and Greek Texts with English Translations*, Vol. 2: *Damascus Document, War Scroll, and Related Documents* (ed. James H. Charlesworth et al.; PTSDSSP 2; Tübingen: J. C. B. Mohr [Paul Siebeck], 1995), 84. Cf. his earlier study, "The *War Scroll* from Qumran and the Greco-Roman Tactical Treatises," *RevQ* 13 (1988): 131-51.

48. Geza Vermes, *The Complete Dead Sea Scrolls in English* (New York: Allen Lane, 1997), 163.

49. Lester L. Grabbe, "Warfare," in *EDSS* 2:965.

50. Bauckham, *Climax of Prophecy,* 212.

the expectation of a messiah who would lead the troops of Israel in a holy war against its enemies comes from the Middle Ages, since "in the Jewish apocalypses of the earlier period [it is] almost absent."[51] In fact, "in apocalyptic proper . . . [the monergistic] tradition predominates."[52]

Third, although calling the Apocalypse a "Christian War Scroll" is provocative, it is problematic in that it could give several wrong impressions: (a) there is a tendency among Christian scholars to simplistically compare so-called "Christian" literature, teachings, and people with so-called "Jewish" literature, teachings, and people. Given the history of Jewish-Christian relations, such overly reified and simplistic comparisons are fraught with pitfalls that are too often ignored by or even invisible to Christian scholars.[53] Moreover, (b) even the terms *Christian* and *Jewish* are clearly anachronistic in the first century, as most scholars now recognize.[54] Bauckham knows better than to make this mistake himself, but the phrase lends itself to such a misunderstanding. Finally, (c) Baukham's terminology could be taken to imply that the Apocalypse of John is essentially like the *War Scroll* preserved at Qumran, *except for its "Christian" character.* That is, the basic purpose, genre, and function of the Apocalypse is similar to that of the War Scroll, save its Christian and therefore theologically different character. Here again, Bauckham is too careful to be guilty of such a mistake himself; nevertheless, his provocative title lends itself to such a misunderstanding.

Any legitimate use of the phrase "Christian War Scroll" as a descriptor of John's Apocalypse must be based on a clear definition of what one means by each of the terms and by the phrase as a whole. There are significant differences between the Apocalypse and the Qumran *War Scroll* in both genre and purpose. Fortunately, Bauckham is fairly clear about what he does and does not mean to claim in such a comparison. He uses the comparison "to draw attention to the emphasis on *human participation* in the eschatological holy war."[55] Thus, Bauckham's article is best understood as an elucidation of the

51. Ibid., 211.

52. Ibid.

53. For a salutary warning about such undertakings, see Alon Goshen-Gottstein, "Hillel and Jesus: Are Comparisons Possible?" in *Hillel and Jesus: Comparisons of Two Major Religious Leaders* (ed. James H. Charlesworth and Loren L. Johns; Minneapolis: Fortress, 1997), 31-55. For my own arguments for why it may be worth the risk to compare the various literatures of Second Temple Judaism, see Loren L. Johns, "The Dead Sea Scrolls and the Apocalypse of John," in *The Bible and the Dead Sea Scrolls*, Vol. 3: *The Scrolls and Christian Origins* (ed. James H. Charlesworth; Waco: Baylor University Press, 2006), 255-79.

54. See, e.g., John W. Marshall, *Parables of War: Reading John's Jewish Apocalypse* (Studies in Christianity and Judaism; Waterloo: Wilfrid Laurier University Press, 2001).

55. Bauckham, *Climax of Prophecy*, 212.

ways in which the Apocalypse of John can be read as a Christian *War Scroll* in terms of *human participation in the eschatological holy war.*

Lastly, the evidence does not suggest that the Apocalypse was written as some kind of response to the *War Scroll*. One could just as well claim that the Apocalypse of John can be read as a "Christian 4 Maccabees" in terms of *human participation in holy war,* with the recognition that 4 Maccabees does not share with the Apocalypse or the *War Scroll* their strong eschatological tone.

The war of the Sons of Light against the Sons of Darkness is clearly conceived in 1QM as an eschatological war: a final cosmic confrontation of good and evil. The two sides of the battle are described in the opening lines of the scroll. On the side of the Sons of Darkness are the army of Belial, presumably made up of the troops of Edom, Moab, Ammon, Philistia, and of the Kittim of Ashur, who are "being helped by those who violate the covenant" (1QM 1.2). Thus the resistance of evil is equated to resistance of Israel's neighbors — more specifically, to resistance of Israel's historical enemies. This identification of Edom, Moab, Ammon, and Philistia in the second or first centuries BCE provides a clue that the *War Scroll* should be read mythologically. That is, whatever its historical context at the time of its writing, the conflict is thrown onto a cosmic, mythological screen.

The words of 1QM seem to belie the often-repeated description of the Essenes in Philo:

> Among those men you will find no makers of arrows, or javelins, or swords, or helmets, or breastplates, or shields; no makers of arms or of military engines; no one, in short, attending to any employment whatever connected with war, or even to any of those occupations even in peace which are easily perverted to wicked purposes; for they are utterly ignorant of all traffic, and of all commercial dealings, and of all navigation, but they repudiate and keep aloof from everything which can possibly afford any inducement to covetousness.[56]

Josephus essentially agrees with Philo in his characterization of the Essenes as quietistic and peace-loving, although he does note that one Essene participated in the first revolt and assumed some military leadership.[57] Josephus

---

56. Philo, *Prob.* 78.

57. See Josephus, *J.W.* 2.567; 3.11, for his mention of "John the Essene." See also Duhaime, "War Scroll," in PTSDSSP 2:85. Duhaime cites Josephus, *J.W.* 2.151-253, as evidence that the Essenes participated in the first Jewish revolt against Rome (ibid., 85 n. 36). However, these lines indicate only that some Essenes were tortured in that war.

also suggests that the Essenes were not pure pacifists in that they carried weapons on trips "for fear of thieves."[58]

As Steve Mason has noted, Josephus's lengthy introduction of the Essenes abruptly interrupts his account of Judas the Galilean, presumably to demonstrate that the rebel faction does not characterize the best or the center of Judaism:

> Significantly, right where we might expect Josephus' account of the Herodian princes' governments, he inserts his lengthy account of the Essenes' politically docile mode of life, in contrast to that of the rebel faction (2.118-166). This interlude is intended to divert the reader's attention from the messy affairs of Judean politics, toward the philosophical heart and soul of Judaism.[59]

Among the better analyses of the witnesses of Philo and Josephus in light of the Scrolls themselves in the matter of non-retaliation is that of Gordon M. Zerbe.[60] Zerbe concludes that the Essenes placed a high valuation on non-retaliation, based on Lev 19:18 and 1 Sam 25:26-39. They interpreted Nah 1:2 as indicating that vengeance belongs to God alone (CD 9.5; cf. 1QS 10.18). Zerbe finds evidence for this in CD 9.2-10; 7.2-3; 8.5-6; 14.22; 1QS 7.8-9; and 10.20. The Qumran covenanters were not to take vengeance or to bear malice. The initiate was required to take a vow not to retaliate against anyone (1QS 10.17-18; 11.1-2). The initiate must also vow not to engage in legal dispute (ריב) with outsiders until the Day of Vengeance (1QS 10.19 [// 4Q260 (4QS^f) 4.7-8]; cf. 1QS 9.16-17, 22-23; 1Q26 frg. 1 line 8; but see also 1QH 10.14).[61] The dispute is *God's* (cf. 1QM 4.12, where one of the banners is to read ריב אל: "[This is] God's Dispute").

On the other hand, the Qumran Community was fascinated with vengeance and encouraged and even *required* hatred of the Sons of Darkness (cf., e.g., 1QS 4.1; 9.16, 21-22; 1QH 4.24; 3.28; 6.10). Although the prohibition of retaliation was apparently warranted by their eschatological views, it is clear that the Qumran Community could not wait until their vengeance could be released in a satisfying way. 1QS 8.6-7 makes clear that the Community has a responsibility to wreak the vengeance of God in the eschaton. If this was the

---

58. *J.W.* 2.125.

59. Steve Mason, *Josephus and the New Testament* (Peabody: Hendrickson, 1992), 91.

60. See Gordon Mark Zerbe, *Non-Retaliation in Early Jewish and New Testament Texts: Ethical Themes in Social Contexts* (JSPSup 13; Sheffield: JSOT, 1993), esp. 106-35. Zerbe's monograph began as a dissertation directed by Professor James H. Charlesworth.

61. Zerbe, *Non-Retaliation in Early Jewish and New Testament Texts,* 134-35.

theological ethic of the majority of Essenes, it must have led to some cognitive dissonance as they nurtured a spirit of hatred against evil and against evildoers while maintaining a covenant of personal non-retaliation — and, at the same time, longing for the final day of judgment in which the Essenes would be let loose to avenge God's justice upon all those Sons of Darkness! However, caution is warranted, since we do not have enough solid evidence to identify a monolithic attitude or ethic of the Essenes toward outsiders, let alone whether these were stable over the years or changed from century to century or from region to region.

As Otto Bauernfeind has noted, "In practice . . . it makes a great difference whether one takes to arms in the rank and file as in all other wars or whether it is expected that God or the Messiah will wage the war so directly that there is no place at all for the idea of human participation."[62] The *War Scroll* is clear about this matter: the final eschatological battle will be a holy war in which the Sons of Light will participate, even if they refrain from retaliation in the meantime.

From 1975 to 1980, John J. Collins and Philip R. Davies carried on a quasi-conversation about dualism and eschatology in the Qumran *War Scroll*.[63] One of the points of contention between the two was the extent to which "the difference between the two books [Daniel and the *War Scroll*] in their basic conception of holy war . . . marks a highly important point of transition in the development of Jewish apocalyptic."[64] Davies challenged Collins for having posited a linear development in "Jewish apocalyptic" that could be followed by means of Daniel and the *War Scroll*. In his 1979 reply to Davies, Collins clarified his position and expressly repudiated "the theory of a straight-line development of apocalyptic."[65] Arguments about historical developments in theology are difficult enough without the knotty problems surrounding the composition history of the *War Scroll*, including deciding whether its first recension predates Daniel.[66] Furthermore, to posit such a de-

---

62. Otto Bauernfeind, "πόλεμος, πολεμέω," in *TDNT* 6:511.

63. The conversation began with John J. Collins, "The Mythology of Holy War in Daniel and the Qumran War Scroll: A Point of Transition in Jewish Apocalyptic," *VT* 25 (1975): 596-612. Philip R. Davies responded with "Dualism and Eschatology in the Qumran War Scroll," *VT* 28 (1978): 28-36. Collins then countered in "Dualism and Eschatology in 1QM: A Reply to P. R. Davies," *VT* 29 (1979): 212-16, to which Davies responded in "Dualism and Eschatology in 1QM: A Rejoinder," *VT* 30 (1980): 93-97.

64. Collins, "The Mythology of Holy War in Daniel and the Qumran War Scroll," 597.

65. Collins, "Dualism and Eschatology in 1QM," 213.

66. See, e.g., Hartmut Stegemann, who speaks confidently about the "pre-Essene foundational composition of the *War Rule*" (*The Library of Qumran: On the Essenes, Qumran, John the Baptist, and Jesus* [Grand Rapids: Eerdmans, 1998], 103).

velopment would require, for instance, that one decide whether 1QM 1, the column that most clearly betrays knowledge of Daniel, comes from the earliest or latest period in that composition's history.[67]

There has been significant conversation about whether the war imagined in 1QM is a "utopian" projection or whether it describes an actual, usable manual.[68] Duhaime seems to reject the possibility of the real life-changing and world-creating power of "utopian" visions when he says that the War Scroll "could have been . . . a genuinely utopian product written for liturgical purposes or for personal meditation, and conveying the dreams and hopes of a community totally deprived of real power within the turmoil of events."[69] Duhaime seems content with identifying the genre as "tactical treatise," even if it is utopian in character. Similarly, Albert I. Baumgarten has recently suggested that tactical treatises need not be considered inimical to utopian literature, citing the example of the military plans of "cargo cults."[70]

---

67. Following P. von der Osten-Sacken, Collins sees 1QM 1 as part of the early stratum of the document. In contrast, Davies sees it among the latest. See P. von der Osten-Sacken, *Gott und Belial* (Göttingen: Vandenhoeck & Ruprecht, 1969), 42-62; and Collins, "The Mythology of Holy War in Daniel and the Qumran War Scroll," 605. Raija Sollamo ("War and Violence in the Ideology of the Qumran Community") sides with Davies. In light of the complex literary problems, Duhaime is reluctant to attempt a clear adjudication of the matter (PTSDSSP 2:83). See also the cautions of Philip R. Davies about making broad generalizations about "the" eschatology at Qumran: "The Qumran scrolls present a remarkably diverse variety of eschatological teachings" ("Eschatology at Qumran," *JBL* 104 [1985]: 39). 1QM does not even manage to include a messiah in its narrative, though the related fragment 4Q285 appears to do so. Even though 1QM does mention the Prince of the Congregation in 5.1 (נשיא כול העדה), Collins seems to stretch too far when he states, "[i]n view of the messianic overtones of both the prince and Balaam's oracle, the burden of proof falls on anyone who would claim that the Davidic messiah was absent at any stage of the War Rule tradition" (John J. Collins, *The Scepter and the Star: The Messiahs of the Dead Sea Scrolls and Other Ancient Literature* [ABRL; New York: Doubleday, 1995], 59). The Prince of the Congregation clearly does not play as important a role in 1QM as does the high priest. Similarly, VanderKam's decision to lump various "titles" from various Scrolls (e.g., Messiah, Interpreter of the Law, the priest, the High Priest, etc.) into one "priestly eschatological figure" is, in my view, questionable. See James C. VanderKam, "Messianism in the Scrolls," in *The Community of the Renewed Covenant: The Notre Dame Symposium on the Dead Sea Scrolls* (ed. Eugene Ulrich and James Vanderkam; Notre Dame: University of Notre Dame Press, 1994), 211-33. Cf. also the contribution by C. D. Elledge in the present volume.

68. For an early round of this discussion, see Hans Bardtke, "Die Kriegsrolle v. Qumran übersetzt," *TLZ* 80 (1955): 401-20; and Leonhard Rost, "Zum Buch der Kriege der Söhne Des Lichtes Gegen die Söhne der Finsternis," *TLZ* 80 (1955): 205-8.

69. Duhaime in PTSDSSP 2:87.

70. See Albert I. Baumgarten's post on the Orion List at http://orion.mscc.huji.ac.il/orion/archives/2000b/msg00201.html.

(Cargo cults originated in Melanesia in the nineteenth century and are an example of non-Western millennial movements.)[71] And there is some evidence that in the complex history of composition, what may have begun as an actual tactical treatise used by the Maccabeans themselves became more dualistic and eschatological over time.[72]

In contrast to the hyper-realistic materialism that rejects any utopian vision as unrealistic, Brian K. Blount argues that language is potential. It creates choice and provides people with the opportunity to create meaning when performed.[73] Even a so-called utopian vision can transform society. The very categories used in the secondary literature on 1QM, for example, "authentic military textbook" vs. "utopian" or "unrealistic," are highly problematic.[74] Much work needs to be done yet in examination of the "rhetoric" of the *War Scroll*. Such work must go beyond a narrow discussion of "genre" or "purpose" to investigate the "persuasive discourse" represented by the work and the interrelationship between the three.

4. Conclusion

In conclusion, not all literature for which identity as God's people was central portrayed that identity primarily as a matter of resistance (e.g., 4QMMT, which nevertheless is keen to carve out a space for *difference*). And some books for which both resistance and identity were crucial concepts did not see the matter necessarily as an eschatological issue (e.g., 1 Maccabees).[75] I have argued that even with the so-called "pure" passive resistance model represented by Daniel, we actually have a clear call for an "active," though nonvi-

---

71. For more information on cargo cults, see "Cargo Cult," in *The Encyclopedia of Christianity* (ed. Erwin Fahlbusch; Grand Rapids: Eerdmans, 1999-), 1:353; Peter Worsley, *The Trumpet Shall Sound: A Study of "Cargo" Cults in Melanesia* (London: MacGibbon & Kee, 1957).

72. See Russell Gmirkin, "The War Scroll and Roman Weaponry Reconsidered," *DSD* 3 (1996): 89-129; cf. also Russell Gmirkin, "Historical Allusions in the War Scroll," *DSD* 5 (1998): 172-214.

73. Blount, "Reading Revelation Today," 398.

74. See, e.g., van der Woude, "Fifty Years," 12.

75. As noted above, Heard and Evans have suggested that Josephus's "fourth philosophy" may have begun as a general, umbrella term for several disorganized bodies united only in their conviction that some kind of resistance to Greek influence was required. If so, it would have included, over the years, Essenes, zealot types, Hasidim, the martyrs of 4 Maccabees, Taxo and his sons, Jesus, the Sicarii, and others who would eventually be included in the "Sons of Darkness" (e.g., 1QM 1.2). In any case, much of the Jewish literature that followed was highly interested in questions of identity vis-à-vis various models of resistance being promoted as faithful.

olent, resistance. Passivity should in most cases be associated with accommodationism — which rarely characterizes the literature of Early Judaism — rather than with resistance. This leaves us with various understandings of *accommodationism,* on the one hand, and various understandings or models of *resistance* on the other. The theology of active resistance witnessed to in 1 Maccabees is essentially non-eschatological and envisages human participation in resistance as marked by violence. The theology of active resistance witnessed to in the final form of the *War Scroll* envisages violent human participation in the eschatological battle. The theology of resistance witnessed to in Daniel and the Apocalypse is both eschatological and nonviolent with regard to the active human participation of the faithful. The primary difference, as Yarbro Collins has noted, is that Daniel does not view the active resistance of the faithful as "effective" in terms of contributing to the battle, whereas the Apocalypse — like the *Assumption of Moses* — does, insofar as it sees the victory of the faithful as participating in the eschatological victory. Worshiping the victorious Lamb provides a kind of realized eschatology to those who offer consistent resistance (ὑπομονή). Although Daniel and Revelation both have a strong eschatological emphasis, the believers in Revelation already celebrate Christ's victory.

All of this suggests the existence of a rich and variegated debate or set of models in the literature of Second Temple Judaism regarding the ethical propriety of human participation in violent conflict. Understanding how this debate and these models developed in the emergence of early Christianity and rabbinic Judaism out of Second Temple Judaism would require a clearer understanding than we presently have of the roles played by the failed revolts against Rome in the first and second centuries CE, by the social location of Jewish communities both in Palestine and in the Diaspora, by the teachings of Jesus, and by the emerging self-definition of Judaism and Christianity over against each other. This is a broad research agenda and yet the importance of the subject matter involved — whether humans should participate in violence connected to religious pursuits and/or beliefs — indicates that it is a matter that not only deserves but requires our serious attention.

Index of Authors

Index of Ancient Texts

---

*For the sake of both precision and consistency, texts are cited primarily according to Q number but are also provided with a parenthetical descriptor, which is taken, in the main, from DJD 39, even if the author of the article did not use both designations or used (only) an alternative descriptor. After the listing by Q number, for convenience, there is a listing of selected texts by descriptive title (e.g., *Rule of the Community, Damascus Document*).

Index of Ancient Texts